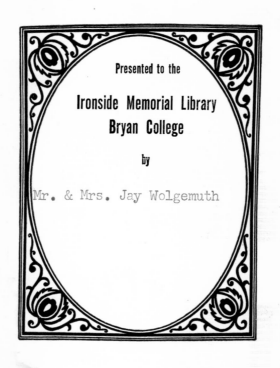

World History In Outline

Lacey Baldwin Smith
PROFESSOR OF HISTORY,
NORTHWESTERN UNIVERSITY

Jean Reeder Smith
SOCIAL STUDIES DEPARTMENT,
EVANSTON TOWNSHIP HIGH SCHOOL

BARRON'S EDUCATIONAL SERIES, INC.
WOODBURY, NEW YORK • 1966

CONTENTS

INTRODUCTION

THIS IS AN OUTLINE OF WORLD HISTORY. The problem is where to begin: 1] with the appearance of man, the central character of this story; 2] with the development of civilized society, the absolute prerequisite to recorded history; or 3] with the advent of global history on which the emphasis of this narrative rests. The last alternative excludes 99.9% of recorded history, for world history cannot be said to have begun until the unification of the globe by the Europeans in the sixteenth and seventeenth centuries. The first possibility trespasses upon anthropology and paleontology and falls outside the scope of this outline. Through a process of elimination, the logical point of departure is with the appearance of civilized man.

A second major problem is what areas to include in the story of civilization. Presumably world history should encompass the four corners of the earth, but certain peoples and civilizations have played key roles in the unification of the globe and their histories have been emphasized to the exclusion of other societies, which have been, up until now, upon the periphery of world history. For instance, the Eskimo has no place in this story; the Aztec only passing emphasis; while the Greek, the Chinese, the Arab, and the Anglo-Saxon among others monopolize a major portion of the theme. This outline begins with the Middle East, which most authorities regard not only as the cradle of civilization but also the crossroads from which civilization spread to India, Europe, and possibly even to China.

LACEY BALDWIN SMITH
JEAN REEDER SMITH

The Middle East

PREHISTORIC PERIOD   Before 3700 B.C.

In order for man to develop the art of living together in static communities, he had to pass through the Old Stone Age, the New Stone Age, and move into the Bronze Age and learn the art of agriculture and the domestication of animals.

THE OLD STONE AGE (PALEOLITHIC)

The longest stage of man's history was the Paleolithic period, dating from about 500,000 years ago to before 6000 B.C. Man sustained life by gathering food and hunting, and he used a roughly chipped stone hand ax as his basic tool. His shelter was generally a cave or a lean-to, and his clothes were made of animal skins. During this period (about 150,000 years ago), fire was used and language was evolved.

THE NEW STONE AGE (NEOLITHIC)

The New Stone Age began in the Middle East about 6000 B.C. but did not come to some parts of the world (the Afrasian desert, Australia, and parts of America) until 1500 A.D. with the colonization of the earth by the Europeans.

During this period man began to produce food by domesticating animals—the dog was probably the first—and cultivating plants, wheat and barley first. Weapons and tools became more refined and were of polished stone.

The production of food meant that man became a settler

1

rather than a nomad and this in turn led to the growth of permanent villages (the earliest cities known were Jericho in Palestine and Bybus [Jubayl] in Lebanon). A reliable food supply also led to a population increase and thus to the development of social order.

From the Middle East, the New Stone Age culture seems to have spread to Africa, Europe, and India. China also developed a Neolithic culture, but historians are not sure whether it was through Indian influence or whether it developed independently. The American Indian seems to have discovered agriculture independently.

THE BRONZE AGE   3700 B.C.

The beginning of what historians call civilization is generally assumed to be the Bronze Age—the era when metal (copper and bronze) was used for tools, when pottery and weaving had been developed (about 5000 B.C. in the Middle East) and the wheel was invented (about 4000 B.C. in Mesopotamia). The use of copper and bronze and finally iron (1300 B.C.), as Mr. Philip K. Hitti said in *The Near East in History,* was "responsible for the greatest advances in industry and, until the advent of the airplane, for the largest measure of progress in transportation." The wheel led to transportation and communication. The plow was invented and irrigation was employed; and men began to specialize, becoming potters, carpenters, and smiths.

The Invention of Writing

With the invention of writing history really begins, for men were able to record their experiences for future generations. The oldest known evidence of writing was found in Uruk in Mesopotamia. The script was called cuneiform because of the wedge-shaped characters produced by a stylus. Egyptian writing followed shortly afterwards, using picture symbols—hieroglyphics.

By 3700 B.C. on the plain of Sumer (Tigris and Euphrates rivers), civilization had developed. Writing, urban life, political organization, social classes, and finally arts and sciences had all evolved. Civilization spread from Mesopotamia to Egypt (3000 B.C.); to the Aegean and the Indus (2500 B.C.) and to China (1500 B.C.).

ANCIENT CIVILIZATION   3700–1000 B.C.

The word civilization stems from the Greek word civis *or* city. *The arts of civilization—writing, literature, political organization, and science—developed in the fertile valleys of Mesopotamia and Egypt, where man first began to experience an urban life.*

THE BRONZE AGE

Mesopotamia   3000–1200 B.C.

The Sumerians in lower Mesopotamia first evolved an urban culture. The city became a city-state, its nucleus was the temple, and the rulers though originally elected, rapidly endeavored to acquire the attributes of a priest-king.

Mesopotamia was never under the rule of one city-state for very long. The rich valley of the Tigris-Euphrates was vulnerable to attack and witnessed many upheavals and conquerors, as peoples fought to gain control of the precious water and land.

The Rulers of the Mesopotamian Area   3000–1100 B.C.

The Sumerians	before 2300 B.C.
The Akkadians	2350–2200 B.C.
The Guti	2200–2050 B.C.
The Sumerians (revival)	2050–1850 B.C.
The Babylonians (Amorites)	1850–1575 B.C.
The Kassites	1575–1180 B.C.

Sargon I, the First Empire Builder
In 2350 B.C. Sargon founded Akkad and conquered the Mesopotamian area, extending its boundaries east through Elam

(Khuzistan) and west into northern Syria. Under his grandson, Naram-Sin (2270–2233 B.C.), the empire was even greater. This was the first time in Mesopotamian history that there was some attempt at an imperial government. Akkadian control was broken by invasions by peoples from the east; by Sumerians who had not been fully assimilated; and then by newcomers from the west, the Amorites.

Hammurabi (1728–1686 B.C.) Was One of the Greatest Rulers of Mesopotamia

Under Hammurabi the first national code of laws was created. There had been earlier attempts at codified law (the code of Bilalama of Eshruma was fifty years older and the code of Lipit-Ishtar of Isim and the code of Ur Nammu were at least one hundred and fifty years older), but this was the earliest code attempting to govern all peoples in a kingdom. It reveals some interesting things about Mesopotamian civilization: the family was the basis of society; there was a rigid class system and wages were fixed for all jobs; the rights of women were safeguarded; and criminal actions were punished on the basis of *an eye for an eye*.

Mesopotamian Religion

For the people of the Tigris-Euphrates valley, the world was populated with hosts of evil spirits. The ruler of the city-state was the agent of the gods. The good life was to obey the family, the ruler, and the gods. The greatest piece of Sumerian literature, the *Epic of Gilgamesh,* is the story of the Great Flood, and it reveals a feeling of insecurity, a search for immortality, and a sense of doom; there was no belief in the doctrine of paradise and salvation. The fact that the theme of this epic is found throughout Middle Eastern literature reveals the strength of Sumerian influence upon all the peoples of the ancient Near East.

Sumerian Contributions

The wheel was a Sumerian invention. In the field of literature the Sumerians far excelled the Egyptians and led the way in mathematics by creating a number system based upon the unit

60 and by discovering geometric formulas. The city-state organization and business organization also originated in Sumer.

Egyptian Civilization

Unlike Sumer, Egypt developed political centralization. Irrigation and control of the Nile were possible because of the predictable nature of the river. The need for an organized effort to regulate flood control was probably the reason for the pharaohs' great power and political supremacy.

The Dynasties of Egypt   3000 B.C.–525 B.C.

A. pre-dynastic   before 3000 B.C.
   Union was attempted between lower and upper Egypt but was not permanent.
B. Thinite (dynasties I and II)   3000–2778 B.C.
   Under King Menes the second union was accomplished.
C. Old Kingdom (III–VI)   2778–2263 B.C.
   This was the height of Egyptian culture.
D. Feudal Period (VII–XI)   2263–2000 B.C.
E. Middle Kingdom (XII)   2000–1788 B.C.
F. Hyksos (XIII–XVII)   1788–1580 B.C.
G. The Empire—The New Kingdom (XVIII–XX)
   1580–1085 B.C.
   The eighteenth dynasty was one of the most brilliant, dynamic, and aggressive. During this period Egypt's empire was at its most extensive.
H. Rule of the Priests (XXI)   1085–950 B.C.
I. Rule of the Libians (XXII–XXIV)   945–712 B.C.
J. Rule of the Nubians (Ethiopia) (XV)   712–663 B.C.
K. Rule of the Natives (XXVI)   663–525 B.C.
Then came the end of independence.

Achievements of Egypt

Despite dynastic change there was a continuity in Egyptian history, as there was in Chinese history. Almost all of the major advances of Egyptian civilization were accomplished during the Old Kingdom. From then on achievement was primarily repetitious.

POLITICAL ORGANIZATION

Egyptian government was based on a priestly monarchy. The pharaoh of Egypt was the child of the sun-god. He owned the land and subdivided it among his people, but he maintained direct control of at least one fifth of the land. The control of wealth as well as religion gave the ruler immense power.

ART AND ARCHITECTURE

The most outstanding aspect of Egyptian architecture was the monumental nature of its buildings, through which the pharaohs endeavored to achieve immortality. The best examples are

1) the pyramid-tombs (Cheops', built in the fourth dynasty, and the Step pyramid, built in the third dynasty, were incredible engineering feats);

2) the Great Sphinx at Gizeh;

3) the Temple of Amon-Re at Karnak, built during the New Kingdom, is the largest columnar structure ever constructed. A single room, the Hypostyle Hall, alone covered 54,000 square feet.

EGYPTIAN RELIGION

Egyptian religion was unlike Mesopotamian religion, for although Egyptians believed in a multitude of evil spirits and gods, and although their gods changed with each dynasty (Re, for example, did not appear until after the collapse of the first dynasty), there was optimism in the Egyptian faith. The pyramid was built for the afterlife; theirs was a belief in eternity. The *Book of the Dead* explains the elaborate system for the preservation of the dead body and the method of embalming, and also states that happiness in the next life is partly dependent upon social behavior in this world.

Cultural Diffusion

The greatest achievement of the Bronze Age civilization in both Egypt and Mesopotamia was the creation and diffusion of the tools of civilization through trade and warfare.

THE COMING OF THE IRON AGE 1300–1000 B.C.

The Iron Age changed the civilizations of the Middle East, for the use of iron tools took control out of the hands of the wealthy and put it into the hands of every man. Iron was plentiful, whereas there had been a small and restricted supply of bronze. The creation and spread of the alphabet by the Phoenicians, which occurred during this period, meant that any man could now control written communication. The Iron Age also made it possible for small groups of people to pursue their own development, and during this period one of the world's great religions was born among just such a small group—the Hebrews. As Hitti says, it is "a paradox of world history that the two countries destined to give birth one to the most accomplished system of writing and the other to the noblest system of religious beliefs were not extensive, military and opulent . . . but relatively small, poor and militarily weak."

The Hittites and the First Use of Iron

During the Hyksos' domination in Egypt (1788–1580 B.C.) a new empire arose in north central Asia. In 1500 B.C. the Hittites reached the height of their power. Little is known about these people, but it is believed that they were the first to develop the use of iron. A desperate struggle occurred with Egypt that weakened the Egyptian empire and destroyed the Hittites around 1200 B.C.

The Phoenicians

Origins

When the Amorites occupied the fertile crescent, the Canaanites were their southern branch (in Syria, Lebanon, and Palestine). The group of Canaanites who were not destroyed or absorbed by Semitic hordes, such as the Arameans, Israelites, and Philistines, and who traded with the Greeks became known as Phoenicians for the purple red cloth they sold. They had been conquered in 1600 B.C. by the Egyptians but the decline of Egyptian power around 1200 B.C. gave them an opportunity to play an independent role.

Colonization and Trade

These people were primarily concerned with trade and became the chief agents of civilized life. They planted colonies in Egypt, Cyprus, and Sicily. One of the most famous Phoenician colonies was Carthage (Tunisia) founded about 814 B.C. Every colony that they developed was independent, yet linked by culture and trade with the mother city-states, particularly Sidon and Tyre. The Phoenicians even reached the Atlantic and possibly England. Legend claims that Europe received its name from Europa, daughter of a Phoenician king. The Phoenicians are believed to have circumnavigated Africa between 600 and 593 B.C. By 727 B.C., however, the mother city-states had fallen to the Assyrians.

The Alphabet

The Egyptians had developed from hieroglyphics forty consonantal signs, but the Phoenicians were the ones who developed twenty-two letters and used them as independent signs and then spread this invention throughout the Mediterranean world.

The Arameans (Syrian is the Greek name)

The Arameans settled in the middle Euphrates around 2000 B.C. and soon established states in inland Syria, founding Damascus (Aram). If the Phoenicians carried civilization by sea, the Arameans carried it inland by caravan. In 732 B.C. they also fell before the might of Assyria.

The Hebrews

Origins

A freak in history, a small, scattered, and insignificant group of people, the Hebrews were able to maintain their cultural unity despite invasions and conquests. A barely civilized people in the fourteenth century B.C., they succeeded by 1200 B.C. in forcing their way, tribe by tribe, into Palestine. One migration was connected with the Arameans in the fourteenth century B.C. and one was from Egypt in the late thirteenth century (1234–1215 B.C.) under the leadership of Moses.

The Monarchy
Faced with a threat from the more advanced and prosperous Philistines, the Hebrews were temporarily unified under Saul in 1020 B.C. This unity lasted only seventy years. Under David (1004 B.C.) Jerusalem was founded and the Hebrew kingdom extended from Lebanon to the Red Sea. Under Solomon (963–923? B.C.) the monarchy reached its height, but with his death it split into the north (Israel) and the south (Judah). Israel was conquered by the Assyrians in 734 B.C. and Judah by the Neo-Babylonians and Nebuchadrezzar in 586 B.C.

Religion
The Hebrews gave to the world the concept of exclusive and ethical monotheism, as well as an unsurpassed literary achievement—the Torah (the Old Testament). By 750 B.C. their god, Yahveh or Jehovah, had been endowed by the major prophets with characteristics unlike any other, for he had become a god of justice *and* mercy. The prophet Isaiah gave to the faith a vision of a different world, a world of universal peace "where wolves shall dwell with lambs." The prophet Jeremiah added the doctrine of individual responsibility as opposed to group responsibility. Each man was responsible for his own soul. The prophet Hosea further expanded the theme of a god of love, and the prophet Micah stated that God required nothing more of man than "to do justly, to love mercy, and to walk humbly with thy god." Judaism had become a religion of righteousness in which salvation was dependent upon the judgment of a just god who punished evil and rewarded good actions on earth. (Compare with Eastern mystery cults.)

CLASSICAL CIVILIZATION   1000 B.C.–500 A.D.

During the classical period of history, the lands of the Middle East were united for the first time under a single empire, first the Persian (sixth century B.C.) and then the Hellenistic empire under Alexander the Great (332 B.C.). By the beginning of the first century B.C., however, the countries of the Middle East were once again divided into the Roman Empire in the west and the Parthians in the east. During the classical era, another of the world's great religions was born in the Middle East—Christianity—but it had little lasting influence on the countries of its origin.

ASSYRIAN DOMINANCE   900–600 B.C.

The introduction of organized cruelty as a political policy, the use of iron for warfare, and the deliberate preservation of the achievements of the past is what the world owes the Assyrians, who began their conquests of the Middle East around 900 B.C. (The fact that Sargon II (721–705 B.C.), one of the greatest of Assyrian rulers, took the name of Sargon of Akkad is an example of the Assyrian preoccupation with the continuity of history.)

In 612 B.C. the Assyrian empire fell, destroyed by a combined army of Chaldeans under the leadership of Nabopolassar (612–605 B.C.) and Medes from northwest Persia led by Cyaxares.

The destruction of the Assyrian empire left four powers to struggle for its legacy: the Medes and the Persians; the Neo-Babylonians or Chaldeans; the Lydians; and the Egyptians.

NEO-BABYLONIANS

The most famous leader of the Chaldeans or Neo-Babylonians was Nebuchadrezzar II (605–562 B.C.) whose reign is known for the hanging gardens of Babylon and for work in astronomy.

LYDIANS IN ASIA MINOR

Croesus (560–545 B.C.) was the last and great king of the Lydians and was responsible for the first use of coinage.

THE PERSIAN EMPIRE

The Conquests

The first modern empire in history was the Persian. Indo-Iranian in language and Zoroastrian in religion, the Persians under their king Cyrus (550–529 B.C.) began their conquests. First the Median yoke was thrown off; then the Lydians were destroyed; then in 539 B.C. the Chaldeans were overthrown. Under Cambyses (529–521 B.C.) Egypt was conquered, and the Persians came into conflict with the Athenians and Spartans in 490 B.C., suffering their first defeat.

The Empire

The Persian Empire was divided into twenty provinces, each having a large measure of autonomy and yet carefully supervised. Common coinage, a postal system, and roads linked the empire together and trade flourished. Compared with the Assyrians, the Persians were lenient, even allowing deportees to return home.

Zoroastrianism

Zoroastrianism began with a Median prophet, Zoroaster, who is believed to have lived about 600 B.C. *Avesta*, the sacred book, explains the fundamental Zoroastrian belief in the dualism of life. Good and evil, light and dark are represented by two deities: Ahura Mazda, who is similar to Jehovah, and Ahriman (or Angra Mainyu), who has the qualities of Satan. A code of ethics is the basis of the faith: good thoughts, good works, and good deeds are necessary to stay out of the hands of Ahriman. Later on in its history, Zoroastrianism became associated with fire worship, for its sacred symbol is the fire that burns perpetually in its temples. The Parsi in and around Bombay, India, are Zoroastrian today, and there are still a few Zoroastrians left in Persia, although Islam has almost destroyed this ancient faith.

Alexander's Motivations for the Conquest of the Middle East

Alexander's father, Philip of Macedon, had laid the original plans for the liberation of the Greek states in Asia Minor.

Alexander had been educated to believe in Greek culture, and Aristotle, his tutor, had instilled in him a devotion to Panhellenic ideals.

The Conquest of the Middle East

Syria fell in 333 B.C.; Tyre, the only Phoenician city that put up a struggle, was taken in 332 B.C.; and Egypt, weary of Persian rule, offered little resistance. Then followed Babylon and Susa, and finally Afghanistan and northwest India.

In 323 B.C. Alexander I died and his empire was divided among four of his generals.

A. Seleucus (312–280 B.C.), the ablest of all of the generals, received Babylonia. He soon acquired most of Asia Minor and encouraged colonization and a standard calendar for the lands he controlled.

B. Ptolemy acquired Egypt.

C. Antigonus received Asia Minor but soon lost most of it to Seleucus.

D. Antipater was given Macedonia.

Hellenistic Culture

The greatest gift Alexander gave to the world was the blending of Middle Eastern culture and Greek ideas and institutions. Intellectual life flourished. Alexandria in Egypt was the symbol of the age, a magnificent city to which scholars from all over the world flocked. The library at Alexandria housed over 700,000 scrolls.

Economic as well as intellectual prosperity was achieved by uniformity in speech, in coinage, and in laws that created the conditions necessary for a flourishing trade.

THE ROMAN EMPIRE IN THE EAST

By the beginning of the Christian era, Rome had conquered Asia Minor, Syria (64 B.C.), Palestine, Egypt (30 B.C.), Northern Mesopotamia, and later part of Arabia.

Intellectual and Religious Life during the Roman Empire in the East

During the Roman Empire one of the greatest of the world's religions was born in the Middle East—Christianity.

Rome carried still further Alexander's attempt to bring Greek ideas and institutions to the Middle East.

Neoplatonism was the attempt to reconcile Platonic and Aristotelian thought with oriental ideas. It combined a contempt for the world of matter with a belief in the purification of the soul, which could be reunited with the godhead through spiritual ecstasy.

Mystery cults flourished in the Roman Empire, particularly during the third century A.D. They preached that true knowledge of God could be achieved only through mysticism and intuition, not through reason. Paradise could be attained by membership in secret societies that practiced ritualistic and emotional rites. The two most popular mystery cults were the Isis-Osiris cult, which was the most bitterly antagonistic towards Christianity, and the cult of Mithraism (originally an Iranian diety).

THE BYZANTINE EMPIRE

Constantine, in 324 A.D., chose the site of an old Greek colony, Byzantium, for his capital. Christianity was recognized as the official religion of his empire.

Constant warfare between Byzantium and Persian troops for the mastery of the Near East was the theme of the Byzantine empire. In 617 the Persians came within one mile of Constantinople, but Heraclius (r. 610–41) was able to turn back the Persian tide, and Constantinople itself survived as the imperial seat of the Eastern Roman Empire until 1453, although during the eleventh century it was dealt a death blow by the Saljuq Turks.

The Christian Middle East

Syria, Lebanon, and Palestine became Christian, although the Syrian church differed in language and ritual and became known as Nestorian, named after the bishop of Constantinople in 428 who argued the divine nature of Christ.

The Egyptian Christian church also deviated from the imperial church, accepting the Arian heresy named after a Greek ecclesiastic, Arius (d. 336), who taught that God was unknowable and Christ was not God) and using Coptic (one of the ancient Egyptian tongues) as its language. The church today is known as the Coptic Christian Church, of which there are about 8,500,000 members in Ethiopia (one half the population) and about 160,000 in Egypt (7 percent of the population).

MEDIEVAL CIVILIZATION 500 A.D.–1500 A.D.

The division between the Christian west and the Persian-Zoroastrian east was to disappear at the beginning of the medieval period, when once again the lands of the Middle East were united under a single empire and a new religion, Islam. For centuries the Moslem empire ruled the Middle East, giving to it a common language, a common faith and a common heritage, but by 920 the Moslem empire was in decline and by 1258 it gave way to Turkish invaders from Central Asia. The medieval Islamic period was probably one of the most impor-

tant in Middle Eastern civilization, for it ended Greco-Roman hegemony and developed the faith and language that are still predominant in the area. Unlike the medieval period in European history, this was an era of learning, progress, and splendor in the Near East.

THE ISLAMIC AGE AND EMPIRE

The Birth of Islam

The founder of the Moslem faith was Mohammed (571–632). Born in Mecca of a camel herder and orphaned at six, Mohammed married at twenty-five a wealthy widow, who gave him the economic means to spend a life of meditation.

Around 610 A.D., he became aware of the message of Allah (God). His faith was not popular among the pagan aristocracy, and his early followers were primarily slaves and lower classes. In 622, because of persecution, Mohammed and 200 followers fled to the city of Medina, a rival of Mecca. The founding of Islam is dated from this flight or hegira. Mohammed's faith soon became so popular that by 630 he was able to return to Mecca, defeat his aristocratic enemies, destroy the 360 pagan idols in the Kaaba (holy shrine) and become head of the state.

The Nature of Islam

An offshoot of Christianity and Judaism, Mohammed's faith accepted the basic doctrine of the sole creator and sole judge. The prophets of the Old Testament were recognized and Christ was believed to be a great prophet, but Mohammed was the last and greatest prophet. Mohammed broke with the Christian faith on several items:

A. The sabbath was changed to Friday;

B. The direction faced during prayer was changed from Jerusalem to Mecca;

C. Pilgrimage to the Kaaba and Mecca was sanctioned;

D. There were to be no priesthood (this was later modified) and no sacraments;

E. Eventually the Koran became the word of God.

The Five Pillars

The religious duties and beliefs of a Moslem are known as the Five Pillars of Islam (the word Islam means submission to the will of God).

A. The creed of a Moslem is "There is no God but Allah, Mohammed is His prophet." This is chanted from minarets by a muezzin (not a priest but an intoner) when he calls the faithful to prayer.

B. Prayers are required five times a day. Prayer is said on a carpet, with the head covered, facing Mecca.

C. Almsgiving is necessary and holy. Orphans and poor are provided for in the Moslem world.

D. Fasting is also required. The holiest fast is Ramadan, which is made in thanks for the Koran and is from daybreak to sunset for a month.

E. Pilgrimage to Mecca is required of every Moslem at least once in his lifetime. After the pilgrimage is taken, a Moslem may add the title of Hadj to his name.

F. Another Islamic belief was elevated by some sects to the position of a sixth pillar. From the beginning Islam was a militant faith, believing that the world was divided into two camps, Moslem and non-Moslem, and that Holy War (Jihad) against the infidel was necessary to salvation. If the non-Moslem was a person "of the book" (the Old Testament) he need not be forcibly converted but could be allowed to pay tribute instead. This was often extended to Zoroastrians and others. Death in Holy War was martyrdom and guaranteed the privileges of paradise. After death a day of judgment decided one's future life.

The Koran

The compilation of the sayings of Mohammed was begun under Abu-Bakr (r. 632–634) and completed under Uthman (r. 644–656). The Koran was the earliest prose work in Arabic and to the Moslem was the word of God as revealed to Mohammed, and was (and still is for some sects) the final authority on everything, not just religious matters. It contained civil law—rules of inheritance, divorce, the treatment of slaves and prisoners, and so on. It authorized polygamy and concubinage but set the limit at four wives; it forbade most stimulants; and it required all good women to practice purdah (veiling).

The Two Branches of Islam

A. The Sunnite Moslem is the orthodox Moslem and believes that the caliph inherited Mohammed's temporal powers only; no one inherited his spiritual ones.

B. The Shiite Moslems were the discontented group and have broken into many splinter groups. Fundamentally they believe that the imam (Moslem priest) is the leader of the faith and has inherited Mohammed's spiritual as well as temporal powers. (Ali Khan's followers, for example, are members of a Shiite splinter group.)

The Caliphate

When Mohammed died in 632 A.D., he left no provisions for a successor. The decision as to who would replace Mohammed as ruler, leader, and commander of the faith led to years of bloodshed within the Moslem world and was never resolved completely. There were three groups who contended for the position:

A. Mohammed's wife's relatives who had fled with him to Medina and those who had supported him in Medina soon joined together to form the Companions, and this was the group who first triumphed.

B. The Legitimists were those who thought that the Caliphate should be an heir of Mohammed. Ali, husband of the prophet's only surviving daughter, Fatimah, was named as the legitimate heir.

C. The traditional heads of the community, the Umayyads, felt that they should be allowed to rule.

The Caliphate   632–1258 A.D.

ABU BAKR   (r. 632–634)

The father-in-law of Mohammed and one of his early followers, he was responsible for conquering Arabia and beginning
the compilation of the Koran.

UMAR   (r. 634–644)

Like his predecessor a simple man, Umar is known for his
piety and virtue. He was killed by a Christian Persian slave.

UTHMAN   (r. 644–656)

Uthman was killed during a Moslem uprising.

ALI   (r. 656–661)

At first acknowledged by both Companions and Legitimists,
he was killed during a dynastic war.

THE UMAYYAD DYNASTY   661–750, with its capital at Damascus

A cousin of Ali's, Muawiyah, governor of Syria, established
the principle of succession in his family, the Umayyads. A branch
of the Umayyads ruled in Cordova, Spain from 929 to 1031.

THE ABBASID DYNASTY   750–1258, with its capital at Baghdad

This was the height of the empire. The Abbasids succeeded
in overthrowing the Umayyads and from then on the position of
caliphate was dependent upon military force.

THE FATIMID DYNASTY   909–1171, with its capital at Cairo

The Fatimid dynasty controlled most of North Africa until
it was overthrown by Saladin.

Islam Conquers the Middle East   632–750

The military campaigns of two of the greatest generals in
history—Khalid ibn-al-Walid and Amr ibn-al-As—were responsible for the success of the Moslem armies. The use of cavalry and
"camelry" gave the Moslems remarkable mobility.

The Conquests

A. In 636 Damascus fell to the Arabs and soon all of Syria
was in their hands. By 637 the Moslems had defeated the Persians
and acquired Iraq, and by 643 were on the borders of India.

B. The battle against Egypt (642) was one of the most spectacular. The Arabs had about 20,000 men and no ships and no siege machines, yet they took Alexandria with her garrison of some 50,000 men and the entire Byzantine navy.

c. From Egypt, north Africa was overrun by 703, and in 711 under Tariq half of Spain was conquered. Musa, jealous of his lieutenant, rushed to Spain in 712 and captured the other half.

d. The first defeat the Moslems suffered was in 720, when they attempted to push on beyond the Pyrenees; and they were finally routed by the Franks at the Battle of Tours in 732.

By 732 the Islamic empire was at its height; the Mediterranean Sea had become a Moslem Lake.

The Islamic Empire and Civilization

The Social Structure of the Empire

Social classes were rigidly defined. First were the ruling Moslems, the original Arab conquerors. Second in the social scale were the neo-Moslems (those who had been converted). They were discriminated against politically and yet outshone the Arabs in their intellectual achievements. Third in the social scale were members of the tolerated sects. They were forced to pay tribute and wear distinctive dress; they thus became known as spotted. But on the whole they were treated fairly well: Jews were better treated than Christians and often held positions of responsibility.

Under the Abbasids (750–1258) the Islamic empire experienced its golden age. Baghdad, built by the Abbasids, was the symbol of the era, and the *Arabian Nights* is an accurate picture of its wealth and splendor, as well as its corruption.

Contributions of the Empire

Probably one of the greatest contributions was the transmission of civilization. Ideas from all over the world were brought together at centers of learning such as Cairo and Gundeshapur (Persia). Greek and Indian influence played an extremely important role. Hunayn ibn-Ishaq (809–873), a prolific translator, was representative of this era during which the major works of other civilizations were translated into the Arabic tongue. For example, almost all the surviving works of Aristotle were translated, and it was in part through these translations that the European world became aware of the Greek world.

Another of the significant gifts to the world was the Arabic tongue. The Middle East, with the exception of Turkey, Persia, and, later, Israel, became Arab.

Important transmissions in the field of agriculture also took place during the Islamic Empire, although the Arabs themselves did not believe in working with their hands. New crops such as sugar cane, cotton, rice, and fruits were introduced into Mesopotamia, Spain, and North Africa, and stock-raising was also brought to many parts of the world.

Trade flourished, manufacturing was increased (the manufacture of linen paper was brought from China and rapidly replaced papyrus), and cities grew throughout the Middle East.

Not only were the natural sciences of Greece thoroughly studied but the Moslems also made important contributions in the field. Arabic numerals and the zero were adopted from India and spread to Europe, making possible significant Arab discoveries in the fields of trigonometry, geometry, and astronomy.

Some of the most outstanding Moslem achievements occurred in the field of medicine. Hospitals were established throughout the empire; extensive work was done on eye diseases; Al Razi (865–925) wrote a book that was the chief source of chemical knowledge in Europe until the fourteenth century. Ibn-Sina (Avicenna), who lived from 980 to 1037, wrote the chief medical guide, *Al-Quanun,* which was to serve in the East until the nineteenth century. Important discoveries in alchemy and botany went hand in hand with medical progress.

A Spanish Moslem, Ibn-Khaldun (d. 1406), was probably the founder of social science, taking into consideration physical facts such as climate and geography in order to understand historical development.

In art the Moslem, influenced by the Persian, created the most exquisite mosaic.

Moslem philosophers "succeeded," according to Philip K.

Hitti in *The Arabs: A Short History,* "for the first time in the history of human thought in harmonizing and reconciling monotheism . . . with Greek philosophy. . . . Islam thus led Christian Europe toward the modern point of view."

THE DOWNFALL OF THE ISLAMIC EMPIRE

General Causes

The continuous problem of the succession of the caliphate became more and more serious as rival dynasties claimed control. Internal problems such as the cleavage among social classes, between north and south Arabia, and within the faith itself also tore the empire apart. Luxurious living, overtaxation, and the depletion of manpower through war added to the causes of the downfall of the Moslem empire.

Invasions Weakened the Empire and Finally Destroyed It

The Saljuq Turks claimed control of Mesopotamia and placed their leader, Tughril, on the thone of Baghdad in 1037, although the caliph was allowed to survive. In 1092, however, the Saljuq rule began to break up.

Militant Christianity Wreaked Further Havoc in the Middle East

The first of the crusades, up to 1144, brought Syria and much of Egypt into the crusaders' hands. The Moslem reaction and the victories of Saladin were a temporary reprieve.

1) Saladin, a Syrian of Kurdish parents and Vizar of Egypt in 1169, recaptured Jerusalem in 1187, and signed a peace with the Europeans in 1192 giving the coast to the Latins and the interior to the Moslems.

2) Saladin was more than a warrior; he devoted his energies to building canals and irrigation ditches and encouraging scholarship.

In Spain, the Christians delivered the death blow to the corrupt Moslem dynasties. In 1031 the Spanish Islamic government had broken up into a conglomeration of Moslem states and then had passed to a Berber dynasty, the Almoravids. At the same time the Christian Spaniards had begun the reconquest of the land. Toledo fell in 1085; and the union between Castile and Leon in 1230 helped the Christian cause. Cordova surrendered in 1236 and Seville in 1248. In 1469 the marriage of Ferdinand of Aragon and Isabella of Castile united all Christian forces, and the Moslems were totally eliminated with the fall of Granada in 1492. By the beginning of the seventeenth century over three million Moslems had been banished or executed.

The Norman conquest of Sicily began in 1060; by 1071 Palermo was in their hands; by 1085, Syracuse; and the conquest was complete by 1091. Contrary to their experience in Spain, however, the Moslems were allowed, until 1154, to retain some of the highest positions under Roger I and II.

The Loss of Egypt

A. The Fatimid Caliphate had established its independence from the rest of the Moslem empire in 909, but it faced the same problems as its cousins.

B. The Mamluk dynasty was the last medieval dynasty in the Arab world. A dynasty of slaves, they ruled the country from 1250 to 1517. Founded by Baybars, the Mamluks were able to defeat the Christian crusaders and check the advance of the Mongols so that Egypt did not suffer the devastation that Iraq and Syria did. The dynasty was noted for its amazing architectural and artistic productivity. Domes, the geometrical arabesque, and Kufic lettering were representative of this period.

C. The Mamluks were finally defeated in a battle by the Ottoman Turks led by Salin in 1516, and Egypt was overrun by 1517.

THE LOSS OF SICILY had been gained by the Moslems in 827.

The Barbarian Invasions

A. In 1216, Jenghiz Khan and 60,000 Mongolian barbarians invaded the Middle East, destroyed the cultural centers and the irrigation works, and laid waste to the land.

B. In 1253, the second wave of Mongols led by Hulagu invaded. In 1258, Baghdad was destroyed and 800,000 people were killed in a single week. Fifty thousand more fell at Aleppo. In 1260 Syria was under Mongol control and Hulagu took the title of Il-Khan. The Mongols may have destroyed the Islamic empire, but in the end Islam triumphed; the seventh khan recognized Mohammed's faith as the state religion.

C. In 1380 Tamerlane (Timur Lang) and his horde of Tartars gained Afghanistan and Persia. By 1393 they were in Baghdad and soon laid waste to the rest of Mesopotamia. By 1401 they had acquired northern Syria, sacking Aleppo in 1400 and Damascus in 1401, and soon afterwards they conquered all of Asia Minor.

D. The final invaders were the Ottoman Turks. This group of people had originated in Mongolia and had mixed with Iranian tribes and established a kingdom in Asia Minor by the beginning of the fourteenth century. By 1517 they had conquered Syria and Egypt.

MODERN CIVILIZATION 1500 to the Present

The modern period in Middle Eastern history began with the conquest of the Moslem empire by the Ottoman Turks, but the founder of modern civilization may be said to be Muhammed Ali (d. 1849) of Egypt, who first began to borrow Western ideas and institutions. By 1900, the Ottoman empire had become "the sick man of Europe," an invalid state financially under Western control, and the only reason it was not totally in Western hands was because the Europeans could not decide how to divide it up. At the end of World War I, however, France and England assumed control under the mandate system. Along with Western influence came nationalism and the demand for independence, and immediately after World War I many of the mandated countries revolted. Order was finally restored and there was uneasy peace until World War II. By the end of the Second World War the situation had changed. The power of Western Europe, particularly France, had declined; Arab nationalism had been further inflamed by German propaganda; and Russia had become a great power, thus giving the Middle East a chance to play off Western Europe against the U.S.S.R. By 1946 most of the Near Eastern countries were free but divided—more divided than they had ever been in their history. There have been some attempts at Pan-Arabism, but the problem of uneven distribution of wealth and the rivalry for leadership of the movement loom large, and so far there seems to have been very little success in achieving unity. A factor that has solidified antagonism toward the West and strengthened Near Eastern nationalism, however, is the existence of Israel.

THE OTTOMAN EMPIRE

Government

The government of the new empire was a military dynastic institution. The Turks were the privileged class in society, and the entire Moslem hierarchy was headed by them. The chief judge of Islamic law, the mufti, soon assumed both religious and secular power. The Ottoman empire enslaved Christian boys (Janissaries), trained them, "turkified" them, and used them as government officials, army officers, and soldiers. The empire was naturally antinationalistic, for it contained so many different ethnic groups.

The Important Sultans of the Ottoman Empire

Osman (r. 1299–1326), the first of thirty-six sultans, is given credit for the founding of the empire.

Muhammed II (r. 1451–81), however, was the real founder,

for it was he who led the troops against Constantinople in 1453, destroying what remained of the Byzantine empire, and establishing Ottoman supremacy. Only his death prevented the conquest of Southern Italy.

Salim I (r. 1512–20) conquered Egypt and Syria and brought Arabia into the Ottoman fold. With the addition of Arabia the Ottomans assumed the position of caliph and became heads of the Moslem faith.

Suleiman the Magnificent's reign (1520–66) was the height of the Ottoman empire. Under his rule law was codified, Ottoman sea power was built, and great buildings were constructed (he is given credit for building 312 structures). Tunisia was invaded in 1534 and became a province in 1574; Tripoli in 1551; and most of Hungary was added to the empire. When Vienna was besieged for the first time in 1529, Ottoman supremacy had reached its greatest extent. Thereafter the empire went into rapid decline, subject to foreign pressures and internal revolutions.

THE DECLINE OF THE OTTOMAN EMPIRE

As early as Salim II (r. 1566–74) the decline of the Ottomans had begun. The state was unwieldy; its population was heterogeneous; it was too far-flung in area; and its purpose seemed to be "warfare rather than welfare." There was never an attempt to improve either industry or agriculture. Other problems plagued it: a lack of established rule of succession; corruption and constant warfare with the Balkans and with Russian ambitions to gain a warm water port.

The Ottomans Were Never Able Effectively to Control Their Far-flung Empire

Egypt was semi-independent from 1801 on; Iraq, incorporated into the Ottoman empire in 1638, was ruled by Egyptian Mamluks, although the Ottomans reasserted their authority in 1831; Lebanon developed independently thanks to two of her rulers, Fekhri-al-Din II and Bashir II; Greece declared her independence in 1821.

Saudi Arabia had also given the Ottomans trouble.

A. In the 1700's a puritanical religious revival, led by Muhammed ibn-Abd-al-Wahhab (d. 1792), was befriended by a petty chief, Muhammed ibn-Saud (d. 1765). To spread the word of Allah, the Saudi family had to capture Arabia. In 1773 they succeeded in seizing Riyad, and this became the Saudi capital. In 1818 the Ottomans finally defeated the Saudi clan and the dynasty was banished. In 1891 Muhammed ibn-Rashid occupied the Saudi capital of Riyad.

B. Then in 1902, twenty-year-old Abd-al-Aziz ibn-Saud, raised in Kuwait from the age of ten, raided Riyad with two hundred followers. In 1913 he seized al-Hasa and by 1917 he had only two rivals left—Rashid in the north and Hussein ibn-Ali (father of Faisal of Iraq and Abdullah of Jordan, who had been installed in Mecca by the Ottomans in 1908) in Hejaz. This was the situation at the outbreak of World War I when the allies turned to Arabia for help against the Turks.

Abd-al-Hamid II's Reactionary Reign (1876–1909) Contributed to the Downfall of the Turks

He replaced his liberal brother, Murad V, on the throne, declared him insane and abolished his constitution.

Repressive measures such as the Armenian massacres of 1894 and 1895, in which 100,000 were killed, were symptomatic of his fear of assassination at the hands of liberal Turks, and his fear for the life of the state, because of uprisings in Bulgaria and Armenia.

He attempted to dam up Western ideas, to control the nation with an iron hand, and to turn the clock back. This finally led to a coup in 1908 by young army officers demanding a constitution and a homogeneous nation. Hamid was deposed in 1909 and his brother, Muhammed V (r. 1909–18), was placed on the throne—in name only, for the government was actually controlled by the Young Turks.

Under the Young Turks the Empire Disintegrated at an Even Faster Rate

Austria annexed Bosnia and Herzegovina in 1908, and in the same year Bulgaria declared her independence; in 1910 Albania revolted; and in 1911 and 1912 Italy occupied Tripoli and Benghazi. Serbia, Montenegro, and Bulgaria allied against the Ottomans, and in 1913 Bulgaria and Serbia agreed to partition Ottoman Macedonia. This agreement led to war, in which Turkey was stripped of most of Eastern Europe (the First and Second Balkan Wars).

EUROPEANS AND EUROPEAN INFLUENCE COME
TO THE MIDDLE EAST

North Africa—the First to Fall into European Hands

Algeria was invaded by France in 1830, and eighteen years later was declared French territory.

Tunisia was then occupied by the French in 1881.

Libya was seized by Italy in 1911.

By 1912 the French and Spanish zones of Morocco had been acquired.

Egypt

From the very begnining of Ottoman rule (1517) Egypt had been under a system of dual control involving the Mamluk governors (beys) and an Ottoman pasha or overlord. Corruption, poverty, and heavy taxation were the themes of the administration.

Westernization and Muhammed Ali

A. With Napoleon's invasion of Egypt in 1798, the situation changed and Western influence began to penetrate Egypt. Muhammed Ali, a Turkish officer of Albanian birth, drove Napoleon's troops out of Egypt by 1801 and became the pasha. He then made his rule virtually independent of Ottoman control.

B. Recognizing the technological superiority of the West, he began a rapid program of Westernization and centralization. He established state monopolies, improved agriculture and industry by introducing rice and Egypt's most important crop, cotton, and by promoting irrigation projects and native industries. He combatted plagues by rigid quarantines, established the first schools of engineering and medicine and the first Arabic press, created a westernized military force and destroyed the Mamluks, and sent 311 students to Europe to study.

C. Muhammed Ali had visions of a pan-Arab state and captured Syria, which Egypt controlled until 1840, and the Sudan, and he even knocked on the gates of Constantinople. This led to the first Western intervention in Egyptian affairs, for the British and French preferred a weak Ottoman state to a strong pan-Arab one.

The second and most important western intervention in Egypt was over the control of the Suez Canal.

A. In 1859, Said (r. 1854–63) granted a concession (ninety-nine years) for a Suez Canal to the French engineer Ferdinand de Lesseps; Said was to receive in shares 15 percent of the profit and provide four fifths of the labor.

B. Under Said's successor, however, the Egyptian government fell further and further into debt. Ismail (r. 1863–74) set up uniformity of jurisdiction, increased the number of public schools, introduced the first post office in Egypt, and bettered communications, but his projects were expensive and reckless (the debt rose from 250 million francs in 1865 to two billion in 1875), and Ismail, in order to stave off bankruptcy, was forced to sell his 200,000 shares in the canal to the British government. But the money from this sale lasted him only a year.

C. The British assumed control of Egypt.

1) After the Egyptian government defaulted on debts borrowed from French and English banks, two controller generals, one English and one French, were established to protect European investments, and they virtually took over the government. They instigated reforms in the government and forced Ismail to abdicate in favor of his son. This caused rioting against foreign penetration led by Ahmad Arabi.

2) War broke out in 1882, and the Egyptians threatened to destroy the canal. Britain sent in troops, seized the canal, and ruled Egypt in all but name until 1914, when she took over total control.

Lebanon and Western Influence

Under Fekhr-al-Din (r. 1590–1635) Lebanon was virtually independent of Ottoman control. During his reign European Catholic missions, which were later to play a large role in the westernization of Lebanon, were permitted in the country.

Again under Bashir II (r. 1788–1840) Lebanon became independent, and Bashir opened up the country to foreign influence. American missionaries arrived in the 1820's, and the French built the first silk factory there in 1841. Civil wars, following the death of Bashir, finally led to European intervention in the 1860's.

Persia

Persia was one of the first Middle Eastern countries to become a pawn of the Western powers. The Safawid, a native dynasty, ruled Persia from 1501 to 1736, and during this period, the Portuguese seized Hormuz on the Persian gulf, controlling it until 1622, when it was recovered by the Safawids with Dutch and English help. From then on it was Great Britain who received the concessions in Persia. (The French, for example, were not allowed to trade with Persia until 1644.)

The Afsharid, a Turkoman tribe, ruled Persia from 1736 to 1746, followed by the Ands, a nomadic Iranian tribe, 1750–79; and then the Qajars another Turkoman dynasty (founded by a eunuch!), 1799–1925. The Qajars ruled the country as an enemy and were far from popular with the people. During their rule the British, French, and Russians bickered among themselves for control of the country.

A. The Anglo-Persian Treaty of 1814 against Russia put Persia at the mercy of British foreign policy; the Russo-Persian Treaty of 1828 put her at the mercy of Russian foreign policy. From then on she was a pawn in world politics; foreigners controlled her economy; the British and the Russians were given more and more concessions; and the Persian government sank further and further into debt.

B. In 1907 Russia and Britain settled their differences, dividing the country between them—Russia taking the northern half as her sphere of influence and the British the southern half.

C. In 1901 a concession for oil was given to William D'Arcy, a New Zealander. In 1909 the Anglo-Persian Oil Company was formed, which built the Aradan refinery, the largest in the world.

WORLD WAR I AND THE DEATH OF THE OTTOMAN EMPIRE

Turkey entered the war on the side of Germany in the summer of 1914. She was unprepared to fight a war on four fronts (Russia in the Caucasus; Anglo-Iranian troops on the Iraqi border; Arab, British, and French troops on the Palestine-Egypt front; and Australian, New Zealand, and English forces in the Dardanelles). Many of the Arabian countries such as Lebanon and Syria welcomed the Allies, and others such as Saudi Arabia fought vigorously against the Turks.

An armistice ending World War I (October 30, 1918 at Mudros) did not end the war for the Turks, nor did the Peace Treaty of Sèvres, signed by Sultan Walud-al-Din on August 10, 1920, bring peace to the Middle East. The Ottoman empire was dismembered by the Treaty of Sèvres: Syria and Lebanon became mandates of France; Iraq and Palestine became mandates of Great Britain; the Hejaz and Armenia were to be independent. Turkey's islands went to Italy and Greece, and foreign troops, primarily Greek, landed in Anatolia.

The Turks were in a state of anarchy. In 1920 a national assembly at Ankara set up a provisional government with Mustafa Kemal (Ataturk) as head. The nationalist government refused to accept the terms of the peace treaty, and Turkey was once again at war. By 1922 the sultanate had been destroyed; by 1924 the caliphate had been abolished, and Ataturk and his forces had pushed the Greek army into the sea. In 1923 the Lausanne peace treaty was signed: Turkey recovered East Thrace and some of her islands, escaped paying reparations, and freed herself from European control.

THE MANDATED AREAS OF THE MIDDLE EAST

Egypt 1914 to Independence

Britain declared a protectorate over Egypt as soon as Turkey had joined Germany, and martial law was enforced throughout the country. Nationalistic hopes and aspirations were raised during the war as a result of frustration with British control and promises made in Wilson's Fourteen Points. Saud Zaghlul led a delegation (the Wafd party) to London demanding independence, and for his efforts he was deported to Malta and then to Aden. Yet in 1922 Britain yielded to nationalistic demands, gave up her protectorate, and declared Egypt to be "independent with reservations" (defense, communications, protection of foreign interests, and the status of the Sudan). Faud (r. 1922–36) was made king of Egypt, and although in some respects he was a tool of the British, Egypt was at least semi-independent.

Syria and Lebanon

The administration of the French mandates was entrusted to generals. The Syrians were opposed to the mandate from the very beginning. Lebanon was in favor, because the majority of her population was Christian and she felt French rule would be protection from Moslem domination. A Syrian congress declared Faisal, son of the Hashmite al-Husayn, to be king of Syria, but the Congress party was put down by French arms (and Faisal was installed by the British as King of Iraq). A period of terrorism and reprisal followed. Men such as Shukri al-Quwatli were jailed; revolt in 1925 led to French bombing of Damascus;

and parliaments were promised, elected, and then prorogued by the French. But after World War II the French were in no position to argue, and Syria became independent in 1945.

Lebanon was a different story. For the first fifteen years there was peaceful progress. In 1926 Lebanon was proclaimed a republic and given a constitution. This constitution has been modified several times but is still in force (Lebanon's tradition of having a Maronite [Christian] president, a Sunnite [Moslem] prime minister and a Shiite [Moslem] speaker of the house is not in the constitution but was initiated during this period). From 1936 on, however, there was a decline in relations between Lebanon and France, and there were further demands by the Lebanese for complete independence. In 1943 France finally yielded, but it required UN action in 1946 to force the last French troops from Lebanon's soil.

Iraq

In contrast to French administration in Syria, leadership under the British mandate in Iraq fell into civilian rather than military hands. In 1921 a revolt was put down by the British at the cost of 400 British and Indian and 8540 Iraqi lives and at the expense of £200,000,000 (plus another £400,000 on Iraq's part). The British quickly learned their lesson and treated Iraq in much the same manner as they had treated Egypt. Faisal was made king of Iraq, and in 1924 she was declared a sovereign state; in 1930 she agreed to consult Great Britain on foreign policy for a period of twenty-five years and to show preference to British advisers; and by 1932 she was considered totally independent and joined the League of Nations.

Palestine and Transjordan

The Creation of Jordan

A. From the outset Palestine resisted the British mandate, and because of the peculiar wording of the mandate, Britain was able to divide the Palestine and Transjordan area into two separate countries.

B. Britain made Transjordan autonomous under Amir Abdullah, brother of Faisal of Iraq. An artificially created state with no geographic unity, no political history, and no economic viability, Transjordan was created by the British as a fortress to guard her oil industry. During World War II the Arab Legion of Jordan supported the Allies, and in 1946 Britain granted a treaty of complete independence so long as Jordan agreed to consult her on all foreign matters.

The Palestine issue was the thorniest in the Middle East and is still causing trouble.

A. In 1917, the Belfour Declaration had announced that it should be England's intention to establish a national home for the Jews in Palestine "without prejudicing the rights of non-Jews." At this time the Arabs (the non-Jews) in Palestine numbered about 700,000, whereas the Jews were a minority of about 70,000.

B. From 1917 on, Zionists (the organization of Jewish people desiring the reestablishment of a national home in Palestine) encouraged immigration into the country. By 1939 Arabs outnumbered Jews by only two to one.

C. In 1928 and again in 1936, Arabs rioted, and in 1939 the British White Paper attempted to end Jewish immigration into the country, but London and Washington were afraid to take drastic steps because they needed to "woo the Jewish vote." Moreover, with the persecution of the Jews by Hitler, the sympathies of the world were naturally with the people who fled to Palestine.

D. In 1948 the United Nations recommended the division of Palestine between the Arabs and the Jews, but in May of 1948 a provisional government in Tel Aviv declared the independent state of Israel headed by David Ben-Gurion as prime minister and Dr. Weizmann as president. War broke out between the Arabs and the Israelis. Egyptian, Iraqi, Transjordan, Lebanese, and a few Saudi Arabian troops invaded the area. In 1949 an armistice was declared, but it was not the end of hostilities.

Arabia Becomes Saudi Arabia

World War I and the Struggle for Mastery of Arabia

A. During World War I the British offered Hussein an independent Arabia—there was definitely a question whether this promise included the entire Arab world—if he would fight against the Turks, and he obliged in June of 1916. Ibn-Saud, however, did nothing during the war for the Allied cause but instead made ready his troops and consolidated his possessions for the battle that was to ensue for mastery of the peninsula.

B. In 1921, ibn-Saud succeeded in eliminating the house of ibn-Rashid, thus gaining control of central and east Arabia. In 1924 he defeated Hussein's son and seized Mecca, in 1925 Medina, and in 1926 he was proclaimed king of Hejaz. By 1932 the Arabian peninsula, with the exceptions of Yemen, an independent principality, and Oman and Aden, both British domains, had been unified and become Saudi Arabia.

Present-day Saudi Arabia

A. Saudi Arabia has been called the world's most feudalistic state. The Koran is the constitution; law is based on ancient Islamic law; only Mecca, Medina, and Jeddah have city governments; and the king of Saudi Arabia is an absolute monarch. Under ibn-Saud technological improvements were made but not many educational ones; about 95 percent of the people remain illiterate.

B. Saudi Arabia received a great amount of aid during World War II, in return for which the United States was allowed an air base at Dhahran, and in March of 1945 Saud declared war on Germany.

C. Oil, discovered in 1936, is controlled by the American Company, Aramco, and one half of the profits go to Saudi Arabia. Another source of income is the pilgrimage to Mecca, which brings about six million dollars a year.

D. Saudi Arabia was the founding member of the Arab

League, probably in hopes of creating and leading a United Arab empire, but she played only a minor role in the war against Israel, and her hopes for leadership of the Arabs have been frustrated by Nasser of Egypt.

E. In 1952 ibn-Saud died, and one of his forty sons, Saud (Saud ibn Abdul Aziz al Faisal al Saud) became king. Saud was more Western than his father, but in 1958 a financial crisis led to a palace revolt, and his brother Faisal took over the government until December of 1960. In 1964 Faisal (Faisal Abdel Aziz al Saud al Faisal) was made the official ruler of Saudi Arabia. In the struggle against Saud, Faisal had most of the young liberals on his side. He promised economic development with conservative financing, modernization with caution, and the limiting of the power of the religious leaders without hurting their feelings.

Persia Becomes Iran

Persia was not part of the Ottoman empire and did not change drastically as a result of World War I. It was not until Reza Khan (1925–1941) took over the government of Persia that a definite break with the past occurred.

A. Reza Khan first brought the tribes of Persia under government control and then set about on a drastic program of reforms similar to those of his contemporary, Ataturk in Turkey. Communications were improved; the Trans-Persian Railroad was built; privileges of the priestly class were curtailed; education was modernized and nationalized; legislation on women's rights was initiated; and in 1938 Reza Khan abolished the capitulations (foreign extraterritorial rights) and acquired more oil royalty for Iran.

B. Reza Khan was forced by the allies to abdicate, because he was pro-Axis during the war. His son, Muhammed Reza, at the age of twenty-two, succeeded him and immediately declared war on Germany.

After World War II the economic conditions of the country were poor, and in April of 1951 the prime minister Muhammed

Mosaddiq, an extreme antiwesterner, nationalized oil. The nationalization of oil, however, proved unsuccessful, for Iran had few technicians and the industry soon closed down. Mosaddiq plotted to dispose of both the Shah and the parliament, and in 1953 he was jailed; oil settlements were reached (the British Petroleum Company Limited, consisting of eight companies, was formed); and Iran received a forty-five-million-dollar grant from the United States to put her back on her feet economically.

Since the war Muhammed Reza has initiated vast land reforms and vigorously attempted to modernize his country.

The Ottoman Empire Becomes Turkey

Once Turkish territory had been regained by the young nationalists led by Kemal, the Republic of Turkey was established with Kemal as president and Ismet as prime minister.

Radical reforms were immediately introduced to change the face of Turkey and create a modern, westward-looking country. Education was taken out of religious hands and made universal; women were granted rights including the franchise; the fez and purdah were outlawed; Islam was disestablished as the state religion; Islamic law was replaced by a new code based on European models; polygamy became illegal; the Arabic alphabet was outlawed and replaced by the Latin one; family names were adopted. (Kemal took the name of Ataturk [father of the Turks] and Ismet took the last name of Inonu.) Although the government was dictatorial, controlled completely by Ataturk and the Republican People's Party, Kemal nevertheless did set up the machinery for a democratic system.

In 1938 Ataturk died, and his policies were carried on by Ismet Inonu. Another party, the Democrat, was allowed to exist and triumphed under Bayer and Menderes (prime minister) from 1950 to 1960. Menderes' Democrat Party revived Islam, and his economic policy in most cases favored the peasants at the expense of the urban population. The Party was overthrown by a coup d'état in 1960 by advocates of the Republican People's

Party. In 1965, however, the eighty-one-year-old Inonu was forced by a vote of no confidence to resign.

Turkey has its problems; over 61.2 percent of the people cannot read or write. The peasant situation still needs attention, but the country is industrializing rapidly and is closely linked with the West, being not simply anti-Communist but anti-Russian.

Turkey is a member of NATO, and initiated the Baghdad Pact; and she received $200,000,000 from the United States in military aid in 1955 and $70,000,000 annually after that. In 1958 she was granted another $359,000,000.

Independent Egypt

In 1936, after negotiations, riots, and more negotiations, Great Britain agreed to withdraw her military forces except in the Suez Canal zone, but she still retained indirect control through King Farouk. In 1937 Egypt was admitted into the League of Nations.

During World War II Egypt declared a state of siege (not war); Cairo and Alexandria were bombed by the Axis powers; and Egypt was occupied by the Allies. She was strategically important in addition to serving as a supply center for the entire Near Eastern region. As a result of the war the country prospered economically and emerged from World War II as the most powerful Arab state.

In 1948 Egypt participated in the Arab League against Israel.

The Fall of the Monarchy

A. Egypt had changed, but the government had not. The monarchy was bound to run into trouble. By tradition and training King Farouk (r. 1936–52) and his father, Faud I (r. 1922–36) were instruments of British influence; they were authoritarian in their rule and they had little concern for the welfare of their people. The Wafds (an antimonarchy party) held a parliamentary majority and yet were not in control of the government.

B. In 1952 General Naguib, hero of the war against Israel, and the army overthrew Faud II, who had replaced his father Farouk. A possible explanation for this was the discredit that the defeat in Palestine had caused the monarchy, but there were many economic and anti-Western motives as well. According to Nasser the original cause of the revolution was "the enslavement of the people by the imperialists and their lackeys, the Egyptian feudal lords and politicians."

Changes Under Naguib, and Nasser's Rise to Power

Immediately, Naguib and the military junta set about changing Egypt: the constitution was abolished; political parties as well as the monarchy were eliminated—Naguib was made president and prime minister of the new republic; and titles were banned. Naguib, however, was not prone to extreme measures and he soon clashed with a young colonel, Gamal Abdel Nasser. In 1954 Nasser took over the government and Naguib was placed under house arrest.

Egypt Under Nasser

Redistribution of land was immediately inaugurated. By the end of 1957 about 600,000 acres or one tenth of the land had been redistributed. Religious laws were modified and a modern civil law created; women were granted rights and Nasser made some progress in breaking down the power of the mufti: In 1960, for example, brushing teeth during the fast of Ramadan was permitted, as was also wife-kissing, and a wife was allowed to sue her husband if he took another wife. Educational improvements were also inaugurated. Between 1950 and 1952 there had been only three schools built per year; in 1953 alone 369 schools were opened and 117 new health centers were built. A six-year plan for clean water was also introduced.

THE SUEZ CRISIS

1) In 1956 the United States and Great Britain withdrew the promise of a seventy-million-dollar loan for the projected Aswan dam project, and Nasser retaliated by nationalizing the Suez Canal.

2) Protests from England and France did no good, and in

October, 1956 the two countries and Israel attacked the Suez area. Under pressure from the United Nations the venture was given up.

3) The Result of the Suez Crisis

A. The Suez became Egyptian government property (before seizure the board of management consisted of one Dutch, one American, five Egyptian, sixteen French, and nine British members); in 1957 the U.S.S.R. agreed to advance 60,000,000 Egyptian pounds for the Aswan dam, and in 1960 offered one hundred million dollars more.

B. The war made matters worse between Israel and the Arabs. Hatred of Israel is the one issue on which all Arabs can unite and has contributed to making Nasser the major leader of pan-Arabism.

C. The crisis weakened British influence, particularly in Iraq where the Kassem coup was a direct result of anti-British feeling.

PAN-ARABISM

1) In 1958 the U.A.R. (United Arab Republic), a federation of Egypt, Syria, and Yemen, was created with Nasser as President and Quwatli as Vice-President. Nasser announced that the aims of the U.A.R. were

A. to create an Arab empire;

B. to equalize the distribution of oil (which obviously Saudi Arabia and a few others did not approve of);

C. to annihilate Israel;

D. to "Egyptianize" Egypt by making her totally independent of foreign influence.

Quwatli announced that "Zionism not communism is the only threat to world peace."

2) Although the U.A.R. broke up in 1961 because of Egyptian interference in Syria, the aims of Nasser remain the same, and in 1963 a new U.A.R. was created with Egypt, Syria, and Iraq as members. This new attempt at Arab unity failed almost immediately, and the three countries remain allied but separate nations.

3) The hope for pan-Arabism seems very slight, because

Saudi Arabia dislikes the U.A.R.; Jordan and Lebanon mistrust her; and Nasser mistrusts the Syrians.

Syria

Independent Syria faced many problems; there was no tradition of self-rule; there were serious economic crises and serious religious controversies. From 1949 to 1955 its government was extremely unstable, and coup d'états were the normal routine. After Quwatli was ousted in 1949 and fled to Egypt a series of military regimes rose and fell one after the other. Reforms were initiated under Colonel Husni al-Zaim, who was assassinated for his efforts. Then under al-Shishakli a military dictatorship was established. In 1954 Quwatli returned to power, but Communist infiltration into the country combined with economic difficulties, of which Moscow took full advantage by giving Syria $100,000,-000 at 2½ percent in 1957, pushed Quwatli into union with Egypt. From 1961 to 1963 Syria was ruled by a series of rather amiable military coups, but in March of 1963 a coup d'état by the Ba'ath Socialist party placed Major Amin el-Hafez in power, and in 1965 a vigorous hate-America campaign was initiated. The first example of this was the torturing, beating, brainwashing, starving, and finally hanging of the naturalized United States citizen, Attassi.

Iraq

The Government of Iraq 1933 to 1958

Faisel I, beloved and efficient, died in 1933, leaving his twenty-one-year-old son Ghazi to rule his country. Corruption and the building of a feudal aristocracy were the results, until Ghazi died in an automobile accident in 1939. He in turn was succeeded by his four-year-old son, Faisel II, and his uncle Abdul-Ilah. Nuri-al-Said became prime minister of Iraq, and his policy was one of cooperation with the British, with the exception of the question of Israel and the Suez Canal crisis, in which he backed Egypt. The Baghdad Pact was signed, allying Turkey, Iraq, Iran, Pakistan, and England, and indirectly NATO.

2. Iraq also had her problems, with nine tenths of her people illiterate, one sixth nomadic, and many minority groups. Ten percent of her population are Kurds, and they constitute 40 percent of Iraq's communists, because they are traditionally in conflict with the government. The Nestorian Christians are another minority that Iraq must contend with, although they were almost totally wiped out by military force in 1933. Nevertheless, Iraq's economy is sound, for she is rich in oil (after 1951 receiving half the royalties), and the money earned has been spent wisely on domestic improvements. Imports in 1956 were 335 million dollars, while exports, without oil, were 36.4 million.

Iraq and Pan-Arabism

A. In 1958 as a countermove to the U.A.R., Iraq joined Jordan in an Arab Federation that had no foundation other than blood ties. That same year the forces of anti-Westernism, antimonarchists, leftists, and pro-U.A.R. people joined in a coup d'état under Abdul Kareem-el-Kassem, who marched on Baghdad, killed King Faisel, his uncle, and the prime minister, as well as two hundred others, and overthrew the government. Kassem immediately set up a military dictatorship, pulled out of the Baghdad Pact (later called the Central Treaty Organization) and tried to walk a middle course between East and West. This was not very successful, and more and more he began to depend on Russian support.

B. Kassem was overthrown in 1963 by the conservative element of the military. He "died with a smile on his face," and Iraq's new government joined the U.A.R. The federation with Egypt never came into being, but Abdel Salem Aref still maintains dictatorial control of Iraq.

Israel

The War Against Israel

A. In 1949 Israel emerged victorious from the war of survival against the Arab League. Her national determination proved stronger than the Arab crusade against her, and her economic, technological, and military strength, which was a reflection of world Zionism, was more than a match for the Arab forces. An armistice was signed between Israel and the Arab League, but no peace treaty followed. Raids by discontented Arabs continued on Israeli land; the boundary question was never solved; and in 1951 Israel's ships were banned from the Suez Canal.

B. By 1956 tensions had again become so great that Israel invaded the Sinai peninsula and the Gaza Strip, where she claimed the nests of raiders were located. (This invasion was in connection with the British and French invasion of the Suez.) The UN ordered Israeli troops to withdraw, but peace between Egypt and Israel has been maintained only by the presence of United Nations troops in the area, for the two countries were unable to come to a final boundary settlement.

Economic Outlook

Israel is proof of what can be done in an underdeveloped area, given enough energy and money. She has done wonders with what few resources she has. The country is 75 percent agricultural; irrigation has been increased; production of food has soared under a collective farm system; and industry has been constructed. Israel has a per capita income of $500, the highest in the Middle East. From 1948 to 1960, tonnage carried by her ships increased from 14,000 to 445,000, and the number of teachers rose from 5964 to 22,400.

Handicaps

Israel's imports are still ten times as great as her exports; she is still dependent on outside aid (receiving $380,000,000 in 1957); she feels she must maintain the cost of a standing army; and the boycott by Arab states means she must go farther for importing and exporting.

In 1963 Ben-Gurion, who was most responsible for the creation of the state of Israel, retired as premier and was replaced by Levi Eshkol.

Jordan

With the creation of Israel, Arab Palestine was merged with Transjordan to form the kingdom of Jordan, and Jordan became one of the leading members of the Arab League, the only one to do any effective fighting. In 1953 Hussein replaced his father as King of Jordan.

Generally, Jordan has been more pro-Western than some Middle Eastern states, but she rejected the Baghdad Pact (although with good reasons, for it was sent as a demand), and she fired General Glubb, the British head of the Arab Legion.

The Iraq revolt in 1958 led to trouble in the Jordan government, and Britain sent troops at Hussein's request to support him. Jordan's bitterness towards the West is primarily due to the Arab refugee problem. There are over 700,000 refugees from Palestine living in Jordan, one third in camps and two thirds in caves or any place they can find.

Hussein's Country Is Plagued with Problems

A. The eastern half has 400,000 people and is 95 percent desert and seminomadic. (Fifty thousand are nomads; 120,000 are seminomadic.)

B. The western half has 1,000,000 people, over half of whom are refugees.

C. Fifty percent of the population is illiterate.

D. Jordan has received £40,500,000 in aid from Great Britain, and the United States gave her $44,000,000 in 1955, but she has little irrigated land, few resources, little industry, no seaport except the Gulf of Acaba, and as a political entity no history, because she was the creation of English policy after World War I.

Lebanon

Lebanon is unique, for she has no nomads, has a history of independent rule, is half Christian, and has thrived for centuries on trade and tourism. Her per capita income is $250 a year, the highest in the Arab countries of the Middle East. Two thirds of her people are literate; four fifths of her children are in school. She has a strong and growing middle class. The Litani Irrigation project initiated under Lebanon's five-year plan (total cost, $230,-000,000) has irrigated some 16,000 acres and quadrupled her hydroelectric power.

This does not mean that Lebanon does not have problems. The religious division in the country (49 percent Moslem, 51 percent Christian) has caused difficulties. The Christian half of the population is very much afraid of losing its identity and being swallowed up by the Arab world. This is the primary reason that Lebanon has been generally pro-West; for example, she was the only Arab country to accept formally the Eisenhower Doctrine. Yet the Arab half of the population desires closer relations with Syria and Egypt. During the Iraq revolution, Lebanon's pro-Western, anti-Nasser regime threatened to collapse, and at the government's request 10,000 United States marines were landed in the country.

Political History

Bisharah al-Khuri was president of Lebanon from 1943 to 1952 and accomplished a peaceful social and economic revolution. He was succeeded by Kamil Chamoun, who had his difficulties in 1958 with strikes and riots in favor of Egypt. Resulting economic and political chaos forced him to turn to the United States for aid. Faud Shibab came to power as Lebanon's third president, in the wake of extensive rioting. He is a soldier, but a constitutionalist, and is more of a neutralist than his presidential predecessors. In 1964 he was replaced by Charles Helou.

The United States provides the greater part of the aid given to Lebanon. (In 1955 Lebanon received $35,000,000.)

The Sudan

Although culturally the south Sudan is a part of Africa, the Sudan's history is closely linked with that of Egypt, and the northern half of the country is Moslem and Arab.

British Control

A. From 1896 the British ruled the country by force, and in 1899 a condominium was formed with joint Egyptian and British rule. Great Britain provided the governor-general and the high officers, and Egypt provided the middle grade officers and four fifths of the military cost.

B. In 1925, however, the condominium was broken, and Egyptian troops were pulled out of the Sudan because of trouble in Egypt and the assassination of the governor-general of the Sudan in Cairo. From 1925 to 1936 there was very little peace in either country.

Independence

During World War II, the Sudanese agitated for independence, but negotiations reached a deadlock primarily because of Egypt's claim of control over the area. In 1948 the first legislative assembly was granted, and in 1953 the British and Egyptians reached agreement that the Sudan should be prepared for independence and in three years could decide whether she wished to join Egypt or be totally independent. In 1953 it appeared as if the Sudan would join with Egypt, but when Nasser overthrew Naguib (Sudanese by birth), the Sudan in 1955 declared her total independence, and in 1956 the British and the Egyptians agreed.

Although originally a constitutional government, the Sudan became a military government under General Abboud and remained so until October of 1964.

Tunisia and Independence

Independence

A. In the 1930's Tunisia began to agitate for independence from the French. The Destour Party led the struggle. Tunisia suffered as one of the battlefields of World War II. Her trade was paralyzed and she was occupied by the Germans for six months.

B. Between 1947 and 1950 the French agreed to some minor reforms, such as giving more offices in the government to Tunisians, but this was not enough and from 1951 to 1954 there were riots and troubles.

c. In 1955 the first all-Tunisian government was granted; in 1956 she became a member of the United Nations, and in 1957 the monarchy was abolished and she became a republic under president Habib Bourguiba.

The Republic

A. Bourguiba is "the most Westernized of Arab Moslem rulers"; he has totally eliminated Islamic law, polygamy has been abolished, and in 1960 he even led attacks against the fast of Ramadan. Land has been redistributed, medical facilities and clinics have been established, elementary education is free and universal, and industry is being built.

B. Tunisia still faces problems. In 1958 there had been a population increase of 60 percent over the last twenty-five years and a production increase of only 25 percent.

Morocco and Independence

Independence

A. Morocco had had a history of freedom. Before 1921 she had been free for eleven centuries. She was not completely pacified by the French until 1933, and in 1934 nationalistic movements began. In 1943 the Istiqlal party was founded, which objected to having no voice in the government, no civil liberties, and the fact that the French owned most of the fertile land in the country.

B. The French had established a dualistic rule in Morocco, retaining the Sultan as a tool of the administration. Muhammed V, on the throne since 1927, was forced abroad at the insistence of the French in 1953 because of rioting in Morocco.

c. In 1955 the French finally agreed to independence and Muhammed V was returned. In 1956 both the French and Spanish pulled out of the country, and in May of 1963 elections were held for Morocco's first parliament.

Morocco is more fortunate than most North African countries, for she is rich in natural resources—phosphate, cork, manganese, and lead. The Istiqlal party is in control of the country but has had trouble from the more anti-Western Riff party. In 1958 pressure from below forced the government to order the withdrawal of all foreign troops (this involved twenty French and four American bases), but the United States has continued to give aid to the tune of forty million dollars.

Libya

Independence

In 1943, as a consequence of defeat in World War II, the Italian administration in Libya was expelled, and Cyrenaica and Tripolitania were put under British military administration and Fezzan under French. In 1949 the United Nations declared that Libya should be independent in January of 1951. A constitutional monarchy with Mohammed Idris as-Sanuai as king, with both spiritual and temporal powers, was formed.

In 1953 Libya joined the Arab League, and in 1957 she became a member of the UN. Eighty percent of the country is engaged in agriculture; 93 percent of the people are nomadic; literacy is less than 40 percent, and per capita income is $35 a year. In 1958 oil was discovered in commercial quantities, an event that may improve the economic picture. But both the Soviet Union and Egypt have been very active in the country.

Algeria—The Last Country in the Middle East to Become Independent

The movement for independence in Algeria was complicated by the presence in 1954 of 934,052 French citizens living among 8,595,674 Moslems. Algeria had always been controlled directly from Paris and was economically closely allied to France (40 percent of her exports are wines). The first demands by natives for reforms were made in 1926; in 1939 the French agreed to allow natives to be elected to an Algerian parliament, but they were never allowed to gain a majority. World War II increased the agitation for independence, and the Free French under Giraud and De Gaulle encouraged the nationalists. In 1950 the Algerian Freedom Front (the M.T.L.D.) and the Nationalist Democratic Union (the U.D.M.A.) began agitation. The Front de Libération Nationale (F.L.N.) received aid from Egypt, Tunisia, and Morocco.

Open war was declared in 1954. The French then tried to eliminate the extremist section, led by Messali Hadj, at the cost of three million dollars per day and the use of 70,000 troops. War raged on and off from 1954 to 1958. In 1958 the French army in Algeria rose against the conduct of the French Algerian parliament, and this led to General De Gaulle's appointment as president of France. But De Gaulle refused to use force against the Algerians. In 1959 he offered the Algerians, after a four-year period of pacification, the opportunity to secede from France or to stay with France and be completely integrated. In 1962 De Gaulle finally negotiated a cease-fire with the nationalists, and now Algeria has achieved total independence.

Until 1965 Ben Bella, who was anti-Western and pro-Nasser, ruled Algeria with an iron fist. He was overthrown by the neutralist, Col. Houari Boumedienne, and the Soviet Union has been informed that Algeria will no longer serve as a "forum for Moscow propaganda."

European Civilization

ANCIENT AND CLASSICAL CIVILIZATIONS
2500 B.C.–500 A.D.

Until 2000 B.C. Europe was in the New Stone Age, while the Middle East, Egypt, and the Tigris-Euphrates valley, the island of Crete, and the Aegean area, had passed the neolithic age at least 1000 years before. Towards the close of the Stone Age, invading Indo-Europeans appeared throughout Europe. The first of them to make an imprint on European history were those who settled in Greece. It is here that the story of European civilization begins. From about 900 to 500 B.C. the Greeks passed from barbarism to the peak of civilization. From tribal organization they developed city-states with concepts of political freedom and democracy. From illiteracy they moved to the philosophy of Plato and Aristotle, the drama of Sophocles, Euripedes, Aeschylus, and Aristophanes, and the historical writings of Herodotus and Thucydides. From primitive art they passed on to the sophisticated sculpture of Phidias and the architecture of Ictinus. From superstition they evolved the foundations of modern science. In governmental organization and military defense, however, they were deficient, and in 146 B.C. the Greek islands were conquered by the Romans, who assembled an empire joining the ancient civilizations of Egypt, Asia Minor, Syria, and Greece to what is today North Africa, Spain, Portugal, France, Switzerland, Belgium, and England. It was to the Romans that Europe owes the trans-

49

mission of the cultures of the East and of Greece, as well as Roman culture, which emphasized political organization, administration, government and law. It was also through Rome that Europe received Christianity, for Christ, being born in Palestine, was a citizen of the Roman world. By the fifth century A.D. the entire Roman world was formally Christian. When the empire collapsed, Roman and classical culture were destroyed, but Christianity continued, becoming the cultural foundation of the new medieval society that slowly evolved in Northern Europe during the tenth and eleventh centuries.

PRECLASSICAL CIVILIZATION

The Mycenean Age or Minoan Civilization 3000–1400 B.C.

This civilization belongs more to the Middle East than to Europe. Borrowing heavily from Egypt and the Mesopotamian valley, the island of Crete developed an advanced civilization based on sea power and commerce, but with the coming of the Indo-Europeans, this Mycenean or Minoan civilization was undermined and ruined. Archeologists have very little evidence of how the society on Crete was destroyed, for there is no indication of violent invasion, volcanoes, or earthquakes.

The Indo-European Invasions   2000–1000 B.C.

The newcomers to the Aegean area were composed of many separate barbaric tribes. The four main ones were the Ionians, who settled in the area of Athens and went across the Aegean to Lydia; the Dorians and the Acheans, who went further south, the Dorians settling in the area of Sparta; and the Aeolians, who stayed in the northern part of the country and crossed the Aegean to Asia Minor.

By 1000 B.C. the expansion into the Greek islands was complete and the older Mycenean civilizations such as Troy on the coast of Asia Minor were destroyed.

The Dark Age or the Homeric Period   1000–750 B.C.

The havoc created by the invasions of the Indo-Europeans led to a temporary eclipse of civilization. Tribes were under the leadership of clan kings, wealth was based on land, and plunder and piracy were the main means of livelihood.

Although Homer wrote of an earlier era (the destruction of Troy by the Indo-European invaders), this period is reflected in his epic poems of the *Iliad* and the *Odyssey*. The people he portrays witnessed the bitter transition from the Bronze to the Iron Age.

HELLENIC CIVILIZATION

The Age of the City-State   750–500 B.C.

By the eighth century B.C. the clan kings had been overthrown by nobles, tribal organization had disintegrated with the increase in landed estates controlled by the nobility, and the city-state had emerged as the political unit throughout Greece.

The Polis (the city-state)

A. The most famous of the city-states to emerge during this period were Athens, Sparta, Thebes, Corinth, Olympia, Argos, and Delphi. They had developed as separate political units partly because of original tribal settlements and partly because of the geographic isolation of the Greek country. People settled in the valleys where fertile soil was available, but in doing so they were completely cut off from their neighbors by the rugged nature of the terrain.

B. The failure to evolve a single and united Greece resulted in each city-state developing its own local patriotism and independence. This led to different types of political, economic, and social structures and explains the great contrast existing between such city-states as Athens and Sparta.

C. There were, however, at least two unifying forces in Greece: the Olympic games, which athletes of all city-states entered, and the oracle at Delphi, which was the center of religious belief for all Greeks.

The Colonization Movement   750–550 B.C.

A. During this period the Greeks planted colonies, which in turn became independent city-states, from the Straits of Gibraltar to the Black Sea. Marseilles, Naples, Syracuse, Segesta, and Istanbul were all originally Greek colonies.

B. The motivations behind the extensive colonization movement were half economic, half social. Land was scarce, the population was increasing, the city-states needed markets for their goods, and there was political and social unrest at home.

C. The obvious effect of colonization was to spread Greek civilization (particularly Ionian), but perhaps an even more important result was the rise to power of nonaristocratic members of society, for trade led to wealth and wealth began to rival birth as the basis of political power.

The Age of Tyrants   600–500 B.C.

A. Opposition on the part of the merchants and the newer elements of society to the power of the nobility led to the rise of tyrants in many city-states. These men were rulers who overthrew the aristocrats with the support of the rising middle classes. Although ruthless, they were the first step in the development of democratic government, for they often extended social rights, patronized the arts, and encouraged the development of law and trade. They were the first great protagonists of freedom. Some of the most famous were Thrasybulus of Miletus, Peisistratus of Athens, and Periander of Corinth.

B. Most of the tyrants were eventually replaced either by an oligarchy of landed aristocrats and wealthy mercantile commoners or by democracies where the citizens became the ruling power.

Athens and the Development of Democracy

In the 700's Athens was ruled by a board of archons, a council of nobles who had assumed the power of the kings.

In 621 B.C. Draco, the chief archon, established a code of law that was extremely severe (the death penalty was given for stealing a cabbage), but it was important because it took punishment for a crime out of private hands and placed it under the control of the state.

In 594 B.C. Solon became sole archon and reformed the harsh system of Draco. Slavery for debt was abolished, the money standard was reformed, skilled artisans were imported into Athens, nobles were put below the law, and the first steps toward democratic government were taken with the development of a citizens' assembly and a people's court.

From 560–527 B.C. Peisistratus, the benevolent tyrant, ruled Athens. He encouraged the development of agriculture, industry, and the arts. At his death, Athens broke into civil war under the harsh rule of his sons, Hippias and Hipparchus.

Cleisthenes took over the government of Athens, and this was the actual beginning of democracy. In 508 B.C. his constitution was formulated, and it placed a definite limit upon the power of government.

A. Citizens were given the right to ostracize one man every year by popular vote. Ostracism meant exile for ten years.

B. Citizenship was extended to include all males over the age of eighteen who were native-born. (This was actually only about 10 percent of the population, the remainder being women, children, foreigners and slaves.)

C. A legislative council of five hundred citizens, from whom the administrative officials of the government were chosen by lot for one year, and a popular court of six thousand citizens were also created. The principle of rotation in office was established.

D. The army was set up under a board of ten generals who were elected by the people.

Pericles (461–429 B.C.) was the unofficial ruler of democratic Athens, for he was both chief general and leader of the popular assembly. His rule, called the Golden Age of Athens, is considered to be the height of Athenian democracy, for as Pericles himself said, "Since our constitution considers not the benefit of the few, but the welfare of the many, we call it a democracy."

Sparta in Contrast to Athens

Sparta's political organization consisted of two figurehead kings, an aristocratic council, an assembly composed of citizens over the age of thirty, and five ephors, who were elected annually by the assembly and were the actual rulers of the city-state. Sparta was a military oligarchy that could not afford the luxury of violent party discord or political revolution, because the helots (pre-Dorian aborigines, on whom the Spartan society depended for its labor) were always a menace to the security of the area.

In order to safeguard against the corrupting influence of wealth and new ideas, no commerce and little outside contact were allowed.

Education was state-controlled and emphasized physical training and military discipline. At the age of seven, children were selected for the army and taken away from their homes to be trained in rigorous discipline. They lived and ate in common and were considered the property of the commonwealth. This was in contrast to Athenian education, which emphasized personal and intellectual as well as physical development. Although Athenian boys went into the army for two years at the age of eighteen, they were trained in music, literature, and art. Women in Athens and in most city-states were educated in household duties only, but in Sparta they had greater freedom and were given physical training for the purpose of breeding future soldiers. On the other hand, they were forced to walk naked in processions in order to play down any idea of sexual attraction and to emphasize the fact that they were not feminine but "merely mothers of Spartans."

The Triumph and Decline of Athens   550–400 B.C.

The Persian Wars

The Athenians were able to withstand the first major threat to their existence, the Persians. The Lydian Empire had conquered the Ionian Greeks in Asia Minor in the sixth century

B.C.; the Persians under Cyrus had overthrown the Lydians in 546 B.C., and under Darius (521–486 B.C.) they ruled their Greek subjects with an iron hand. In 499 B.C. the Ionians, led by the city-state of Miletus and supported by Athenian aid, revolted, and they were not brought back under Persian control until 494 B.C. Darius wanted revenge against Athens.

PERSIAN WAR I

In 490 B.C. Darius invaded Greece. The Athenians were outnumbered two to one, but under the leadership of Miltiades, the Persians were defeated at Marathon, 26 miles northeast of Athens. It was during this battle that Philippides ran 140 miles to Sparta for aid (and that today is the distance of a marathon).

PERSIAN WAR II

1) Under Xerxes, the successor of Darius in 486 B.C., the Persians tried again to conquer Greece, with a large amphibious operation in which the Persian troops crossed the Hellespont and then marched through Thrace, Macedonia, and Thessaly.

2) The Battle of Thermopylae Pass

Three hundred Spartans and Leonidas, their King, put up a heroic but futile stand in which they were slaughtered to a man.

3) The Athenians evacuated Athens while the Persians burned the city, but at the Straits of Salamis the Athenians won a brilliant naval victory as a consequence of the imagination and leadership of Themistocles.

4) At the battle of Plataea, a combined Greek force defeated the Persians, forced them to retreat, and liberated Ionia.

Significance of the Greek Victory

1) The victory meant that Europe had triumphed over oriental despotism.

2) It gave control of the Aegean Sea to the Greeks, allowing their culture and commerce to spread.

3) It led to the growth of Athens as a great power.

The Athenian Empire and Its Downfall

A. The Delian League was formed in 477 B.C. by the eastern city-states as a defensive measure against the possibility of further attempts by Persia. Ships and money were contributed by the member states and this became the foundation of the Athenian empire, for in 454 B.C. the treasury of the League was moved from Delos to Athens. Athens used force to prevent secession from the League (Lisbos in 482 B.C. attempted to revolt and as punishment its people were sold into slavery), and spent the tribute on the beautification of the Athenian state. (The buildings on the Acropolis—the Parthenon and the Propylaea—were constructed with League money.)

B. The Peloponnesian League was formed by Sparta and Corinth, who were rivals of Athens. Wars between Athens and Sparta began in 431 B.C. At the same time, Athens was experiencing the worst plague in her history, which killed one fourth of her people, including Pericles, and led to lawlessness and terror in the city. In 421 B.C. a peace was concluded that did not last long, and Alcibiades, the egotistical leader of Athens, led an attack on Sicily in 415 B.C., losing all his forces. Persia, seeing Athen's weakness, aided Sparta and in 404 B.C. Athens surrendered and became a puppet state ruled by Sparta. (In 371 B.C. Thebes defeated Sparta and ruled both cities until 362 B.C.)

The Contributions of the Greeks to Western Civilization

Systematic political science was born and set forth in the *Republic* of Plato (427–347 B.C.) and the *Politics* of Aristotle (384–322 B.C.).

A. Plato believed that the state's function was to satisfy the common good, and he outlined the first utopia, founded on justice, with workers providing the necessities of life, warriors acting as guards, and philosophers as rulers, where there was no private property or family organization, and education was regulated by the state.

B. Aristotle, the student of Plato and tutor of Alexander the Great, classified all known fields of knowledge and founded biology, formal logic, and deductive reasoning (the syllogism).

C. Plato and Aristotle were the men who established the

basis of Western philosophical thought, and each attempted to answer the question of what is reality.

1) Plato believed that ideas had an existence apart from matter. He rejected the concrete world as a source of knowledge. To Plato truth was unchanging and reality was found in abstract ideas.

2) Aristotle, on the other hand, denied Plato's Theory of Ideas and claimed a changing dynamic universe. He believed that every concrete object was composed of form and matter and neither had existence apart from the other.

The Greeks were the first to write history rather than myth and legend.

A. Herodotus (485–425 B.C.), the "father of history," traveled over much of the known world attempting to find out about the past, and wrote the *History of the Persian Wars.*

B. Thucydides (460–400 B.C.), one of the ten generals of Athens in 424 B.C. and exiled for twenty years, wrote on the Peloponnesian Wars and was perhaps the first scientifically critical historian. He thought of history as utilitarian: man could learn from study of the past.

The creation of the drama with the addition of the second actor was accomplished by Aeschylus of Athens (525–455 B.C.). Some of the greatest of all tragedies, *Oedipus Rex* and *Antigone,* were written by Sophocles (497–405 B.C.), and Euripedes (480–406 B.C.) has eighteen or nineteen extant plays. Aristophanes (446–385 B.C.) was famous as the originator of comedy.

The foundations of the mathematical sciences were laid by Euclid, who worked out the principles of geometry, and by Fratosthenes, who in 200 B.C. concluded by mathematics that the earth was a sphere and computed its size. By the first and second centuries before Christ, writers and encyclopedias passed on the knowledge of Greek science to later generations—Strabo in geography, Galen in medicine, and Ptolemy in astronomy.

In the fields of architecture and sculpture, the Greeks reached their artistic zenith in Athens in the fifth century B.C. Moderation, proportion, and poise are the themes of such famous edifices as the Erechtheum, the Temple of Wingless Victory, and the superbly proportioned Parthenon. Three types of columns were used—the simple Doric with no base and topped by a simple capital, the more elaborate Ionic with a base and spiral decorations on the capital, and the Corinthian (employed more by the Romans) with columns topped with acanthus leaves. The human body was magnificently protrayed in sculpture. Polyclitus (430 B.C.) was the first to change the traditional stance of the rigidly upright figure of man by putting weight on the advanced foot; Myron's Discus Thrower is famous for its balance and restraint. The greatest of sculptors was Phidias, who carved the friezes of the Parthenon.

THE HELLENISTIC WORLD

Philip II of Macedonia, through a policy of "divide and conquer," was able to control the disunited and anarchistic Hellas. In 338 B.C. he defeated the Greek forces of Athens and Thebes at the battle of Chaeronea.

After Philip's assassination in 336 B.C., Alexander the Great (356–323 B.C.) succeeded to the throne of his father and led his army into Asia in 334 B.C., conquering the Persian Empire in 331 B.C. and reaching India. His ultimate aim was to create a world government, involving the fusion of races and ideas, but his empire broke up soon after his death at the age of thirty-three.

Nevertheless, Alexander had accomplished a great deal. Greek thought, art, and language were spread far and wide, and a new type of culture was born uniting the Greek and oriental minds.

ROMAN CIVILIZATION

The Migrations into Italy

Italic tribes, probably from central Europe, infiltrated into the peninsula somewhere between 2000 and 1000 B.C., followed by Etruscans from Asia Minor in the ninth century B.C. and

Greek colonies in the south of Italy around 750 B.C. Celts invaded the area around 390 B.C.

Etruscan Rule

The Etruscans ruled Rome during the sixth century B.C. and gave to the area the arch, certain religious traditions, and a pattern of government. In 509 B.C. they were expelled from Rome by popular revolt, and this was the beginning of the Roman Republic.

The Roman Republic 500–30 B.C.

Two consuls elected annually held executive power and appointed members of the senate; it was this group of men who ruled the Republic.

Social and political power was in the hands of the patricians, the wealthy landlords who constituted about 2 percent of the population, and this soon resulted in class struggle with the plebians (nonaristocrats). Gradually the plebs did win legal and political rights. In 494 B.C. they were granted tribunes to protect their interests; then they received an assembly that could enact resolutions or plebiscites, which could become laws if approved by the senate; and finally in 287 B.C. they gained the Hortensian law, which said that plebiscites were law without the consent of the senate. But government remained essentially aristocratic because office-holding was expensive and, unlike the situation in Athens, officials received no pay.

Territorial Expansion

In 509 B.C., three hundred square miles of territory was all that was controlled by the Romans; by 275 B.C. they had control of southern Italy and 10,000 square miles of land.

Conquest of the western Mediterranean was accomplished between 264 and 146 B.C.

In the First Punic War (264–241 B.C.) over the control of

Sicily, the Romans defeated Carthage by sea power. In the Second (218–201 B.C.), Hannibal of Carthage crossed the Alps and reached the Po valley with 30,000 men, waging a "colossal contest between the nation Rome and the man Hannibal," for he received no supplies or aid from Carthage. After the Third Punic War (149–146 B.C.) Rome captured and destroyed Carthage, burning the city to the ground, selling its people into slavery, and plowing the land with salt in order to destroy its fertility. During these three wars Rome annexed Sicily, Corsica, Sardinia, Spain, and parts of North Africa.

Conquest of the eastern Mediterranean, including the lands of Macedonia, Greece, Asia Minor, Syria, Judea, and finally Egypt (annexed by Augustus) was begun in 200 B.C. and was complete by 30 B.C.

Almost all of what is today Western Europe was also conquered by the Romans. Caesar conquered Gaul (France and Belgium); later parts of what are today the Netherlands, Germany, and Switzerland were added; Britain was taken by Claudius in 43 A.D.; and by 117 A.D. the empire had reached its greatest extent.

Results of Imperialism

A. The Roman world was unified by a single imperial administration and law. The entire Mediterranean world could claim Roman citizenship, and a system of military roads, a single currency, and one language (Latin) united the empire.

B. The areas conquered gained by the transmission of civilization, but at home imperialism resulted in the decline of the small farmer, who had to leave his land to fight in the wars and who was driven out of business both by wheat brought into the country from conquered lands and by the growth of the latifundia (large estates owned by senators and worked by slave labor). This led to the unemployment of peasants, who flocked to the cities with no jobs and no homes, which in turn led to the destruction of the Republic, because no one could maintain order in the city of Rome except the army and an emperor—who was always a general.

The End of the Republic and the Beginning of the Empire

The Senate was unable to cope with the political, social, and economic problems caused by the acquisition of an empire. Radical reforms were necessary, and benevolent despotism seemed the only solution. The Roman society was deteriorating—corruption, brutality, divorce, and idleness were all on the increase. Greek vices were imitated as well as Greek virtues. (It has been said that the only civilized and decent sport practiced by the Romans was chariot racing.)

The reorganization of the army into a professional volunteer army meant that the generals replaced the state in gaining the loyalty of their men and became independent powers able to use military force in politics. The dictator Sulla (82–79 B.C.), Pompey and Caesar, Antony, and Octavian all rose to power in this way.

A. Marius was the first military leader in politics, but it was Caesar who officially ended the republic. The first triumvirate of Caesar, Crassus, and Pompey ruled from 60 to 50 B.C. Crassus died, and Caesar won over Pompey and established himself as dictator.

B. Despite the fact that Caesar rebuilt and beautified Rome, reformed the administration of the provinces, introduced the twelve-month calender and was a great general, politician, and statesman, his rule ended in the same way it had begun—by violence and military take-over.

C. The second triumvirate consisted of Antony (in Egypt), Lepidus, and Octavian (in Rome). After defeating Antony and Cleopatra, Octavian became Augustus Caesar (29 B.C.–14 A.D.) and the first emperor of Rome.

This chaotic era was the golden age of Roman literature. During the period from 70 to 43 B.C., Cicero composed his oratorical writings, Catullus his lyric poems, and Caesar his historical works. The era of Augustus brought tight imperial censorship but literary patronage, and Vergil (70–19 B.C.), famous for his epic *Aeneid*, Horace (65–8 B.C.), famous for his satire and insight, Ovid, famous for his poetry, Livy, famous for his prose, and Seneca, famous for his tragedy, flourished during this period.

The Pax Romana   30 B.C.–170 A.D.

Two centuries of relative peace started with Augustus and lasted through the rule of Marcus Aurelius. Commerce expanded, the speed of travel possible on the highways was not surpassed until about 1800, government armies patrolled and controlled the provinces, and lawyers worked on the body of legal principles known as Roman Law, which favored the authority of the state and argued that the source of law rested with the enlightened intelligence and not with historic custom. (These principles, together with more specific codes on debt, marriage, and so on were to have a great effect on European history. Today Roman law is the basis of law in Italy, France, Spain, Japan, Scotland, and Latin America. English Common Law, based on precedent and custom and not on national codification, is found only in England, Ireland, the United States, Canada, Australia, and New Zealand.) Justinian (527–565), who codified Roman law, said that there could be only "one empire, one law, one church."

The Fall of the Empire

There were many reasons for the gradual collapse of the Roman Empire: increasing despotism and suppression of personal liberties, civil war and rebellion, the decline of Italy as the eastern provinces grew in importance. But there were three main causes for the fall.

Economic Problems

A. The basis of the Roman economy was agriculture and there was little industry, partly because the Romans considered trade degrading and also because mining, pottery, and so forth were done by slave labor and therefore no laborsaving devices needed to be invented. Over the years gold was being drained out of the country for the luxuries of the East that Roman industry failed to produce. Eventually this led to the bankruptcy of the Empire and the decline of trade.

B. With the growth of large estates, areas of the Empire became self-sufficient. This cut trade between parts of the Empire still further and in turn led to increased independence and self-sufficiency, which broke down any sense of loyalty to the whole Empire and destroyed the feeling of imperial citizenship.

The Problem of Succession

Three conflicting sources of imperial power existed in the Roman Empire—the election by the senate, the right of inheritance, and the strength of the army. Senatorial sanction became nominal, succession by inheritance was never established absolutely, and more and more emperors tended to base their claim on their position as generals. Consequently, Rome was often afflicted with civil war.

The Barbarian Invasions

A. Germanic infiltration began long before the Germanic invasions. Tribes of settlers were allowed into the Empire, particularly in Gaul, and as the manpower of the Empire declined, hired German mercenaries were used in the armies. Even some of the emperors were German.

B. With the barbarian invasions came the final blow. About 450 A.D. the Angles and the Saxons overran Britain and the Franks moved into Gaul. The West Goths sacked Rome in 410 and reached Spain in 420. In 476 A.D. the western kingdom fell to Odovacer. (This is traditionally considered the end of the Roman Empire in the West.)

C. The invasions were most destructive in the West. In the East, the Empire (Byzantium) successfully resisted the barbarians and with its center in Constantinople lasted another thousand years.

D. The Germans were totally agricultural, thus breaking down trade even further and increasing the tendency toward self-sufficiency and decentralization. They were also tribal, and thus imperial political unity collapsed as the Western Empire broke up into warring tribal states of Franks, Lombards, Burgundians, Saxons, and others.

Christianity

The Origins of the Christian Faith
There were four major sources of Christianity:

A. Oriental, Eastern mystery cults from which the Christians received the doctrine of grace, of a personal and approachable god, of salvation and an after life, and of monotheism (a belief in a single, universal divine source of power).

B. The Hebrews from whom they received the concept of God as a judge and of salvation based on righteousness. The Old Testament of the Christian faith is approximately the same as the Torah.

C. Classical philosophy, which contributed the Platonic concept of the existence and hierarchy of ideas, with the good as the highest abstraction. In Christianity the Platonic good became the Christian God. Also, the Greek concept of a universe that could be understood by man was taken over by the Christians, producing one of the main precepts that God and His universe are rational and capable of being understood by human reason.

D. Jesus of Nazareth himself, who revealed the Word of God to the Christians and offered redemption for mankind.

1) About 4 B.C. Jesus was born in Jerusalem in Palestine. About 28 A.D. he began to preach against the vices of his era, the selfishness of the rich, and the self-righteousness of the Jewish priests. He taught a gospel based upon love of one's fellow man. Soon Jesus began to attract a number of followers, and when he came to Jerusalem to attend the Passover he was greeted by crowds who regarded him as the promised Messiah of the Jews.

2) In 33 A.D. (?), Christ was crucified after having been condemned for blasphemy by the Sanhedrin, the Jewish high court that enforced the law of Moses. His Messianic claims were considered to be seditious, and Pontius Pilate, the Roman procurator of Judea, allowed the Sanhedrin to crucify him.

3) Under the leadership of one of his followers, Paul, a

man of Jewish birth, Roman citizenship, and Greek culture, Christianity began to make converts, for Paul eliminated many of the narrow characteristics of the faith, making no distinction between Jew and Gentile and introducing Greek philosophy into Christianity. It was also through his influence that Jesus was recognized as the Christ, the son of God who had died to atone for the sins of man. (The disciples Paul and Peter died in Rome under Nero about 67 A.D.)

The Effects of Christianity
Christians taught that there was only one God from whom all mankind came and only one path to salvation. The idea of the world as a single whole was therefore important, and this sense of human unity meant that Christianity was essentially intolerant and crusading, since all mankind was in need of salvation.

Christianity brought to Europe a new sense of human life, for it taught that all men were equal in the sight of God and that beauty, wealth, and power were only superficial.

THE NEW TESTAMENT

A number of documents, written by early Christians, were selected in the seventh century to compose the Christian creed, or the second half of the Christian Bible.

The Spread of Christianity
A. Through the efforts of the disciples Christianity spread from Judea throughout the Jewish communities in Athens, Antioch, Corinth, and Rome. Because of this connection with the Jews, the Christians enjoyed the benefits of their immunities until 64 A.D.

B. However, the attitude of the Christians toward the Roman Empire led to popular antagonism toward them. The Christians were not concerned with this world; they refused to participate in public and pagan festivals; they excluded non-Christians from their gatherings; and they were monotheistic, thus committing treason by denying the divinity of the emperor.

1) At first accepted mainly by the discontented, the slaves,

and the poor, by the second century educated and well-to-do adopted Christianity.

2) Under Nero the early Christians were brought to trial on a charge of arson (the burning of Rome in 64 A.D.), but they were punished in the same manner as magicians and sorcerers— by crucifixion, burning, and wild animals in the arena. Persecutions of the Christians varied from ruler to ruler and province to province, but in 250 A.D. the emperor Decius began the first attempt to abolish the faith throughout the whole Empire by issuing an edict ordering all citizens to perform public acts of worship to the gods of the state. Refusal meant death. In 303 A.D. Diocletian renewed the persecutions. Edicts were issued calling for the destruction of Christian churches and books, imprisonment of the Christian clergy, and the worship of state gods by all persons. Nevertheless, the majority of Christians remained true to their beliefs, and finally, in 311, Galerius issued the edict of toleration.

c. Constantine invaded Italy in 312 and defeated the forces of Maxentius, successor to Galerius. According to legend, before the battle at Milvian bridge just across the Tiber from Rome, Constantine had a vision and ordered his men to mark their shields with a Chi and Rho, for Christ. Victory followed, and from then on Constantine looked upon himself as designated by the Christian God to rule the Roman Empire. He thus transformed the empire into a Christian state, although he was too wise to force pagans to change their ideas.

d. When Christianity became the state faith it was weakened by the church's growing wealth and power and by its enslavement to the emperor, yet it was the only institution of the Empire that survived the collapse of the Empire in the West.

e. As the barbarians invaded the Empire, they were converted to the faith. The most important conversion was that of the Franks under King Clovis in 496. In 590, under Gregory the Great, monks were sent to England and Ethelbert of Kent was converted. Bishop Boniface brought about the conversion of Germany in the 700's.

The Organization of the Christian Church

A. At first the Christians formed independent communities directed by an elected committee of elders or overseers (bishops) and assisted by deacons.

B. By the third century, the organization became centralized in the hands of a single bishop from each community, who controlled the elders or the priests. The laity gradually ceased to participate in the government of the church. About this time a dispute occurred over the question of whether all bishops should have equal authority or the bishop of Rome supremacy.

C. The late Empire witnessed an extension of the power of the bishop of Rome and he became known as pope (father). Leo I (440–461 A.D.) claimed the primacy of Peter. A rival to his power, however, developed in the patriarchate of Constantinople, but the patriarchs never acquired the power and independence of the popes of Rome, for they were dependent on secular authority and support of the emperors. In the West, however, the clergy began to occupy a privileged position in the state. The bishops soon had a definite place in municipal administration, and as imperial authority collapsed, they became the leaders of the Romans in their contact with barbarian conquerors. By the end of the sixth century, the pope became the virtual ruler of Rome.

MEDIEVAL CIVILIZATION 500 A.D.–1500 A.D.

The blows of the barbarians broke the unity of the Roman world and divided it into three parts—Byzantium, the Arabic world, and Europe. Europe was in chaos, and the Germans who had overrun the Roman provinces were able to maintain political organization only on the local level. The West broke up into self-sufficient, localized villages with little contact with the rest of the world. Trade withered, cities died, and the Roman roads fell into disrepair—Europe was in the "Dark Ages." Only one institution remained that was capable of providing unity—the Christian church. It attempted to win protection and reestablish the empire

*by crowning the king of the Franks, Charlemagne, emperor in
800, and although a certain degree of unity was achieved, his
empire did not last. There were more barbarian invasions (Magyars and Scandinavians) in the ninth century, and by the tenth
century the church as an institution was fragmented and localized
and its creed was a mixture of pagan and Christian doctrines.
About 1000 A.D., however, Europe began to change, developing a
system known as feudalism, which provided a decentralized defensive system against further barbarian invasion; created a
professional and constantly ready military protection in an age
of no money; and preserved a minimum amount of political
unity. Peace and security were thus secured. Gradually, technological advances in the field of agriculture led to an agricultural
surplus, which in turn led to the growth of towns and new commercial classes who desired independence from feudal lords. At
the same time, feudal kingdoms began to grow in power, and a
secularization process commenced that led to a new era of thought
and feeling known as the Renaissance. It was then that modern
civilization began.*

Feudalism

Feudalism as a Form of Political Organization

The Feudal Contract

Feudalism evolved slowly out of the dying Roman world. Its
purpose was to supply a minimum of political order in a society
that was falling to pieces, had no money economy, and had no
defense against invaders. Feudalism was a political relationship
between two men in which one gave land in return for military
service. This arrangement was perhaps clearest in England. William the Conqueror, who invaded England in 1066, claimed all
lands, kept one fifth as crown lands, and gave one quarter to the
church and the rest to 170 Norman barons. In return, the barons
had to provide the king with a fixed number of mounted and
armed knights. The barons, in order to meet their obligations,
gave their land to lesser tenants. This continued on down the

line until one knight held one manor (in theory a unit of land large enough to support him and his armed retainers).

FEALTY AND HOMAGE

Feudalism was a contractual relationship in which each party was bound by certain obligations:

1) The obligations of the overlord or baron were to provide justice and protection for his vassal.

2) The obligations of the vassal were to do homage and fealty to his lord, to fight for his lord for forty days a year, to take his disputes to his overlord's court, to give advice to his lord (this gave the vassal what he later claimed as an historic right to advise the king and became the germ of parliamentary government), to pay feudal aides (a form of taxation), and to defray certain costs such as the knighting of the lord's son, the dowry of his daughter, and the ransoming of the lord in time of war.

FEUDAL KINGSHIP

1) The essence of feudalism was anarchy. Real power rested with the baron, and kings had only nominal authority.

2) Kings were often elected by the curia regis (great council) of the barons and wise men of the kingdom. In 987 Hugh Capet was chosen king of France; in 911 a German king was elected, and crowned emperor in 962; but in England there was a more centralized form of feudalism, for William, Duke of Normandy, had conquered, not been elected.

Chivalry Was the Only Means of Keeping the Feudal Contract

A. Originally, knighthood was a secular ceremony in which the vassal swore fealty to his overlord, but in the twelfth century religious vows were added, which meant that in breaking his feudal vows the knight was endangering his soul. This concept of the ethical duty of the vassal to the lord was absolutely necessary, for there was no coercive instrument by which the overlord could compel his vassal to do his duty except by full-scale military attack to deprive him of his fief, and any respectable castle could maintain a siege of forty days, the normal length of military service.

B. Despite the chivalric code, real power did not rest at the top of the social and political pyramid but at the bottom, with the individual baron in his castle who had political, military, and judicial power. This was particularly true in the German empire, which eventually broke up into almost six hundred semi-independent petty states recognizing only nominal allegiance to the German emperor.

Feudalism as an Economic and Social Institution

The political structure of feudalism rested on an economic structure called serfdom. Serfdom was an effort to regulate the labor supply in an era when there was a shortage of labor and an abundance of land. The peasant was not a slave, but he was tied to the land. The lord of the land did not own his serfs, but he did own a percentage of the fruits of the land that were the product of the serf's labor. Thus he could claim a certain percentage of the serf's labor (often three to four days a week) as well as a percentage of his productivity in the form of wheat, and so on. The serf was at the mercy of his lord and received justice only if his lord cared to give it. It must be remembered, however, that "medieval Europe was the first complex human society not to have slavery as its economic base."

THE HOLY ROMAN EMPIRE

In 962 the Holy Roman Empire was proclaimed. In theory, medieval Christianity was divided between pope and emperor: temporal power wielded by the emperor, spiritual authority by the pope. In actual fact, the emperor's authority was limited to Germany and northern Italy, and even in these areas he was unable to make his rule effective, primarily because of the elective nature of his office.

Throughout most of medieval history there was a long struggle between pope and emperor over ultimate authority. The great Saxon emperors (919–1039) were able to resist papal supremacy, and Otto the Great (936–973) came close to turning the pope into an imperial appointee. Imperial authority reached its height under Henry III (1039–1056). In the end, however, the popes won out and forced Henry IV (1056–1106), at Canossa in 1077, to do penance to Pope Gregory and accept papal supremacy. After Henry IV, the Empire became weaker and weaker, the states of the Empire (the Electors) becoming stronger and stronger. Eventually it was as Voltaire said, neither holy, Roman, nor an Empire.

The Church

Attempts to Reform and Reunify the Church

Pope Nicholas II proclaimed in 1059 that popes should be elected by cardinals. This was an attempt to keep them free of lay control and was not always successful.

Pope Gregory VII, known as Hildebrand (1073–1085), was responsible for such reforms within the church as enforcement of celibacy and the creation of an independent and self-contained clergy centralized under the leadership of the pope. In effect, the church became a state within a state, having its own laws, government, and jurisdiction.

The height of the medieval papacy was achieved under Innocent III (1198–1216). He succeeded in establishing the papacy as the absolute moral and spiritual leader of the Christian world, and he virtually controlled Europe, intervening in politics and acting as feudal overlord to kings of all countries. He brought John of England into submission by the use of his power of interdict.

The Position of the Christian Church in the Medieval World

In 1300 Europe was primarily a religious community. Religion and the church were omnipresent. The vows between lord and vassal were religious oaths; the king was crowned by the church, merchant guilds were religious brotherhoods with patron saints, the drama and art were all concerned with faith, the church was the largest landowner in all countries, and the clergy were a privileged class. To the common man the church was everywhere, from the cradle to the grave.

The church was the agency of Christ, the intermediary between God and man. It alone possessed the means of salvation. Men had originally lived in a state of perfection, but Adam and Eve, of their free will, fell from paradise, and thus all mankind was damned. Christ, through his crucifixion, gave to man the opportunity to win salvation. The church gave to man the sacraments by which he could gain God's grace—baptism, confirmation, the mass, penance (such as prayer, fasting, and pilgrimages), extreme unction at the time of death, ordination (giving the priest spiritual power the common man did not possess), and matrimony.

The Church Had Three Principal Weapons by Which It Enforced Its Teachings

A. Canon law to punish crimes such as usury, sorcery, blasphemy, and perjury (the Inquisition began in the thirteenth century as a means of punishing such crimes);

B. Excommunication, which meant exclusion from the church and thus exclusion from the means of salvation; and

C. Interdict. Excommunication punished single people, interdict was excommunication of whole groups. This was first used in 998 against France and then against John of England.

The Scholastic Philosophy

In the twelfth century new knowledge poured into Europe from the Arabs in Spain, who had studied and translated the Greek masters. Aristotelian and Platonic works were to have the most influence on the European mind. The greatest of the scholars was Thomas Aquinas, who maintained that faith and reason were not in conflict with one another but led to a greater understanding of God. By reason he meant precise definition of words and concepts and Aristotelian logic. The schoolmen argued that God was a rational deity, capable of being comprehended by human reason. That man could not understand his

God and his universe was explained in terms of human failings. Reason was the sword of Hercules in the hands of a pygmy. Although Scholasticism, as this philosophy was called, was not encouraging to the development of natural science, it gave new dignity to intellectual study, philosophies, and universities. The official doctrine of the church was never as extreme as that of some of the scholastics; it insisted that God was beyond man's reason and could be accepted only on faith.

EXPANDING EUROPE

The greatest threat to the existence of Europe seemed to be militant Islam, which was moving into Spain but was stopped at the Pyrenees in 732. Finally, in the eleventh century, Europe took the offensive when the Seljuk Turks occupied the Middle East, conquered the Holy Land, and endangered Constantinople.

The first crusade (1095) was a military success. Asia Minor was conquered in 1097 and Jerusalem fell July 15, 1099. Afterwards, however, the political situation in Jerusalem, which was characterized by political strife, conflict between clergy and laity, and mingling of infidel and Christian, undermined the successes of the first crusade.

In 1144 the second crusade was advocated after the fall of Edessa to the Turks. This was a military failure.

In 1187 Jerusalem was recaptured by Saladin and this led to the third crusade. Frederick I of Germany, who died before he could play an active part, Philip II of France, and Richard the Lionhearted of England were all involved in the failure, which cost endless lives and gained only Acre.

The fourth crusade, in 1201, resulted in the increase in power and wealth of Venice and the weakening of the power of Constantinople.

The remaining crusades; Childrens' in 1212, fifth in 1219 to 1221, sixth in 1229, and the seventh in 1270, were all disastrous. The effects of increased contact with the East were, nevertheless, important and were the really significant result of the crusades.

Elsewhere Christendom was on the move. About 1100 the

Normans won Sicily from the Arabs, and by 1250 the Christians in Spain succeeded in throwing back the Moors and gaining most of the peninsula except Granada. Although there was still to be trouble from the Ottoman empire, Europe had proved herself capable of resistance.

THE BREAKDOWN OF FEUDALISM AND THE MEDIEVAL WAY OF LIFE

The Growth of Towns and Trade

A. Agricultural innovations that created a food surplus were the vital steps in the rise of towns and trade. A heavier plow enabling the farmer to cut a deeper furrow; a horse collar enabling the horse to pull a much greater load; windmills creating a new source of power; and the three-field system of rotation whereby two thirds of the land was cultivated and one third left fallow were all developed. The results were increased agricultural productivity that allowed a larger population and the means to feed urban areas.

B. The new towns soon demanded freedom from the control of feudal lords. The Italian cities were first to gain complete independence, and they developed as city-states. In the Holy Roman Empire, towns became small republics owing only nominal allegiance to the emperor; but in England and France the feudal kings were too powerful, and the towns received charters of liberties, not complete independence. This difference explains in part the creation of the national state in England and France long before Germany and Italy.

C. The obstacles to trade in the feudal era.

1) The self-sufficiency of the manor or fief did not encourage trade.

2) Early in the history of the town, merchants and craftsmen developed guilds to control their products, supervise their affairs, and eliminate competition. Neither church nor guild advocated an economic approach to life. The merchant who lived by the laws of supply and demand or who charged excessive rates of interest imperiled his soul. Instead, the proper charge and profit were based on the just or moral price.

3) The church refused burial to and had the wills annulled of anyone who made usurious interest on money.

4) Pirates, tolls, and duties added to the discouragement of trade, but nevertheless trade gradually began to increase.

D. The towns and trade were part of the undermining of feudal society, not only because they were independent of it, but also because they brought money back into circulation and offered freedom and occupation to those who wanted to escape from serfdom. The increase in money also led to the increase in the power of the monarch.

E. A new type of man began to emerge known as the entrepreneur. He usually started out as a merchant, buying and selling materials in an extensive market, and he often ended up a banker. Two examples of this new man were Giovanni de Medici of Florence (d. 1429) and Johann Fugger (d. 1408) of Augsburg. These two families were representative of

1) The wealth that would later finance the art of the Renaissance and the commercial revolution.

2) The existence of nonfeudal elements that could buy out the feudal nobles and even determine royal policy.

The Hundred Years War

This war, fought between England and France during the years 1337 to 1453, made chivalry a mockery, cost the British all their territory in France except Calais, which remained English until 1558, and led to the centralization of France under the French monarchy.

The Rise of the National Monarchy and the Centralization of Legal and Territorial Power

Slowly kings began to demand money (shield money) instead of military service from armed knights in payment for the use of land, and they began to supervise their interests by instituting such royal officials as the sheriffs and justices of the peace in England and the baillis and intendants in France. Besides this, they began to extend royal justice and the authority of royal courts. This obviously led to baronial opposition: the Magna Carta in England (1215) was a document requiring John to reconfirm the historic rights of freedom of his barons.

With the growth of towns, merchants and manufacturing classes began to demand protection and rights from their kings.

Representative assemblies were called to explain the king's policy and to ask for money. This occurred all over Europe: the first Cortes met in Spain in 1188, the first Estates-General in France in 1233 and then in 1302, the first diet in the Holy Roman Empire in 1255, and the first parliament in England in 1295. (Much of this dating is dependent on the definition of representative bodies; in England the date is often given as 1265). England, however, was the only country

A. To develop an effective two-house system in which a very small number of great barons (about fifty to eighty) sat in the House of Lords and the lesser aristocracy (the knights of the shire) sat along with the representatives of the charter towns (the burgesses) in the House of Commons.

B. Where the power of the crown was such as to demand that members of parliament be sent with sufficient authority to commit the constituency to policies initiated by the king. Therefore the English kings used their parliaments, whereas the monarchs of Europe did not.

The Unification of the State

THE BREAKDOWN OF RIVAL ALLEGIANCES

With the new wealth from taxation, monarchs were able successfully to demand the total loyalty of all subjects. This was in contrast to the medieval past in which individuals had tended to give their loyalty to their immediate overlord, to their village, to their profession, to their class, or to some combination of these.

THE GROWTH OF THE FEUDAL STATE

The growth of the feudal monarchs reached a high development in England under Henry II and Edward I, and in France under Philip IV. The growth of central power in both countries, however, received a serious setback by the successful revolt of the great nobles—in England the Magna Carta of 1215 and the civil wars of 1470 to 1485, and in France the Hundred Years War, 1337 to 1453.

THE "NEW MONARCHIES"

1) In both France and England, monarchy was successfully revived. The "New Monarchs" came to England in 1485 with the Tudor dynasty, and to France with Louis XI in 1461.

2) In Spain, the union of Aragon and Castile in 1469 under Ferdinand and Isabella created a unified Spanish state. In Spain, however, the new sense of nationalism had religious overtones, being closely linked to Catholicism and the crusading instinct that led eventually in 1492 to the total defeat of the Moors and the conquest of Granada.

The Kings of England (1066–1485) (The significant ones are starred.)

*William the Conqueror	1066–1087
William II	1087–1100
*Henry I	1100–1135
Stephen	1135–1154
*Henry II	1154–1189
(founder of Plantagenet line)	
Richard I the Lionhearted	1189–1199
John	1199–1216
Henry III	1216–1272
*Edward I	1272–1307
Edward II	1307–1327
Edward III	1327–1377
Richard II	1377–1399
Henry IV	1399–1415
Henry V	1415–1422
(King of France 1420–1422)	
Henry VI	1422–1461

(King of France and England)

Edward IV	1461–1483
Richard III	1483–1485
*Henry VII	1485–1509

The Kings of France (987–1483) (The significant ones are starred.)

Hugh	987–996
(first of the Capets)	
Robert	996–1031
Henry	1031–1060
Philip I	1060–1108
Louis VI	
the Fat	1108–1137
Louis VII	1137–1180
*Philip II	1180–1223
(Augustus)	
Louis VIII	1223–1226
*Louis IX	1226–1270
St. Louis (the strongest monarch	
of his age)	
Philip III	1270–1285
*Philip IV	
the Fair	1285–1314
Louis X	1314–1316
Philip V	1316–1322
Charles IV	1322–1328
(last of the Capets)	
Philip VI	1328–1350
(of Valois)	
John the Good (II)	1350–1364
*Charles V	
—the Wise	1364–1380
Charles VI	1380–1422
Charles VII	1422–1461
*Louis XI	1461–1483

Science and Technology Destroy the Medieval Way of Life

Gunpowder and printing were doubtless the two most important inventions that led to the breakdown of feudalism.

A. Gunpowder, probably brought from China, meant the end of the power of the feudal castle and increased the ability of the monarch to wage war against the feudal baron.

B. Printing, the Gutenberg movable type invented around 1448, put education within the reach of the masses, made the circulation of the Bible possible (the first printed Bible was set in 1454), and thus influenced not only the Renaissance but also the Reformation.

The compass, brought from China through Spain, and geographical knowledge, an Arab contribution, made possible the discovery of the New World during the 1500's and the commercial revolution in Europe.

A Change in the Way of Thinking—Humanism

In Italy a new concept of man was evolving. A sense of man's tremendous capacities and potential was replacing the concept of man as a frail creature in need of God's grace. Man was becoming a subject worthy of study in his own right and not merely of interest as an example of God's creation. This nonreligious orientation can be seen in the development of the writing of history as opposed to theology, in biography in contrast to the history of saints, and in portrait-painting as opposed to scenes of religious inspiration.

A. Though his *Divine Comedy* is the highest literary expression of medieval thought, Dante (1265–1321) broke with tradition by writing in Italian rather than Latin and by stressing happiness on this earth.

B. Petrarch (1304–1374) has been called the father of humanism, because he was among the first scholars to desert medieval learning and to revive interest in Greek and Roman literature.

C. Literature reflected this new concern for man. It advocated a cult of humanity and human powers and imitated the writings of the ancients.

D. In painting, the new concern with things human can also be found. Although art remained more religiously oriented than other disciplines, studies of anatomy, concern with perspective, and recognition of individual personalities reflect the new concept of man.

E. Machiavelli produced a handbook of statescraft called *The Prince* (1513), which was the first purely secular treatise on politics. In many ways he diagnosed the era, which was becoming more secular, in which kings were breaking with the power of the church and the national state was demanding the loyalty of its people.

Humanism Outside Italy Was Different

A. Humanism spread into north and central Europe nearly a century after it had begun in Italy. The humanism of the north has often been called Christian humanism, because it was more a blend of the old—the religious—and the new—the concern for humanity.

B. The greatest of all northern humanists was Erasmus of Rotterdam. He ridiculed the scholastic philosophers, called for the reform of the clergy, urged the translation of the Bible into vernacular languages, and placed his faith in education, reasonableness, and laughter. His greatest work was the *Praise of Folly*.

MODERN CIVILIZATION   1500 to the Present

The beginning of the modern history of Europe is also the beginning of world history, for from 1500 to 1763 Europe unified the world and from 1763 to 1914 she dominated it, spreading Western civilization to the remote corners of the globe, ruling directly Africa, India, and Southeast Asia and controlling indirectly China, the Ottoman Empire, and the Americas. Never before had one small area so dominated the rest of the world. The story of European history up to 1914, therefore, is the story of how Europe came to control the world—the unique features of religious, economic, industrial, scientific, social, and political revolution that made it possible. The spreading of these peculiar qualities of Western civilization was Europe's triumph as well as her decline, for in giving to the rest of the world her science, her industry, and her political philosophies, she gave to it the technological and ideological means to rebel successfully against her domination, and this is the essence of her history from 1914 to the present. As A. J. Toynbee says in his article, "Encounter Between Civilizations," "Future historians will say, I think, that the greatest event of the twentieth century was the impact of western civilization upon all the living societies of that day."

Europe   1500–1763

The five basic movements that marked the transition to modern civilization were (1) the achievements in art, literature, and thought of the Renaissance, which restored to importance man and this world; (2) the birth of nations, which destroyed the ideal of political unity and gave rise to a faith in the national state; (3) the discovery and exploration of the New World, which led to an economic revolution; (4) the revolt against the papacy, which destroyed the spiritual unity of Europe; and (5) the scientific discoveries and experiments of the seventeenth century, which led to technological changes that in turn made Europe more powerful than any other area in the world.

The Renaissance

The change in the way of thinking, the new attitude toward man, not only led to the breakdown of feudalism and the medieval way of life but also created the conditions that made possible the Reformation and the commercial and scientific revolutions.

The height of Renaissance individuality and art was from 1450 to 1559. Politically, the Italian city-states were in the hands of either French or Spanish armies and the peninsula was in chaos, yet it was during this era that Europe produced the greatest figures of the Renaissance.

The Men of the Renaissance

Michelangelo (1475–1564) was a sculptor, painter, engineer, and architect. Examples of his work are the Medici tombs, the dome of St. Peter's Cathedral, the fresco on the ceiling of the Sistine Chapel, and the statues of David and Moses.

Benvenuto Cellini (1500–1572) was one of the great artists of the Renaissance, but he is best known for his work in silver and gold.

Leonardo da Vinci (1452–1519) was the Renaissance ideal, the universal man, experimenting in mathematics, architecture, geology, botany, physiology, anatomy, sculpture, painting, music, and poetry. Two of his most important works are the "Mona Lisa" and the "Last Supper."

Raphael Sanzio (1483–1520) was another of the great painters and artistic experimenters of the Renaissance.

Much of the literature of the period was imitative of Greek and Roman works, yet outside Italy Sir Thomas More of England (1478–1535) wrote the *Utopia,* the first important book describing conditions necessary for an ideal state since Plato's *Republic,* and William Shakespeare (1564–1616) attained new heights in drama and poetry. In England, Christopher Marlowe (1564–93) wrote *Doctor Faustus;* in Spain, Cervantes (1547–1616) produced *Don Quixote* and Lope de Vega his seven hundred dramas; in France, Montaigne (1533–92) wrote his essays.

The Reformation

Causes of the Reformation
ECONOMIC CAUSES

A. The economic practices of the merchant and the manufacturer clashed with church doctrine, especially on the issues of just price and usury.

B. The fiscal demands of the church were an economic drain on Europe, and monarchs soon came into conflict with the church over the control of ecclesiastical revenues.

POLITICAL CAUSES

The growth of the national state and the resulting clash between the church and the monarch on the question of ultimate sovereignty was another cause of the Reformation. The fact that the Reformation was supported in Germany was due in part to the desire of German patriots to use the religious question to further the cause of nationalism at the expense of an Italian-controlled empire and church.

INTELLECTUAL CAUSES

The vast intellectual revolution was an influential factor in the revolt against the Roman Catholic Church. The humanism of the north, the great concern with humanity and with reform, combined with the secularization of life, played an important part in the desire of men to find a way of attaining salvation without renouncing life or depreciating the importance of man.

FAILURE WITHIN THE CHURCH

A. The conflict between officially sanctioned ideals of society and actual practice of man and church was causing increased desire for reform. Ideally the church was universal and concerned with things of the spirit, yet in practice it maintained a luxurious court, extracted high rents from church land, charged fees for services such as burial and the sacraments. It was "trading upon its monopoly of the means of salvation in order to raise money largely for secular purposes."

B. The Great Schism in the church (from 1378 to 1417 there were two popes—one at Avignon in France, the other at Rome) caused doubt about the divinity of the papal office (articulated by such men as John Wycliffe of England and John Huss in Bohemia) and weakened the authority of the church.

The Reformation

The Reformation began when Martin Luther (1483–1546), Professor of Bible at the University of Wittenberg, posted Ninety-five Theses directed against the selling of indulgences. Luther claimed that the source of spiritual authority was not the church but scripture and the individual reader. The church, he said, was not necessary to salvation, because only faith could save man. This is the famous Lutheran doctrine of "justification by faith alone." After the Diet of Worms in 1520, in which he refused to recant, Luther was excommunicated, and Lutheranism was formed in defiance of the Roman Catholic Church.

The Spread of Protestantism

A. A social and political reformer, Zwingli (1485–1531), broke with Luther and in Zurich, Switzerland formed many of the ideas of Congregationalism. Robert Browne of England (1550–1633), however, is known as the founder of the Congregational faith.

B. John Calvin (1509–1564) in his *Institutes* articulated the theory of predestination and the doctrine of the elect and was the father of the French Huguenots, the Puritans, and the Presbyterians. John Knox founded the Presbyterian church but differed little from Calvin.

C. Henry VIII of England broke with the Roman Catholic Church in 1534 because the pope refused to allow him to divorce his wife, and although Henry broke without first adopting any Protestant principles, intending only to be his own pope in an English Catholic church, eventually the forces of reform were too great and the Anglican or Episcopalian church developed.

Protestants, Although Each Sect Differed, Had Certain Beliefs in Common

A. All rejected papal authority and the supernatural character of the priesthood.

B. All replaced Latin with the vernacular language of the country, and accepted the authority of the Bible.

C. All believed in, although they interpreted differently, justification by faith alone.

D. All rejected purgatory, transubstantiation, and obligatory confession.

E. All reduced the number of sacraments, usually to two or three.

The Catholic Counter-Reformation

At the Council of Trent, sitting irregularly in 1545–1547, 1551–1552, and 1562–1563, the Roman Catholic Church was reformed and rejuvenated. In Spain the Renaissance spirit and paganism had not taken over, and it was here that Catholicism became revitalized and militant. St. Ignatius Loyola established The Society of Jesus (the Jesuits), a monastic order dedicated to active participation in world affairs and acting as a missionary force throughout Asia and the Americas. The Inquisition was established to enforce conformity throughout the Catholic world.

The Wars of Religion

From the middle of the sixteenth century to the middle of the seventeenth century, wars raged in Europe—often referred to as the wars of religion, although in most cases the motives were basically political and economic.

A. France from 1562 to 1595 was engaged in a civil war between Catholics and Huguenots.

B. War broke out in Germany in 1546 between Lutheran princes and the Holy Roman Empire led by Charles V. In 1555 the Peace of Augsburg was concluded, recognizing the religious stalemate and giving each individual prince the right to decide whether his territory would be Lutheran or Catholic.

C. From 1568 to 1609 (or 1648, the Treaty of Westphalia), the Netherlands fought for independence from Spanish control. This was in part a religious war between Catholics and Calvinists, but it was also an economic conflict.

D. In 1588 England defeated her Spanish rival when she destroyed the Spanish Armada by a combination of English seamanship and "Protestant weather."

E. The Thirty Years War (1618–1648) was in part a German civil war fought over the Catholic-Protestant issue and constitutional issues and in part an international war between France and the Hapsburgs, Spain and the Dutch. The Peace of Westphalia finally terminated this bloody struggle, recognizing again the religious stalemate in Europe.

F. In 1642 England's Civil War began, and although the

Puritans triumphed temporarily, the religious issue was not
solved until 1660, when Charles II and the Anglican Church
were restored.

The Commercial Revolution

The Discoveries and Explorations

A. Spain and Portugal led the way in explorations of the
New World primarily because they were two of the first politically united states in Europe.

B. In 1498 the Portuguese Vasco da Gama rounded the Cape
of Africa and discovered a new route to Asia, the source of valued
commodities such as spices and silk. Because of this new route
the cost of Eastern goods was reduced considerably, for there
were no more transshipments, unloadings and reloadings, or dependence upon Arab middlemen. Portugal was soon making
profits of ten to thirty times the cost of goods in the East Indies.

C. In 1492 Columbus, sailing under the flag of Spain,
thought he had reached the Indies. In reality he had discovered
the New World, and in 1520 Magellan and a Spanish expedition
sailed into the Pacific, discovering the Philippines and circum-
navigating the globe. Hernando Cortez of Spain conquered the
Aztecs of Mexico between 1519 and 1521, and Francisco Pizarro
destroyed the Incas of Peru in the 1530's. Between 1500 and 1660
Spain received 18,600 tons of silver and 200 tons of gold from the
New World alone.

D. Decline of the Iberian Empires

Inflation, wars in Europe, corruption, the hidalgo spirit
(the belief that the gentleman did not work with his hands), internal disunity, and the growth of the northwestern European
states led to the decline of Spain and Portugal. The defeat of
the Spanish Armada in 1588 was proof that the Iberian powers
were no longer masters of the seas.

The Commercial Revolution and Its By-products

A. The commercial revolution was the change from a self-
sufficient town-centered economy to a capitalistic nation-centered
economy.

1) The entrepreneur was the first to break with the town and the guild.

2) The putting-out system or the domestic system of rural household industry was another step in the breakdown of the restrictive practices of towns and guilds. The system applied mostly to the manufacture of cloth. Cottagers received the wool and made it into thread or cloth, and the finished article was then collected by an agent who paid the cottager for his work.

3) The first industry to change to a capitalistic economic base was the cloth industry, but certain other concerns were capitalistic from their formation (mining, book printing, armaments, all required large outlays of capital and mass production).

B. A monetary revolution was one of the by-products of the commercial revolution. With the discoveries of precious metals in the New World their value declined, prices rose, and inflation resulted. The monetary crisis affected all levels of society:

1) Monarchies soon quarreled with their parliaments over a demand to increase taxation. This led to a constitutional crisis and this in turn to a rise in royal absolutism throughout Europe (but the triumph of parliament in England).

2) In the country the position of the peasant went up and the feudal lord down. (In Eastern Europe the reverse occurred.)

C. Mercantilism was a direct result of attempts by states to acquire more money. Kings endeavoured to assist merchants, force people to work, and create a favorable balance of trade. Companies with exclusive trading monopolies were formed; the most famous were the East India Companies founded by the British in 1600, the Dutch in 1602, the French in 1664. It was through these companies that Northern European nations began to encroach on the Spanish and Portuguese monopolies in the New World and the Far East, and it was through them that England, France, and Holland were to establish their commercial empires.

D. New wealth and prosperity of Europe from the profits of trade led to changes at home, for the commercial aristocracy began to rival the landed aristocracy in social and political power.

The Scientific Revolution of the Seventeenth Century

The essence of science is the union of observation with reason and the denial of all authorities that cannot be proved by experimentation. As Bacon cried, "I should burn all the books of Aristotle, for the study of them can only lead to a loss of time, produce error and increase ignorance."

Nicholas Copernicus (1473–1543) of Poland

In 1543 Copernicus wrote against the Ptolemaic theory that the sun revolved around the earth and advocated a heliocentric theory that was mathematically simpler than the geocentric.

Kepler (1571–1630) of Germany

Kepler carried Copernicus' theory further and discovered that the orbits of the planets were ellipses.

Galileo (1564–1642) of Italy

In 1609 Galileo built one of the first telescopes, reconfirmed the Copernican theory, and suggested that planetary bodies were made of the same substance as the earth. Galileo threatened existing philosophy and theology and was forced to recant by the Roman Catholic Church.

Francis Bacon (1561–1626) of England

Bacon insisted on the inductive method of acquiring knowledge and the usefulness of knowledge.

René Descartes (1596–1650) of France

Descartes, the developer of coordinate geometry, believed that nature could be reduced to a mathematical formula and advanced "the principle of systematic doubt."

Isaac Newton (1642–1727) of England

In 1687 Newton published the *Mathematical Principles of Natural Philosophy* showing that all motion could be described by the same mathematical formula. Gravitation was the force that moved matter. Until Einstein his theories remained unshaken, but now it has been proved that they do not apply to subatomic structures.

The Effects of Scientific Discovery on Man's Thinking

A. Although the effects of the new science were important in navigation, in the development of calculus, in the science of map-making, in warfare, and so forth, the effects on man's mind were the most profound. Man was no longer the center of creation, but nevertheless man had discovered the laws of the universe—and therefore everything seemed possible to human reason.

B. Political science and the study of man and society were effects of the scientific revolution. The question of what is "right," or "natural law," was uppermost in men's minds. Two of the most important political thinkers of the era were Thomas Hobbes (1588–1679), who wrote in justification of absolutism, and John Locke (1632–1704) who supported constitutionalism.

The Rulers of Europe   1483-1760

The Kings of France (The most important are starred.)

Charles VIII	1483–1498
Louis XII	1498–1515
*Francis I	1515–1547
Henry II	1547–1559
Francis II	1559–1560
Charles IX	1560–1574
Henry III	1574–1589
*Henry IV	1589–1610
(the first Bourbon)	
Louis XIII	1610–1643
*Louis XIV	1643–1715
Louis XV	1715–1774

The Kings of England (The most important are starred.)

*Henry VII	1485–1509
(the first Tudor)	
*Henry VIII	1509–1547
Edward VI	1547–1553
Mary	1553–1558

*Elizabeth the Great (I)	1558–1603
James I	1603–1625
(the first Stuart)	
*Charles I	1625–1649
*Cromwellian Rule	1649–1658
Charles II	1660–1685
James II	1685–1688
William and Mary	1689–1702
Anne	1702–1714
George I	1714–1727
(the first of the Hanoverians)	
George II	1727–1760

The Kings of Spain (The most important are starred.)

*Ferdinand and Isabella	1479–1516
Philip I	1516–1519
(first Hapsburg)	
*Charles I (V)	1519–1556
*Philip II	1556–1598
Philip III	1598–1621
Philip IV	1621–1665
Charles II	1665–1700
Philip V	1700–1746
(first Bourbon)	
Ferdinand VI	1746–1759
Charles III	1759–1788

The Hapsburg Emperors (The most important are starred.)

Rudolf I	1273–1291
(the first Hapsburg Emperor)	
Frederick III	1440–1493
Maximilian I	1493–1519
*Charles V	1519–1556
Ferdinand I	1556–1564
Maximilian II	1564–1576
Rudolf II	1576–1612
Matthias	1612–1619

Ferdinand II	1619–1637
Ferdinand III	1637–1657
Leopold I	1658–1705
Joseph I	1705–1711
Charles VI	1711–1740
Charles VII	1742–1745
(not a Hapsburg)	
Francis I	1745–1765
(husband of Maria Theresa)	

The Rivalry Among the European Powers

With the explorations, commercial exploitation, and wealth of the New World came further conflict on the European continent as well as in the colonies. The resolution of this struggle ends the first section of modern European history.

At first the Dutch were the most successful in the competition with the Iberian peninsula for overseas control, for they had an efficient merchant ship (the flyboat) that was able to challenge Portuguese control in the East Indies and establish Dutch interests in the New World. The Netherlands monopolized whaling in the Arctic, the trade in the Baltic, and temporarily—until 1664—they controlled New Amsterdam (New York); the northeast coast of Brazil until 1654, and the Cape of Good Hope in South Africa. But Holland became entangled in a series of wars with France and Britain, and she lacked manpower and resources to compete with her mightier neighbors.

Britain and France became supreme in the commercial rivalry of the eighteenth century, in part because of their high industrial production and in part because of the fact that their governments were organized on a national scale. Over half of Great Britain's trade became transoceanic, whereas only one third of France's trade was involved overseas—the other two thirds were in Europe and the Near East.

The decline of the Netherlands and the Iberian powers left Britain and France to fight for the mastery of the New World and to maintain a balance of power on the European continent.

A. Conflicts for control of North America, India, and eventually Africa, as well as for supremacy at home were fought 1689–1679 (King William's War) and 1701 to 1713 (the War of the Spanish Succession, or Queen Anne's War). The Peace of Utrecht in 1713 partitioned the Spanish empire: Belgium, Naples, Sicily, and Milan went to the Austrian Hapsburgs; Sardina to the Duke of Savoy; and Minorca and Gibraltar to England. Great Britain also acquired Nova Scotia, Newfoundland, and the Hudson Bay country from France.

B. Then followed the War of the Austrian Succession (King George's War) 1740–1748 and the Seven Years' War of 1756–63. Although there were eight years between them, they were essentially the same war, for their causes were the same:

1) A struggle between Britain and France for colonies, trade, and mastery of the seas.

2) A duel between Prussia and Austria for power in Central Europe.

C. THE WAR OF THE AUSTRIAN SUCCESSION

This war did not accomplish Prussia's purpose, for the Hapsburg empire was not destroyed, but it was forced to surrender Silesia; this doubled Prussia's population and more than doubled her resources, thus upsetting the balance of power in Europe. An about-face in allies occurred after this war: in 1756 Great Britain and Prussia became allies; and France and Austria joined forces—Louis XVI was married to Marie Antoinette, one of the daughters of Maria Theresa.

D. THE SEVEN YEARS' WAR

The final struggle for supremacy began in America but soon spread to Europe. On the continent, it was merely another war of partition. In 1761, when France was losing, she made an alliance with Spain, but England and Prussia were able to defeat her. The situation overseas, however, solved what might have been an endless struggle on the European continent. The Marquis of Montcalm was finally defeated by James Wolfe at Quebec, as was Dupleix by Robert Clive in India. The deciding factor in the colonies was the superior strength of the British navy. When the Treaty of Paris was signed in 1763, Britain was the most powerful nation in the world, for she controlled North America and India, and her supremacy of the seas was secured. France surrendered the St. Lawrence Valley and all territory east of the Mississippi in America. Spain lost Florida to the British, and France lost all her fortifications in India.

EUROPE 1763–1914

During the period 1763 to 1914, Europe became mistress of the world. The explanation of how this was possible can perhaps be found in three revolutions—the economic, scientific, and ideological, which changed the face of Europe during the eighteenth century and made her physically and spiritually able to dominate the rest of the world. It was the transmission of these three revolutions to the rest of the globe that was to be Europe's gift to the non-Western world. In 1914 seven European countries held 115 colonies (Britain had 55, France 29, Germany 10, Belgium 1, Portugal 8, the Netherlands 8, and Italy 4) representing a population twice as large as the mother countries and an area almost three times as great. The economic revolution in part inspired the seizure of these colonies, and the scientific revolution, which was an integral part of the economic and industrial change, made it possible to exploit them, to penetrate Africa, and to subdue those who objected. At the same time that these two revolutions were occurring came ideological changes: the development of constitutional government, the rise of nationalism, the growth of liberalism, and the development of socialism and communism. But with imperialism and nationalism came conflict among the states of Europe that spilled over into the globe, becoming world war.

Economic Change and Revolution

Commercial capitalism produced new wealth. Huge private fortunes were amassed and governments became more and more susceptible to the wishes of the wealthy. When rich merchants and financiers withdrew their support, collapse of the government was almost inevitable; this was in part the cause of the French Revolution of 1789.

The Industrial Revolution

A. According to R. R. Palmer in *A History of the Modern World,* "the process of shifting from hand tools to power machinery is what is meant by the industrial revolution." In the nineteenth century the use of the steam engine and the power-driven machine led to modern industrialization.

B. The country that led the way was Great Britain, beginning around 1770. There were two primary reasons for the industrial revolution occurring first in England:

1) Improvements in agricultural production (inventions such as the machine drill, fertilization, crop rotation, and scientific breeding of livestock) and the private ownership and consolidation of land, known as enclosure, had led to a sharp rise in productivity. Improved productivity provided food for the new industrial cities; changes in land ownership produced the necessary mobile labor supply for the new factories.

2) The new markets opened up by the control of India and the Americas along with growing prosperity at home produced an insatiable demand for manufactured goods.

C. Technological improvements were first introduced in the textile industry. In 1773 John Kay invented the flying shuttle, which increased the productivity of the weaver; in 1769 Richard Arkwright introduced the water-frame (spinning machine), and, more important, in the 1780's used the steam engine (first invented by Newcomen in 1702 and improved by James Watt in 1769) to drive the spinning machines.

1) The use of steam necessitated the growth of factories. Since the machine could no longer be taken to the labor supply, labor had to be brought to the machine.

2) The demand for raw cotton led to further inventions: Eli Whitney, an American cotton grower, invented the cotton gin in 1793.

3) At the same time the wood shortage that was caused by steam-run machines increased the demand for coal, and led to the Darby process and, in 1859, the Bessemer process for the large-scale manufacture of steel.

D. By 1815 Great Britain had become the workshop of the world. Her production in coal rose from 6 million tons in 1770 to 57 million in 1861 and in iron from 50 thousand to 3800 thousand tons. After 1870, however, she faced competition from the major nations of the continent. This competition was in part responsible for the grabbing of the colonies and the scramble for concessions throughout the world, since the great industrial powers were anxious to control markets for their goods.

The Scientific Revolution

Hand in Hand with Economic Change and Industrialization Went Science

In the sixteenth and seventeenth centuries great progress had been made in physics, chemistry, and mathematics; in the eighteenth century chemistry was further advanced by Antoine Lavoisier's writings and by Joseph Priestley who isolated oxygen in 1755; but the nineteenth century witnessed the hey-day of scientific discovery.

Sir Charles Lyell did extensive study on the formation of the earth in 1830; George Mendel worked in the field of biology and made significant contributions to the principles of heredity in the 1860's. William Wiendt made contributions in psychology in 1872; and Louis Pasteur did important work in medicine —the germ theory of diseases, in 1864. The first modern psychoanalysis was introduced by Sigmund Freud in 1895; and in the field of natural sciences, Charles Darwin and his theory of evolution, *On the Origin of Species,* was to have an astonishing influence on the minds of men. These were just a few of the major names and accomplishments of the century.

Effects of the Scientific and Industrial Revolutions

International

A. The industrial and scientific revolutions made possible the exploitation of the globe—railroads, canals, steamships, and most important, armaments made the European mobile and dangerous. Medical science made it possible for him to exist in the tropics.

B. Another international effect was economic interdependence of the world. The entire globe became a single market and dependent upon the fluctuation of prices and demand in other parts of the world.

Social and Economic Effects in Europe

A. At home, the population boomed (Great Britain and Ireland tripled from 1750 to 1850) and new cities rose—steel centers such as Birmingham, shipbuilding in Newcastle, cotton works in Manchester. The rapid urbanization and industrialization caused unheard-of problems: housing was poor, children were forced by their parents into factories, hours were long, family life and morality broke down, but eventually the factory towns improved and were more desirable than rural slums. The very concentration of people ultimately led to improvement of their conditions and to the organization of labor unions.

B. Another serious effect of the industrial revolution was technological unemployment. The cotton gin, for example, reduced the number of people required from fifty to eight.

C. In the long run the total increase in wealth led to a general rise in the standard of living. For example, increased industrial productivity meant that child labor was no longer an economic necessity, and it required the existence of an educated labor force.

Political Results of the Revolutions

A. Industrialization meant a further increase in the power of the bourgeoisie.

B. At the same time, it led to the rise of labor as a political force. Ferdinand Lassalle formed the German Socialist party in 1848. In 1871 it had 124,655 votes out of 3,892,160; by 1874 it won 351,952 votes out of 5,190,254. Louis Blanc organized the first socialist party in France around the same period. The British workmen were more advanced and more successful in forcing collective bargaining on their employers and thus they were slower in forming workers' political parties. The British Labour Party was not formed until 1900 and was less socialistic than those on the continent. (The new ideology of socialism was one of the intellectual and cultural results of the industrial revolution.) (See pp. 107–08; 247; 252.)

Imperialism Was in Part a Result of Industrialization

The Urge to Imperialism

After 1870, European expansion, which had been going on for four hundred years, is referred to as imperialism. The causes of the scramble for possessions and concessions were

Economic Factors
Surplus capital looking for overseas investment, an expanding population, the need for raw materials, and the urge to find markets for industrial goods contributed to imperialism. The competition with rival European nations and the desire for protection by tariff was also a factor.

Political Factors
Rivalry among the European powers eventually led to a projection overseas of inter-European rivalries. Strategic reasons, such as the need for naval bases and coaling stations, were also involved. The newly unified Germany and Italy also contributed to the acute competition for power on the European continent.

Personalities Influenced the Demand for Colonies
Without such men as Disraeli, prime minister of England from 1874 to 1880, to encourage her, Great Britain might never have entered the scramble. Norway, for instance, whose merchant fleet was second only to Britain's, did not enter the struggle. Germany, whose industrial capacity was greater than France's in the 1880's, did not enter the race until the beginning of the twentieth century because Bismarck refused.

Ideological Revolution

The Background to the Political Revolutions of the Eighteenth Century

THE GREAT REBELLION AND THE GLORIOUS REVOLUTION

A. The first step in the radical change in relations that was to occur between those who governed and those who were governed was the Great Rebellion of 1642. The lrst country to develop effective representative government was Great Britain.

B. In 1642 conflict between king and parliament led to civil war. At issue was the right of parliament to tax and to control governmental policy. Charles I argued that governmental initiative rested solely with the king and that parliament was just an advisory body. By 1646 the parliamentary forces were victorious, and in 1649 the monarchy was overthrown and Charles executed.

C. The period from 1649 to 1660 is called the Interregnum; it was an era of extremism in politics and religion, culminating in the theocratic dictatorship of Oliver Cromwell.

D. In 1660 the monarchy was restored; Charles II returned from exile. Parliament's right to raise money was recognized, but the complete victory of parliamentary government and control was not reached until the Glorious Revolution of 1688–1689, when James II was overthrown and replaced by William and Mary. Though England remained a monarchy in name, she was in fact an aristocratic oligarchy until 1832, ruled by parliament, which in turn was controlled by men of landed wealth.

THE AGE OF ENLIGHTENMENT

The Age of Enlightenment was the five decades that preceded the French revolution. It was a period of scepticism toward tradition, secularization of thought, a new attitude toward government, a view of the state as the main instrument of welfare, and a profound belief in reason. It had its origins in the works of men like Locke, Bacon, and Descartes, but the heart of the movement was Paris.

A. The most momentous work of the era was the *L'Encyclopédie* or the "reasoned dictionary," edited by Diderot and d'Alembert and containing a compilation of all scientific and historical knowledge.

B. Three writers symbolize the movement—Voltaire, Montesquieu, and Rousseau, and their writings were to have a profound influence on the fate of the French nation.

1) Voltaire (1694–1778) wrote for the new bourgeois middle class. His main concern was freedom of thought. Around 1740 he became a crusader, preaching religious tolerance and crying against bigotry, censorship, and the power of the clergy. He held England up as an example of freedom of thought and religious liberty. He attacked superstition and stupidity and was the first to present a secular concept of world history.

2) Montesquieu was an aristocrat rather than a member of the middle class, and his most famous work, *The Spirit of Laws* (1748), advocated constitutional monarchy but stated that types of government were dependent upon climate and circumstances. He also developed an intricate system of separation and balance of power (and in part inspired the American constitution). He too held England up as a model of good government.

3) The maladjusted, penniless Rousseau (1712–1778) was unlike either of his contemporaries. He preached that society was evil, that man should return to the state of nature from which he came. But in his *Social Contract* (1762) he argued that governments were formed by an agreement among the people themselves, that every person should feel that he belonged to the state, since it was a product of the "General Will." This theory contained within it the seeds of democracy, nationalism, and also enlightened despotism. His novel *Emile* had the most immediate effect. In it he pointed out the artificiality of aristocratic life.

C. Enlightened despotism was a characteristic of the age of enlightenment.

1) It was rational, reformist, and despotic, and was caused in part by the writings of the philosophers but also by the wars of the eighteenth century (1740–1748 and 1756–1763), which increased the need for efficient government.

2) In Spain and Naples, Charles II was enlightened and despotic.

3) In Austria, Maria Theresa pushed through internal consolidation and began to attack serfdom, but it was her son Joseph II, who came to the throne in 1780, who abolished it, established equality of taxation and punishment, and permitted toleration of all religions. But in so doing he also built up a police state.

4) In Prussia, Frederick the Great held the title of "enlightened" because of his intellectual ability. He revised law and established public education and religious freedom, but he maintained a highly stratified society.

5) Catherine the Great's claim to enlightenment in Russia is somewhat dubious.

6) In England, of course, there was neither enlightenment nor despotism, but during this era her thirteen American colonies revolted, and these American leaders were a part of the enlightenment. Thomas Paine not only wrote *The Crisis* (propaganda for the American Revolution) but also *The Rights of Man* and *The Age of Reason*.

7) Though France was the home of enlightened ideas, her government was one of the most clumsy and inefficient, and this in part explains the downfall of Louis XVI.

THE AMERICAN REVOLUTION 1775–1783

The American Revolution for independence had significant repercussions in Europe.

A. It overburdened the French treasury and thus contributed to revolution.

B. It led to revolts for independence and civil rights throughout Europe.

C. It changed the great nations' attitudes toward their colonies, and England, particularly, began to accept the fact that some day all her colonies would be independent.

D. It had a decisive influence on the French Revolution, and even the French Declaration of Human Rights and the constitution of 1791 were in many ways drawn from the United States.

Tom Paine himself was a member of the French National Assembly during the French Revolution.

The French Revolution,   1789

CAUSES

A. The philosophers' writings, the new ideas about the nature of man and society, the new attitude toward authority—all were significant causes.

B. The political and tax structure of France: The bourgeoisie had little voice in the government, which was still controlled by the prestige classes (nobility and church). The tax burden rested most heavily on those least capable of paying, and people of great wealth, both noble and bourgeois, escaped their fair share of taxation.

C. There was general dissatisfaction with the church in France, for it was a political power and the greatest of all landowners.

D. A rising proletariat (wage-earning group), although not class conscious, was also a necessary ingredient of the successful revolution.

E. The property system was outmoded, for it remained in large part feudal.

F. The financial bankruptcy of the government precipitated the crisis, although it was certainly not a cause in itself (the French national debt stood at 4 billion livres, but this was only half what Great Britain's was). The government's efforts to tax the nobility led to the summoning of the Estates-General (parliament) and in this way initiated the revolution.

THE REVOLUTION

A. A meeting of the Estates-General was called for the spring of 1789; it had last met in 1614. There were to be three hundred representatives from the first estate (the Church), three hundred from the second estate (the nobility), and six hundred from the third estate (the number of the third estate was in itself a revolutionary step). The issue immediately arose as to whether the estates should sit and vote by estates or as one assembly. The third estate demanded a National Assembly, consisting of all three estates. This led to a two-month struggle in the beginning of July in which the third estate, joined by certain members of the other estates, created their own National Assembly.

B. The battle happened to coincide with severe depression in the countryside, and on July 14, 1789 the Parisian mob marched on the Bastille to get arms and to demonstrate in favor of the National Assembly. This saved the assembly, for Louis, instead of disbanding them, was shocked into turning the government over to them.

THE REVOLUTIONARY GOVERNMENTS

A. On August 4th serfdom was abolished and the nobility voluntarily gave up their feudal rights. On August 26th the Declaration of the Rights of Man and Citizen was announced, declaring that "Men are born and remain free and equal in rights," assuring "liberty, property, security and resistance to oppression," and promising freedom of thought, religion, due process of law, taxation only by consent, and separation of powers of the government.

B. But in September of 1789 came dispute over the powers of the king, and insurrection and violence followed. Then the National Assembly moved to Paris and soon fell into the hands of the more radical elements (the Jacobin Club).

C. In 1791 a constitutional monarchy was formed. This lasted ten months. The reasons for the collapse of this government were

1) France was at war.

2) The government failed to win the support of the masses. It gave the franchise to only 50,000 landed men.

D. In 1792 the National Convention was organized, but it lacked control and also failed.

E. Then, under the guidance of Robespierre, the Reign of Terror began in order to bring about a "republic of virtue." It was due in part to the pressure of war and the acute economic crisis. Seventy percent of the 40,000 who died during the Terror were peasants and laborers. Robespierre died the way he had lived, by the guillotine.

f. In 1795 the Directory, under conservative bourgeois control, was placed in power, followed in 1799 by the Consulate.

THE SPREAD OF FRENCH REVOLUTIONARY IDEAS

a. The three great principles of the French Revolution were liberty (the right of self-determination and self-government), equality (the destruction of all forms of feudal privilege and the equality of all men before the law), and fraternity (the brotherhood of all men). French ideas (often enforced by French armies) produced revolutions in Holland, Milan, Naples, Spain, Switzerland, and many of the states of Germany. Though most of these revolutions were in the name of liberty, most ended up in dictatorship. Fraternity tended to deteriorate into nationalism, and the only effective ideal was equality, which led to the abolition of aristocratic privileges and the end of serfdom.

b. Napoleon, the Enlightened Despot, 1799–1814

1) The man most responsible for the spread of the ideas of the French Revolution was Napoleon Bonaparte, who assumed control of the French government first as consul in 1799 and then as emperor in 1804.

2) At home Napoleon's rule was that of an enlightened despot, standardizing taxation and codifying laws.

3) He then set out to impose a political unity on the European continent by conquest. The results were to force reforms upon the conquered areas. Religious tolerance was enforced, serfdom was abolished by decree, and guilds were destroyed.

4) Territorially, the height of the empire was between 1810 and 1811. Napoleon controlled the entire European continent except the Balkan peninsula. Nationalist movements sprang up in protest to Napoleonic rule and became both anti-French and antiautocratic. In England hatred of France and all French ideas eclipsed the misery of industrialism and delayed political reform for thirty years, until 1832. The British fought against Napoleon's Continental System, which was intended to destroy Great Britain by killing her commerce and shipping and aimed at developing the economy of continental Europe, particularly France. In Spain, reaction to Napoleon caused guerilla war against him, known as the Spanish Ulcer. In Germany, it

made the people acutely conscious of their German origins (nationalism).

The Governments of Europe   1760 to the Present

THE GOVERNMENT OF ENGLAND

A. THE MONARCHS OF ENGLAND (The most important are starred.)

*George III	1760–1820
George IV	1820–1830
William IV	1830–1837
*Victoria	1837–1901
Edward VII	1901–1910
George V	1910–1936
Edward VIII	1936
George VI	1936–1952
Elizabeth II	1952–

B. PARTY GOVERNMENT

Liberal Party	—Gladstone	1868–1874
Conservative	—Disraeli	1874–1880
Liberal	—Gladstone	1880–1885
Conservative	—Salisbury	1885–1886
	—Gladstone	1886
	—Salisbury	1886–1892
	—Gladstone	1892–1894
	—Rosebery	1894–1895
	—Salisbury and Belfour	1895–1905
Liberal	—Campbell-Bannerman and Asquith	1905–1915
Coalition	—Asquith	1915
	—Lloyd George	1916–1922
Conservative	—Bonar Law and Baldwin	1922–1923
Labour	—MacDonald	1924
Conservative	—Baldwin	1924–1929
Labour	—MacDonald	1929–1931

Coalition	—MacDonald	1931–1935
Conservative	—Baldwin	1935–1937
	—Chamberlain	1937–1940
	—Churchill	1940–1945
Labour	—Atlee	1945–1951
Conservative	—Churchill	1951–1955
	—Eden	1955–1957
	—Macmillan	1957–1963
	—Douglas-Home	1963–1964
Labour	—Wilson	1964–

THE GOVERNMENT OF FRANCE

Louis XVI	1774–1792
First Republic	1792–1804
The Terror	1793–1794
The Directory	1795–1799
The Consulate—Napoleon	1799–1804
The Empire—Napoleon	1804–1814
The Restoration—Louis XVIII	1814–1824
—Charles X	1824–1830
July Monarchy—Louis Philippe	1830–1848
Second Republic	1848–1852
Second Empire—Napoleon III	1852–1870
Third Republic	1870–1940
German Occupation (Vichy France)	1940–1945
Fourth Republic	1945–1958
Fifth Republic (De Gaulle)	1958–

THE GOVERNMENT OF SPAIN

The Monarchy—Charles III	1759–1788
—Charles IV	1788–1808
—Joseph (Bonaparte)	1808–1813
—Ferdinand VII	1813–1833
—Isabella II	1833–1868
—Alfonso XII	1868–1885
—Alfonso XIII	1885–1932

The Republic	1932–1936
The Civil War	1936–1939
Franco Regime	1939–

THE GOVERNMENT OF AUSTRIA-HUNGARY

*Maria Theresa	1740–1780
*Joseph II	1780–1790
Leopold II	1790–1792
Francis II (the end of the Holy Roman Empire—1806)	1792–1835
Ferdinand I	1835–1848
Francis Joseph	1848–1916
Charles I (the end of Austria-Hungary)	1916–1918

THE GERMAN GOVERMNENT

The Emperors—William I (in 1871 he took the title of Emperor; in 1861 he became King of Prussia)	1871–1888
—Frederick III	1888
—William II	1888–1918
The Weimar Republic	1919–1933
The Third Reich (Hitler)	1933–1945
Allied Military Occupation	1945–1949
The German Federal Republic (West)	1949–
The German Democratic Republic (East)	1949–

THE ITALIAN GOVERNMENT

The Emperors—Victor Emmanuel II	1861–1878
—Humbert I	1878–1900
—Victor Emmanuel III	1900–1946
The Italian Republic	1946–

Liberalism—a Part of the Ideological Revolution

A. Liberalism was essentially the doctrine of individualism in which

1) The state was viewed as the aggregate of all individuals.

2) The individual was assumed to be responsible for his happiness and to know his own interests.

3) All restraints that impeded the individual from realizing his full capacity and achieving his own self-interest should be abolished.

B. In government this meant the extension of suffrage and freedom of speech, press, and religion. In economics this meant the doctrine of laissez-faire (no interference on the part of government in the economic life of the nation) and free trade. In philosophy it meant the insistence upon the dignity of man and that every minority (even a minority of one) must have the right to express its ideas.

C. Liberalism was first introduced in Great Britain. The Reform Bill of 1832 constituted a revolution; suffrage was extended and the seats of parliament were redistributed so that the new business class were as well represented as the old aristocracy. From 1832 to 1872, social reform legislation was passed. Slavery was abolished (1833), a poor law was adopted (1834), local government was modernized, parliamentary votes were allowed to be publicized, and the army and the civil service were open to competitive examination. In 1847 the Ten Hours Act was passed, limiting labor of women and children in industry to ten hours a day. In 1846 the Corn Laws, which kept up the price of food, were repealed, and the suffrage was further extended in 1868.

Socialism—a Part of the Ideological Revolution

A. Socialism was an offshoot of industrialism and the problems it created, as well as a part of republicanism and the new attitude toward the state and what it should do for the individual.

B. The early socialists regarded an economic system based on private property, free enterprise, unrestrained competition, and the liberal doctrine of the absolute freedom of all individuals —even to starve to death—as unjust. They all favored communal ownership of the means of production and rejected the doctrine of laissez-faire. They demanded both social and economic equality.

c. Robert Owen (1771–1858) experimented at New Lanark, Scotland with a cooperative community scheme. In France, Saint Simon advocated a planned society, and the journalist Louis Blanc wrote against the private capitalist and organized the first socialist party. After 1830 socialism spread rapidly, and in France and Germany it became more violent than in Great Britain. All these early socialist movements tended to be highly idealistic, moralistic, and pacifistic, and they were branded by the father of communism, Karl Marx (1848) as Utopian and "unscientific."

d. Communism was a branch of the socialist movement and differed essentially in demanding violent overthrow of the existing conditions. (See pp. 247; 252.)

Nationalism—a Part of the Ideological Revolution

A. Modern nationalism was in part the product of the nineteenth century. The French Revolution fostered it. The mass army, the indoctrination that every man was a citizen with a duty to serve the state, and the loyalty to the state rather than the estate (class or group) were ideas of the Revolution. Nationalism also sprang up as a resistance movement to French imperialism and Napoleonic dictatorship.

B. Nationalism is an emotion characterized by intense loyalty to the nation, no matter the kind of government; unreasoning love of the land; and extreme pride in the cultural and economic achievements of the state.

c. In the nineteenth century nationalism was a force for the unification of states whose peoples had been divided into a multitude of states.

1) The Unification of Italy

Two men were responsible for the unification of Italy.

A) Giuseppi Garibaldi (1807–1882) with his one thousand Redshirts seized Sicily and then invaded the Kingdom of Naples in 1860. He planned to march on Rome and unify Italy by conquest, but he was forestalled by Cavour.

B) Count Camillo Di Cavour (1810–1861), prime minister of the Kingdom of Sardinia, whose liberalism had been influenced by the British, drove the Austrians out of Lombardy in

1859. In 1860 other areas in central Italy joined Sardinia by plebiscite. In 1861 the Kingdom of Italy was proclaimed under the ruler of Sardinia, Victor Emmanuel. Venetia was then acquired by war with Austria in 1866; the papal state and the city of Rome were not absorbed until 1870.

2) The Unification of Germany

A) The two states of Germany that had ambitions to unify the German states of the defunct Holy Roman Empire (abolished in 1806 by Napoleon) were Austria and Prussia. William I (King of Prussia from 1861 to 1888) had grandiose plans of a united Germany, but it was his prime minister, Otto von Bismarck (1815–1898), who was really responsible for the expansion of the Kingdom of Prussia into the German Empire.

B) In 1864 Bismarck gained Schleswig and Holstein from Denmark by military action. In 1866 he went to war against Austria and forced her to give up her rights to interfere in the states of Germany.

c) The ability of Prussia to combine the German states into a unified Germany dominated by Prussia was in large measure a result of prestige. When it became clear that France was trying to prevent German unification, Bismarck tricked France into declaring a war in which she was overwhelmingly defeated. In the wake of military triumph the German Empire was proclaimed in 1871 at Versailles. During the Franco-Prussian War France lost Alsace-Lorraine and was forced to pay an indemnity of one billion dollars.

D. By the beginning of the twentieth century, however, nationalism was no longer a unifying force, for it had spread into east and central Europe. Here it could only succeed by destroying the old regimes of Austria-Hungary and the Ottoman empire.

1) The Ottoman Empire (See pp. 24–27.)

2) The Austro-Hungarian Empire

The Austro-Hungarian Empire was a collection of peoples in central Europe brought together by the accidents of history and ruled over by the Hapsburg monarchy. The three main national divisions of the empire were the Germans of Austria, the Magyars of Hungary, and the Slavic peoples of Serbia. The history of the Empire in the nineteenth century was primarily that of the efforts of the monarchy to prevent these three elements from forming separatist movements and destroying the empire. By 1914 the days of the Hapsburg empire were numbered; separatist movements, particularly in Serbia, were becoming more desperate, and the monarchy was becoming increasingly irresponsible in its handling of the minority elements within the state.

E. As Europe moved into the twentieth century, nationalism became more and more militant and jingoistic, breeding misunderstanding and hatred among the states of Europe, and leading to the debacle of the First World War.

F. Nationalism also spread to the four corners of the globe in the wake of European imperialism and liberal ideas. Though European nationalism seems to have subsided, elsewhere it remains one of the most potent and unsettling forces in the world.

EUROPEAN CIVILIZATION   1914 TO THE PRESENT

The twentieth century has been given many names. It has been referred to as the Age of Industrialism and the Age of Science and Technology. It has been described by Ortega y Gasset as the era of *The Revolt of the Masses,* the century of the mass man. Others have called it the "Age of the Political Collapse of Historic Europe," for in 1900 Europe ruled over 20 million square miles of non-European territory with one-half billion people, and she guided the destinies of countless others. By 1918 she was declining; by 1945 Europe was no longer the greatest power in the world; and a decade later her colonies had dwindled to almost nothing. Another perspective of the period is that of R. Aron, who has called the years following 1914 *The Century of Total War,* and it is around this concept that the other epithets for the twentieth century are best understood and organized.

The war that broke out in 1914 was in some ways more significant than the second one of its kind in 1939. The First World War was a momentous and unique situation in human history. War was no longer confined to the battlefield, and the total energies of all the citizens of the nations were mobilized. The war was a war for survival, fought to the point of exhaustion, and unbelievably destructive, destroying four empires and wiping out a decade of Europe's growth. It was fought on the land and above it, on the sea and under it; war for the first time in history had become three-dimensional. The Second World War, lasting six years and one day, was the same kind of war, fought in part for problems that were left unsolved or were caused by the First World War. The period between the wars has in fact been referred to as the "Long Armistice."

Near the end of World War II, atomic energy was discovered and two bombs were made and dropped on Hiroshima and Nagasaki in Japan. The advent of atomic war has added to the totality of war, making war for the first time in history totally destructive, even of the human race. During the twentieth century, the U.S.S.R. and the U.S.A. rose as the greatest powers in the world, yet Western Europe, taken as a whole, surpassed both of them in population and in economic potential. The economic and political future of Europe remains in doubt, but there are signs that a united states of Europe may evolve, establishing a third power in the balance of power.

Causes of World War I

Nationalism was the primary cause of the First World War. (See p. 108.)

Colonial Conflicts

At the beginning of the twentieth century (between 1895 and 1911), there were six major collisions in the colonial field. Three of these were to lead Europe to the brink of war because the nations involved felt that their national interests were at stake.

A. Britain and France clashed over the question of Egypt in 1898. This was resolved when the two nations agreed to a monopoly for British interests in Egypt and French interests in Morocco.

B. Britain clashed with the Boers in South Africa, which led to the Boer War of 1899.

c. Britain and Russia argued over control in Persia. Here again a solution was reached by agreement. Persia was divided into two spheres of influence in 1907.

4. Russia and the Austro-Hungarian Empire were at odds over dominance in the Balkans. Austria-Hungary controlled most of the area, but Russia was supporting nationalistic revolts among the Slavs in hopes of gaining access to a warm-water port. This was the particular crisis that led to the World War in 1914.

E. Russia and Japan struggled over which would be the dominant power in Manchuria and Korea. This was solved by war between the two countries in 1905, in which Japan was victorious.

F. Germany and France clashed over Morocco, and this conflict almost precipitated war in 1911.

European Conflicts

A. Another standing feud between France and Germany was Alsace-Lorraine, taken from France in 1871, and much of French policy after 1871 was aimed at getting the lost province back.

B. The growing Anglo-German naval and commercial rivalry, which threatened England's control of the seas, was another European conflict that led to war.

c. The conflict between Austria-Hungary and Serbian nationalism precipitated the war.

The System of Alliances

One of the most important elements in projecting local conflict into total war was the European system of alliances.

A. Germany's desire to isolate France so she could not regain Alsace-Lorraine had led to a defensive alliance with Austria-Hungary in 1879 (the Dual Alliance). In 1882, Italy joined the alliance for her own expansionistic reasons, making it the Triple Alliance.

B. In 1890, Germany failed to renew Bismarck's Reinsurance Treaty tying Russia to Germany, and France saw an opportunity to break her isolation. In 1894 she achieved her objective through a military alliance with Russia. In 1904, England and France entered into an understanding (a gentleman's agreement), and in 1907 England and Russia did the same, thus creating the Triple Entente. The Triple Entente consisted of a binding alliance between France and Russia, but only of agreements of mutual understanding between England and France and England and Russia. In 1914 the great unsolved question was whether England would in fact go to war if Germany invaded France or Russia.

c. Each crisis tended to tighten the bonds between the members of the alliance systems, and by 1914 the balance of power was so perfect that neither side could risk the defection of any member of the alliance. This gave great influence to the secondary partners, Austria-Hungary and Russia, just at the moment when both countries were becoming increasingly irresponsible.

The Sarajevo Crisis Turns into War

On June 28, 1914 a young Bosnian revolutionary, a member of the Black Hand (a Serbian nationalistic secret society), assassinated the Archduke Francis Ferdinand of Austria-Hungary. The Austrians decided to end once and for all the Slavic separatist movements led by Serbia, which were tearing the empire apart. Before commencing any action against Serbia, they demanded and obtained from Germany the promise of her support no matter what the consequences (known as the Blank Check). Austria then sent a drastic ultimatum that demanded Serbian submission. The Serbs, after having received encouragement from Russia, rejected the ultimatum, and Austria declared war. Russia mobilized her army on both the German and Austrian frontiers. Germany, receiving no answer to her demand for Russian demobilization, declared war on Russia on August 1 and on France two days later (France had also mobilized on August 1). Russia dragged France into the battle and Austria-Hungary dragged in Germany. Ironically, Austria-Hungary and Russia, of all the major countries, had the least to lose.

The Germans, pleading military necessity, marched through neutral Belgium, and on August 4 England declared war on Germany. The invasion of Belgium created a justification for Great

Britain's entry, but her reasons were much more involved than this. She did not dare let one great power control the Low Countries, and she did not dare interpret the buildup of German naval power as anything but a threat to her supremacy of the seas.

Montenegro declared war on the Central powers on August 10, and on August 23 Japan, following the treaty with Britain of 1902, did the same. (Her only interest was in grabbing German possessions in Asia.) Among the original members of the alliance blocs only Italy and Rumania stayed out of the conflict for the time being.

World War I

The First Year

The war, which lasted four years and three months, started out as a European war. It was essentially a war between the great powers over imperialistic and nationalistic interests. No one thought it would last longer than six months. At the beginning of the war, the Central Powers had the advantage of superior organization and strategic position.

THE VON SCHLIEFFEN (chief of staff of Germany 1891–1901) PLAN

The plan of a swinging hammer through Belgium and northern France before Russia could mobilize was brilliant, and if it had been carried out in full, it might have succeeded. In six weeks the Germans had reached the Marne. There they were stopped.

THE BATTLE OF THE MARNE RIVER

Under the leadership of General Joffre, the French and British threw back the Germans. By the end of September, 1914 the two armies were facing each other along a line that extended across northern France and a corner of Belgium. The weapons of defense (the machine gun, barbed wire, and the trench) were superior to those of offense, and Europe settled down to prolonged trench warfare.

THE BATTLE AT SEA

The Central Powers were stronger than the Allies on land, but the British fleet, commanded by Admiral Jellicoe, was almost complete master of the seas by the end of 1914.

The Second Year Becomes World War

A. Turkey joined on the side of the Central Powers in 1914. A secret treaty of alliance had been signed between Germany and Turkey in August, but it was not until the end of October, 1914 that Turkey provoked the Allies into declaring war on her.

B. By 1915 the Europeans were forced to spread the conflict geographically and politically. In February of 1915 the Gallipoli campaign through the straits of the Dardanelles failed. In the same year the London Treaty was signed with Italy. She decided to join the Allies primarily because in April it looked as if they were winning.

C. In October of 1915 Bulgaria sided with the Germans; in August Rumania chose the Allies. By the end of 1916, all the Balkans were involved in the war.

D. On both the eastern and western fronts the war was deadlocked. There were four major battles in 1915 in which the Allies attempted to break through enemy lines, but with no success. In 1916 both the battles of Verdun and the Somme were costly and futile.

E. On the sea both Germans and British were cautious (although in 1915 the British liners, the Lusitania and the Arabic, were sunk without warning by submarines). The Battle of Jutland on May 31, 1916 confirmed the supremacy of the seas for the British. It was then that the Germans decided to gamble in order to bring Britain to her knees by cutting off supplies to the island country. They decided to wage unrestricted submarine warfare against any and all ships headed toward Britain. They knew that if they did, they risked the United States' entry into the war, but the German high command was overpowered by political pressures in Germany demanding victory. In April, May, and June of 1917, German subs sank a monthly average of 700,-000 tons of Allied shipping.

1917—The Crucial Year of the War

A. In March of 1917 there was revolution in Russia; in November the Bolsheviks came to power; and in December the Russians surrendered to the Germans, liberating German troops for a final drive on the Western front.

B. The decision to wage unrestricted submarine warfare was part of the reason for the United States entry, and her entry in April 6, 1917 was sufficient to tip the scales in favor of the Allies, not just in manpower but, more important, in the production of pig iron and steel. In 1914 both the Allies and the Central Powers produced 22 million tons of pig iron apiece. In 1917 (after the U.S.A. entry), the ratio was fifty to fifteen in favor of the Allies. In 1914 the Allies produced 19 million tons of steel to 21 million of the Central Powers. In 1917 the Allies were producing 58 million tons and the Central Powers had dropped to 16 million.

C. The entry of the United States led not only to a change in the balance of power but also to a new statement of the ideals of the war. In April of 1917 Woodrow Wilson, President of the United States, declared that the war was a fight for democracy, for the self-determination of nations, and for a lasting peace, and that peace would be made on the promises of his Fourteen Points, presented in January of 1918, guaranteeing "open covenants openly arrived at," freedom of the seas, the reduction of tariffs, disarmament, and the self-determination of nations (in the Baltic, Poland, Yugoslavia, Czechoslovakia, and elsewhere). The fourteenth point was the establishment of a "general association of nations."

Victory

A. At the end of 1917, with the use of detection devices, depth charges, mines, and the convoy system, the British regained control of the seas.

B. Baghdad fell in the spring of 1917 to the British, and in December they captured Jerusalem and moved into northern Syria.

C. By the winter of 1917–1918, German airplanes were

bombing London but were more of a nuisance than a menace. The final German offensive came in March–July of 1918. It was successfully repelled by the Allies under the command of General Foch. American troops participated (nine United States divisions in the line and one-quarter million landing per month in France). By July the Germans under Ludendorff were in full retreat.

D. On September 30, 1918, the Turks surrendered; the Bulgarians had surrendered on October 30. On November 3, 1918 the Austrians surrendered, and on November 9 the German Kaiser, Wilhelm II, was forced to abdicate. Two days later—the eleventh hour of the eleventh day of the eleventh month—the armistice was signed.

The Cost of the War

A. The number of known dead has been placed at about 10,000,000, with 20,000,000 wounded. Great Britain had 947,000 dead and 2,122,000 wounded; France had 1,385,000 dead and 3,044,000 wounded; Russia had 1,700,000 dead (actually it may have been many more) and 4,950,000 wounded; Italy had 460,000 dead and 947,000 wounded; the United States had 115,000 dead and 206,000 wounded; Germany had 1,808,000 dead and 4,247,-000 wounded; Austria-Hungary had 1,200,000 dead and 3,620,-000 wounded; and Turkey had 325,000 dead and 400,000 wounded.

B. The total direct cost of the war is figured at about $180,-500,000,000 and the indirect cost at $151,612,500,000.

C. Four great empires disintegrated as a result of the war: the Russian, Ottoman, Austro-Hungarian, and German.

The Treaty of Versailles and the New Balance of Power

There were two basic tasks that faced the victors of the war: the settlement with Germany and the redrawing of the political boundaries of central and eastern Europe.

THE GERMAN PROBLEM

1) The settlement in Germany immediately led to disagreements between France, America, and Britain. The French demanded total demilitarization of Germany; they would have preferred dismemberment. Clemenceau was under great pressure to achieve military occupation of the Rhine. Both Lloyd George of England and Wilson of the United States objected.

2) The Settlement

A) Alsace-Lorraine was returned to France.

B) Germany was not to fortify the left bank of the Rhine, and a demilitarized zone was established on the right bank.

C) Germany's army was to be reduced to 100,000, and she was forbidden to build up her military potential. No more than six battleships of 10,000 tons, twelve destroyers, and six cruisers could be built. Military aircraft and submarines were prohibited, but planes for commercial purposes were allowed.

D) The coal of the Saar was to go to France for fifteen years with the territory administered by the League of Nations. In fifteen years there was to be a plebiscite to decide the nationality of the Saar.

E) Germany was stripped of all her colonies, the Far East going to Japan, Africa to France and Britain, German New Guinea to Australia, and German Samoa to New Zealand.

3) Reparations were another touchy problem.

Clemenceau demanded 200 billion dollars from Germany, Lloyd George and Wilson about 30 billion. The amount of reparations were never decided but Germany was to begin paying immediately. She was really signing a blank check.

In order to persuade the French to agree to these terms, the United States and Britain promised to sign treaties to protect France. There was only one catch: Britain would not aid France unless the United States did, and the United States Senate refused to ratify the military guarantee and treaty; therefore Britain was not under obligation and France felt she had been tricked. The defection of the United States destroyed one of the main props of French security and was in part responsible for the next war.

The new states of Poland, Lithuania, Czechoslovakia, Estonia, Latvia, and Yugoslavia were created, and Rumania was greatly enlarged. Austria lost three quarters of her area and three fifths of her population; Hungary gave Rumania more territory than she was allowed to keep.

Evaluation of the Peace

PRO

The aim of the settlement was idealistic, but unfortunately the concepts were rarely achieved. The peoples of Europe did achieve greater self-determination than ever before, and the organization of the League of Nations was an important step.

CON

The peace failed at general disarmament. The colonial settlements under the mandate system became mere "legal fig leaves"; they were important from a theoretical point of view, but failed to protect the colonies. Self-determination was in many cases impossible, as in Yugoslavia, but the principle was never applied to Germany. The Tirol, which was German in population, went to Italy; the Polish corridor cut Germany in half and caused repercussions; and the western fringe of Czechoslovakia was almost solidly German. The Treaty of Versailles left a France that felt she was not strong enough, a United States not interested in carrying out her commitments in Europe, an England with a guilt complex, feeling that Germany had been mistreated, and a resentful and bankrupt Germany.

The League of Nations

The League was weak from the beginning: the United States refused to join, and few of the great powers were ever members at the same time. Germany was a member from 1926 to 1933, Russia from 1934 to 1939, Japan from 1920 to 1933; and Italy from 1920 to 1937. Only Britain and France were continuous members.

THE FUNCTIONS OF THE LEAGUE

1) To prevent war: This was obviously unsuccessful except in the case of the Greeks in Bulgaria in 1925. Here it was a matter of two small powers.

2) Disarmament: The only progress made in disarmament was in reducing naval strength at the Washington Conference in 1922, and this was accomplished outside of the League of Nations.

3) Social and economic fields: Here the League had its greatest success. In the fields of international communications, health, protection of children, and so forth, they were successful, and every one of the specialized organizations of the League of Nations was carried over into the United Nations.

The League was only a league and had no independent coercive power. All it could do was try to influence a government.

The 1920's

The 1920's were generally a period of optimism; democracy seemed to have triumphed, the League of Nations had had some success, naval armaments had been reduced at the Washington Conference in 1922; peace had been assured by the Locarno pacts in 1925 and the Kellogg-Briand Pact in 1928. As late as 1928 most people were assured and self-confident, yet by 1935 there was a general feeling of despair. Totalitarianism had triumphed in Yugoslavia, Poland, Italy, Germany, and Hungary. Hitler had defied the Versailles Treaty in 1935. In 1931 the Japanese aggression in Manchuria could not be stopped by the League of Nations, and in 1935 Italian aggression in Ethiopia was successful. Part of the explanation for this change was the world depression that began in 1929 and did not run its full course until the beginning of World War II in 1939.

The World Depression

Postwar Economic Conditions Lead to Depression
A. The European economy was in a state of dislocation after World War I; overseas markets were lost (the U.S.A. began

trading heavily with Latin America, and Asia turned to Japan for goods), and inflation of currency was aggravated by a production slowdown.

B. The breakup of the old empires in central Europe caused economic nationalism. Each new country raised its tariffs, expanded its industry, and wanted to sell but not to buy.

C. Europe's wealth had declined as a result of the war. Before the war Great Britain had been the largest creditor nation in the world; during the war she had had to liquidate 25 percent of her overseas investments (almost a billion pounds); and after the war New York became the financial capital of the world.

D. The position of the United States was more to blame for the depression than any other single factor.

1) Between 1913 and 1924, gold poured out of Europe to the United States (she had half the total supply in the world by 1924). Almost fifty percent of the total war debt was owed to her, and she insisted that it be paid in full. Britain and France, in order to pay their debts, had to collect reparations from Germany, but in turn Germany had to borrow the money from the United States or export at a time when tariffs were never higher.

2) The world, therefore, depended upon the financial stability of the United States, yet the situation in the U.S.A. was anything but stable. She imported more than she exported, there was extreme economic imbalance within the country (though industry was booming, agriculture was seriously depressed), and although productivity increased by 43 percent, wages did not rise proportionately, and poverty and agricultural depression cut the domestic market. Her banking system was incapable of weathering the storm when it did come.

E. International financing was unstable. Only short-term loans had been given by the United States, and they were subject to sudden recall. This made capital investment skittish and susceptible to whims and prone to easy panic. This meant that when the United States market collapsed, so did the world.

The Depression
A. On October 24, 1929 the American stock market crashed. The repercussions in Europe were tremendous and immediate.

Loans were withdrawn, prices fell, producers of primary goods lost their markets, and workers lost their jobs, further reducing the demand for goods.

B. Between 1929 and 1932 world production fell by 42 percent and world trade by 65 percent. By 1930 unemployment had increased by 50 percent, and in 1931 came the complete collapse of the financial structure of Germany and Austria—and total depression.

The Consequences of the Depression

A. The depression resulted in further intensification of economic nationalism. (Great Britain, for instance, abandoned free trade, which she had maintained since 1846.)

B. To meet the economic crisis, more and more power was vested in the state, which in countries with no democratic tradition often led to totalitarianism and dictatorship. (The only country in Eastern Europe that survived as a democracy was Czechoslovakia.)

C. Internationally, it furthered ill feeling among nations, and governments were so concerned with their own affairs that they ignored what was happening in other countries. The colonial world suffered as the demand for raw materials dropped and their demands for independence grew louder.

D. In Germany it was directly responsible for the rise to power of Hitler.

The Failure of Democracy and the Rise of Fascism

Italy and the Rise of Fascism
THE WEAKNESS OF THE POSTWAR GOVERNMENT

The postwar government of Italy lacked experience and was plagued by economic problems; unemployment of servicemen, the decline of tourism, and rural overpopulation all contributed to dissatisfaction. In 1920 came a crisis: workers in Milan seized the factories and the leftists took over the government. But the leftist revolution failed

A. primarily because most of the leftists were orthodox Marxists who were willing to sit and wait for the revolution,

B. and also because the leftists were overconfident.

REACTION LEADS TO FASCISM

A. In reaction against the left, industrialists and the army combined. In the election of 1921, this new party known as the Fascist Party carried only twenty-five seats, whereas the leftists captured 122, but the following year the Fascists had taken over the government.

B. Mussolini (1883–1945) was originally a socialist but broke with the party over the socialist position that the world war was a capitalist-imperialist war and should not be supported by the proletariat, and in 1915 he joined the army. In 1919 his fascist movement began, drawing support primarily from ex-soldiers but also from property owners and intellectuals. There was nothing in common among these groups except supernationalism and a fear of communism.

C. By 1922, 40,000 men had joined the party, and Mussolini threatened that "either the government will be given to us or we shall march on Rome." The government resigned and Victor Emmanuel III turned control over to Mussolini as prime minister.

THE MUSSOLINI GOVERNMENT

A. Order was immediately restored, strikes were suppressed, and unemployment was eased by the building of public works. In 1924, however, total dictatorship was inaugurated. Between 1925 and 1928 all political parties except the Fascist were dissolved, property of dissenters and communists was confiscated, communications were taken over by the government, and in the 1928 elections there was only *yes* or *no* on the ballot.

B. The aim of fascism was to increase the power and the glory of the state. Mussolini championed nationalism, imperialism, and war. A one-party state with government control of industry, labor, and employment (the corporative state) was introduced.

Germany and the Triumph of Nazism

POSTWAR GERMANY—THE WEIMAR REPUBLIC

A. Germany was given a democratic government after the war. The republic was bicameral in structure and based on universal suffrage with proportional representation. The President of the Republic was elected by the people and he in turn appointed the chancellor, who was generally the head of the largest party. The power of the president was excessive, for in case of emergency he could dismiss the chancellor and rule by decree, and the judiciary had no power of declaring a law or a decree unconstitutional.

B. The postwar problems faced by the government could not be solved.

1) The most serious problem was reparations. Thirty-three billion dollars was finally demanded in 1921, but protectionist tariffs in other countries meant no markets for Germany, and no markets meant no money, and no money meant no payment of reparations. By 1923 the Germans could no longer pay reparations, and the French retaliated by invading the Ruhr.

A) The Dawes plan in 1924 was one of the first attempts to deal with reparations on an international scale. The decision that reparations be based on world economic conditions and Germany's prosperity eased the situation and set the stage for German recovery.

B) The Young plan in 1929 set reparations at a definite sum to be paid off by 1988.

C) From 1924 to 1930, Germany paid a total of $1,994,-566,695 in reparations. By 1930, however, reparation payments went into a state of limbo, and they were terminated at the Lausanne Conference in 1932.

2) Inflation destroyed the German economy. In 1920 one dollar was worth sixty to seventy marks; by November 12, 1923 the dollar was worth 840,000,000,000 marks; by November 20, 1923 the dollar was worth 4,200,000,000,000 marks. This almost destroyed the middle class in Germany by wiping out their savings and investments.

3) The Weimar Republic failed to win the support of the people, for it was associated from the very beginning with Germany's defeat and it had been forced to sign the Versailles Treaty.

4) In foreign policy the Republic had the most success. In

1922 the first break in Germany's isolated world position occurred when Germany signed the Treaty of Rapallo with Russia. In 1926 she joined the League of Nations, and in 1928 Allied occupation forces evacuated the Rhine. But she could not achieve what the Germans demanded—the reannexation of the Saar, a union with Austria, the end of the Polish corridor, and the reunification of the fatherland.

THE NAZI REVOLUTION

A. An essential reason for the success of fascism in Germany was Adolf Hitler (1889–1945).

1) Frustrated during early life, Hitler found himself during World War I, when he experienced a sense of comradeship and dedication. In 1920 he formulated his program for National Socialism. This program was a blend of supernationalism, state control of industry, and the offering of the Jews and communists as the scapegoats for all Germany's troubles and defeats. He demanded the union of all Germans, the revision of the Treaty of Versailles, living space for Germany's surplus population, and a homogeneous state. He listed the three main threats to Germany as communists, Jews, and democracy. The driving force behind the Nazi revolution, however, was not the program but Hitler himself, who was ruthless, paranoiac, and magnetic, having the ability to use propaganda and to sway the masses.

2) After his unsuccessful coup in Bavaria in 1923 Hitler was jailed, and it was then that he wrote the Nazi bible, *Mein Kampf*.

3) The official title of the party Hitler organized was the National Socialist German Workers Party; both party and state were means of enhancing the "German Volk" and upholding the superiority of the "Aryan Race."

B. The depression was an important factor in the Nazi rise to power.

In 1929, 1 million out of 20 million were unemployed in Germany; by 1933 there were 6 million unemployed. By 1930 the Nazis had become the second largest party with 107 seats (whereas in 1928 they had held only 13 seats), and by 1932 they had 230 seats. (The communists also gained during this period, and part of the reason for the Nazi gain was middle class fear of a leftist revolution.)

   c. The steps to power

   1) During the depression economic recovery programs could not be passed through the Reichstag, because the government was composed of a coalition of the Catholic Center Party (conservative) and the Social Democratic Party (socialist). The president used his special power and parliamentary democracy died in fact even before the Nazis came to power. Between 1930 and 1933 intrigue, party maneuvering, and backstairs politics, along with the skillful use of propaganda and hard work on the part of the Nazis, increased their strength tremendously. Hitler promised a revitalized Germany, jobs for all, and the end of communism and Judaism. By July of 1932 the Nazis had won 230 seats; in August Hitler was offered the vice-chancellorship in a coalition government, which he refused. At the beginning of 1933 Hitler allied with the Nationalists, a highly conservative party, and on January 30, 1933 he was appointed chancellor.

   2) If the three other major parties in Germany (the communists, the socialists, and the Catholic Center) had been willing to form a coalition government, Hitler's rise could have been prevented, but the communists were forbidden by the Comintern to cooperate with bourgeois parties.

   3) The destruction of the communists

In February of 1933 Hitler moved against his most powerful rival, the communists. On February 27 the Reichstag (parliament building) was burned, and this was blamed on the communists. Civil liberties were suppressed and all communist deputies were arrested.

   4) The destruction of the trade unions

The next power Hitler destroyed was the trade unions. In May of 1933 the unions were brought under control by the use of Hitler's storm troopers.

   5) The end of political parties

The only party that had any strength was the Social Democrats, and in May of 1933 their assets and property were seized by the Nazis; in June the party was outlawed. (The smaller parties just liquidated themselves.) By July the Nazi party was the only legal one.

6) Centralization

In March of 1933, all local state governments were taken over by force and governors were made directly responsible to Hitler. Never before in German history had there been such a degree of political centralization.

7) Hitler became chief executive in name as well as in fact.

In August of 1934, von Hindenburg died and Hitler became both chancellor and president of the Third Reich, which had been established in 1933. As president, he also became commander-in-chief of the armed forces.

D. Hitler carried through his plans without any serious opposition. This is a characteristic of the twentieth century: that the masses can be easily controlled by a shrewd and ruthless leader and that totalitarianism is a phenomenon of mass civilization. Hitler made good his promises; public works created new jobs. The rearmament (1935) further stimulated production. The Nazis, however, were not interested in economic stability for its own sake. Hitler's domestic policy was a step to the ultimate aim of making Germany strong enough to go to war once more.

Spain, from Monarchy to Republic to Fascism
THE POSTWAR GOVERNMENTS OF SPAIN

During World War I Spain was neutral, and war had brought tremendous industrial expansion and prosperity; but with the end of the war prosperity ebbed and discontent increased. In 1923 King Alfonso, who had had twelve cabinets from 1918 to 1923, gave in to the demands of Madrid that General Primo de Rivera head the government. Rivera was an absolute dictator: jury trial was suspended, censorship of the press was enforced, the Cortes was dissolved, and textbooks approved by the church were the only ones permitted. (All these acts were by permission of King Alfonso.) De Rivera did, however, build public works and clean up the bureaucracy. The intellectuals rose up against de Rivera's educational and censorship policies, and

King Alfonso was forced to ask for de Rivera's resignation in 1930. General Berenguer, who then took over the government, reversed many of Rivera's policies, and when censorship was ended the monarchy was flooded with criticism. Alfonso finally had to give in to public opinion, and in April of 1931 he allowed elections to be held.

THE REPUBLIC

The republican parties (the leftists) were victorious, Alfonso left the country, and Azana became prime minister until 1933, when the tide swung to the right. In the 1936 elections, however, a coalition of socialists and communists under the popular front policy were victorious, and Azana once again became prime minister.

THE CIVIL WAR 1936–1939

A group of army officers (the Spanish fascists known as the Falange) revolted in 1936 against the program of the Spanish popular front. When neither side was immediately victorious, each received aid from the outside. Italy and Germany aided General Franco (Italy sent over 100,000 troops and Germany sent mostly supplies and her air force), and Russia aided the popular front. Britain and France decided to stay out of the issue, but some unofficial aid did come from both countries and from the U.S.A. Forty thousand foreigners were fighting for the popular front (the loyalists), 3,000 of whom were Americans. In March of 1939 the surrender of Madrid to General Franco ended the Civil War.

Fascism in Spain meant rule by the army, the Catholic church, and the upper classes. In 1939 Spain signed the Anti-Comintern Pact and withdrew from the League of Nations. Although she remained neutral during World War II, she was an important base of supplies for Germany.

In Japan democracy also failed, and a type of fascism took control of the government when Japan conquered Manchuria (1931) and moved into north China.

In Russia democracy had failed before the end of the war with the collapse of the provisional government and the takeover of the Bolsheviks.

In Poland, Yugoslavia, and Hungary dictatorship also triumphed.

The Long Armistice: Basic Causes of World War II

Nationalism

All the causes of the war can be tied to the rise of supernationalism, the glorilcation of the state. World War I had heightened jingoism and statism in all the countries of Europe, and Hitler's Germany became the most extreme example.

Imperialism

So called have-not powers—Germany, Japan, and Italy—demanded "living room" for their overcrowded populations and raw materials for their new industries, and Japan wanted a chance to compensate for her sense of inferiority. The British had access to eighteen out of twenty-five essential raw materials in their own empire, whereas Germany had only four and the Italians and the Japanese had almost none. This economic situation was further complicated by mounting tariff barriers and the collapse of world trade after 1930.

Revisionism

Discontent with the Versailles Treaty and particularly with the boundary settlements also led to war. Germany was extremely resentful, Hungary was dissatisfied, and even Italy felt she had been badly treated, not getting as much of the Alpine Tirol as she wanted.

The Failure of the League

The failure of the League was not so much a cause as it was a reflection of the other causes. It failed to protect all nations, disarmament negotiations floundered, and it could do nothing about Japan's aggression in Manchuria, Germany's breaking of the conditions of the Versailles Treaty, or the Italian invasion of Ethiopia.

Division in the West

Without division in the West Hitler might have been stopped before he got any further than invading the Rhine. But

France and Great Britain were at odds. The British felt that Germany's east frontiers were of little vital significance, that concessions should be made to Germany, and that a strong, prosperous Germany was an asset to English industries. France wanted desperately to keep the status quo of the Versailles Treaty and to keep Germany poor and militarily weak.

The Road to War

1930–1936

Hitler's actions led directly to war, and although Germany's guilt as far as starting the First World War is questionable, there is no doubt about the Second World War. Indirectly, the refusal and/or the inability of England and France to stop Hitler during the early years of his career (the policy of appeasement) also contributed to war.

In October of 1933, Hitler withdrew from the disarmament conference and the League of Nations. The following year he signed a ten-year nonaggression pact with Poland. In 1935, when Germany gained the Saar in a plebiscite, he announced that Germany had no more territorial interests in the West.

Then in March of 1935 he boldly announced the creation of an air force and obligatory military service. In June a naval agreement was signed with Great Britain, which was a violation of Versailles and which the British hoped would calm Hitler down.

In 1935 Mussolini attacked Ethiopia, and although the West imposed economic sanctions, oil and coal, the two vital military commodities, were not included, and by May of 1936 Ethiopia was overrun. The League had proved worthless. The failure of the League to stop Italy as well as Japan was the last bit of encouragement Hitler needed, and in March of 1936 he sent his troops into the demilitarized section of the Rhine. In October the Rome-Berlin Axis was signed; in November the Anti-Comintern Pact was signed with Japan, and the following November a similar pact was signed with Italy.

Appeasement

UNION WITH AUSTRIA

On February 16, 1938 the Austrian Nazis were admitted to the Austrian cabinet—after pressure had been exerted. On March 11 Hitler presented an ultimatum to Austria that Seyss-Inquart (the pro-German minister of interior) take over the government and that two thirds of the seats go to Austrian Nazis. On March 13 union was announced. France and England did nothing, even though German occupation of Austria made a mockery of France's military alliance with Czechoslovakia, for French troops could no longer reach the country should it be threatened by Germany.

In April Britain concluded an agreement with Mussolini, recognizing Italy's position in Ethiopia and pledging mutual friendship.

THE SUDETEN CRISIS AND THE MUNICH CONFERENCE

1) The Sudeten area of Czechoslovakia was the center of the armaments works and the fortifications of Czechoslovakia. It contained, however, three and a half million Germans and only 300,000 Czechs. Henlein organized a Sudeten Nazi party and was told by Hitler in 1938 to agitate for an autonomous province. Czechoslovakia tried to make concessions, and Hitler concentrated his troops on the border. The crisis subsided temporarily when Britain objected, but in September, 1938 Hitler suddenly demanded self-determination for the Sudetens. Four days later, Britain and France backed him with a formal note to Benes, president of Czechoslovakia. On September 22 Hitler raised the price again, demanding not only self-determination but the incorporation of the Sudetenland into the German Reich. A conference was proposed by Chamberlain.

2) The Munich Conference met on September 28, 1938. Hitler, Mussolini, Daladier of France, and Chamberlain of England were the only representatives (Czechoslovakia and Russia were omitted). By September 30 an agreement was reached: Hitler got what he wanted: one fifth of Czechoslovakia, 4 million of her people, the fortifications of the Sudetenland, and the crucial Skoda armament works.

3) In March, 1939 Hitler violated the Munich Pact and took over the rest of Czechoslovakia.

With the takeover of Czechoslovakia, Britain and France were finally shocked into realizing that appeasement would not stop Hitler. In April, 1939 they guaranteed the defense of Poland, but they failed to reach agreement with Russia, primarily because of mistrust on both sides.

The Nazi-Soviet Pact was announced on August 23, 1939. This was Hitler's grand strategy of assuring Russia's neutrality and isolating Poland. (The same arrangement had been made in the eighteenth century between Catherine the Great and Frederick the Great.) The pact meant that Hitler could attack Britain and France in the west without worrying about the eastern front; then, when the right time came, he could turn on Russia.

On September 1, 1939 the German army invaded Poland, and the Second World War had begun.

World War II   September 1, 1939 to September 2, 1945

The Second World War Differed from the First

A. Warfare became mobile; airpower was an essential factor in victory. Not as many soldiers were killed in the second war of survival as in the first, primarily because the war was one of movement and also because of new discoveries in medicine. Yet perhaps more civilians were killed than men in uniform. The Axis powers in the war lost more people than the Central Powers had in World War I.

B. The Second World War was more truly a world war, for, with the exception of the American continent, the whole world was a battlefield, and twenty-six nations fought on the side of the Allies. The major nations involved in the war were still the same as they had been in World War I, except that Turkey and Italy had switched sides.

C. The war also differed from the first in that atrocities were committed that were unparalleled in the history of man.

D. Science and invention played a vital role in World War

II. The British invented radar in 1939; rockets, from the portable bazooka to the German V-2's that fell on London in September of 1944, became practical weapons of war; and finally, atomic research and the development of the two atomic bombs, which the Americans dropped on Hiroshima and Nagasaki (the whole project that led eventually to the building of the two atomic bombs cost $2,000,000,000), inaugurated a new age of warfare.

At the beginning of the war Germany had many advantages. Her military leaders had developed advanced types of tanks and planes, achieving high speeds and great mobility and fire power. The Allies, on the other hand, still believed in the World War I theory that well-fortified positions were impregnable; the Maginot Line had been built by France, stretching from the Belgian frontier to Switzerland.

The War Begins on the Eastern Front

On September 1, 1939 Germany invaded Poland; on September 17 Russia followed suit; and ten days later Poland surrendered and was partitioned. Then the Baltic states were brought under Russian control, and on February 1, 1940 the U.S.S.R. declared war on Finland. On September 3, 1939 France and Great Britain had declared war, but nothing happened on the Western front until Hitler had settled matters in Eastern Europe.

The Western Front

On April 9, 1940 Hitler began the hot war in the west by attacking Denmark and Norway. (Reaction in Britain to this campaign led to the fall of Chamberlain's government and the organization of a National Wartime Government under Winston Churchill.) Then Hitler proceeded to sweep through the European continent; Luxembourg surrendered in three days; Belgium and the Netherlands were invaded on May tenth. The Dutch capitulated in five days, the Belgians in eighteen. By the twentieth of May the Germans had reached the English Channel, cutting off the British from the main French forces.

THE BATTLE OF DUNKIRK

Between May 27 and June 4, 1940 almost 340,000 British

and French troops were evacuated from Dunkirk by sea with every available boat the British had. This was one of the most spectacular evacuations in military history.

THE SURRENDER OF FRANCE

1) On June 10 Mussolini joined the war on Hitler's side and invaded southern France. The Germans entered Paris on June 14. There were many who wanted to continue the fight, Prime Minister Reynaud and such men as General Charles de Gaulle, who later formed the Free French movement. On June 16, however, Reynaud was forced to resign in favor of Petain, one of the strongest advocates of surrender.

2) On June 22 the treaty was signed; two fifths of France was left under French control (the Vichy French), and France was to pay the cost of the German occupation of the other three fifths. The French prisoners of war were to remain hostages.

GREAT BRITAIN ALONE AGAINST THE AXIS—ENGLAND'S "FINEST HOUR"

1) Luckily for Great Britain, German leadership was divided, Hitler's plans were disorganized, and the German air force could not make up its mind what its strategy should be. But the Battle of Britain was not won only by luck; it was won by the British R.A.F. and the courage of the British people, who refused to let the bombs break their will to fight.

2) The Battle of Britain started in July and came to a climax in September. It was fought to establish air control over the English Channel, the preliminary step to any invasion. In October Hitler abandoned his invasion plans. This change of plans may have lost him the war. Twelve hundred forty-four German planes were destroyed, against 721 lost by the R.A.F. during August and September, and the British had the advantage that they could save many of their pilots. By the spring of 1941 Britain was retaliating by bombing Germany.

Africa and the Middle East

In the meantime Britain had to spread her forces too thin, for Italy moved into Egypt in the autumn of 1940. The British, however, succeeded in driving them out, in removing Iraq's pro-Axis faction, and in clearing out the Vichy government of Syria. In 1941 Russia and Britain occupied Iran, thus providing a supply route to the U.S.S.R.

The Eastern Front and the Invasion of Russia

The Germans and Russians soon came to blows over the question of supremacy in the Balkans. From December to May, 1941 Germany invaded the Balkans, primarily for the sake of oil and also in preparation for war with Russia. Bulgaria willingly joined the Tripartite pact with Germany, Yugoslavia and Greece submitted not so willingly. By June 1 Germany had full control of the peninsula. Russia in the meantime had signed a neutrality pact with Japan (April, 1941), which at least secured her eastern front. On June 22 Germany invaded Russia. By December her troops were within twenty-five miles of both Leningrad and Moscow. The Germans were stopped by the cold, the collapse of their supply lines, and General Zhukov's offensive, which began on December 6.

The United States Entry

Long before December 7, 1941 the United States had become the "arsenal of democracy"; she had in effect chosen sides and was shipping supplies to Great Britain.

1) The Neutrality Act of 1937 had placed an embargo on arms to any belligerent nation, and this acted as an aid to the Nazis, but in 1939 the United States passed a somewhat less neutral Neutrality Act, which allowed arms to be sold to any belligerent if they were paid for in cash and transported by the warring nations (the Cash and Carry Act). This in essence meant she had chosen to side with Great Britain.

2) In 1940 Roosevelt began to release more arms and some old destroyers to Britain in exchange for naval bases in the Caribbean. Then in March, 1941 the Lend-Lease Act was passed: in effect the Act came close to being a declaration of war, since the bill gave the President of the United States the right to lend resources to any nation whose defense was necessary to United

States security. (Lend-Lease aid amounted to $50 billion between 1941 and 1945.)

3) In August, 1941 Roosevelt and Churchill signed the Atlantic Charter, in which they pledged their countries to the spread of democratic principles; and it established eighteen points similar to Wilson's Fourteen Points of World War I and also stipulated that a "permanent system of general security" should be established at the end of the war (the origins of the United Nations).

THE UNITED STATES ENTERS THE WAR

1) Background to the Japanese attack

In 1940 to 1941 Japan was obtaining four fifths of her oil and a great deal of scrap iron from the United States. In 1941, after Japan had taken over Indochina, Roosevelt froze Japanese assets in the United States and placed a severe embargo on Japan.

2) On December 7, 1941 Japan retaliated by attacking the naval base and the airfields at Pearl Harbor on Oahu Island in Hawaii. The same day she also attacked the Philippines, Hong Kong, and Malaya, and the next day, the American bases on Guam and Wake islands.

3) On December 8, 1941 the United States, the United Kingdom, Canada, South Africa, the Netherlands, and Luxembourg declared war on Japan. Now the war had become global.

The entry of the United States finally defeated the Axis both because of the addition of American soldiers on the battlefield and also because of United States production. The output of the U.S.A. between 1943 and 1944 was one ship per day and one aircraft every five minutes. During the entire war the Germans sank 23 million tons of Allied shipping, but the Allies built 42 million tons of new shipping.

THE UNITED NATIONS DECLARATION January 1, 1942

The Big Three (U.S.A., U.K. and U.S.S.R.), along with China and twenty-two other nations, signed the United Nations declaration, which pledged them to a common effort to defeat the Axis, promised not to make a separate peace, and agreed to the "common program of purpose and principles" as laid down in the Atlantic Charter.

The Far Eastern Theatre

Japan was initially very successful; only the Philippine Island fort of Corregidor held out until May. Malaya and Singapore fell in February of 1942, and by March Japan had virtual control of Burma and the Dutch East Indies.

Occupied Europe

Poland's lot was the hardest; almost all her political leaders and her Jewish population were exterminated. All of Eastern Europe suffered, for the area was just behind the battle lines. The brutality of the Nazis was unbelievable.

A. Medical experiments carried on by the Nazis involved the resistance of an individual to air pressure, to cold water, and to inoculation with fatal diseases (100,000 were sacrificed in this way). The tortures employed by the Gestapo (the secret police) were equally brutal although more conventional. To avenge an assassination in Prague a town was razed to the ground, and in Prague itself the army shot seventy people taken indiscriminately off the streets during a nine-day period.

B. Nazi brutality was even more ferocious against the Jews. In two days in the Ukraine 33,771 Jews were shot. Of 500,000 Jews in Warsaw, only two hundred lived to see the end of the war. The concentration camps and extermination camps were first established by Hermann Goering in 1933. At Treblinka B, 10,000 Jews from Warsaw were gassed to death every day for a week. Seventy to 80 percent of the people in these camps died (the other 20 to 30 percent were those who had been imprisoned the day the peace was signed). In all, it has been estimated that at least 10,000,000 were killed by the Germans in extermination and concentration camps.

The Turning Point—the Winter Months of 1942 to 1943

AFRICA

In November 1942 under General Eisenhower, Anglo-American troops landed in North Africa. The British under Montgomery pushed Rommel out of Egypt to Tripoli, and in May 250,000 German and Italian troops surrendered.

THE EASTERN FRONT

By 1942 the Germans had reached Stalingrad. The defense of Stalingrad was crucial to the Russians, for if captured it would have isolated Moscow and Leningrad. Under General Zhukov the Russians made a last-ditch stand, and by January of 1943, 300,000 Germans had surrendered. From then on Russia was on the offensive. Kiev was recaptured in 1943, and by 1944 the Russians had reached Odessa.

THE INVASION OF ITALY

In June, 1943 the Allies captured Sicily; then began a long and badly handled invasion and conquest of Italy. In July, 1943 Mussolini's government fell, but it was not until July, 1944 that the Allies were able to reach Rome. Italy had surrendered, although Italian troops, aided by Germany, continued to fight in the north.

THE BATTLE IN THE AIR

The British flew at night and the Americans by day, bombing cities to break the morale of the German people and destroying strategic bases, ammunition, and supplies. The battle in the air was vital to victory.

THE BATTLE AT SEA

Shipment of supplies was endangered by German submarines. Sometimes over 600,000 tons a month of Allied shipping was destroyed, but the aircraft carrier, the destroyer escort, and the bombing of submarine bases helped alleviate the situation. The other essential reason that the Allies won the battle at sea was the fast production of more and more tons of new shipping.

THE PACIFIC THEATRE

A. The Pacific Theatre was under three different commands: the Northwest Pacific under General MacArthur, the Pacific Ocean under Admiral Nimitz, and the China-Burma-India area under General Stilwell. In August of 1943 a separate Southeast Asia Command was established in India under Vice Admiral Mountbatten.

B. For a while the Allies played a waiting game in the Far East while they slowly built up supplies and concentrated their troops in Europe. Then in 1942 came the first Japanese defeat, the Battle of the Coral Sea, followed by the Battle of Midway Island in which the Japanese lost four aircraft carriers, two cruisers, and many pilots. Then in August of the same year came the Battle of Guadalcanal. The Allies were now on the offensive. Tokyo was bombed for the first time in April, 1942.

c. The Road Back to the Philippines

First New Guinea was captured by the Allies, then Morotai, then the Marshall Islands. From there the Allies moved on to Saipan and Guam, in June, 1944. Then the Palan Islands were taken in September, 1944, and the Allies were finally ready to move back to the Philippines.

d. Flying the Hump

The most important aspects of the war in India were the defense of India (Japan penetrated into the Assam valley) and the problem of getting supplies to China. This involved flying over the Himalayas (17,000-foot mountains). The Chinese, nevertheless, were not easy to work with, and Stilwell and Chiang Kai-shek often came to blows on strategy. Stilwell was recalled from the front in October, 1945. In January, 1944 the Allies began the invasion of Burma.

V-E Day

a. V-E Day began with the invasion of Normandy on June 6, 1944. Under the unified command of General Eisenhower, five divisions landed on the Normandy coast. By July, 1,000,000 had been landed—the American First Army under General Bradley, the British-Canadian Twenty-first Army under General Montgomery, and the Third Army under General Patton. Six months later the Allies had reached the German frontier.

b. On December 16, 1944 Germany made her last desperate counterattack in northern France. The Battle of the Bulge took a month to resist. At the same time, Germany began to bomb London with flybombs (V-1's) and rockets (V-2's). Nine thousand people were killed in those few months.

c. On March 1 the Russians crossed the Oder; on March 7 the Americans and British crossed the Rhine; and in April Vienna fell.

D. On April 30 Hitler committed suicide, and on May 8 victory in Europe was proclaimed.

V-J Day

A. As defeat followed defeat, the Japanese government was disgraced and began to topple; in July, 1944 Tojo resigned as prime minister; in April, 1945 his successor Koiso resigned, and Suzuki took over and began to sue for peace.

B. The Battle of Leyte Gulf, the largest naval engagement in the war, was fought in October, 1944. As a result Japan's naval power was wiped out.

C. Then, in January, 1945 the Allies captured Luzon. In the spring of that year, Iwo Jima and Okinawa fell, and from there the Twentieth Air Force began the systematic bombing of the homeland. Between May and August of 1945 the greatest air offensive in history destroyed the remnants of the Japanese navy and her industry. Forty thousand tons of bombs were dropped on Japan's industrial centers in one month.

D. The Japanese government still refused the American demand for unconditional surrender, so Churchill and Truman (Roosevelt had died in April) decided to use the atomic bomb. Hiroshima was destroyed on August 6; on August 9 Nagasaki suffered a similar fate. On August 14 the Japanese accepted the terms of unconditional surrender, and on September 2, 1945 they signed the surrender papers on board the U.S.S. Missouri. The second total war had come to an end.

The Cost of the War

At the end of the war forty-six countries were fighting on the Allied side, eight on the Axis. Over 15 million soldiers were killed or missing. The casualties of the United States were 295,-904; of the British Commonwealth, 452,570 (305,770 from the U.K.); of the U.S.S.R., 7,500,000; of France, 200,000; of Germany, 2,850,000; of Italy, 300,000; of China, 2,200,000; and of Japan, 1,506,000 (330,000 were civilians, and of these 78,150 died at Hiroshima alone).

The cost of military operations is figured at 1.5 trillion dollars.

There was more physical destruction in the second total war than in the first. Ground fighting ruined western Russia, and air fighting reduced whole cities to debris. Industry and transportation were destroyed, and refugees swarmed homeless over Europe. Most overseas investments were lost, and Europe was reduced to bankruptcy.

The Conferences of World War II and the Peace Settlements

The Foreign Ministers Conference—1943

In October, 1943 the foreign ministers of the Big Three (Hull, Eden, and Molotov) met in Moscow. It was decided that Italy, who had surrendered in September, should have a democratic government and that Austria should be liberated and made a free and independent nation. Also, Hull was able to get Molotov to pledge Russia to a system of collective security after the war. This was the first definite commitment to a postwar substitute for the League of Nations. The conference was relatively free of differences, for the need of military cooperation was still great.

The Teheran (Iran) Conference—1943

Churchill, Roosevelt, and Stalin met for the first time in Teheran in November of 1943. Before this, Roosevelt and Churchill had met in Cairo with Chiang (Russia would not meet with Chiang since the U.S.S.R. and Japan had a neutrality pact) to assure China's rights after the war.

A. At Cairo it was agreed that Japan would be stripped of all gains in the Pacific since 1914; Manchuria and Formosa would be returned to China; and Korea would be free and independent.

B. The Teheran Conference was essentially military and was the high point of Allied cooperation. It was agreed that a second front would be opened in either May or June of 1944 (it was here that Churchill argued for the invasion of the "soft underbelly of Europe"—the Balkans). The question of Poland's boundaries was broached but never solved, and it was agreed that Germany should be eliminated as a strong military power after the war.

The Yalta Conference—1945

The single most important conference was Yalta in February, 1945. There was still hope of compromise and Russian cooperation regarding each country's postwar role, and policy had not yet been clearly formulated. The aims of the three major powers were

1) The United States wanted agreement on the United Nations organization, and this took precedent over all other matters. She also wanted a definite commitment that Russia would enter the war in the Pacific.

2) Great Britain wanted to arrive at a friendly settlement on specific items and political problems, especially the questions of Greece and the Middle East.

3) Russia wanted territories and rights in the Far East and to strengthen her security against Germany by a belt of nations on her western border friendly to the U.S.S.R.

THE SETTLEMENT

1) No real agreement was reached on postwar Germany. The big stumbling block was again over reparations. Russia was now taking the French position in World War I (that is, to make Germany pay for the war). It was agreed, however, that until a peace treaty was signed there would be four zones of military occupation. Churchill and Roosevelt argued that Germany should not be dismembered; Stalin did not commit himself. The only decision totally agreed to by Russia was that France should participate in the zones of occupation.

2) The fate of Eastern Europe was decided, although the West was unaware of the consequences. The Poles would have a coalition government between the Lublin government (the government in Moscow) and the government in exile in the west. This would be a provisional government until free elections could be held—they never were. All the Eastern European nations were to have free elections—they never did.

3) The settlement in the Far East can be understood only by realizing that the United States felt that Russia was still necessary in the war against Japan. Military advisers had forecast the end of the war in the Pacific to be as far off as December, 1946 and were convinced that the invasion of the home islands of Japan would be necessary to bring about Japanese surrender. Russia refused to consent to war without a price. She agreed to enter two or three months after the conclusion of the war in Europe; she entered after the first atomic bomb was dropped. In return, Mongolia was to remain as it was, a Russian puppet; Manchuria was to be a Russian sphere of influence under Chinese sovereignty; and Russia was to acquire the Kurile Islands and the southern half of Sakhalin Island.

The Potsdam Conference—July and August, 1945

A. There was no longer room for diplomacy, for the situation had changed. Germany had surrendered in May, and America was on her way to winning the war against Japan. Most of the agreements were disagreements. There was no fundamental meeting of minds, and all that was settled was a kind of bargain unfavorable to both the Russians and the West.

B. Two major questions were to be settled: one was Allied economic policy for Germany, and the other Russia's position in Eastern Europe. Stalin wanted reparations from Germany and recognition of the Communist regimes in Eastern Europe (this was in violation of the Yalta Agreement). Truman and Churchill (and later Attlee) opposed him. All that could be agreed upon was that

1) Three areas should be placed under Polish administration: the section of Germany lying to the east of the Oder and Neisse rivers, the free city of Danzig, and the southern portion of East Prussia. This was not a final commitment, although Poland and the U.S.S.R. treated it as such.

2) A Council of Foreign Ministers was established that would draft the peace treaties for Italy, Rumania, Bulgaria, Hungary, and Finland.

3) It was decided that there would be no central govern-ment for Germany; each zone would be different. A control council, however, was set up to decide on joint policies for Ger-many as a whole. Within each zone Germany was to be demil-itarized and denazified. The amount of reparations could not be decided upon, but it was agreed that they were to be paid by the removal of German industrial plants and capital equipment. The Russian share was to come from her own zone plus one quarter of the industrial equipment removed from the three western zones. Russia, in turn, was to supply the other zones with foods and raw materials (she gave no goods but got most of her one quarter).

4) Berlin was divided into four zones, separately governed by Russia, the United States, the United Kingdom, and France.

The European Peace Treaties

A. In 1947, peace treaties were signed with Italy, Rumania, Bulgaria, Hungary, and Finland.

1) Certain territorial changes were made. Italy lost land on her western frontier to France, the Dodecanese Islands to Greece, and the island of Saseno to Albania. She lost all her colonies, which were put under United Nations auspices. Finland ceded to the U.S.S.R. the northern province of Petsamo, a strip of land along the frontier, and the area of the Karelian Isthmus (12 percent of her country). She was also required to lease a naval base to Russia for fifty years. Rumania ceded Northern Bukovina and Bessarabia to the U.S.S.R.; Hungary ceded a strip of territory on the Danube to Czechoslovakia.

2) Reparations were agreed upon: Italy paid $360 million (100 million to the U.S.S.R. and 125 million to Yugoslavia); Ru-mania paid $300 million (to Russia); Bulgaria paid a total of $70 million (to Yugoslavia and Greece); Hungary paid $300 million (200 million to the U.S.S.R.); Finland paid $300 million (to Rus-sia).

B. Austria

Austria was also divided into four occupation zones, with the capital city of Vienna administered in the same way as Berlin (four zones of occupation). The Austrian peace treaty was concluded in 1955, much to the Western world's amazement, for Soviet occupation had given the U.S.S.R. valuable bargaining power in negotiating a German settlement. Austria delivered $150,000,000,000 worth of goods and $2,000,000 in cash, plus one million tons of crude oil annually for ten years to the U.S.S.R.

c. No peace treaty was agreed upon for Japan and Germany.

In 1951 peace was made with Japan (with neither of the two Chinas invited to sign, and the U.S.S.R. refusing to sign). In 1956 the U.S.S.R. finally agreed to a declaration ending the state of war with Japan.

In 1949 the German Democratic Republic (East Germany) was proclaimed. In 1955 a treaty was signed by the U.S.S.R. that recognized the full sovereignty of the Republic. In 1951 the British, French, and Americans announced the formal termination of the state of war with Germany. On May 5, 1955 the Occupation Statute was revoked and West Germany regained full sovereignty.

The Nuremberg Trials

For the first time in the history of war the men who had led the world into conflict were put on trial for their actions: war had become a crime against humanity.

In October, 1946 an international military tribunal was set up by the Allies in Nuremberg to try the top Nazis. These men were charged with causing the war, with crimes against humanity, and war crimes (breaking the Geneva Convention of 1924). Three men were freed; seven received ten years to life imprisonment; and twelve were condemned to death—Joachim von Ribbentrop, minister for foreign affairs; Hermann Goering, commander in chief of the air force; Wilhelm Heitel, chief of the high command; Ernest Kattenbrunner, chief of the security police; Alfred Rosenberg, minister for eastern occupied territories; Julius Streicher, general in the S.A. (Storm Troopers); Hans Frank, governor-general of Poland; Wilhelm Frick, director of central office for all occupied territories; Fritz Sanckel, general plenipotentiary for the employment of labor; Martin Bormann, secretary to the Fuehrer; Alfred Jodl, chief of operations in the supreme command; and Artur Seyss-Inquart, chancellor of Austria. (Most of these men were generals in the S.S.—the elite guards—and held other positions as well.)

There were twelve more trials held in Nuremberg, but these were under United States auspices; as a result of these trials, 185 men were indicted and twenty-four were put to death. The major responsibility for denazification, however, was turned over to the German tribunals under Allied supervision; in these, 1,635 people were judged major offenders and 600,000 received some punishment.

In Japan the leaders of the war party were also tried.

The United Nations

The United Nations was formed by the Allies in the summer of 1945 in San Francisco. Like the League of Nations, it was a voluntary organization of sovereign states, dependent upon the cooperation of its members. Unlike the League, it had the support of the United States.

At the creation of the U.N. there were fifty-one member nations; now there are more than twice that many (114).

The Structure of the U.N.

A. The General Assembly, in which all nations have one vote, is purely an advisory body. The organ with the responsibility for action is the Security Council, consisting of five permanent members—the United States, the Soviet Union, Great Britain, France, and Nationalist China—and six nations elected for a two-year term. Decisions must be agreed upon by seven of the eleven nations and all five of the permanent members. This implies a veto power and means that the Soviet Union has been capable of blocking most important actions. The Security Council's only major peace-keeping operation was made possible by the U.S.S.R.'s walkout in 1950. Without Russia the Council ordered "police action" in Korea.

B. The principal organs of the U.N. are the international court of justice, the economic and social council, the security council, the trusteeship council, and the secretary-general (and the secretariat). The secretary-generals of the U.N. are recommended by the Security Council and voted on by the General Assembly. There have been three

   1) Trygve Lie of Norway (1945–1953)
   2) Dag Hammarskjöld of Sweden (1953–1961)
   3) U Thant of Burma (1961–   )

The Hammarskjöld decade witnessed two important operations for keeping peace—the Suez and Gaza Strip crisis and the civil war in the Congo.

C. In 1964–1965 the whole structure of the United Nations has been questioned. The National Assembly may have to be rebalanced on the basis of "weighted voting"; the financial crisis with Russia may lead to a reevaluation of the U.N.'s effectiveness; and the withdrawal of Sukarno's Indonesia has certainly shaken the organization. The Cyprus crisis was momentarily averted by a U.N. force of 6,150, but whether the U.N. can handle a showdown between Greece and Turkey is another question.

The New Balance of Power at the End of World War II

There were only two world powers after World War II— the United States and the Soviet Union. The rivalry between these two nations has deeply affected Europe's postwar history, for she was the center of this rivalry and the prize to be won. Ever since the seventeenth century there had been a multilateral balance of power consisting of a half-dozen nations of relatively equal strength. In the years following the Second World War, however, the old diplomacy broke down because the world was divided into two camps dominated by two giant states, and though certain nations remained neutral, they did not influence the balance between the U.S.A. and the U.S.S.R. It was most important to both the U.S.S.R. and the U.S.A. that Europe choose their side, but there was a decisive difference in their approaches—the U.S.S.R. had more to gain by chaos on the continent and an internationally weak Europe, while the U.S.A. had more to gain by rebuilding Europe. This is what the United States set out to do almost immediately after the war.

The Cold War

In March, 1946 Churchill announced that "From Stettin in the Baltic to Trieste in the Adriatic an iron curtain has descended across the continent." Churchill was one of the first statesmen to recognize the new balance of power and Russia's ultimate designs. It took the rest of the West longer to perceive the true nature of her plan. In 1947 the Cominform was established, and there was no longer much pretense about Russia's ambitions. In 1947 the Greek civil war began, and it was Great Britain who had to muster her resources and fight against the communists (although $400 million in aid did come from the U.S.A.). Then in February, 1948 Czechoslovakia was taken over, and in June of the same year Russia blockaded Berlin. The United States then inaugurated the policy of containment, an attempt to alleviate the economic conditions on which communism bred by such plans as the Marshall Plan and the Point 4 program of technical aid and to protect Europe by military aid (the Truman Doctrine in 1947, followed by the creation of NATO in 1949).

The Marshall Plan

A. The creation of the United Nations Relief and Rehabilitation Administration (U.N.R.R.A.—an agency that developed from Allied wartime cooperation) was the first economic effort at saving Europe. Between 1943 and 1948 it distributed millions of tons of food, clothing, farm equipment, and industrial machinery, saving thousands of lives and speeding the world's economic recovery.

B. On April 3, 1948 the European Recovery Program (the E.R.P.), called the Marshall Plan, was signed by President Truman. The United States' plan to keep Europe in the American camp was to finance the recapitalization of European industry by making available American dollars.

1) Congress appropriated $6.8 billion dollars for the first fifteen months, and in the next four years assistance in E.R.P. aid amounted to over $13 billion, and assistance to NATO to almost $11 billion.

2) The O.E.E.C. (Organization of European Economic Cooperation) was set up to distribute the funds according to need. Most of the money was in the form of outright grants, and each nation receiving these grants had to match the amount in "counterpart funds." "Counterpart funds" could also be spent only with American approval. The O.E.E.C. continued even after the Marshall Plan had terminated in 1952 and played an important role in reducing trade and currency barriers in Europe.

NATO

A. The Truman Doctrine in 1947 was the first step by the United States towards a European defensive alliance. Truman announced that it must be the policy of the United States "to support free people who are resisting attempted subjugation by armed minorities or by outside pressures."

B. In that same year Britain and France signed a defensive alliance. The following March, Belgium, the Netherlands, and Luxembourg joined with them in the Brussels Treaty.

C. In June, 1948 the United States passed the Vandenburg Resolution that a regional defense organization should be established.

D. In April, 1949 the North Atlantic Treaty Organization (NATO) was formed. The member nations were the United Kingdom, France, Belgium, the Netherlands, Luxembourg, Denmark, Iceland, Norway, Italy, Portugal, Canada, the United States, Greece, Turkey (in 1951), and finally West Germany (in 1955).

1) NATO was a defensive military pact with command under the direction of Supreme Headquarters Allied Powers

Europe (SHAPE). General Eisenhower was the first commander (1949–1952), followed by Matthew B. Ridgway (1952–1953), Alfred M. Gruenther (1953–1956), Lauris Norstad (1956–1963), and currently Lyman L. Lemnitzer.

2) At present (July, 1963) NATO has 12,143 aircraft, 234 submarines (17 nuclear), 27 cruisers, 39 carriers, 661 escorts, 523 minesweepers, and 83 other ships; and a combined army of 3,101,500 men. These figures do not include missiles. All the countries of NATO have nonstrategic missiles except Canada, Iceland, Luxembourg, and Portugal. The United States and the United Kingdom have by far the most.

3) NATO's foundations have been shaken, however, by France's Charles de Gaulle's objection to a nuclear fleet armed with missiles and manned by mixed crews.

Postwar Europe

Great Britain

The major change in the United Kingdom after the war was nationalization and socialization.

A. Nationalization, or government ownership, was not new in Great Britain; the B.B.C. (British Broadcasting Company) had been taken over by the state in 1927, the telegraph and telephone had been under post office jurisdiction from the start, the London transport system had been nationalized in 1933, and the government had assumed control of the mineral rights of coal mines in 1938, and during the war all aspects of life were regulated and controlled by the government.

B. In 1945, when the Labor Party came to power in England, a far more extensive program of nationalization took place. The Bank of England, the cable and wireless service, and civil aviation were put under government auspices. The operation of coal mines, railroads, canals and docks, electricity and gas were also nationalized. None of this was done by confiscation; in each case the owners received compensation. In 1949 steel and iron were nationalized, but in 1953 the Conservative Party denationalized the steel industry as well as the trucking business. In 1964 the Labor Party came back into power under Prime Minister Harold Wilson but with a very slim majority, and whether they will renationalize steel remains to be seen.

c. In 1946–1948, four major acts were passed that changed Britain into a welfare state. The National Insurance Act provided for health, old age, and unemployment insurance; the National Health Act provided for further compensation in industrial injuries; the National Health Service Act gave free medical, hospital, and nursing care (with a slight charge for dentists and spectacles); and the National Assistance Act provided for anyone not covered under the National Insurance Act.

d. At the same time the United Kingdom began to provide for the economic and social development of her colonies. The British Colonial Development and Welfare Acts of 1945, 1950, and 1955 provided £220,000,000 to be spent by 1960 on colonial improvements (although rationing at home was not completely ended until July, 1954).

e. Although Britain's Gross National Product was up 7.5% from 1963 to 1964, her financial situation after the war was not as cheery as was forecast. British industry has not been modernized enough to compete on the world market, and the trade gap is greater than ever. In hopes of solving financial problems, the Labor Party has succeeded in passing a new and severe budget with exchange controls, curbs on foreign travel, and higher taxes.

France
France suffered not only economic but political problems at the end of the war.

a. In 1944 De Gaulle, as head of the Free French, took over the government and named a cabinet as the provisional government. During this period De Gaulle himself governed by executive decrees. He too was forced to nationalize certain industries because of the dislocation and disorganization caused by the war. Coal mines, aircraft, and banking were nationalized, and in 1946 coal, gas, and electricity were also nationalized.

b. In 1945 the communists were the largest single bloc in the Chamber of Deputies, yet De Gaulle still maintained control. In

1946, however, he "retired" in a huff over the issue of military credits, and in October, despite protests from De Gaulle, a new constitution was ratified and the Fourth Republic was created. In 1947 De Gaulle reentered politics, advocating a rightist national state. This made French politics more unstable than ever. Between 1947 and 1958 there were nineteen cabinets. By 1956 the communists were again the largest party and the socialists the second largest.

c. In May, 1958, however, the French army leaders seized power in Algeria and demanded the return of De Gaulle. In June De Gaulle took over the government on his own conditions and has been running it ever since. In September, 1958 a new constitution was ratified that gave dominant power to the president (De Gaulle), who is elected for a seven-year term, who can dissolve parliament and in emergency assume the powers of a dictator (which De Gaulle in fact assumed), and the Fifth Republic was proclaimed.

d. Overseas, De Gaulle was responsible for the French Community of Nations, replacing the highly centralized French Union. Internal autonomy was granted and the executive of the French Community (the premier of France and the heads of the member nations) controlled foreign affairs, defense, and overall economic planning.

Italy

In 1946 Italy was declared a Republic and ever since has been ruled by coalition governments. Thirty-one percent of the Italians vote communist and there is a heavy socialist vote. The Catholic Church is still an extremely strong power. It is the only church that receives state subsidies, and religious instruction is compulsory in all state schools. Italy, primarily an agricultural country, has nevertheless made great strides in industrial development since the end of World War II.

Germany

a. East Germany, or the German Democratic Republic, is still under Soviet control in fact if not in name. Otto Grotewohl (an ex-Social Democrat) is premier; Wilhelm Pieck is president; and Walter Ulbricht is chairman of the politburo (all this as of 1963). Berlin remains divided, East Berlin resembling East Germany and West Berlin a part of West Germany. Both Berlins send nonvoting representatives to their respective parliaments.

B. West Germany, or the German Federal Republic, contrasts sharply with East Germany, for it has established a democratic government and a prosperous economy.

1) In 1949 a constitution was drawn up in Bonn, Germany, the new capital of West Germany's government. Power is vested in the chancellor and the cabinet. A combination of direct and proportional representation is used in electing the lower chamber. Germany has in essence become a two-party state with the Christian Democrats (Konrad Adenauer, 1949–1963, and Ludwig Erhard as chancellors) holding 243 seats in the Bundestag and the Social Democrats (which control many of the local states as well as Berlin) having 190 seats. In 1956 communism was outlawed.

2) Comparative economics of Germany, Great Britain, France, and Italy.

After 1950 Germany made great strides in industrial and agricultural growth and today is again the major West European economic power.

A) Germany's phenomenal economic growth can be seen in the following comparative figures on industrial production. In 1957 Germany's index of industrial production stood at 147; it was 100 in 1953; France's was 145, 100 in 1953; and Great Britain's was 138, 100 in 1948.

B) In steel production West Germany produced 24.5 million metric tons in 1957; Great Britain, 21.7 million; France, 14.6 million; and Italy, 6 million.

C) In the production of cars, again West Germany leads Western Europe. In 1957 she built 1,212,260 automobiles, Great Britain built 861,000, and Italy, 350,000.

D) In the size of her merchant marine, Great Britain still leads the world (with 19,500,000 tons carrying on 50 percent of the world's shipping, and building 35 percent of the world's new ships), but since the war Germany has almost replaced her wartime losses (4,492,708 tons).

E) Germany is second in the world in the export of machinery items.

The Decline of Europe

After World War II Europe no longer guided the destinies of the world; her colonies had been reduced to a mere handful and her prestige had suffered. Economically she cannot compete, not so much because she lacks the money (Europe as a whole has greater industrial potential than Russia or the U.S.A.) but she lacks political unity. If Europe were politically united, she would constitute a third major power along with the U.S.A. and the U.S.S.R. There have been steps towards unity.

A. In 1951 France, Germany, Italy, Belgium, the Netherlands, and Luxembourg formed the European Coal and Steel Community—a federalized organization creating free markets for coal and steel. The result was a production boom.

B. In March, 1957 the same nations set about a more ambitious plan: they formed the European Economic Community (the Common Market) and the European Atomic Energy Community (Euratom). The Common Market's purpose is to promote free trade among its members by slowly (in twelve to fifteen years) eliminating all tariff barriers. Euratom is a common market for nuclear raw materials, technicians, and equipment. For the first time in history, the European nations have surrendered certain portions of their sovereignty willingly.

C. The Council of Europe was set up in May, 1949, and although it has very little power, it has fostered interparliamentary cooperation among its sixteen member nations. Representation is according to size and the council is a policy-formulating body, doing such things as legally guaranteeing civil rights throughout Europe and bringing member nations together to debate over foreign policy.

Despite the fact that Europe is no longer the economic and

political center of the world, her influence has never been greater, for her three revolutions—industrial, scientific, and ideological (liberalism, socialism, nationalism, communism)—have swept the world. Even the United States and the Soviet Union's achievements are in large measure European in origin. Though Europe may be in decline, her heritage remains triumphant.

The Vestiges of European Influence

Possibly the most important and certainly one of the last remaining vestiges of European influence is the British Commonwealth of Nations, an enormous but unstructured association of eighteen states, all of which were originally members of the British Empire.

1) The commonwealth received statutory status by the Statute of Westminster in 1931, but its origins go back to the time when Canada received dominion status within the British Empire (1867).

2) In 1931 there were six white (mostly Anglo-Saxon) member states—Great Britain, Canada, Australia, New Zealand, South Africa, and Newfoundland. Today there are eighteen, and only four are predominantly white. (Newfoundland lost its dominion status in 1933 and joined Canada in 1949; South Africa voluntarily left the Commonwealth in 1961.)

The United States and Anglo-Saxon Migrations

It is traditional to commence North American history with Christopher Columbus' voyage of discovery in 1492. In actual fact, however, European interest in the New World was limited to Florida and Central and South America for the next hundred years. It was not until 1607, when three ships of Captain Christopher Newport anchored in Chesapeake Bay, that the development of North American civilization began. Since there is nothing but modern history in North America, it is necessary to divide the story into five parts, all of which fall into the recent period. They are the exploration, settlement, and independence of the United States (1492–1783); the growth of American institutions and way of life (1783–1840); internal discord and westward expansion in Canada and the U.S.A. (1840–1877); economic, political, social, and international change in the U.S.A. and Canada (1877–1917); and the United States and Canada as world powers (1917–1965). Australia and New Zealand are both discussed throughout the chapter for contrast and comparison.

The Exploration, Settlement, and Independence of the United States   1492–1783

The white settlers who came to the northern half of the New World faced a different situation from that faced by their

Iberian brothers who traveled south into Mexico, Peru, and the Argentine. They were also there for a different purpose—the French to trade, the English to settle. The Indians of North America, numbering only about 200,000 east of the Mississippi, were too few and too backward to be a real threat to colonization, and the English white settlers soon became more interested in making the country their new home than in the gold and plunder that brought the conquistadors to the south. (It was much to English disgust that no precious metals were found.) The geographic features of North America also played an important part in its future history. The Atlantic coast was dotted with bays and inlets which contributed to the growth of small colonies (thirteen in all) rather than large ones, gave America a wide variety of institutions, and eventually led to the creation of a federation of states, not a monolithic nation. Geography also contributed to a speedy opening up of the entire continent once the first settlers had passed the Alleghenies. Once England controlled the Ohio River it was inevitable that a great flood of English-speaking people would move westward along the vast water system formed by the Ohio, Mississippi, and Missouri rivers.

THE EXPLORATION OF AMERICA

The Iberian world led the way in the discovery and exploration of the New World.

Portugal was first led into Africa in 1415, as a consequence of her long-standing conflict with the Moslems. It was Henry the Navigator who inspired and financed Portugal's initial attempts to explore the whole coast of Africa looking for the southern limits of Islam and searching out a water route to China and India. Christopher Columbus, however, promised a shorter route to the East by sailing not east but west to Cathay, and finally in 1492 he persuaded the Christian monarchy of Spain to finance him. On October 12 Columbus sighted the Bahamas and mistakenly thought that he had reached the Indies. (This is the origin of the name West Indies.)

Spanish Exploration

Though in 1497 John Cabot discovered and claimed Labrador for England and in 1500 John Cabral claimed Brazil for Portugal, the Spanish monopolized the early decades of colonial discovery.

In 1497 Amerigo Vespucci explored Puerto Rico, Central America, and Mexico.

In 1508 Alonso de Ojeda settled Panama.

In 1513 Vasco Nuñez de Balboa discovered the Pacific; and in 1519 Ferdinand Magellan claimed the Philippines for Spain while making the first circumnavigation of the globe.

The first Spanish expedition to North America came in 1508, when Ponce de Leon, who had subdued Puerto Rico, explored Florida.

Estevan Gómes, a Portuguese in the employ of Spain, made the first survey of the Atlantic coast between 1524 and 1525.

Spain never took the same interest in North America as she did in South and Central America because the north lacked gold and silver. Nevertheless, Hernando de Soto discovered the Mississippi River in 1541 and Franciso de Coronado explored West Texas, Colorado, and New Mexico.

French Exploration

As Spain grew rich from the easy profits of the New World, the rest of Europe sought to emulate Spanish conquests and deprive her of her colonial wealth and holdings. The French were the first to singe the Spanish beard in the New World.

In 1523 Jean Fleury raided Spanish ships returning from the New World, and the following year, under French colors, Giovanni de Verrazano explored the North American coast from Newfoundland to North Carolina (known as New France).

Jacques Cartier explored the St. Lawrence River in 1534, and St. Augustine, the first permanent settlement in North America, was established by Spain in 1565 as a military base to prevent French seizure of Florida.

Newfoundland was a haven for French fishermen and was to become the foundation of French wealth in America.

The French explorer Samuel de Champlain, having established Quebec in 1608 as his headquarters, traversed the Great Lakes region, and the Jesuit Père Jacques Marquette, with Louis Joliet, discovered the mouth of the Mississippi in 1673.

French backwoodsmen explored the Hudson Bay country and, when punished for their behavior by the governor of New France, sold out to England and the Hudson Bay Company in 1670. The French also founded New Orleans in 1718.

THE SETTLEMENT OF NORTH AMERICA

The English Arrive

The English rift with Spain did not become decisive until the reign of Elizabeth I. In 1557 Drake's voyage of plunder around the world brought the situation out in the open, and the Spanish Armada of 1588 gave the British temporary supremacy of the seas.

Between 1585 and 1587 Sir Walter Raleigh engineered three expeditions to the New World to found a settlement on Roanoke Island (North Carolina). His lack of success was in part responsible for the assumption of the task by joint stock companies.

The Settlement of Virginia

A. In 1606 the London Company was chartered by James I to settle Virginia; in 1607 Captain John Smith founded Jamestown. By 1619 there were only two thousand settlers, but that same year ninety maidens arrived, a representative government was formed, and the first (Dutch) ship landed twenty Negro slaves.

B. By 1625, 5,500 people had been sent to Virginia, four thousand of whom had perished and three hundred of whom had returned. That year Virginia was made a royal colony. In the 1650's, 15,000 settlers had taken the ocean trip to Virginia and some of them had moved on to the Carolinas. Tobacco exports rose from 20,000 pounds in 1619 to 60,000 in 1624.

The Pilgrims

Pilgrims who had fled to Holland entered into commercial negotiations with the London Company: in return for passage to Virginia, they were to give the Company seven years of labor. In 1620 the Mayflower sailed with 102 people aboard (half of whom died within a year). Instead of landing at Virginia, they disembarked by accident or design at Plymouth and formed an independent colony. In 1691 Plymouth was absorbed into the Massachusetts Bay Colony.

Massachusetts Bay Colony

In 1629 a group of Puritan merchants founded the Massachusetts Bay Colony and sent John Winthrop with nine hundred settlers to establish eight cities, one of which was Boston. That same year, Archbishop Laud began a heavy-handed campaign of enforced Anglicanism on all Englishmen, and many Puritans decided to emigrate. By 1640 there were 25,000 people in the new colony. Boston grew from 1200 in 1640 to 6,700 in 1700. In 1636 a college to train the clergy of the Society of the Saints was founded. (In 1638 John Harvard gave the library and half his estate.) Public education was established by law throughout the colony, but there was no religious tolerance for the non-Congregationalists, and many dissenters were expelled.

The Dutch Arrive

French seapower began to decline, and it was the Dutch who immediately took over the seas. The Dutch were more anti-Spanish than the French (having rebelled against Spanish rule in 1566), and rivalry in the New World became intense as the Dutch established the Dutch West India Company as well as the Dutch East India Company.

In 1614 an armed fur-trading post was built near Albany and trade was established with the Iroquois. This failed, but in 1624 the Dutch returned, and the Iroquois, the most powerful Indian confederation, agreed to support the Dutch in return for the exclusive use of Dutch firearms.

In 1626 the Dutch West India Company bought Manhattan

Island and established the prosperous community of New Amsterdam (New York).

The Thirteen British Colonies

Though the British colonial experience on the Eastern seaboard varied from colony to colony (New England tended to be Puritan and organized on the basis of town government, the South was Anglican and organized by parishes), within one hundred years of the establishment of the thirteen colonies a general system of colonial government had taken shape. Connecticut and Rhode Island were exceptional in being almost completely self-governing commonwealths. The other colonies, regardless of whether they were proprietary (controlled by private individuals) or royal (chartered by the crown), all had much the same political structure. The King or the proprietor appointed the governor who governed (except in Massachusetts) through an appointive council. Governors tended to be English, councillors American, and very shortly the councillors developed into an upper legislative chamber. Every colony had its representative assembly, which was often in conflict with the governor but was able to resist royal pressure because of its popular nature and control of taxation.

The New England Colonies
RHODE ISLAND AND CONNECTICUT

1) Among the dissenters expelled from Puritan Massachusetts Bay Colony were Roger Williams, who founded Providence, Rhode Island, in 1635, and Anne Hutchinson, who established Portsmouth, Rhode Island, in 1638. The area was joined into a single colony in 1644 and granted a very liberal crown charter in 1663.

2) Religious dissenters also migrated into the Connecticut valley under the leadership of Reverend Thomas Hooker (in 1662 the colony of Connecticut was formed, also with a liberal charter). Connecticut and Rhode Island were completely self-governing commonwealths choosing all their own officers. In 1639 the freemen of Connecticut drew up the Fundamental Orders of Connecticut—the first written constitution in the Western world.

NEW HAMPSHIRE (AND MAINE)

These areas were also settled largely by Puritans from Massachusetts, and Massachusetts exercised political control over New Hampshire until 1680 and over Maine until 1820.

MASSACHUSETTS (See section "The English Arrive.")

The Middle Colonies

The Middle Colonies were more tolerant, varied, and cosmopolitan than New England. By the time of the Revolutionary War, New York, New Jersey, Pennsylvania, and Delaware had about 700,000 people.

PENNSYLVANIA AND DELAWARE

Pennsylvania was unusual from the start. Most of the other colonies were formed by commercial companies as business ventures, but the Carolinas, Maryland, and Pennsylvania were given by the English crown as estates to private individuals. British, Dutch, and Swedish settlers had come into the area of Pennsylvania and Delaware, and in 1681 William Penn, the Quaker son of an admiral, was given the charter to form the "perfect commonwealth." Pennsylvania was based on Quaker principles, representative government was established, freedom of religion was allowed, and Philadelphia became the "city of brotherly love." Delaware was made an independent colony in 1704.

NEW YORK

Manhattan was gained by conquest. The Dutch settlement of New Amsterdam was autocratic and a constant commercial and military menace to the English. In 1664, during the Anglo-Dutch war, three warships were sent against the settlement. The Dutch gave in without a struggle and New Amsterdam became New York and was given a government by the Duke of York.

NEW JERSEY

James, Duke of York, created New Jersey when he sold it to two friends in 1664 who ruled as proprietors. It became a royal colony in 1702.

The Southern Colonies

Almost exclusively rural, there was more class distinction in the South. Socially and religiously they tended to be patterned after England. Slaves were introduced from the start, and by 1770 a little less than half the population in Virginia were slaves, and in South Carolina the Negro outnumbered the white by two to one.

MARYLAND

Maryland was a proprietary grant land, given to Sir George Calvert, Lord Baltimore. His first settlers arrived in 1634. Maryland was free of religious intolerance but slow to receive any form of popular government.

THE CAROLINAS

These too were proprietary grant land. The proprietors attempted to populate the land with tenant farmers, but in 1729 a combination of economic problems forced the proprietors to sell Carolina back to the crown. The country was then split into two royal colonies.

GEORGIA

The convict colony of Georgia was created in 1735 for those who were in trouble or debt in England. This action infuriated the Spanish, and Georgia's boundaries were not finally settled until Florida was purchased in 1819.

VIRGINIA (See section "The English Arrive.")

Population Statistics

In 1675 the mainland colonies had 50,000 people; in 1700 they had 100,000; and by 1750 there were about one and a half million people; by 1780, 3,250,000.

Menaces to British Settlement

The Dutch were a threat to British settlement in Connecticut, the French to those in the north; but the most important menace was the Indian. Many of the Indian tribes were small; the most powerful were the five or six nations of the Iroquois family of western New York. In the southeast the Creeks also had a strong confederacy, and in the northwest the Sioux reigned supreme. War against the Indians was of three types:

The conflict was first with the small local tribes such as the Pequot War of 1637 in the Connecticut valley and the Powhatan War in Virginia in 1622.

The next stage of conflict was when the Indians established alliances for resistance. This happened during the Tuscarora War in North Carolina and the Yamassee War in South Carolina. The most famous of the wars of this type was against the Narragansett Indians in 1675 (King Philip's War), which ended the Indian menace in southern New England. (Surviving Indians went north and joined the French in Canada.)

The Indians then found European allies—the French to the north and the Spanish to the south—but the Iroquois remained friendly to the British and even aided the settlers.

New France

In 1535 Cartier had discovered what was to become the site of Montreal but did not succeed in his attempt to colonize the territory. It was not until 1608, when Samuel de Champlain laid the foundations of Quebec, that the French began to come to North America. In 1628 the Company of New France was formed by Richelieu, and the colonies were vigorously supported by Louis XIV. In 1663 New France was made a royal colony under Count Frontenac (1672) and his associate Sieur de La Salle, who was responsible for establishing French posts on Lake Ontario and in Illinois.

The French, however, came to America only in small numbers, and their chief interest was to trade in fish and furs. When the struggle for control of North America came, the British had twenty men for every one the French had. In 1754 there were 1,500,000 British and only 100,000 French. The British also had a better navy and better leadership.

Conflict for Control of North America

With British expansion into the interior, conflict was bound to come. In northern Canada the Hudson Bay Company was intruding on French trading, and in New York the Iroquois were persuaded to strike at pro-French tribes of the Great Lakes. This led to King William's War (1689–1697).

The French continued expansion into Illinois, Detroit, and Louisiana (1699), contributing to the outbreak of the War of the Spanish Succession, or Queen Anne's War (1701–1713). Again the British won, and by the Treaty of Utrecht in 1713 the French surrendered the Hudson Bay country, Newfoundland, and Acadia (Nova Scotia).

War broke out again in 1744 (the War of the Austrian Succession, or King George's War), but the final struggle came in 1754 with the Seven Years' War. French and Indian raids, along with the conflict for the control of the Ohio valley, were the chief causes of the war in America. By the Treaty of 1763, England gained all of Canada from the French and Florida from the Spanish.

THE ESTABLISHMENT OF THE UNITED STATES OF AMERICA

The Causes of the Revolutionary War

The Seven Years' War

A. One of the major effects of the Seven Years' War was to lessen America's dependence on Great Britain because of the disappearance of the French threat.

B. Another major effect of the war was the change in Britain's attitude toward the colonies. Her administrative control over them was tightened, and the mercantile system that had long been in existence was suddenly enforced in an effort to put the empire on a rational and economic foundation. Just at the moment that the French threat was removed, Great Britain insisted that the colonies pay for their own defense.

Economic Grievances

A. The mercantile or navigation acts injured the northern colonies. They had few staples to exchange for manufactured goods and had to pay in species. Species could be obtained only by trading with the West Indies, but this was prohibited by the Molasses Act of 1733 and the Sugar Act of 1764. The export tax on non-English goods shipped to the colonies was raised in 1764 from 2.5 percent to 5 percent.

B. The South faced a different economic problem. The southern colonies were heavily in debt to British merchants (the Virginia debt at the beginning of the revolution was computed at £2,000,000). In 1764 Parliament forbade the printing of paper money in the colonies, and all debtor groups joined the ranks of those opposed to British rule.

Parliament

Misunderstanding over Britain's desire to centralize also caused problems, and the fundamental theoretical disagreement over the power of Parliament led to war. Parliament maintained that all the colonies were subject to its decisions and laws. The colonies, on the other hand, said the crown alone had authority and could get money only by asking for it from the colonies themselves—in other words from the colonies' own parliaments, which were regarded as the equals of the Parliament in Westminster.

The Road to War

The first step to the war for independence was rioting. The Stamp Act of 1765 led to violence in Massachusetts, New York, Virginia, and North Carolina, in which mobs destroyed the stamps and expelled the tax collectors.

Then came economic boycott of everything British. The Townshend Act of 1767 placing duties on tea, paper, glass, and printers' colors hit Massachusetts the hardest, and economic boycott was followed by violence in which four Bostonians were killed in March, 1770 by British Redcoats. The reaction to the

Boston Massacre caused the British parliament to repeal the duties except on tea.

The next step towards war was the establishment of committees of "correspondence," or propaganda societies, by men determined to keep the revolutionary spirit alive. Sam Adams of Massachusetts established the first intercolonial correspondence committee.

The Leaders of the Revolution Were of Two Types

A. The group of intellectuals, men of education, who started the impetus towards revolution included, among others, Samuel Adams, John Adams, John Jay, James Otis, Alexander Hamilton, Benjamin Franklin, Thomas Jefferson, and John Rutledge.

B. The group of radicals with little or no education who were the spirit behind the actual revolt included such men as Alexander McDougall, Isaac Sears, and John Lamb of New York, Patrick Henry of Virginia, and Timothy Bloodworth of North Carolina.

The Coercive Acts

On December 16, 1773 the Boston Tea Party, the dumping of over three hundred chests of tea into Boston Harbor in reaction to Parliament's granting of the monopoly of trade to the East India Company, took place. Boston was once more in revolt. Reaction to the destruction of private property scandalized even the pro-American members of Parliament, and by way of discipline the British Government passed the Coercive Acts (the Intolerable Acts) in 1774, which included the quartering of troops in private homes, the closing of Boston port, and the right to try offenders in England. Colonial resentment was further outraged by the Quebec Act, granting an independent government for ex-French territory in Canada, giving freedom of worship to all Catholics, and preventing the coastal colonies from migrating into the Northwest Territories.

The last step towards war was then taken. Revolutionary legislatures were established. The first was in Virginia in 1774. Then came the first Continental Congress, with an agreement to boycott British goods. A Continental Association was created to supervise this, and munition dumps were established by the Association. Britain sent troops to Boston, and General Gage marched to destroy a munition dump at Concord. On April 19, 1775 the minutemen (men called out by Paul Revere) met the Redcoats and the revolution had begun.

The Revolutionary War

In May, 1775 the second Continental Congress met and appointed George Washington commander-in-chief of the revolutionary forces. By January, 1776 there was no turning back, and Thomas Paine published his book *Common Sense,* which proclaimed the growing attitude on the part of the Americans. "There is something absurd in supposing a Continent to be perpetually governed by an island." By May of that year most colonies had set up independent state governments and were at war with Great Britain.

The war was characterized by great bravery, brilliant and absurd maneuvers, treason, brutality, and difficulties on both sides in getting men to fight. The decisive battle of the war was Saratoga in 1777, for the Americans were able to keep the British forces divided and the victory led to the entrance of France into the war on the side of the colonists. After 1780 the war became a world conflict in which Great Britain had to fight the French, the Spanish, and the Dutch. In October, 1781 Cornwallis, blockaded by Washington on the land and a French fleet on the seas, capitulated, and the war in the colonies was as good as over.

The Treaty of Peace   1783

In 1783 America south of the Great Lakes and west to the Mississippi was proclaimed free. Two concessions were made by the Americans: British creditors were allowed to sue for debts and loyalist property was to be restored. (Congress could not control the states, however, and most loyalist property was not regained.) Canada remained an English colony until 1867.

THE GROWTH OF AMERICAN INSTITUTIONS
AND WAY OF LIFE   1783–1840

Though the colonies had won their freedom, it still remained to get them to cooperate in peace as well as in war, and the early years of the new republic were taken up in forming a federal government that would safeguard states' rights yet prevent anarchy and link the colonies into a nation. There were 3,250,000 people in the new republic in 1783, of whom about one third (not including the Indians) were either slaves or in jail. New York, the capital of the new nation until 1790, had a population of only 30,000. By 1796 Kentucky and Tennessee had become states, the Mississippi and Ohio valleys had become the frontier, and by 1820 the republic had grown into twenty-four states, had more than doubled in area, tripled in population, and quadrupled in wealth. Cities were growing faster than rural areas. Along with expansion westward, the two most significant themes of the era between 1783 and 1840 were the growth of democracy and the rise of nationalism in America.

THE GOVERNMENT OF THE UNITED STATES

The Articles of Confederation

In March of 1781 the Articles of Confederation were adopted by the states. The new congress was little more than a conclave of ambassadors representing sovereign states and had very little authority. There was no system of courts, no true national executive, and the government could not levy taxes or enlist troops. States joined the union and ceded from it at will.

The only real authority that the new congress had was over the territory between the Appalachians and the Mississippi, and the Northwest Ordinance, passed in 1787, was its only achievement. The Ordinance divided the territory into five potential states, which would be admitted to the union on the same basis as the original members once any state had a population of 60,000 people. This was to become the precedent for all future states admitted to the United States.

Economic chaos caused by inflation, tariffs, lack of coordination between states, and no control over the printing of paper money finally led to the summoning of a constitutional convention.

The Constitutional Convention

The second convention (the first failed) met in May, 1787 and included delegates chosen by each of the state legislatures. The most learned men present were Benjamin Franklin, James Madison, and Alexander Hamilton, and George Washington's presence was important to the success of the convention. Many of the men most active in the revolution (Jefferson, Paine, Sam Adams, John Adams, and Patrick Henry) were absent, and this was significant, for it meant that the more radical elements were not represented.

The Constitution of the United States

Three distinct branches of government were established. The eighteenth-century concept of a balance of governmental power was employed. Judicial, executive, and legislative branches were formed, each equal and each checked by the other two.

A. The legislative branch consisted of two houses—the Senate and the House of Representatives. The small states were given equal representation with the large states in the Senate. The House was elected by direct popular vote and the Senate—until 1912—by the state legislatures. All laws passed by Congress had to be approved by the executive branch of the government.

B. The executive was the President and Vice President,

elected by an electoral college in which each state had as many representatives as it had Senators and Representatives. Most appointments and all treaties signed by the President had to be approved by the Senate, and the executive could be impeached by Congress.

c. The Judiciary, the Supreme Court, consisted of judges appointed for life (on good behavior) by the President with the consent of the Senate. Their task was to judge the constitutionality of the law. They could also be impeached.

d. The variety in terms of office (two years in the House of Representatives, six years in the Senate, four years in the presidency, and life in the Supreme Court) was also a check, for no complete change in personnel could be accomplished except by revolution.

The Powers of the Government

The powers of the Federal Government were carefully specified, and (by the Tenth amendment) all residual powers were granted to the states. Taxation, the borrowing of money, control of imports and exports, the coining of money, the fixing of weights and measures, copyrights and patents, post offices, the creation of an army and navy, and control over interstate commerce and international relations were granted to the Federal Government. Its strength was also added to by the amending process and by the vagueness of phraseology of the Constitution, which did not spell out the powers of the chief executive and said nothing about the cabinet or the committee system of Congress.

Amendments to the Constitution

The Constitution was passed on the understanding that the first ten amendments guaranteeing the rights of freedom of speech, religion, and so on would be included.

The new government went into force in the spring of 1789, with George Washington unanimously elected as its first president.

The Presidents of the United States 1789–1841

PRESIDENT	INAUGURATED	PARTY
George Washington	1789	Federalist
John Adams (chosen president by three electoral votes)	1797	Federalist
Thomas Jefferson (tied with Aaron Burr for president and thus the vice-presidential election system was amended)	1801	Democrat-Republican
James Madison	1809	Democrat-Republican
James Monroe (reelected by all but one vote)	1817	Democrat-Republican
John Quincy Adams	1825	Democrat-Republican
Andrew Jackson	1829	Democrat
Martin Van Buren	1837	Democrat

Political Parties

No date can be named for the beginning of political parties in the United States. At the outset the Federalists (those who supported the Constitution) had no effective opposition. It was Thomas Jefferson who came out violently against the Federalist policies (particularly on the issue of support of the French treaty). It was in part due to party strife that Washington retired in 1796. The names of the political parties are confusing.

The election of 1796 put the Federalists in power once more, but Thomas Jefferson received sixty-nine votes (Adams 71), and Jefferson triumphed in 1800. His party was originally called the Republican and then the Democratic, but neither term should be confused with the present Republican and Democratic parties.

The Democrats did not enter the political picture until 1825, when Andrew Jackson became their leader.

In 1833–1837 the Whig Party was formed, but it lacked any effective or constructive program and consisted mainly of those people who were opposed to Jacksonian policy.

The Republican party (the ancestor of that of the present day) was formed in 1854 in opposition to the Democrats and the Kansas-Nebraska Act.

THE GROWTH OF DEMOCRACY

Early Contributions

Pennsylvania led the way in the establishment of democratic government by granting representation by population and by abolishing property qualifications for voting in 1775–1776.

Though it is hard to generalize, loyalists, especially in the mid-Atlantic and New England states, were often of the wealthy and more conservative element in society, and their exodus during the revolutionary war tended to foster the growth of democracy.

Much of the privileged status of the upper classes was destroyed when in the South primogeniture was outlawed and the Anglican Church's authority challenged.

The Bill of Rights

The first ten amendments to the Constitution guaranteed to all men freedom of worship, speech, press, and petition, the right to bear arms, protection against the quartering of soldiers and from search and seizure, the right to jury trial and a speedy trial, the sanctity of private property, protection from cruel punishment, and the rights of the states to the residual powers of the Constitution.

Thomas Jefferson's Contributions

Thomas Jefferson posed as the champion of the common man, but his championship tended to be highly aristocratic and paternalistic in form. He did, however, encourage immigration, favor agricultural interests over commercial and financial ones, and in the name of the equality of all men abolish honorific titles. Though Jefferson was doubtful about the extent of the authority vested in the Federal Government by the Constitution, he was responsible for the stretching of the powers of the Federal Government by the acquisition of Louisiana.

Andrew Jackson's Contributions

Jackson, a military hero of the war of 1812, was one of the "common people" and the first President to have a belief in these people. Brought to power by the Democratic party, which consisted mainly of farmers in the West and laborers in the East, he set about to establish economic and social equality. He destroyed the eastern monopoly of control of finance (the Second Bank of the United States). He reduced the working day in Massachusetts to ten hours. The ballot throughout many of the states became freer during his administration, and the battle for public education reached its climax. At the same time, Jacksonian policy forced up the price of land and contributed to speculating by

Evacuating the Indians;

Leaving internal improvements solely to the states;

Fiscal policies directed against the Second Bank of the United States. In 1833 Jackson began removing government deposits from the Bank of the United States and distributing them to "pet banks" in the states. The deposits were loaned by the banks to speculators. Then in 1836 Congress tried to alleviate the situation by distributing the treasury of the Bank proportionately by electoral vote. This started a speculative spiral in the western states and precipitated the financial crash of 1837, the first of the major financial busts following periods of speculation that plagued the economy until the Great Depression of 1929 and the advent of Government control of credit.

NATIONALISM AND UNITY

Hamilton's Contributions

Hamilton played a major role in the movement toward a stronger national government. As Washington's Secretary of the Treasury, he set up the Bank of the United States and the National Mint, and the Federal Government took over the state debts. He encouraged the development of national industries, taxed liquors, and made propertied men dependent upon the Federal Government for their continued well-being. There was no justification in the Constitution for his acts, but he asserted that it was an "implied power" of the executive. He further strengthened the national government by sending out a force of one thousand national militiamen to smash the Whiskey Rebellion.

The Defeat of the Federalists

The Alien and Sedition laws (1795) of John Adams, which included censorship of the press, the extension to fourteen years of residence requirement for citizenship, and an attempt to make a crime of political opposition, ultimately led to the defeat of the Federalists, for they granted the Federal Government too much power over individual liberties.

Jefferson's Contributions to the Growth of the National Government

Jefferson, who advocated a stricter interpretation of the power of the Federal Government, in contrast to Hamilton, inadvertently strengthened the powers of the Government by

Doubling the area of the nation with the Louisiana Purchase (for $15,000,000). No clause in the Constitution permitted this; he acted without the consent of Congress.

Attempting to maintain neutrality during the Napoleonic wars by an embargo act that forbade all foreign commerce. This was eventually replaced by a nonintercourse law (and limited to Great Britain), which became one of the causes of the War of 1812.

The War of 1812

The poorly fought, unnecessary war between the British and the Americans in 1812 also contributed to the growth of national unity. The few successes that the Americans had (primarily at sea), the comradeship in arms, and the general dissatisfaction with those who would not fight knit the Republic together.

John Marshall and the Supreme Court's Contributions

Chief Justice of the Supreme Court John Marshall (1800–1835) probably did more to strengthen the hand of the Federal Government and the Constitution than any other single man. He established, among other things,

The right of the Supreme Court to review any law of Congress or of a state legislature.

He established that the Federal Court had the final judgement on any case, not a particular state court.

He stood behind Hamilton's insistence that the Constitution gave to the Government powers that were not necessarily stated (implied powers).

Division

One issue, however, was beginning to split the country asunder. The sugar, cotton, and tobacco states of the south were bringing in thousands of slaves. In 1818 there were ten slave and eleven free states. In 1819 Alabama and Missouri applied for admission into the union. Alabama had to be a slave state, but the free states said that Missouri must not be a slave state. A compromise was reached whereby Maine was brought into the union as a free state and Missouri would be admitted without restriction (she was admitted as a slave state), and Congress decreed that slavery should be excluded from the remaining portions of the Louisiana Purchase, north of 36°30'. The problem was only temporarily solved, and the slavery issue became the rock upon which national unity foundered.

THE WESTWARD MOVEMENT

People flooded to the northwest and southwest after the revolution. Hunters and trappers went first, followed soon afterwards by farmers and, finally, doctors, shopkeepers, preachers, land speculators, and others.

Chicago was a trading village in 1830. Within a lifetime it had become a wealthy metropolis. The city grew from five hundred to four thousand between 1830 and 1840, the price of land rose from $1.25 an acre to $100 in 1832, and a few years later to $3,500.

The Indians were evicted to the Great Plains under Presidents Monroe and Jackson, and by 1840 nearly all the Indians east of the Mississippi had been forced to emigrate. The Cumberland Road (1811) of six hundred miles, the Ohio River, and most important, the Erie Canal, were the instruments of the westward movement. By 1840, 3,326 miles of canal were taking people and goods across the country.

The Following Twenty-six States Were Admitted to the Union between 1787 and 1840

Alabama	1819
Arkansas	1836
Connecticut	1788
Delaware	1787
Georgia	1788
Illinois	1818
Indiana	1816
Kentucky	1792

Louisiana	1812
Maine	1820
Maryland	1788
Massachusetts	1788
Michigan	1837
Mississippi	1817
Missouri	1821
New Hampshire	1788
New Jersey	1787
New York	1788
North Carolina	1789
Ohio	1803
Pennsylvania	1787
Rhode Island	1790
South Carolina	1788
Tennessee	1796
Vermont	1791
Virginia	1788

FOREIGN AFFAIRS   1787–1840

The War of 1812

Causes

The United States' policy of neutrality and the British policy of searching neutral ships and taking deserters (and sometimes aliens) during the Napoleonic wars resulted in misunderstandings on both sides. Between 1804 and 1807 United States ships lost six thousand men, and reluctantly Madison asked for war.

Sectional dissension within the United States delayed the invasion of Canada, and it was not until September of 1813 that Toronto was invaded and the Canadian parliament houses were burned. In turn, in August of 1814, the British burned the White House and the Capitol. The war was fought badly and mishandled from the beginning, and the Treaty of Ghent did very little except to bring peace.

The Effects of the War

Eventually commissions set up by the Treaty of Ghent did determine the boundary between the United States and Canada (except for Maine) and insure the demilitarization of the Canadian-United States border.

THE EFFECTS ON CANADA

1) In 1812 there were three strains of population in Canada: the French who had been in the St. Lawrence Valley since the seventeenth century; the loyalists who had fled the United States during the revolution and settled in the maritime provinces, Upper Canada, and Ontario; and recent immigrants from Great Britain.

2) The War of 1812 increased Canadian nationalism and made her more willing to depend politically upon Great Britain for military security.

The Monroe Doctrine 1823

The most outstanding example of American diplomacy between the years following the revolution and 1840 was the Monroe Doctrine. Two ideas were presented by Monroe in his annual address to Congress in 1823—one, that Europe should be forbidden to establish any new dependencies in the Western hemisphere, and two, the older doctrine of American nonintervention in the affairs of Europe. The address was prompted by Russia's claim to territory south of Alaska and by the threat to Latin America by the Quadruple Alliance. Also standing behind the Monroe Doctrine was Great Britain's encouragement and her navy.

INTERNAL DISCORD AND WESTWARD EXPANSION
IN CANADA AND THE UNITED STATES   1840–1877

The main theme of the years between 1840 and 1877 was the growing division within the United States. The split between the North and the South had been on the increase since 1830. The North had become more outspoken in its denunciation of slavery, demanding that it should be abolished as it had been in the British empire in 1833. The South was increasingly worried by the introduction of antislavery states into the union and the consequent upset of the political balance within the Senate. Although the South had a total white population of about 6 million in 1850, only 347,725 people owned slaves. Yet it was with the large slave owners (about 3,000 or 4,000) that wealth and, more important, political power rested. The slave population was on the increase, rising from 1,500,000 in 1820 to almost 4,000,000 by 1860. The schism between North and South had been artificially mended by the Missouri Compromise of 1820, but when Texas applied for admission into the union, it tore wide open again.

There were many other themes of importance between the years 1840 and 1877. The expansion of United States territory (by 1877 fifteen new states had been added to the union), the growth of the Republic (in 1854 alone almost 430,000 immigrants came to the United States), and the industrial revolution and urbanization (by 1860 one fifth of all Americans lived in places of 2500 population or more) were major factors in these years.

At the same time that the United States was changing Canada was beginning to work out her future, and in 1867 the Dominion of Canada was established and a federal constitution approved.

Economic and Social Change in the United States— the Industrial Revolution

The Beginnings of Industrialism

In 1750 the industrial revolution—the use of heavy machinery powered by water or steam and operated by a disciplined factory labor force—had begun in England, especially in the spinning and weaving industries. The introduction of Eli Whitney's cotton gin, which allowed the production of mass cotton for the mass spinning and weaving in English factories, was a key step in the industrial process, which by 1820 was beginning to appear in New England and the mid-Atlantic states.

Eli Whitney played a major role in forwarding the concept of industrialism in the United States. More significant than his invention of the cotton gin was his introduction of the principle of mass production. The first successful American factory (1791) was small, but by 1812 there were hundreds like it. The first "new model" factory was opened in 1816 by the Boston Manufacturing Company, a totally integrated textile factory, employing young women whom they sheltered and fed. It was an instantaneous success.

America's Advantages

America had important advantages to insure rapid industrial and technological growth:

A plentiful supply of raw materials including coal, oil, and iron, and eventually electric power.

A good transportation system linking the Ohio River basin with both the Mississippi and the Hudson.

Originally a labor shortage, which required the increased use of labor-saving machines and then a labor supply that was constantly renewed through immigration.

An expanding domestic market.

A government that encouraged industry as well as protected it against foreign competition and prevented the growth of interstate barriers.

The Extraordinary Speed of the Industrial Revolution

Between 1820 and 1837 investment in industry rose from $50 to $250 million.

The Middle West became the leader in the manufacture of agricultural machinery, and this machinery ranked above any in the world. (In 1854, in a thresher competition, an American machine threshed 740 liters of wheat in a half-hour, an English machine 410, and a French machine 250.)

The 1840's and 1850's saw the sewing machine, the vulcanization of rubber, and the production of inexpensive steel and petroleum. In 1856 came the telegraph, in 1866 the cable, and ten years later the telephone. (Within twenty-five years of the first telephone, American Telephone and Telegraph incorporated with a capitalization of a quarter of a billion dollars.) In 1873 the typewriter was invented, in 1878 the arc lamp, followed by the incandescent lamp, and in 1882 the first generating and distributing station was built in New York. In the 1890's came the gasoline motor car. Between 1860 and 1900, 676,000 patents were granted. In those same years the total number of wage earners increased from 12 million to 29 million.

An electrolytic process made aluminum commercially available in 1887, and by 1900 over 7 million pounds of aluminum were being produced. Oil was struck in Pennsylvania in 1859, and in five years production had increased to more than 2 million barrels.

The Railroads

Hand in hand with industrial progress and invention went the railroad. In 1840, with 3,000 miles of track, it led the world; by 1850 it had added 5,500 miles more, and by 1860 another 21,000 miles. By 1860 one and a half billion dollars had been invested in the railroads.

Urbanization

Urbanization was an immediate result of the industrial revolution. New York had over a million people by 1860, and Philadelphia, Baltimore, and Boston were not far behind. Chicago had 110,000 and St. Louis and Cincinnati 160,000.

THE MOVEMENT WEST

Oregon

The first group of settlers arrived in Oregon in 1841. By 1843 two hundred families had gone to Oregon on the "great emigration," and by the middle 1840's the Oregon Trail had become a great highway from the Missouri River to the Columbia. In 1849 Oregon was made a territory and in 1859 a state.

Utah

The Mormons, led by Brigham Young, fled from Illinois and settled in the Great Salt Lake Valley. By 1850 Utah had become a territory.

Texas, California, and the Southwest Taken from Mexico

In 1835 settlers in Texas revolted and finally won their independence from Mexico. In 1845 Texas was annexed by the United States.

The American element in California was also growing (about 1,200 by 1846). The dispute over Texas' boundaries with Mexico led to war. At the end of the war, the United States had gained California and the Southwest (New Mexico and Arizona), 918,000 square miles of land.

The Following Twenty-four States Were Admitted to the Union After 1840

Alaska	1959
Arizona	1912
California	1850
Colorado	1876
Florida	1845
Hawaii	1959
Idaho	1890
Iowa	1846
Kansas	1861
Minnesota	1858
Montana	1889
Nebraska	1867

Nevada	1864
New Mexico	1912
North Dakota	1889
Oklahoma	1907
Oregon	1859
South Dakota	1889
Texas	1845
Utah	1896
Washington	1889
West Virginia	1863
Wisconsin	1848
Wyoming	1890

THE GROWTH OF AMERICA

Between 1850 and 1860, 2,452,000 immigrants flooded to America. In 1870 in the United States, 435 out of a thousand people were native-born whites with native parents; 292 were native-born with foreign-born parents; 144 were foreign-born; 127 were Negro; one was Indian; and one was Chinese. Most of the immigrants before 1860 were from the British Isles and Ireland. Between 1846 and 1932, 18,000,000 people migrated from Great Britain and Ireland.

THE CIVIL WAR

Background

The proposed annexation of Texas and the Southwest brought the slavery question to a head once more. Texas had slavery already, but the issue arose over California, New Mexico, and Utah. The Wilmot Proviso that these territories be admitted only on condition that slavery be prohibited raised the constitutional issue of whether Congress had the right to regulate the existence of slavery in the states. The South threatened to secede from the union if the Wilmot Proviso was passed. Henry Clay's compromise of 1850 that California be free and Utah and New

Mexico be organized as territories without qualification, and that a law enforcing the return of fugitive slaves to their masters be passed, satisfied no one but brought temporary peace.

The Road to War

The North never cooperated with the Fugitive Slave Law, and became more blatant in its encouragement of the "underground railroads" (the illegal channel by which slaves could go north, established in 1833).

Then in 1854 the South demanded the right to open up the entire Missouri valley to slavery (forbidden by the Missouri Compromise). On Douglas' instigation the Kansas-Nebraska Act was passed in 1854. It repealed the Missouri Compromise by opening up the area to popular sovereignty on the issue of slavery. The effect of the act was to

A. Turn Kansas and Nebraska into a hotbed of contention between the North and South as freeholders and slave owners poured in to grab territory.

B. Eventually kill the Whig party and make it possible for the Republicans to rise to power. The Republicans, appealing to eastern business as well as western farmers, demanded that slavery be excluded from all territories.

In 1857 in the Dred Scott case, the Supreme Court announced that Congress had no power to exclude slavery from the territories.

In 1858 Lincoln and Douglas, running for a seat in the Senate from Illinois, debated the issue of slavery and did much to awaken the country to the constitutional as well as moral problem.

In 1859 John Brown and a small band of followers invaded Virginia to liberate the slaves and were hanged for their efforts.

The division in the country was not caused totally by those who advocated slavery and those who were against it. The South and North were extreme opposites. The South was rural, with little manufacturing; it did not want protective tariffs or centralized banking, and it was receiving few of the immigrants. On each side there was fear and mistrust of the other.

The Rise to Power of the Republican Party

In 1860 the Democratic Party split when radicals demanded that Congress pass laws protecting slavery and nominated John Breckinridge as their candidate for president. (The other half of the party nominated Douglas). The split in the party was disastrous, not only to victory but also to union. In the election Lincoln won with a clear majority of the electoral votes, but not with the popular votes.

In December, 1860 South Carolina seceded from the union, then Mississippi did the same, and in the following February seven southern states organized the Confederate States of America with Jefferson Davis as provisional president. In April of 1861 the South fired on Fort Sumter.

The Civil War 1861 to 1865

In reply to the fall of Sumter Lincoln called out 75,000 volunteers and the uncommitted states chose sides. Maryland, Delaware, Kentucky, and Missouri stayed with the union, and Virginia, North Carolina, Tennessee, and Arkansas filled out the ranks of the rebels. The war had begun.

The South's hope for victory lay in immediate triumph, the North's in delaying tactics until she could mobilize her superior industrial and human resources. During the first year and a half of war the South, better led and fighting on inside lines, was generally the victor, but inconclusively so, and time was running in favor of the North. On September 22, 1862 the Emancipation Proclamation was announced by Lincoln, which changed the conflict from a constitutional one (that is, defending the integrity of the union) into a moral one. Then, in July, 1863 the turning point came when General Grant took Vicksburg and split the Confederacy and Meade conquered Lee's army at Gettysburg. By September, 1864 Sherman had begun his march through Georgia. On April 2, 1865 General Lee evacuated Richmond, which had held out for nearly a year, and on April 9 he surrendered to Grant at Appomattox. The war between brothers was over.

The Results and Cost of the War

The war was one of the most destructive that the world had yet experienced. Union deaths reached 360,000 and Confederate deaths 260,000 (which was one fifth of the South's white male population). Many southerners died of malnutrition, epidemics, and riots as a result of the aftermath of the war. The war cost the North 4 billion dollars, but much of this had been invested in industries. The Confederacy, on the other hand, had spent about 2 billion but lost everything.

The South was in economic chaos. The labor system was totally disorganized, the area was bankrupt (between 1868 and 1874 the southern states' debt rose to close to $125,000,000), factories were forsaken, and ex-slaves wandered homeless. In Mississippi alone there were 10,000 orphans, and there was no one to alleviate the situation or to assume the reins of government.

The situation in the South might have been alleviated if one of the most tragic events of the war's fanatic aftermath had not taken place. On April 14, 1865 the hero of the victorious Union—and the only man who might have saved the South—was murdered. This was a misfortune to all, for the man who replaced Abraham Lincoln as President of the United States, Andrew Johnson, was not the President for the task, because he was unable to control the northern radicals in Congress, who came within one vote of impeaching him and who forced through a Carthaginian reconstruction of the South.

Hatred between North and South was another tragic result of the war. Not for twenty years would a Democrat (Grover Cleveland was the first) live in the White House, and not for fifty years would a southerner by birth (Woodrow Wilson was the first) become President of the United States.

But the war had achieved its purpose. The Union was preserved, and the Thirteenth Amendment (ratified at the end of 1865) abolished slavery forever.

Reconstruction 1865–1877

Andrew Johnson, the new President of the United States, could not control his Congress, and the radicals in the North imposed on the South

A. Military occupation.

B. The Fourteenth Amendment of equal rights for all, and the Fifteenth Amendment granting the ballot to all.

C. Using poor whites and Negroes and fortune hunters (carpetbaggers) to set up the new state governments.

Reconstruction did a great deal of harm, but by 1876 only the governments of Louisiana, Florida, and South Carolina were still in the hands of carpetbaggers, and in 1877 the last Federal troops were withdrawn.

The South was eventually transformed. Although she remained basically rural (sharecroppers solved the labor situation), new industries began to grow. Tobacco began to rank as one of the foremost industries, and by 1888 Durham had become the largest producer in the world. Iron was discovered in Birmingham, and the South soon produced one fifth of the world's pig iron. The textile and oil industries also grew by leaps and bounds.

The Presidents of the United States 1841–1877

President	Inaugurated	Party
9th—William Henry Harrison	1841	Whig
10th—John Tyler	1841	Whig
11th—James Knox Polk	1845	Democrat
12th—Zachary Taylor	1849	Whig
13th—Millard Fillmore	1850	Whig
14th—Franklin Pierce	1853	Democrat
15th—James Buchanan	1857	Democrat
16th—Abraham Lincoln	1861	Republican
17th—Andrew Johnson	1865	Republican (originally a Democrat)
18th—Ulysses S. Grant	1869	Republican

CANADA

At the same time that the United States was facing problems of division, Canada was having sectional difficulties.

Background of the Canadian Government   1791–1860

The Canada Act

A. In 1791, by the Canada Act, Great Britain had created two provinces in Canada—one French (Lower Canada) and one English (Upper Canada). Each province had its own governor, an appointed legislative council (appointed by the Governor), and an elected assembly. Colonial laws could be disallowed by Great Britain within two years of passage.

B. The new governments were faced with economic as well as political problems.

The Revolts of 1837

In 1837 revolts broke out in both Lower and Upper Canada. The primary cause was the constitutional conflict between governor and legislative council on the one hand and the elected assemblies on the other. The grievances were over revenue, church control, and the judiciary. The situation was much worse in Lower Canada, for here the British minority controlled the governor and the legislative council.

The Durham Report

The following year Lord Durham was sent to Canada as Governor, and in 1839 he reported that Canada should be reunited and allowed a "responsible government" with an elected assembly.

The Union Act

In 1840, as a result of Durham's Report, Canada was reunited, given one governor and an elected national assembly. But the legislative council appointed by the Governor was retained until 1856, when it too was made elective.

The British North America Act 1867

The new Government set up in 1840 had autonomy in internal matters only and failed to solve the French problem. Federalism had to be the final answer. A federal constitution was drafted in Canada by Canadians and finally passed through the British Parliament in 1867. The British North America Act granted Canada dominion status in the Empire and gave her provincial governments, a federal government with a parliament of two houses elected by the people, a prime minister, and a governor-general representing the British crown. Sir John A. MacDonald became Canada's first prime minister.

Canada Expands

The original provinces were Quebec, Ontario, New Brunswick, and Nova Scotia. The Canadian Government purchased the land owned by the Hudson Bay Company for $1,500,000 in 1869. In 1870 Manitoba was added, in 1871 British Columbia, in 1873 Prince Edward Island, in 1905 Alberta and Saskatchewan, and in 1949 Newfoundland. These provinces and the Yukon territory and the Northwest Territories make up what is today Canada.

By the Treaty of Washington in 1871 the Canadians ironed out the major obstacles in their relations with the United States.

The Growth of Canada

Agriculture remained Canada's primary industry, although fishing, forestry, and mining played an important role in her development.

In 1836 the first Canadian railroad was built, and by 1881 the Canadian Pacific Railroad had been begun (finished in 1885), linking the country from coast to coast with 2905 miles of track.

Between 1840 and 1932 5,200,000 people immigrated to Canada.

Australia

Australia faced many problems that were similar to those in the United States and Canada. She too needed a federal system of government, and here too economic sectionalism caused problems, as it did in both Canada and the United States.

Background: The Settlement of Australia

The Dutch first explored the north and south coasts of Australia. Then, in 1769, the English Captain Cook explored the east coast and sent home a favorable report, recommending colonization.

In 1788 717 English convicts were transported to Sydney (New South Wales). Free settlers followed in 1793. As more settlers and more convicts reached Australia, the country was opened up. In 1829 Perth was established in West Australia; in 1834 South Australia and Victoria were founded.

In 1840 the last convicts were brought to Sydney. Since 1788 60,000 to 75,000 had been transported, but by 1840 only 25,000 still remained under sentence, and the free population greatly outnumbered them. In 1853 transport of convicts to Tasmania ended (67,000 had been landed), and in 1870 the last were brought to West Australia (since 1853 10,000 convicts had settled there).

The Government of Australia

In 1842 Sydney (New South Wales Colony) was granted a large measure of autonomy, and in 1850, by the Australian Colonies Government Act, the colonies were given virtual self-government. They elected their own legislatures, could alter their constitutions, could determine their own tariffs, subject to British confirmation. All the colonies were granted internal autonomy— Queensland, Victoria, South Australia, North Territory, North Australia, and New South Wales. In 1870 the British withdrew their troops from the continent.

More and more agitation for a federation led to a federal convention in 1897–1900. The convention succeeded in drafting a constitution, and in 1901 the Commonwealth of Australia came into being. A political system with a bicameral parliament, a supreme court, and a check and balance system (very close to the United States) was established. The chief executive was the prime minister, and the governor-general was the crown's representative. (Today the governor-general is always an Australian and is appointed only on the advice of the prime minister. This is true of all the dominions.)

The Growth of Australia

The original and primary occupation of the settlers was sheep-raising, but the discovery of gold in 1851 contributed to the rapid growth of the continent. In the first ten years, the Victoria Fields produced £80,000,000 worth of gold.

In 1850 the population was 400,000 people, and within ten years it had doubled. Victoria rose from 77,000 in 1851 to 333,000 in 1855. Between 1840 and 1932, 2,900,000 Europeans immigrated to Australia. In 1902, in order to bar oriental immigration, a new Immigration Act was passed that made literacy in a European language the requirement for admission.

NEW ZEALAND

Background: The Settlement of New Zealand

New Zealand was inhabited to the north by about 100,000 natives (Maoris) who were cannibalistic and warlike, and although permanent settlements were established by convicts who escaped from Australia, Great Britain had a difficult time encouraging immigration to the country. In 1826 the first New Zealand Company was formed to bring white settlers to the country, but these settlers preferred to go on to Australia.

Then in 1837 a New Zealand Association was formed and succeeded in encouraging immigration. In 1840 the British government assumed the protection of the settlers and in exchange for the Maoris' acknowledgement of Britain's sovereignty, England promised to protect natives' rights and grant them lands (which was not always done and led to several wars with the Maoris).

The Government of New Zealand

In 1852 a constitution granted the provincial governments control over most affairs, and until 1875 New Zealand remained essentially disunited. In 1870, after the conclusion of the Maori War, the British Government withdrew its troops from the country.

In 1875 district councils were abolished, and New Zealand was thenceforth under one government. In 1907 she was given the status of a dominion within the British Empire.

The "Great Britain of the South"

New Zealand turned into an amazing country, for it became the pioneers in labor reform, in social legislation, and in democratic government. In 1855 Victoria Colony introduced the secret ballot; in 1893 woman suffrage, workmen's compensation, and old-age pensions were granted.

New Zealand produced few artists, scholars, or writers (with the exception of Katherine Mansfield), yet she has the best per capita book market in the British Empire.

New Zealand is agricultural. Fruit, wheat, and wool were its main crops, but in 1882 meat refrigeration for transoceanic shipment led to prosperity, for sheep now were raised for meat as well as wool, and New Zealand also became a great dairy state.

In 1861 gold was discovered, and the population rose from 100,000 to 250,000 by 1870. Then followed a period of depression and serious efforts to encourage immigration. The result was that the population rose from 256,000 whites in 1871 to about 772,000 in 1901. Between 1840 and 1932 594,000 Europeans immigrated to New Zealand. In 1881 New Zealand became worried about the oriental problem (as Australia had been) and passed a Chinese Immigrants Act that almost totally barred them from the country.

Economic, Political, Social, and International Change in the United States and Canada   1877–1917

The change in the United States between 1877 and 1917 was even more rapid than it had been during the previous three decades. In 1860 she had been the fourth industrial nation in the world; by 1894 she was first. Between 1860 and 1900 the number of industrial establishments increased three times, the number of wage earners four times, and the value of manufactured products seven times. But industrialism was not without its problems, and the end of the nineteenth century witnessed the growth of large combines and trusts and the virtual control of the United States by the "robber barons." The same period in foreign affairs was one that many Americans are not proud of: the Americans joined with "the Christian nations" who were "subduing the world, in order to make mankind free." Japan was opened up, Latin America was controlled, the Caribbean became an American sea, the United States went to war against Spain and meddled in everyone's affairs. The end of the era, however, changed the situation, for the United States found herself involved in World War I.

The Growth of Big Business

The aftermath of the Civil War, the economic boom in the North, the demand for railroads going west, and the application of science to industry made possible the era of the capitalist.

The Railroad Boom

Between 1865 and 1873, 30,000 miles of track were built. At the same time the railroads were being consolidated. Small lines were bought out or forced out of business. The most spectacular examples of consolidation were the transcontinentals.

A. In 1862 Congress chartered the Union Pacific and the Central Pacific and granted them huge tracts of land. Construction companies made large and shady fortunes from these deals.

B. Before 1873 three other transcontinentals were chartered and given land, but only the Northern Pacific ever made it to the coast.

By 1893 the United States had 170,000 miles of railroad, capitalized at $10,000,000,000, and the capitalists behind them had amassed huge fortunes.

Corporations

The use of the corporate form of business led to dramatic growth in industry, for the liability of the capitalist was now limited to his own investment (called limited [Ltd] liability companies in England), and this encouraged risk-taking.

The Stock Market

The rise of industrial corporations led to the expansion of the stock market, and despite its evils, without it American industry could not have grown with the speed it did.

The Growth of Trusts and Monopolies

The steel industry grew because of the enterprise, skill, and capital of Andrew Carnegie, who entered the steel business in 1872. The panic of 1873 made it possible for him to buy out other men, and by 1890 he was described as being in "almost absolute control," but in 1901 his power was challenged and he preferred to sell out rather than fight. His holdings were merged into a new organization, the United States Steel Corporation. J. P. Morgan engineered the transaction and John D. Rockefeller made large profits from his control of the Mesabi mines. The

Carnegie Company was one of six hundred iron and steel establishments, but the United States Steel Corporation absorbed most of them, came to control two thirds of the steel products of the country, and was the nation's first billion-dollar corporation.

The oil industry, along with the railroad network, is an excellent example of the growth of big business and monopoly. John D. Rockefeller was the man most responsible. As he himself said, "The day of combination is here to stay. Individualism has gone, never to return." In 1870 he organized the Standard Oil Company. In two years its capitalization rose 150 percent. By 1879 he had made a deal with the railroads and controlled 90 percent of the refining capacity of the country and most of the world market for his products.

Almost every product on the market became a monopoly. Meat-packing was dominated by Armour, Wilson, Swift, and Cudahy; the reaper business by McCormicks; sugar by the Havemeyers; tobacco by the Dukes; milling by the Pillsburys and the Washburns; copper by the Guggenheims. This, however, did not compare with England, where industrial amalgamation was even more common.

The money trusts, led by the house of Morgan, came closest to nationwide consolidation of the railroads. In 1912 the banking houses dominated by Morgan and William Rockefeller held 341 directorships in railroads, coal, copper, steel, oil, and other industries, with resources of 22 billion dollars.

By 1904 319 industrial trusts had destroyed 5300 independent concerns, and 127 utilities had absorbed more than 2400 smaller ones.

Businessmen dominated Congress and voted in high tariffs and hard money. As early as 1865 it was reported that in New York there were several hundred men worth a million dollars, and some worth 20 million.

America might not have grown as fast without the Morgans, Rockefellers, Vanderbilts, Carnegies, and others, but there were certainly sad effects of the huge trusts.

A. Trusts tended to be conservative. Original ideas were

often ignored, and one of the best examples of this was the fact that at first General Motors Company could not keep up with Ford, who refused to be bought out.

B. Price-rigging, political lobbying, and lack of concern for conservation, high accident rates, child labor, long hours, and dreadful working conditions, along with the growing dehumanization of industrial machines, were characteristic of the giant corporations.

Labor

The organization of labor in the United States was slow for several reasons

A. There was always a supply of cheap labor coming into the country every year. Between 1850 and 1870, 5 million immigrants came to the United States, and they were willing to work for almost any wages and under almost any conditions. (Yet, fortunately for labor, there was an escape valve—the west—and many left the industrial cities for the open land.)

B. States, not the Federal Government, had control over labor conditions, and this meant that although there was labor legislation in some states, the great majority did nothing.

By 1898 more than 17,000,000 worked in American factories, and only 500,000 of these were members of labor unions. In 1881 the first labor union organized for the welfare of labor rather than for political goals was formed by Samuel Gompers. The American Federation of Labor started out as a union of craft unions, and by 1900 it had a membership of 550,000 and had won many rights for its workers.

Between 1881 and 1905, 37,000 strikes occurred. And even as late as 1900 only a small segment of labor had won basic rights, and these did not include any welfare plans.

Reaction—the Progressive and Reform Movements

As trusts grew larger and working conditions did not improve, protests became louder, particularly among the middle classes. The Social Gospel Movement, the General Federation of Women's Clubs, the National Consumer's League, and muck-raking magazines reached thousands of people. The midwestern states began to pass laws attempting to alleviate the situation. Wisconsin under the governorship of the Progressive Robert M. La Follette (1901–1906) led the way.

A national child labor committee was organized in 1904, and by 1910 twenty-five state committees had joined. Between the years 1902 and 1909, forty-three states adopted child-labor laws.

The Progressives began to realize that the root of the problem was in the political system, the various machines that were running the country, especially in the big cities. They began agitation for the direct primary, and by 1916 forty-five states had adhered to it. Then came demands for the direct election of United States senators, and in 1912 the Seventeenth Amendment was passed through Congress. By 1914, however, women's suffrage was permitted in only eleven states. (It was finally achieved through the Nineteenth Amendment in 1919.)

The first successful regulation of big business concerned the railroads. Midwestern states had passed laws limiting rates of railroads going through their territory. These laws were upheld by the Supreme Court in 1876. Next came the Interstate Commerce Act of 1887, which set up a commission to supervise rates, pools, services, and so forth on the railroads. This law was for a long time ineffective.

To keep the Progressives quiet, the Sherman Antitrust Act was passed in 1890. This too remained ineffective for years.

Theodore Roosevelt was the hope of the Progressives, but when he became President in 1901 he actually did very little. The Pure Food and Drugs Act of 1906 was passed but remained useless. Roosevelt, however, did succeed in

A. Attacking the Northern Securities Combine in 1902–1904.

B. Arbitrating for the workers in the mines of Morgan's Reading Railroad and settling the strike with a 10 percent increase in pay.

C. It was during Roosevelt's administration that the Hepburn Act of 1906 was passed. This set up an interstate commerce commission with the authority to set maximum railroad rates.

D. The Aldrich-Vreeland Act of 1908 was the forerunner of the Federal Reserve Act of 1933.

William Taft, it has been said, was "an immense figure physically," but "as a symbol of Progressivism he was an uncomfortable and uncompromising pigmy." Yet the Progressives in Congress were able to push through more reforms under him than under Roosevelt.

A. The Mann-Elkins Act, passed in 1910, gave the Interstate Commerce Commission the right to suspend objectionable rates on railroads.

B. The parcel post and the postal savings bank were established.

C. A separate Department of Labor and Commerce was created.

D. The Sixteenth Amendment was passed, making the income tax legal.

Under Wilson, before the First World War, three very important acts passed Congress

A. The Underwood Tariff of 1913 lowered the traiffs. (They had been raised by each of the presidents since the Civil War.)

B. The Clayton Antitrust Act of 1914 set up the Federal Trade Commission.

C. The Owen-Glass Act of 1913 established the Federal Reserve System and thus gave the United States a flexible currency.

THE PRESIDENTS OF THE UNITED STATES 1877–1917

PRESIDENT	INAUGURATED	PARTY
19th —Rutherford B. Hayes	1877	Republican
20th —James A. Garfield	1881	Republican
21st —Chester A. Arthur	1881	Republican
22nd—Grover Cleveland	1885	Democrat
23rd —Benjamin Harrison	1889	Republican
24th —Grover Cleveland	1893	Democrat
25th —William McKinley	1897	Republican

26th —Theodore Roosevelt	1901	Republican
27th —William H. Taft	1909	Republican
28th —Woodrow Wilson	1913	Democrat

THE WEST—THE END OF THE FRONTIER

In 1860 California had 400,000 people, Oregon some 50,000, and Utah about 40,000, and most of the rest of the western lands were occupied by the Indians—the Sioux, the Blackfoot, and the Crow in the north; the Ute, Cheyenne, and Kiowa in the middle areas; the Comanche and Apache in the south; and the Pueblo in the Rio Grande valley. Thirty years later the frontier was gone; the Indians had been defeated and all but extermi-nated, and the Great Plains had been conquered by the farmers.

The miners came first, in search of the gold in California, Montana, Dakota, and Wyoming. With them they brought wealth and, most important, the railroads.

The cattle barons were next, claiming the grasslands as their own, but they could not keep out the farmers who flooded across the Great Plains. The Homestead Act of 1862 opened the plains to free settlement, but it was President Arthur and Presi-dent Cleveland who demanded that the cattlemen stop fencing water rights and ordered the grasslands open to homesteaders.

The Agricultural Revolution

The conquering of the Great Plains by the farmer was a part of the agricultural revolution—the application of science to agriculture. Without barbed wire, better plows, irrigation methods, and deep-drilled wells it could never have been done.

Between 1860 and 1900 land held by farmers doubled from 407,000,000 acres to 841,000,000 acres, and the acreage of land under cultivation trebled. This was made possible by the new land opened up, but even more by the new inventions.

A. The plow was faced with steel in 1837 and improved steadily from then on. The reaper was first introduced in 1840, and in the 1880's came the reaper-thresher (the combine). Four men could now do the work formerly done by three hundred.

B. The agricultural revolution took place west of the Mississippi. In 1920 the farmers of Iowa alone had a larger investment in machinery than did all the farmers in New England and the mid-Atlantic states combined.

The Farm Problem

Nevertheless, as the farmer produced more and fed more cities, the agricultural debt began to rise. Farmers were heavily mortgaged for farm machinery. This precipitated the growth of the Populists and the battle between the silverites (cheap money and easy credit terms) in 1896, represented by William Jennings Bryan, and the advocates of the gold standard (hard money). Although Bryan lost, the United States was not to hear the end of the problem.

FOREIGN AFFAIRS—THE IMPERIALISTIC ERA

Background

America's "manifest destiny" to expand had started with the war against Mexico in 1846. Then, in the 1850's, Commodore Perry and Townsend Harris opened up Japan to western trade. In 1856 the United States Government allowed naval officers to raise the American flag on Pacific islands where guano (fertilizer) was found. In 1867 Russia sold Alaska to the United States. Although it was never admitted, the imperialistic urge continued to grow. American businessmen were laying financial empires in Latin America, and in the 1880's the United States began building a navy "to be second to none." By 1898 only Britain and France outranked her in naval power, whereas earlier she had been only twelfth.

Hawaii

Missionaries from New England settled in Hawaii in the 1820's. The native population began to decline, and at the same time the French and the British began to show an interest in the islands.

After 1876 sugar was admitted free of duty to America from Hawaii, and in return, in 1887, Hawaii agreed to yield Pearl Harbor to the United States as a naval base.

Anti-American feeling was on the increase, however, for the American missionaries virtually controlled the government and three quarters of Hawaii's arable land. In order to quiet discontent, Hawaii was quickly annexed in 1898 and in 1900 was granted full territorial status.

The War Against Spain

The Cuban insurrection against Spain in 1895 created anti-Spanish feeling in the United States. Rebels deliberately attacked American property in order to force the United States to intervene, and McKinley became president on a platform calling for Cuban independence.

It has never been proved that the blowing up of the *Maine* in Cuban waters on February 15, 1898 was the fault of the Spanish, but nevertheless it was the justification for the war that was declared on April 25.

The Spanish-American War lasted four months and cost the Americans seven thousand men, 90 percent of whom died of disease.

As a result, the United States acquired Guam, Puerto Rico, and the Philippine Islands (for $20,000,000), and virtual control of Cuba.

Latin America

Troubles in Latin America began in 1891 when rioting occurred in Chile between American sailors and Chileans. This almost led to war. More serious yet was the boundary dispute between British Guiana and Venezuela in which the United States interfered.

Harrison's Secretary of State, Blaine, brought the Latin

American nations together at the first Pan-American Conference in 1889. His purpose was to get trade concessions. He failed, and as a consequence the United States raised the tariff on Latin American goods.

Under Taft "dollar diplomacy" (the interference on the part of United States private business concerns in the political affairs of South America, and the United States Government's support of those businesses) became even more extreme.

The Panama Canal

A. Theodore Roosevelt's determination to build a canal that the United States alone controlled led to an American initiated revolution in Colombia, aimed at separating Panama from Colombia. (After Roosevelt's death, the United States paid an indemnity of $25,000,000 to Colombia.)

B. The canal was opened to ships in 1914 at a cost of $375,000,000.

C. The existence of the canal made United States policy more and more interventionist in the Caribbean.

Under Wilson the United States intervention in Mexico was probably one of the most notorious examples in American history.

The Pacific

The port of Pago Pago on the Pacific island of Samoa was acquired by the United States in 1899 as a result of an agreement among the United Kingdom, Germany, and the United States.

In China Secretary of State Hay advocated the Open Door Policy, leaving the country free for trade, but the United States still participated in the smashing of the Boxer Rebellion. She contributed 2,500 men and received an indemnity of $24,000,000, most of which she did return.

At the end of the Russo-Japanese War (1905), Roosevelt negotiated the treaty because, he said, it was vital to American interests in the Philippines.

WORLD WAR I

The Commonwealth Goes to War

As soon as Great Britain entered the war against Germany, Australia and New Zealand and Canada pledged their support.

Canada

By the end of September, 1914 30,000 men had volunteered to go to England. By the end of the war Canada had supplied 640,886 men and had spent $1,500,000,000. In September, 1917 a coalition cabinet was formed and compulsory military conscription was begun, yet most of the Canadian forces were volunteers.

New Zealand

New Zealand supplied 117,000 men. Most of these were volunteers, though conscription was begun in 1916.

Australia

Australia was never able to pass a conscription law, but she provided 329,000 men.

The United States

"Neutrality"

A. Unlike the Commonwealth, America hoped to remain neutral during the "European" war. She immediately became irritated with Great Britain's naval blockade and her seizure of neutral ships. Sentiment, however, remained sufficiently pro-British that the United States did not follow her policy of 1812, and she quietly acquiesced to the blockade of Germany. This was the first step away from neutrality.

B. By 1916 United States business with the Central Powers had almost totally disappeared. (In 1914 it had been worth $170,-000,000.) By the end of 1916, the United States investment in the Allied cause in terms of loans stood at $2,500,000,000.

C. Although by 1916 the United States had in fact, if not

in theory, committed herself to the Allies, Wilson was able to win reelection on the slogan "He Kept Us Out of War." As soon as he was reelected, he doubled the size of the army and started a three-year naval building program.

D. In 1915 the British vessel *Lusitania* was sunk without warning by German submarines, and 128 Americans died. Germany then promised to stop unrestricted submarine warfare, but early in 1917 she reopened it in order to starve England into submission. Eight American vessels were sunk within the first month, and in February, 1917 the United States severed relations with Germany. On April 2, Wilson asked for war; on April 4 the House agreed; and on April 6, the Senate followed suit.

The United States' part in the actual fighting was small, but it was her industrial production that decisively tipped the balance in favor of the Allies.

THE UNITED STATES AND CANADA AS WORLD POWERS
1917 TO THE PRESENT

By 1918 the United States and Canada had become world powers. Canada's international status was changing. She was represented in the United States by a Canadian resident minister in 1926, and diplomatic representatives were sent to Japan and France in 1928. Emotionally, however, the United States remained isolationist, and in March, 1920 she rejected the League of Nations and the Treaty of Versailles and pledged herself to a return to "normalcy," which meant "business as usual" and no entangling alliances. In doing so, she played a major role in the coming of the Second World War, for the League was helpless without the backing of the nation that had inspired it, and United States economic practices contributed to the economic decay of Europe. The Second World War brought greater responsibility to the United States than any people had known before in history. The rehabilitation of the Western world, the strengthening of democracy, and the sustaining of those who wanted to be free all over the world fell squarely on her shoulders. Generally, the United States has accepted these responsibilities, for she realized that only the United States and Canada had the moral and economic vigor to lead the non-Communist world.

THE RETURN TO "NORMALCY"

The Defeat of the Treaty of Versailles

Wilson made a series of mistakes at the end of the war; one was in not taking a Republican (the majority party in Congress) to the peace conference with him; another was in not being willing to compromise on Article 10 of the League Covenant (to submit all disputes to arbitration and to employ military and economic sanctions against nations resorting to war in disregard of the League's orders), which was regarded by the Senate as an abridgment of United States sovereignty. These two errors led to the defeat of the Treaty of Versailles in the Senate and kept the United States out of the League of Nations.

In March, 1920 the Treaty and the League Covenant were rejected, and America became isolationist.

Economic Isolationism

In 1920 an emergency high tariff bill was passed, which Wilson vetoed on the grounds that economic nationalism would endanger the peace. But after the Republican victory of 1920, first the Fordney-McCumber tariff and then the Smoot-Hawley tariff were passed, both of which raised duties to the highest they had ever been in American history.

The United States had become, as a result of the war, the creditor nation of the world, and she tended to ignore the mounting economic distress in Europe and demanded the payment of all war debts. As President Coolidge put it, "They hired the money, didn't they?"

THE GREAT DEPRESSION

Although American industry prospered as an aftermath of the war, agriculture suffered. Between 1920 and 1932 farm income declined from $15,500,000,000 to $5,500,000,000.

Never before had American society been so interested in making money. Sinclair Lewis' *Babbitt* was the symbol of the era. Yet much of the prosperity of the 1920's was specious. By one reckoning, in 1929 a family needed a minimal income of $2000 to buy basic necessities, but almost 60 percent of all American families earned less than $2000.

There are many causes for the Great Depression that struck the United States and the entire world in 1929, but in America two causes were fundamental:

A. Loss of confidence in the industrial growth and prosperity of the land, which was reflected in the collapse of the stock market.

B. The failure to find some way of distributing the wonders of mass production to the people who were making them. Such a small percentage of the profits of industry was finding its way into the pockets of the workers that the laboring man was unable to buy (except on time) the products of industry.

By the end of October, 1929 Americans had lost $15 billion on the stock market; by the end of that year the total reached $40 billion. By 1932 12 million people were unemployed in the United States, 5 thousand banks had crashed, and 32 thousand commercial businesses had failed. The national income declined from over $80 billion to $40 billion.

The New Deal

The Hoover administration did not take drastic action against the effects of the depression, although it did attempt to spend money on public projects, appropriating $300,000,000 for farm loans and lending $2 billion to industry, banks, insurance, railroads. But these measures did not alleviate the situation.

In 1930 the Democrats captured Congress, and in 1932 Franklin D. Roosevelt was elected President by a landslide victory with a popular majority of 7 million votes.

Government legislation associated with the New Deal was not new. Farm relief, conservation, labor legislation, trust regulation, even judicial reform had all been attempted before, and many of the laws were already on the statute books. The thing that made the New Deal new was not the laws themselves but the philosophy that stood behind them—the doctrine that the government can and should interfere in the affairs of individuals and the unrestricted economic laws of supply and demand in order to create a society in which all men would be able to profit. The paramount doctrine in the nineteenth century had been one of no government interference in the economic life of the country. By the 1930's this older view had been largely replaced by the doctrine of the welfare state, in which it was the responsibility of the government to restrict and direct the economy (especially finance) of the country; and poverty became the responsibility of the state, not of the individual.

Relief

The new administration immediately began loans to business, to housing projects, and to public works. Unemployment relief was the first problem tackled. By 1940 $16 billion had been spent on direct relief and $7 billion on public works. The Civil Conservation Corps provided hundreds of jobs; cultural sponsorship kept artists from starving; and public works and the Tennessee Valley Authority provided jobs for thousands.

The Farm Problem

Farm relief was finally achieved by payments to farmers who would devote part of their land to "soil-conserving crops." By 1939 farm incomes were double what they had been in 1932.

Banks

All banks were closed and then reopened under stricter supervision and with the government's guarantee of bank deposits.

Labor

The acts passed concerning labor were to have lasting effect on the American labor situation.

A. The Wagner Act of 1935 gave labor the right to collective bargaining and to union organization, and set up a Labor Relations Board to hear disputes.

B. In 1932 there were only 3,000,000 Americans in labor unions. Then, in 1937, a group within the A.F. of L. (American Federation of Labor) led by John L. Lewis formed the C.I.O. (the Congress of Industrial Organization), a union for the unskilled laboring man that was organized on the basis of entire industries and not individual crafts. By 1941 the C.I.O. had a membership of 5,000,000, whereas the A.F. of L. had 4,500,000 members. In 1955 these two unions were united and had a membership of 15,000,000.

C. The Fair Labor Standards Act of 1938 placed "a ceiling over hours" (a forty-hour week) and "a floor under wages" (a minimum wage of 40 cents per hour).

D. In 1935 a series of Social Security Acts were passed that provided unemployment insurance, aid to dependent mothers, and pensions for the aged.

Certain measures of the New Deal were declared unconstitutional—the NRA (the National Recovery Administration), which attempted to use trade associations to administer business codes and which little business found rigged to big business and which big business disliked, and the A.A.A. (the Agricultural Adjustment Act), which attempted to raise prices of farm staples by reducing acreage sown (in 1933 thousands of acres of crops were plowed under).

Canada

Canada suffered equally from the depression and was also hurt and irritated by the American tariff legislation against Canadian products in 1929. In 1930 she in turn passed the Dunning tariff, giving Great Britain preferential treatment.

During the depression the Liberal Government failed to provide relief for the unemployed, and the Conservatives came to power.

Relief
A. In 1930 $20,000,000 was voted for relief of the unemployed and another $21,000,000 for railroads.

B. Tariff duties were again increased, and in 1931 a tariff revision cut off two thirds of the goods previously imported from the United States. In 1932 preferential tariffs were agreed upon by members of the Commonwealth.

C. In 1934 came a series of acts regulating the prices of marketing and investing and shareholding, and the Bank of Canada was formed under Government supervision.

D. Social legislation was carried through in 1935. A wheat board was established, legislation against monopolies was passed, and the Employment and Social Insurance Act provided unemployment insurance, while the Limitation of Hours and Work Act provided an eight-hour day and a forty-eight-hour week. By 1936 Canada as well as the United States had achieved a form of welfare state.

Australia

As in all countries, the war brought an extension of the Federal Government's powers; in 1920 the Commonwealth Government was given authority to regulate state employees, and in 1927 it took over state debts. This meant that it could act when the depression hit.

Australia was quicker to recover from the depression, primarily because of the rising price of gold and wool after 1933.

New Zealand

New Zealand, on the other hand, suffered a heavy blow in 1930, for she was totally dependent upon primary products.

In 1935 the Labor Party pushed through a series of acts that in many cases reestablished rights that had been neglected following the war. The Reserve Bank was nationalized, a Primary Products Marketing Act guaranteed that the government would buy farm products at a set price, the States Advances Corporation Act regularized loans, the Industrial Conciliation and Arbitration Amendment Act reestablished compulsory arbitration of labor disputes, and the Government Railways Amendment Act put the railroads under government control. In 1936 the basic wage for a family of five was set at three pounds, sixteen shillings per week. Of all the democracies, New Zealand had gone farthest by 1939 in developing the welfare state.

WORLD WAR II

Canada, Australia, and New Zealand immediately pledged their support to Great Britain, but the United States' reaction was to pass strict neutrality legislation (1935–1937). This attitude was a result of disillusionment from the last war, fear of involvement, and a policy of peace at any price.

In 1940 Britain stood alone and Churchill announced that "we shall never surrender" and that if the Germans were to invade and conquer England "our Empire beyond the seas . . . would carry on the struggle, until, in God's good time, the New World, with all its power and might, steps forth to the rescue and liberation of the Old." The Americans' hatred of nazism in Germany; the realization that should England fall the United States would stand alone in a world dominated by fascism; and the efforts of F. D. Roosevelt to reeducate the American people and bring them out of isolationism led to a reevaluation and change in American policy.

Rearmament was hastily begun, and Roosevelt called for 50,000 planes to be built in 1940.

A joint board of defense was established with Canada.

Fifty old destroyers were given to Britain in exchange for leases on naval bases extending from Newfoundland to British Guiana.

In 1940 Wendell Willkie ran against Roosevelt, but both men stood irrevocably for the policy of aid to Britain.

Then at the end of 1940 came lend-lease, and in December, 1941 the United States entered the war.

The United States provided 16 million men, and all records of production were broken. In 1942 Roosevelt called for 45,000 tanks, 8 million tons of shipping, and 60,000 new planes (48,000 were built). In 1943 the United States built 85,930 planes and

19,396,000 tons of new shipping, and in the last year of the war 300,000 planes and 55,000,000 tons of shipping. The war cost the United States $350,000,000,000 ($50,000,000,000 of which went to lend-lease). At her peak strength during the war there were 12,300,000 men fighting, and 291,557 battle deaths.

Canada's peak strength was 780,000, with 37,476 battle deaths; Australia's 680,000, with 23,365 battle deaths; and New Zealand's 157,000, with 10,033 battle deaths.

THE UNITED STATES AND CANADA AS WORLD POWERS

Most of North America's prewar history is directly con-.cerned with European or Russian affairs and has been explained elsewhere in this outline.

The United Nations

The United Nations, a creation of Roosevelt and Secretary of State Hull, came into being in 1945, and both the United States and Canada pledged their support. The new organization was considerably stronger than the old League but still faced many problems. Nevertheless, action was taken in Korea, in the Congo, and in the Middle East with some success, and both the United States and Canada provided troops.

The Cold War

The United States took a strong international stand immediately after the war. The Marshall Plan appropriated $12,000,-000,000 for European recovery; between 1947 and 1950, thanks to the Truman Doctrine, $660,000,000 went to Greece and Turkey. In 1949 NATO was formed, and by 1954 $400,000,000 had been spent by the Point Four Program to bring modern medicine and technology to underdeveloped areas.

Then, in 1950, came the Korean War. Both the United States and Canada sent troops, and United States casualties were higher than in any war except the Civil War and World War II.

But the policy of containment (keeping Communism contained to the area it had acquired after the war) had at least partially succeeded.

United States policy in China, however, was a failure: $2,000,000,000 was spent on the shaky and corrupt regime of Chiang Kai-shek before 1949. The Marshall Mission failed to bring peace. Chiang fled the country before the war was over, yet the United States pledged her support to Chiang's government on Formosa and refused to recognize the Communist government of Mao Tse-tung. This policy has led her into difficulties with her allies, certain of whom recognize China and trade with her, and has also caused a serious military and moral question of whether to protect the offshore islands.

On November 1, 1952 the first hydrogen bomb was successfully exploded and a new age was ushered in—an age in which both Canada and the United States tried desperately to attain some kind of atomic test ban, and which in 1963 was in part achieved by the signing of a treaty with the U.S.S.R.

On October 4, 1957 the Russian Sputnik I ushered in the Space Age, and the space race with the Soviet Union began. Despite a slow start, the United States and Russia are today (1966) about equal in their space achievements.

The Presidents of the United States
1917 to the Present

President	Inaugurated	Party
28th—Woodrow Wilson	1913	Democrat
29th—Warren G. Harding	1921	Republican
30th—Calvin Coolidge	1923	Republican
31st—Herbert C. Hoover	1929	Republican
32nd—Franklin D. Roosevelt	1933	Democrat
33rd—Harry S. Truman	1945	Democrat
34th—Dwight D. Eisenhower	1953	Republican
35th—John F. Kennedy	1961	Democrat
36th—Lyndon B. Johnson	1963	Democrat

The Social and Economic Growth of Canada and the United States—the Affluent Society

In area Canada is the second largest country in the world and immensely wealthy in undeveloped resources, but she has a population of only 18,900,000. The United States' population, on the other hand, is 186,847,000. Together the North American countries are the richest in the world.

In 1945 it was reported that the American standard of living was three times as high as an Englishman's, six times as high as an Italian's, and forty times as high as an Indonesian's. In the United States in 1960 the average income of a family before taxes was $6250 against $5290 in 1947. The United States and Canada have 22.6 percent of the world's food but only 7.5 percent of the world's population. The United States' Gross National Product in 1963 was $554.9 billion, in contrast to that of the Common Market, which was $222.7 billion.

In 1961 the United States exports and imports (in millions of dollars) were 5100.2 exported to Canada and 4634.3 imported from her; 6440.4 exported to Europe and 4149.8 imported from her; 2229.3 exported to South America and 2360.3 imported from her.

The most important social development in the United States since 1945 was the Supreme Court's decision in 1954 that stated that racial segregation must end. Most of the nation's recent domestic interest and much of its legislation has been devoted to the problem of segregation and to an effort to achieve a reasonable degree of equality between Negro and white in education, working conditions, and economic opportunity. These aims were incorporated into the Civil Rights Act of July 1964.

On November 22, 1963 President Kennedy was assassinated, presumably by Lee Harvey Oswald. (Kennedy was the fourth president to be killed in office; the others were Lincoln, Garfield, and McKinley.) Within thirty minutes of his death Vice President Lyndon Johnson was sworn in as the thirty-sixth President of the United States.

A. In November of 1965 Lyndon Johnson was elected President in his own right in a smashing victory in which he received 61.4 percent of the vote.

B. The Johnson administration has inaugurated the "Great Society," a concerted war on poverty, in an effort to improve the standard of living of the bottom fourth of the nation's population. So far the government has passed

1) The $6 billion-a-year Medicare bill.
2) The $1.3 billion aid-to-education bill.

Canada has grown and prospered greatly since World War II. She is the largest exporter of nonferrous metals, the largest producer of nickel and asbestos, the second in cobalt and gold, the third in silver and lead, and the fourth in copper and iron. In 1963 her population stood at 18.9 million. Prosperity has been accompanied by a stable two-party system—the Conservatives and the Liberals (along with a number of splinter groups).

CANADIAN PRIME MINISTERS SINCE 1921

1921–1926	W. L. MacKenzie King	Liberal
1926	Arthur Meighen	Conservative
1926–1930	W. L. MacKenzie King	Liberal
1930–1935	Richard B. Bennett	Conservative
1935–1948	W. L. MacKenzie King	Liberal
1948–1957	Louis S. St. Laurent	Liberal
1957–1963	John Diefenbaker	Conservative
1963–	Lester Pearson	Liberal

Politically, Canada appears to be an exception to an almost universal rule: she is a federal state moving in the direction of decentralization.

PROBLEMS OF CANADA

1) Growing pains: Canada is today, on a small scale, the melting pot of the world and has the potential to become one of the giant states.

2) Fear of the U.S.A.: The United States is the greatest consumer of Canadian exports (59 percent, against the U.K.'s 15

percent) and the greatest supplier of her imports (69 percent, against the U.K.'s 9 percent).

3) Separatism: Agitation for varying degrees of autonomy (even independence) continues in the province of Quebec, which is 80 percent French-speaking.

Russian Civilization

ANCIENT AND CLASSICAL CIVILIZATIONS
1000 B.C.–500 A.D.

The civilization of Russia is young compared with that of China, India, the Middle East, and Europe. Consequently, there is no ancient and very little classical history. The history of Russia is usually considered to begin in the ninth century A.D. with the wave of Viking migrations and conquests that swept over all of Europe including Russia and the Mediterranean area. The history of Russia can just as easily be dated about 1000 B.C., when Slavic tribes moved in from central Asia; but very little is known about these peoples until 650 A.D.

THE SLAVIC MIGRATIONS

The Slavic peoples moved from the foothills of the Carpathian Mountains to the fertile western part of the Eurasian plain. By the eighth and ninth centuries B.C. they had dispersed through the Dnieper River Valley as far north as Novgorod and as far south as Kiev.

The Slavs were tribal and had no central organization. Agriculture was the basic economic occupation, and all property was held in common. Their religious concepts resembled those of the early Indo-European peoples.

The Khazars

The first attempt to unify the land was made by the Khazars. They were essentially a trading empire in the Kiev area. Accord-

ing to most authorities they followed the Jewish faith and were
peace-loving people, but in 737 A.D. they were scattered and defeated by constant Arab invasions.

MEDIEVAL CIVILIZATION 500 A.D.–1500 A.D.

*The medieval era of Russian history must be regarded as
Russia's first period of recorded history. The age witnessed
the migrations, invasions, and settlements (in the city of Kiev) of
the Vikings and the Mongols (in Sarai). This period is historically
important for the penetration of Byzantine influence and the
foundation of the Russian Orthodox faith, as well as the development of a sense of unity among the tribes of Slavic background.*

THE KIEV PERIOD AND THE INTRODUCTION OF BYZANTINE CULTURE AND THE GREEK ORTHODOX FAITH 878–1237

The Varangians

Because the western Eurasian plain was exposed to constant
Arab invasions, the Slavs turned to the Varangians (or Vikings)
for aid and protection. According to legend Rurik, king of the
Vikings, was called upon for help in 862 A.D. The protectors soon
turned into conquerors, and it was under the leadership of Oleg,
who succeeded Rurik at Novgorod, that Kiev was conquered in
879. Through this period of Varangian rule, however, there was
no Russian state, but the name Russia itself was of Swedish-
Viking origin.

Christianity and Vladimir

Vladimir (known later as Vladimir the Saint), who won the
throne of Kiev in 977 by murdering his older brother, was converted to Eastern Christianity in 988 after having explored all
the other major faiths. He seems to have chosen Christianity not

because of its theology but because of the splendor and beauty of its churches. (This concern with the ornamental elements of religion was to remain a characteristic of the Russian Orthodox faith.)

In 990 Vladimir was allowed to marry a Byzantine princess in return for protecting the Byzantine Emperor, thus making the ties with the Eastern world stronger.

For the masses, converted by the sword, Christian ritual was only a thin coating on top of deep pagan superstition.

The Characteristics and Effects of Contact with Byzantium and the Greek Orthodox Faith

Though no Russian state was created during this era, a degree of unity was achieved through the introduction of Christianity and of Byzantine civil law.

Church Slavonic became the language of the church in Russia, and during this period a native literature evolved, but the use of the vernacular narrowed Russia's intellectual horizons, for it "closed the door in Russia upon Greek culture."

The Collapse of Kiev

With the death of Yaroslav the Wise (1019–1054) any form of centralized state ruled from Kiev came to an end, for he divided the land among his five sons. The growing number of Russian princes struggling for control of land, along with a number of raids by nomads from the east, further weakened the city. In one year there were 64 principalities, 293 princes, and 83 civil wars.

Kiev lost its economic significance once the Mediterranean Sea was opened for trade by the Crusades, and her trade with Constantinople was blocked by nomadic invasions along the shores of the Black Sea.

Novgorod in the north took the place of Kiev as the main center of trade in Russia.

THE SARAI PERIOD AND MONGOL DOMINATION 1237–1472

The Mongol Invasions

In 1237 Batu Khan, the grandson of Genghis Khan, and his Golden Horde invaded Russia and by 1240 had captured most of the great Russian cities. Only Novgorod remained an independent area.

Results of Two Centuries of Mongol Rule

The Mongol onslaught was devastating. Towns and settlements were burned (it took eight centuries for the Russian city population to recover), captives were slaughtered, and a huge tribute was exacted. Skilled craftsmen were taken to the Mongol capital at Sarai and some were eliminated altogether. Industry and commerce were extinguished. Russia was further isolated from Western Europe and unity was shattered. The fortunes of the peasants were worsened and they fell further and further into debt.

The Mongol Rule Led to the Rise of Russian Autocracy

A. The Mongol state was founded upon the principle of universal service and submission to the ruler. Many of the forms of despotism in the government of the czars were inherited from the Mongols.

B. The Sarai government treated city and country alike (the Kievan period had not), thus strengthening the basis for common subordination of all subjects to the monarch.

C. An efficient system of taxation, which czars were later able to use to their advantage, was introduced.

The Mongols' toleration of religion permitted the church to grow richer and more powerful. After the devastation of Kiev, the metropolitan (bishop of the Eastern church) moved to Moscow. This was later of significance in the rise to importance of the Muscovy state.

Ivan Kalita (Ivan I)   1322–1341

From the time of Ivan Kalita (Moneybags), the title of sovereign prince of Russia was held by the princes of Moscow. In 1326 the seat of the metropolitan was moved from Vladimir (originally it had been in Kiev) to Moscow, and in 1328 Ivan was made responsible for the collection of tribute for the Mongols. These two events gave the princes of Moscow power to extend their influence and their territory.

The Successors of Ivan

> Simeon the Proud (1341–1353)
> Ivan the Red (1353–1359)
> Dmitry of the Don (1359–1389)
> Vasily (1389–1425)
> Vasily II, the Dark (1425–1462)

Under the successors of Ivan Moscow continued to grow. Each prince added new lands, increased the wealth of the principality, and strengthened the position of Moscow vis-à-vis Sarai. By 1400 Russia comprised approximately a 250-mile radius of land around Moscow.

The War Against the Mongols

Divisions within the ranks of the Golden Horde brought opportunities to Moscow. In 1378 the Russians won victories at Vozha River and in 1380 at Kulikovo, but in 1408 Moscow was ravaged by the Tartar army. During the reign of Vasily II (1425–1462), the Golden Horde suffered as Tamerlane advanced and Mongol centralized authority collapsed. However, it was not until Ivan IV's reign that the remnants of Tartar power were driven from Russia. In 1480 Ivan's father had defied the Golden Horde by refusing to pay tribute, and in 1552 Ivan IV conquered Kazan and four years later Astrakhan. In 1583–1584 the Siberian Khan was defeated.

MODERN CIVILIZATION   1500 to the Present

RUSSIAN HISTORY   1462–1703

The modern period begins in 1462 with the growth of the Muscovy state and the power and influence of Ivan III and his descendants. The capital of Russia became Moscow, and it was during this era that Russia developed many of the characteristics that have lasted to the present day. The concept of czardom evolved, and the centralization of government in the person of a despot was established. The church was subordinated to the state; the peasant was tied to the land; the middle class lost all its power and influence and became a tool of the government; and the imperialistic expansion of Russia began. It should also be remembered that this period corresponded in time with the Renaissance in Europe, and in contrast Muscovy was uncultured, illiterate, and backward. The same year (1645) that Charles I of England was defeated by parliamentary forces, serfdom was formally acknowledged in Russia.

The Czars of Russia   1462–1689
(The most important are starred.)

*Ivan III, the Great (1462–1505)
Known for his consolidation of power and territorial acquisition, Ivan married the orphan niece of the last of the Byzantine emperors, thus establishing his claim to be Czar of Russia.

*Vasily III (1505–1533)
Vasily, son of Ivan III, extended the work of his father. When he died he left two children by his second wife. The eldest (aged three) became Ivan IV.

*Ivan IV, the Terrible (1533-1584)

Ivan IV is known for his cruelty and love of torture, his paranoic cunning, and his establishment of full autocracy in Russia. Two years before his death he struck his eldest son with an iron staff and killed him. Fedor, the second child of his first wife, Anastasia Romanov, was left to rule.

Fedor (1584-1598)

Fedor was feebleminded and inherited an empire seething with discontent, and power inevitably fell to men behind the throne, first Nikita Romanov and then Boris Godunov.

Boris Godunov (1598-1605)

Friend of Ivan IV, he was the power behind the throne under Fedor and was finally "elected" czar.

Dmitry—Vasily—Dmitry (The Time of Troubles 1605-1613)

When Fedor died in 1598, the line of princes was extinguished, for his brother Dmitry had died in 1591 under circumstances not unlike the English Little Princes in the Tower. The results were also similar, for many fictitious Dmitrys appeared throughout the period, 1598-1613. When Boris died in 1605, Russia fell apart. The crown went from one pretender to another, and the Russian country was in constant revolt.

Michael Romanov (1613-1645)

Elected as a compromise candidate, he was not a strong czar, and his true importance is that he was the father of a line that ruled Russia until 1917.

Alexis (1645-1676)

Alexis was somewhat stronger than his father, Michael, but generally both Romanovs were mediocre men.

Fedor (1676-1682)

Peter and Ivan under Regency of Sophia (1682-1689)

Alexis left two sons, Fedor and Ivan, by his first wife and one, Peter, by his second wife. Both Fedor and Ivan were sickly children. Fedor died six years after he became Czar. Sophia,

Ivan's sister, then ruled as regent over the dual czardom of Ivan and Peter. (Peter, however, lived on the outskirts of Moscow with his mother, while Ivan lived with his sister in the Kremlin.)

The Establishment of the Russian State   1462–1703

Ivan III, Vasily III, and Ivan IV

A. Ivan III and his son, Vasily III, referred to themselves as "czar and autocrat by the grace of God of all Russia." In 1547 Ivan IV was officially proclaimed Czar. The Russian state was established during the reigns of these three princes of Moscow. The Tartars were driven from the land; the separate, independent principalities were gathered in; and government was centralized in the person of the czar. The era dominated by the princely family had ended, and the Russian national state was born.

B. Ivan III and Vasily III ruled Russia in cooperation with the boyarskaya duma, a council of hereditary landed aristocrats (boyars). Although this system worked fairly well under Ivan the Great (III), the grand prince of Moscow more and more came into conflict with the ancient aristocracy. It was Ivan the Terrible (IV) who was to make himself supreme autocrat in Russia by destroying the power of the aristocracy.

1) He struck at the influence of the boyars by dividing Russia into two parts, half controlled (in theory) by the boyar councils and half controlled directly by a new body, the Oprichnina, a council of one thousand men personally responsible to the czar. The Oprichniks' main task was to destroy those who represented a challenge to Ivan's power, specifically the boyar class (although all classes were subject to the terror).

2) The boyars lost their special privileges, such as the right to transfer allegiance to another prince and their hereditary right to their lands. The nobles became merely servants of the state, bound to act as officials for the prince of Moscow, and land ownership was made contingent upon loyalty and allegiance to the czar. In effect, a new landlord class was created.

3) Once the boyars were eliminated there was nothing in

Russia to compete with the czar's authority, although the church did offer momentary resistance.

The Time of Troubles and the Zemsky Sobor

A. Ivan IV's government was totally dependent upon the personality of the czar, and when Ivan died in 1584, having killed the son he had named as successor and leaving his feebleminded son Fedor and the infant Dmitry (the son of a dubious seventh marriage), he bequeathed to Russia years of anarchy and civil war. The real Dmitry was killed, and with Fedor's death in 1598 the line of succession ended and the Russian state fell apart. By 1611 the Poles controlled the southwest including Moscow and Smolensk, and the Swedes had the northwest. There was no government, no leadership, and the land was devastated.

B. The results of fifteen years of chaos were disastrous. The boyars were extinct as a class, the peasant had no choice but to sink further and further into the clutches of the gentry, and the country was on the brink of economic collapse.

C. In 1612 the assembly of the land, the Zemsky Sobor, representing all classes, met and elected Michael Romanov czar. Although the assembly of the people had brought the Romanovs to power, the idea of a representative government never took hold.

1) It was never intended that the assembly should assume permanent powers.

2) The assembly never developed into an independently functioning body because of lack of unity. Consequently, the Zemsky Sobor was not capable of opposing the will of the supreme autocrat and was called upon only when the czar wished ratification of a policy.

3) The Romanovs were new rulers, but they continued the policy of forcing everyone to serve the state.

The Russian Orthodox Church and Its Conflict with the State

The Russian Orthodox Church, from the moment of its conception, was linked with the power of the state. During the sixteenth and seventeenth centuries it became subordinate to the state, and in the following centuries it deteriorated into a mere tool of the czar.

The Moscow Patriarchate

The creation of the Moscow patriarchate (archbishopric) was Boris Godunov's achievement in 1589. It was the patriarch Job who assisted in Boris' election as czar. The patriarchate, from its creation, was therefore closely allied with the state.

Nikon

A. Within the ranks of the clergy there was a desire to reform the Russian church by drawing it into closer unity with the Eastern (Greek Orthodox) church. In 1652 Nikon was elected Russian patriarch and began the revision of the service books. The church split over the issue; the old believers (schismatics) refused to accept the reforms. Nikon triumphed with the aid of the state, but in doing so he forecast the destruction of the independent power of the church and its subordination to the state.

B. With ambition similar to that of the great Western ecclesiastics, Nikon attempted to make the church stronger than the state. He was finally deposed and exiled. The effect of his efforts was to precipitate the decline of the power of the church and to identify religious dissent with movements against the government's authority.

C. No other patriarch in Russian history ever again dared challenge the authority of the state in secular matters.

The Peasant and Serfdom

Once an independent farmer, the peasant became a tenant during the fourteenth century primarily because he had been driven into debt by Mongol taxation and felt the need for protection. At first he was free to move, although there were agreements among landowners not to accept him. By the middle of the fifteenth century the peasant could leave the land only during a two-week period before and after St. George's Day (November

26). Vasily II, however, forbade the peasants on certain monastic estates to move at all.

Although serfdom did not become official until 1645, the peasant was in bondage much earlier. As a tenant, he soon fell further into debt, since he was paying rates of interest as high as 33 percent. Those who were not in financial bondage to a lord were nevertheless subject to fines for leaving the land and were forced to pay annual rent amounting to one quarter of the capital value of their homestead, which meant they could not afford to leave their land either.

In 1645, under Alexis, a new legal code divided the people into rigid classes. Townspeople were bound to the towns, the church and the nobility were declared closed classes, and most peasants were bound to the land by law. Thus the condition of serfdom that had existed for so long was made official.

The landlord exercised judicial, fiscal, social, and legal authority over his serfs, but the peasant did not accept his fate submissively. All Russian history from this period on is characterized by peasant uprisings. In 1650 a rebellion raged in Pokov; during the plague of 1655 constant revolts occurred in the central regions of Russia; in 1662 there was revolution in Moscow and seven thousand were executed; and finally, in 1670 one of the most famous rebellions of all took place. This uprising, led by Stenka Razin (whose ultimate fate was torture and quartering alive), was symptomatic of peasant dissatisfaction and anarchy.

The Imperialistic Expansion of Russia

Ivan III and Vasily III

A. The extent of Moscow-controlled lands was trebled during the reign of Ivan the Great (1462–1505). This was accomplished by both war and diplomacy. By 1489 the northeast was under Muscovy domination, but the campaigns in the west were less successful. Ivan III was not militarily strong enough to challenge Poland-Lithuania.

B. Control of the prosperous city of Novgorod and its lands

was one of Ivan's objectives. Under his son the *veche* bell, symbol of Novgorod's independence, was removed to Moscow, and leading families were exiled.

Ivan IV

Ivan defeated the last remnants of the Golden Horde by 1556. The conquest of Kazan opened up for colonization the fertile land of the middle Volga. Western Siberia was claimed in 1584, but in the west Ivan lost a twenty-year war against Sweden and Poland-Lithuania.

The Time of Troubles and the Romanovs

A. During the time of troubles (1605–1613) Russia lost much of her newly acquired land, and during the reign of the first Romanov she remained militarily weak and on the defensive. She did expand eastward across Siberia, however, and southward into the Amur basin. (This led to conflict with China.)

B. It was not until Alexis' rule (1645–1676) that Russia again went on the offensive. She moved against Poland's control of the Lower Dnieper in 1649, and in 1667 the Ukraine was split by the truce of Andrusovo. The right bank of the Dnieper (except Kiev) was to remain Polish, and Moscow gained the left bank and Kiev (for a two-year period only, according to the treaty, but in actual fact Poland never succeeded in regaining control). Russia had not controlled this part of the Ukraine since the Mongol invasions of the thirteenth century.

1703–1917

This era's most outstanding characteristic was contact with, influence from, and reaction to the West. The period commences when Peter the Great moved his capital to St. Petersburg on the Baltic, which he called his window to the West because he hoped it would be the port into which would flow Western ideas and culture. Beginning with this first superficial attempt at westernization, the period ends with the greatest manifestation of Western influence—the Russian Revolution.

The Czars of Russia   1689–1917
(The most important are starred.)

*Peter I, the Great (1689–1725)

The fourteenth child of Alexis, at the age of seventeen Peter became czar by military coup, although his mother controlled the reins of government until her death in 1694 and Ivan (his half brother) was nominal co-czar until his death in 1696. As cruel as Ivan IV (he put his own son Alexis to death by torture and executed nearly two thousand during the revolt of the Streltsy), as autocratic as any of the previous czars of Russia, Peter had one characteristic that made him different from his ancestors: he was aware of the West. Educated by foreigners in the German suburb of Moscow where he lived as a youth, he became acquainted with western techniques; and here he played at war with children who were later to form the nucleus of his army and navy. War, expansion, and attempted westernization were the themes of Peter's reign.

Catherine I (1725–1727), Widow of Peter I

When Peter I died, the only male Romanov who could claim the throne was his grandson Peter, son of Alexis. However, it was Peter's palace guards who were to determine policy until 1801, and they decided that Peter's widow, the Baltic servant girl Catherine I, should rule.

Peter II (1727–1730), Grandson of Peter I
Died of smallpox at the age of 15.

Anna (1730–1740), Daughter of Peter's Half Brother, Ivan

Ivan VI (1740–1741), Son of Anna's Niece
The newborn boy reigned for a year and was then deposed.

Elizabeth (1741–1762), Daughter of Peter I and Catherine I

Peter III (1762), Son of Elizabeth's Sister, Anna

*Catherine II, the Great (1762–1796), Wife of Peter III

A palace revolt put Catherine, a petty German princess who had married Peter III in 1745, on the throne of Russia. Peter died a few days later in a futile fight with his captors, and Catherine announced that her husband had died of a hemorrhage.

Paul (1796–1801)

The son of Catherine the Great and a dubious father (possibly her lover, Saltykov, or possibly Peter III, whom Paul resembled in the instability of his character) was mistreated by his mother, and he spent most of his reign trying to undo everything she had done.

*Alexander I, the Great (1801–1825)

Paul was assassinated during a palace revolution and was succeeded by his son. Alexander I was called "the sphinx" by Napoleon, and with good reason, for his motivations were never clear nor his actions consistent. He wavered between a desire for reform and a fear of revolution.

Nicholas I (1825–1855)

When Alexander the Great died at the age of forty-eight, he left two brothers. Constantine, the elder, had had a common law second marriage, and therefore Alexander had left a manifesto naming Nicholas, a younger brother, czar. It was not until almost a month after Alexander's death that Nicholas agreed to rule. His reign witnessed an intensification of the police state, censorship, and tyranny.

*Alexander II (1855–1881), Son of Nicholas I

Although famous for his "liberation" of the serfs, Alexander II was the friend and ally of the nobility and of conservatism.

*Alexander III (1881–1894)

Alexander II was assassinated, and this had a marked effect on his son's personality and political attitude. Since reform had ended with murder and treason, he reasoned that it was time to undo what his father had accomplished and set the clock back to the good old days before 1861.

Nicholas II (1894–1917)

Alexander III was a strong enough czar to halt the revolutionary tide, but the last Romanov and the last czar of Russia,

Nicholas II, only inherited from his father the principle of autocracy, not the ability to maintain it.

The Growth of Autocracy and the Russian State

Peter the Great strengthened autocracy by further subjugating the church, the nobility, and the serfs to the will of the sovereign. Everyone owed service to the government and anyone who resisted faced brutal punishment. Service, in any form, was demanded for life, and the Table of Ranks established a hierarchy of fourteen grades based on merit. If a man achieved the eighth rank, he was allowed the privileges of a nobleman, owning serfs and property. The gentry were educated at the command of the czar. It was not until Peter III's reign (1762) that a manifesto was proclaimed emancipating the nobility from military, administrative, and economic obligations to the state.

After Peter the Great's death the power of the state actually rested in the hands of his personal guards, and they had the ability to make and unmake czars. From 1725 to 1762 six rulers were created and deposed. Even Catherine II, although she restored political stability, owed her supremacy to them.

Despite Catherine II's liberalism, she was as autocratic as any of the czars of Russia, and she strengthened the hold of the despot over the lives of her people. By the end of her reign, landlords had more control over their serfs, the peasant's bondage was extended, literary censorship had begun, and minorities were forced to conform to the Russian mold. Paul attempted to amend Catherine's charter of the nobility by dissolving their assemblies and once again subjecting them to corporal punishment. Further than this he dared not go, but he succeeded in alienating the mainstay of autocracy, and in March 23, 1801 he was strangled by his guards, and his son Alexander (who was involved in the plot) was placed on the throne.

Alexander I, Nicholas I, Alexander II, Alexander III, and Nicholas II, all attempted to maintain autocracy and the power of the despot, with varying degrees of success. In 1864 Alexander II did reconstruct the system of local self-government by issuing the Zemstvo law, giving considerable freedom in local law, education, and taxation. Nevertheless the principle of unqualified absolutism remained, and after an attempted assassination Alexander quickly changed this policy. In 1905 Nicholas II was forced by revolution to grant a constituent assembly, but it was allowed very little control over Russian affairs.

The Russian Orthodox Church

The church as an independent power in Russia no longer existed after the 1700's. First Peter the Great outraged religious orthodoxy by cutting all noblemen's beards (symbols of piety), and then he humbled it by abolishing the office of Patriarch in 1721 and creating in its stead the Holy Synod, a council of ecclesiastical members subject to a layman, an overprocurator, who was in turn subject to the will of the czar. This was the final step in ensuring that the church would be identified with the autocrat's wishes. (It also ensured that the church would suffer the same fate as the monarchy in 1917.) The church could no longer oppose the Czar's reforms, and Peter now had control of its wealth.

The Peasant and Serfdom

The Extension of Serfdom
PETER THE GREAT

A. The fate of the peasant was to finance the czar's schemes of westernization and war. Serfdom was tightly enforced, and the law was extended to new classes of free peasants. Taxes were levied on all males, and thus distinctions among different categories of bondsmen were obliterated. The serf laborers in mines and factories suffered the most. The building of St. Petersburg in 1721 is the classic example: thousands of lives were sacrificed to clear the swamps and build the parks, fountains, cathedrals, and palaces.

B. Between 1704 and 1711 there were three peasant revolts,

but, as in most agrarian revolutions, they failed because they lacked program, unity, and organization. (Compare this with England in 1381 and China up to 1857.)

CATHERINE THE GREAT

Catherine's liberalism in no way extended to the peasant. It stopped short with affairs of state and was totally extinguished by the French Revolution and the Russian peasant revolt of 1773–1774.

A. Serfdom was further extended under the German Czarina: by 1783 the whole of the Ukraine was subjected to it. The peasants of the Don country and most of the Caucasus were no longer free either.

B. Of a total population of 36 million, 34 million were peasants, of whom 20 million were serfs on private estates and 14 million were state or crown land peasants (legally not serfs but certainly in bondage). On the majority of private estates there were at least one hundred serfs, and usually the figure was closer to one thousand.

C. In 1767 an imperial decree prohibited complaint by a serf against his master. There was no redress except revolution.

The Pugachev Rebellion 1773–1774

A. Of all peasant uprisings in Russian history perhaps the Pugachev rebellion was the most important, for it was to leave a scar that no reform healed. The suppression of the rebellion left behind a desire for revenge; peasants did not soon forget the punitive measures of Catherine II.

B. Led by the revolutionary leader Emelian Pugachev, peasant serfs, serfs in the mines of the Urals, minorities opposed to russification, and religious dissenters wreaked havoc for a year in the countryside of Russia. Landlords were tortured, farms were burned, officials and priests were hanged. Even the regular detachments sent to put down the revolt turned against their officers and slaughtered them. But in 1774, with carefully picked troops, Catherine had her revenge. The revolt was crushed, and Pugachev himself was carried off to Moscow in an iron cage and executed.

The "Emancipation" of the Serfs 1861

A. Alexander I

Despite his liberal tendencies, Alexander made no attempt to emancipate the serf. In 1801, however, he extended the right to own land to all free classes and to state peasants. In 1802 he passed a law granting serfs the right to purchase land from their masters (of course this was rare), and he also banned the sale of serfs on the open market.

B. During Nicholas I's reign some peasant reforms were attempted, but they had very little effect. There were 556 peasant uprisings during his rule.

C. Alexander II, after the humiliation of the Crimean War, recognized the need to reform and in 1856 announced that "It is better to abolish serfdom from above than wait until it begins to abolish itself from below." But the act that came in 1861 was too little and too late. Moreover it was done more for military than humanitarian reasons.

D. The Terms of the Emancipation Act 1861

The peasant was allowed to purchase land from his landlord on credit supplied by the government and repaid over a period of forty-nine years.

E. The Results of Emancipation

1) The land was overvalued and peasant holdings were of uneconomic size. Nor did the land really become the peasant's private property. It was transferred from the landlord to the village commune, which became responsible for the collection of payments due the government for the land and became in fact the peasant's master.

2) The peasant was now free but not equal. He continued to pay a poll tax, he alone was subject to corporal punishment, and he was bound to the commune by an internal passport system whereby written permission was necessary before a peasant could move. (Internal passports are now used by the Soviet Government.)

The Influence of the West—Liberalism and Revolutionary Russia

Liberalism and revolution in Russia went hand in hand with the influence of Western culture and ideas, and cannot be separated.

Borrowing from the West

Peter the Great brought the Russian state into contact with the West, but it was superficial contact from the beginning. His interest was primarily in Western military might, not Western culture and thought, and piecemeal innovations were forced upon the Russian people.

A. In 1697 Peter, in the company of two hundred nobles went abroad to study shipbuilding and Western techniques. He returned to Russia and promptly reorganized the military and created a navy.

B. In order to equip his new army and navy, the Czar expanded small mills and foundries, laying the foundations of Russia's industrial development in the Urals and Central Russia. Foreign technicians, engineers, and teachers were brought to Russia to train and advise. But the continuation and strengthening of the bonds of serfdom along with the commanding economic leadership of the nobility were obstacles to further westernization of the Russian economy.

C. Fundamentally the reforms under Peter were concerned with the expansion of Russian power, although he did find time to reduce the alphabet to thirty-six letters, create a new calendar beginning with January 1 instead of September 1, and sponsor the first newspaper.

D. The superficial quality of Peter's reforms, however, was revealed when the Czar decreed that everyone should wear European dress and shave their barbarian beards. This he felt would make the Russians equal to the West. Even Peter's educational reforms indicate that he failed to understand the basis of the superiority of the West: he in no way encouraged intellectual training—only specific technical objectives.

The Enlightenment

Although Catherine the Great is traditionally grouped with the enlightened despots of Europe such as Joseph II of Austria and Frederick the Great of Prussia, her claim is somewhat dubious. Although the cultural and court life of Russia were brilliant and her armies conquered the northern shores of the Black Sea and the nobility spoke French and read Voltaire, Catherine did nothing to improve the lot of the majority of her people, and her reforms remained largely on paper. As R. D. Charques in his *A Short History of Russia* said, "Enlightenment in Catherine was, indeed, not much deeper than her vanity; despotism, on the other hand, was implicit in her ambition."

A. In 1766 Catherine summoned a Legislative Commission to prepare a new codification of the laws. After a year and a half of work an impressive liberal document was produced—but that was all, and when war broke out with Turkey the Commission was disbanded. The Commission, however, did bring to the attention of the Czarina local abuses and corruption, which Catherine remedied in part by reforming provincial governments.

B. In 1785 Catherine's charter of the nobility reinforced the privileges that they had won since Peter the Great's death. The aristocracy was exempt from service, taxation, loss of rank, and corporal punishment. Authority in local government was reserved for them.

The First Liberal Czar

A. Educated in the court of the "enlightenment" by his grandmother, Catherine II, and his republican Swiss tutor, La Harpe, Alexander I was perhaps the only true liberal to sit on the throne of Russia. During the first years of his reign he restored civil rights to thousands, closed down the secret political police, granted permission for students to travel abroad, and allowed the importation of foreign books. He attempted to grant certain freedoms to the serfs but never dared emancipation.

B. In 1809 Michael Speransky was commissioned by the Czar to devise a system of constitutional government. The draft that was drawn up was a remarkable piece of work but remained on paper only. A duma, or parliament, was to be created for each district. On the top of the local institutions was to be an elective duma for the entire country and a state council of advisers appointed by the crown. (Ironically, the Bolsheviks adopted this as their system of representation by soviets.) Speransky, of course, was a threat to bureaucratic vested interests, and he was accused of treasonable relations with France and exiled in 1812.

c. Although Alexander did fulfill his liberal promises in foreign parts, a period of reaction set in in 1812 when war broke out against Napoleonic France, and most of the reforms he had made were undone.

1) Military colonies, perhaps the most hated feature of his entire reign, were established in 1816. Nearly 500,000 local state peasants were made exempt from taxation and were trained for military service in colonies where every aspect of their life was dictated and regimented (not unlike the communes in China).

2) Illiberalism in education was also manifest. Dangerous thoughts were rooted out of the classrooms by purging university faculties and by strict censorship of materials, but this came too late, and it was among the group of educated lower nobility that disturbing and unorthodox ideas were spreading.

The Decembrist Revolt December 14, 1825

A. The revolt led by a secret society of the young educated lower nobility and junior officers of the guard who had served in the army of occupation in France during the Napoleonic wars (less than three hundred people) was in one sense the last of the palace revolutions, but, more important, it was the beginning of a new revolutionary tradition in Russia. It was a rebellion not only to overthrow the Czar but also to establish a more representative government.

B. Paul Pestel, one of the influential leaders, sought revolution and a republic, murder of the Czar, and a temporary dictatorship (compare with Lenin).

c. The revolt failed because of lack of planning and initiative; 120 were brought to trial and thirty-six condemned to death; five were actually executed.

Nicholas I, Alexander III, and Reaction

A. The Decembrist Revolt was to have a definite influence on the internal policy of Nicholas I. As he declared, "a revolution stands on the threshold of Russia, but I swear it will never enter Russia while my breath lasts." His purpose, he said, was to retard the development of Russia by fifty years.

B. Under Nicholas I the secret police were allowed to rule Russia, disciplined conformity was required of all subjects, secondary and higher education were restricted to the nobility, in 1835 the universities were brought under control, and in 1848 the number of students in all fields except theology and medicine was reduced. Censorship was strictly enforced (and yet Russian literature was at its height).

C. Western influence manifested itself in the quasi-philosophical arguments between the Westerners and the Slavophiles, who believed in a unique Russian inheritance. The Westerners triumphed but in doing so became infected with Slavophile notions, and out of the mixture of the two there developed a new social movement called the populist movement.

D. What liberalism there had been in the years between 1825 and 1881, such as the Zemstvo law and the emancipation of the serfs, was destroyed by Alexander III.

   1) Antiwestern, antiliberal, and authoritarian to the core, Pobedonostsev, procurator of the Holy Synod and Alexander III's tutor, became the principal ideological influence of the reign.

   2) Russification (intolerance and persecution of minorities, particularly the Jews) was increased and censorship was enforced. Nevertheless, there were limited economic concessions made to the peasants, and industry was expanded during Alexander's reign.

The Revolution of 1905

A. Nicholas II continued the paternalistic rule of Alexander III, but he did not have the strength to control the revolutionary forces at work in Russia. With the humiliating defeats that Russia suffered during the Russo-Japanese War, liberal demands for reform (freedom of speech, industrial and agricultural legislation, and an elected national assembly) became louder and louder.

B. The spark that set off the revolution was Bloody Sunday —January 9 (22), 1905. A priest, Father Gapon, led 200,000 unarmed workers to the palace gates in St. Petersburg in order to demand an eight-hour day, a minimum wage of a ruble a day, and a constituent assembly. The workers were fired upon by the guards and over five hundred were killed and thousands wounded.

C. Bloody Sunday united the dissatisfied bourgeois, proletariat, and peasants. By the end of 1905, 1500 government officials had been assassinated, peasants had seized estates, a strike committee had been set up by Trotsky, and one of the most complete general strikes in history followed. The life of the country came to a standstill. Soviets (councils) of workers were established all over Russia and pressed the demand for a representative assembly.

D. The Czar finally gave in and by the October Manifesto granted a legislative duma, but Nicholas maintained control of foreign policy and was allowed to disband the assembly and pass decrees when they were not in session. In actual fact, therefore, the duma had little or no power.

Expansion and Foreign Policy 1695–1905

Peter the Great

Under Peter the Great, expansion and westernization went hand in hand. It was for the purpose of military conquest that he borrowed European technology and skills, industry and administration. His main interest was the establishment of two warm-water ports, one on the Baltic and the other on the Mediterranean. (This meant war with the Turks over the control of the Dardanelles and with Sweden over the command of the Baltic.)

AZOV

Peter's first attempt at conquest was Azov on the Black Sea. In 1695 he moved against the city unsuccessfully, but when in 1696 he built a fleet of river galleys in order to blockade the fortress, Azov surrendered. His dream of possessing Constantinople and the outlet to the Aegean was the reason for his travels in Europe in 1697, where he sought technical knowledge and

THE GREAT NORTHERN WAR AGAINST SWEDEN   1700–1721

1) Failure to convince the West of the desirability of dismembering the Turkish empire turned Peter's attention to another warm-water port and outlet to the Baltic. In order to achieve victory against the Swedes, the local and central government of Russia was reformed, a new standing army was created, and the iron foundries in the Urals were developed. Three years of vigorous preparation culminated in twenty-one years of tragic war.

2) Sweden was initially victorious at Narva, and if she had not postponed the invasion of Russia in order to fight a six-year war with Poland, the final outcome of the Great Northern War might have been very different. As it was, Peter had time to recover from defeat, reorganize his army and seize the marshland on the eastern tip of the Gulf of Finland. It was here in 1703 that a fort was built, named St. Peter and St. Paul, and in 1721 that Peter constructed his window to the West—the city of St. Petersburg.

3) Victory at Poltava in 1709 (followed by the conquest of Livonia, Estonia, and Karelia) turned Peter's eyes once again towards the Crimea and the Turks. He was defeated and lost Azov as well as his ambition in the south.

4) The war continued in the north against Sweden. The first Russian naval victory in history was won in 1714, and finally in 1721 the Treaty of Nystadt was signed. The Baltic coast from Viborg to Riga was gained by Russia, as well as part of Karelia.

Peter now turned his ambitions towards Persia and won, temporarily, the western coast of the Caspian.

During the period 1725–1762, Russian diplomacy and expansion were erratic. In 1757 the Russian army invaded East Prussia, but what saved Frederick the Great of Prussia was the death of the Czarina Elizabeth and the subsequent reversal of Russian foreign policy. The only thing that was clear during this period was that Russia was a power to be contended with in the West.

Catherine the Great

Russian territorial aggrandizement was greater during Catherine's reign than any since Ivan IV. As Peter had moved against Sweden, Catherine was to tackle the Polish and Turkish threats. Her main objective was the outlet to the Mediterranean, the capital of the Turkish empire, Constantinople.

POLAND

A. In 1767, by armed force, Catherine established a protectorate over Poland, allowing the country to maintain a loose aristocratic constitution, but in 1772 the Czarina had to agree to end the protectorate and to a partial division of Poland-Lithuania. (The Hohenzollerns gained the most; the Hapsburgs acquired Galicia; and Russia gained only a part of Lithuania.)

B. In 1793 Poland was partitioned for a second time, and this time Austria did not share in the spoils. Russia gained White Russia and most of the remaining Polish Ukraine. Poland's constitution was annulled and once again she became a Russian protectorate.

C. In 1795 a third partition wiped Poland off the map. Russia gained the rest of the Ukraine, Lithuania, and Courland.

TURKEY

A. In 1770 Turkey was incited by France to declare war on Russia. The Pugachev revolt put Catherine in a position where compromise peace was the only solution. By the Treaty of Kuckukkainardji (1774), Russia lost Walachia and Moldavia (trans-Danubian provinces) but gained the whole northern shore of the Black Sea, except the Crimea.

B. In 1783 Catherine annexed the Crimea, and in 1787 Turkey and Russia were again at war; and in 1792 Turkey, by the Treaty of Jassy, was forced to confirm Russian control of the Crimea.

The Napoleonic Wars

A. In 1799 Russia joined the brief second coalition against Napoleon, and Suvorov invaded northern Italy. Finally, however, Paul came to terms with Napoleon, for the Czar was convinced that it was England, not France, which was the real threat to his ambitions, and in 1801 a force of 20,000 unprepared troops marched on India. Paul died and the campaign ended.

B. Alexander made peace with the English soon after he became Czar, and in 1805 he joined the third coalition against France. In 1807, after defeat at Friedland, Alexander signed the Treaty of Tilsit with Napoleon (compare with the Nazi-Soviet Pact of 1939). During this period of uneasy truce, Russia overran Finland (part of Sweden) and incorporated her as a grand duchy. Then she resumed the war with Turkey, gaining only Bessarabia in 1812.

C. By 1812 Russia was again at war with Napoleon. The war bears certain similarities to 1941. The Russian front was overextended, Alexander had no coherent strategy, and if Napoleon had attempted to please the civilian population by liberating the peasantry, perhaps the conclusion would have been different. It was only after Moscow was occupied that the war became a "war of the fatherland."

D. At the Congress of Vienna, Russia's aims were clear—the Balkans, the Baltic, and the issue of Poland were her chief concerns. Russia allied with Austria, Prussia, and England in the Quadruple Alliance to enforce the Vienna peace treaty and insure the future peace of Europe by a series of congresses of the representatives of the four powers. Later in 1815 she signed the Holy Alliance with Austria and Prussia to preserve monarchy, aristocracy, and godliness in Europe, which, according to Castlereagh, was a piece of "sublime mysticism and nonsense." Alexander did keep his promise to grant Poland a liberal constitution and to emancipate the peasants in the Baltic.

Nicholas I

A. In 1831 Poland was absorbed into the Russian empire and brutally Russianized.

B. Nicholas then turned his eyes towards the "sick man of Europe," the Turkish Empire, and the control of the Dardanelles. In 1829 Russia gained a protectorate over the Danubian provinces, but she soon came in conflict with British and French interests in the Middle East. In 1833, the Sultan accepted Russian aid against Mohammed Ali, but in 1841 Russia had to abandon her privileged status in Constantinople and all foreign warships were banned from the Dardanelles.

c. The Crimean War

In 1853 Nicholas' army invaded Moldavia and Wallachia; war between Russia and Turkey ensued, and in 1854 France and Britain entered on Turkey's side. The war was disastrous for all concerned, and incompetence, intrigue, lack of supplies, and inferior equipment led to Russian defeat. In 1856 Alexander II asked for peace.

Russia Turns East

A. In 1860 China lost the lower course of the Amur River to Russia, and Vladivostok was built. (In 1867, however, Russia sold Alaska to the United States.)

B. In central Asia, Tashkent was captured (1865) and Samarkand fell to Russian troops in 1868. In 1891 the Trans-Siberian railroad was begun.

C. In 1877, however, Russia was again at war with Turkey, and the map of the Balkans was transformed as a result.

D. The Russo-Japanese War

1) After the Boxer Rebellion in China in 1900, Russia's lease on Port Arthur became in actual fact annexation, and she became more and more concerned with Japanese penetration in Korea.

2) Nicholas II made no attempt at compromise with the Japanese, and war broke out in February, 1904 in which Russia suffered an overwhelming and humiliating defeat.

1917 TO THE PRESENT

This era begins with the end of 450 years of czarist rule and the establishment of the Union of Soviet Socialist Republics. Change is the dominant theme of the period as Russia moved from what is called today an underdeveloped area with an agricultural economy based on serfdom to a modern industrialized nation. She moved from a highly inefficient form of absolutism in government to a twentieth-century totalitarian state; she changed from a society led by an aristocratic elite based on land and blood to a state led by the Communist Party of the U.S.S.R. whose membership is limited to about 2 percent of the population. Yet if there was change, there was also continuity; the peasant problem still exists, the concept of russification is carried even further than under the czars, and the imperialistic desire to control the Black Sea and the Baltic has remained.

The February Revolution—the Liberal Revolt February (March), 1917

Causes

A. World War I: The February Revolution was a direct outgrowth of wartime conditions.

1) Poor Leadership

There were few generals who were trained in modern warfare, and they clung to the concept of positional old-style fighting dating back to Napoleon. Most of the generals were jealous of each other, and there were incidents in which they refused to fight together. The situation was made worse when the Czar took over personal command at the front in February, 1915.

2) Lack of Industry

At the beginning of World War I Russian industry was hardly capable of taking care of a peacetime economy, let alone wartime demands. (By 1917 men were going to the front with one rifle for every ten men.) What industry there was, was located in the Ukraine and was quickly overrun by the advancing Germans.

3) The Agricultural Situation

Russian agriculture was based on manual labor, and once the war began to take the peasant from the land the country was faced with starvation. Most of the rich agricultural land lay in the vulnerable Ukraine, and poor transportation further aggravated the problem, for the cities were soon starving. (By 1916 the government had no grain reserves left.)

4) The Scorched Earth Policy

The policy of burning everything as the enemy approached had defeated Napoleon's army, but it did not prove as effective in World War I because of modern transportation. An already acute food shortage was made worse by the burning of wheat, and social discontent was increased by the addition of starving peasants who flocked to the cities.

B. The ineffectual government of the Czar was another cause of the revolution.

Nicholas II was more concerned with his family than with the management of the government, and once he had decided to go to the front, St. Petersburg was left in the hands of his wife, Alexandra. She was completely under the control of Rasputin, a man who professed to be a monk and who was able, by the use of hypnotism, to relieve the suffering of the Czar's only son who had hemophilia. Even after Rasputin's murder by members of the aristocracy in December, 1916, the Czarina continued to hold seances with him and continued to persuade her husband not to listen to the cries for reform.

The Course of the Revolution

A. The revolution began as a strike and a demand by the people of St. Petersburg for bread. Government troops were sent out to break up the demonstration but instead they joined the strikers. The arsenal was seized, prisons were opened, and police headquarters was fired upon. A Soviet (council) of Workers and Soldiers was organized.

B. The government collapsed, and the Duma was the only body left capable of taking over. This Duma was the third and most conservative in Russian history (the only socialist was Kerensky). The conservative, Prince Lvov, was made head of the provisional and "liberal" government. On March 15, Czar Nicholas II abdicated.

The Failure of the Liberal Government

A. The major weakness of the government was its failure to end the war. The government felt that it must keep the bargain with the Allies and not make a separate peace.

B. It was a provisional government until elections could be held. Therefore the members felt that they could not put through any of the necessary economic and social reforms until they had received popular sanction.

C. In the end its very liberalism defeated it, for the new government allowed complete freedom to all groups. There was no censorship of the press, there was little control within the army, and the leftists could do what they pleased.

D. The Kornilov Affair

This was the final act that undermined the power of the provisional government. In September General Kornilov, commander-in-chief of the army, decided to restore order in St. Petersburg at the cost of overthrowing the Kerensky government. (Kerensky had replaced Lvov as head of the government.) The only place the provisional government could turn for help was to the soviets (controlled by the Bolsheviks). The Bolsheviks were thus armed and became the heroes of the city.

The October Revolution—the Bolshevik Revolt October (November), 1917

Rival Political Creeds at the Time of the October Revolution

THE SOCIAL REVOLUTIONARIES

This was a group supported by the great majority of the people; their appeal was primarily to the peasantry. (In the 1918 elections they captured 410 seats out of 707 in the constituent assembly.) They had no organized plan of action and often resorted to terrorism and assassination. Their leader was Yevno Azev, who was for years the head of the Social Revolutionary fighting organization as well as a czarist police spy.

THE LIBERALS

Only a small minority of the population were liberals. Their very moderation and tolerance were their greatest weakness. The main body of liberals was called the Constitutional Democrats (Cadets) led by Miliukov, who advocated parliamentary government.

In 1903 the Social Democratic Party of Russia (Marxist) split into the Mensheviks and the Bolsheviks. The main issue was the question of the immediacy of the revolution. The Mensheviks believed that Russia had to go through the stage of bourgeois capitalism first. They were more inclined to be orthodox Marxists, believing that the revolution would be inevitable —so why create it? The Mensheviks also advocated a free organization with looser control than did their cousins, the Bolsheviks. At the time of the revolution in Russia they were more popular than the Bolsheviks.

THE BOLSHEVIKS

The Bolsheviks were a small, tightly knit group of professional revolutionaries who advocated "democratic centralism," whereby there could be no disagreement once a plan had been accepted. They were Marxists who believed in an immediate and violent revolution.

Reasons for the Bolshevik Triumph

A. The organization itself and its ideology.

B. Their leader, Lenin, born Vladimir Ulianov (1870–1924)

1) A dedicated revolutionary who was willing to "eat, sleep, and breathe" the revolution, Lenin urged, in his pamphlet *What Is to Be Done?*, the formation of a compact and strongly centralized party whose membership would be strictly confined to active revolutionaries. It was Lenin who was chiefly responsible for the split between the Bolsheviks and the Mensheviks.

2) The April Thesis—the Blueprint for Revolution

A) When Lenin returned from exile in Switzerland in April, 1917, he immediately took command of the Bolsheviks, and at the railroad station he delivered his blueprint for revolution called the April Thesis. By this time Stalin had returned from exile in Siberia, and a month later Trotsky returned from Brooklyn, New York.

B) The blueprint stated that the Bolsheviks would

(1) refuse support to the provisional government and demand that all power go to the soviets,

(2) gain control of the soviets from the Mensheviks and the Social Revolutionaries,

(3) advocate the goal of peace, bread, and land,

(4) spread propaganda at the front and in the industrial centers.

The Revolution

A. The actual take-over of St. Petersburg was almost bloodless. On October 25, 1917 the Bolsheviks seized the principal buildings in the capital. In other large cities the same procedure was followed. The only place where there was active resistance was in Moscow, by a body of about 3000 military cadets who fought for a week.

B. The Bolsheviks did not control the greater part of the Ukraine, the Cossack lands, the Transcaucasus, or the Russian countryside. Control of these areas was to come later with the civil war.

The Lenin Era 1917-1927

Founding a New State

In December, 1917 the first general election in Russian history was held. The Social Revolutionaries won the greatest number of votes, but in January, 1918, at the command of the Bolsheviks, the soldiers dissolved the Constituent Assembly, and the newly created Bolshevik secret police (Cheka) were ordered to arrest, try, and execute anyone who was an "enemy of the state."

THE CIVIL WAR 1918-1921

The Bolsheviks then began to tackle the problem of taking control of the Russian countryside. The civil war was a military triumph. The reasons for Bolshevik success were

1) militarily they had control of the major cities.

2) Trotsky reorganized the Red Guard into an effective fighting force, secured by the Cheka in the rear.

3) The forces opposing the Bolsheviks had no organization and were not united.

ALLIED INTERVENTION

Lenin had to fight western troops as well as his own people in order to secure his hold on Russia.

1) In February, 1918 the Soviet Government cancelled all debts and nationalized all foreign property, and in March they signed a separate peace with Germany.

2) In the autumn of 1918 Allied troops invaded Russia in the north, the south, and the east. Allied motivations for intervention were mixed.

A) The Americans wanted to protect Allied munitions supplies in north Russia.

B) The Japanese were imperialistically interested in Russian territory in the Pacific.

C) Britain and France wanted to prevent the Germans from transferring their troops to the western front.

3) By November the military reasons for intervention had ended with the surrender of the Germans, and yet the Allies remained. By 1921, however, Western attempts at organizing the forces opposing the Bolsheviks had failed, and the only foreigners who remained were the Japanese in Siberia (until 1922).

THE NEP—THE NEW ECONOMIC POLICY   1921–1926

1) After the military take-over of Russia Lenin still had problems. Industry was in a disastrous condition since the workers had been given control; peasants were refusing to grow crops and miners to mine; and in March of 1921 the Kronstadt sailors revolted, demanding freedom of speech and the abolition of the specially privileged position of the Communist Party. The primitive mixture of Communist theories and practical necessity used during the civil war was not working: the proletariat was revolting against the dictatorship of the proletariat. Lenin realized that concessions must be made if his government was to last.

2) The NEP was introduced in 1921. Private ownership of land was restored, private retail trade was recognized. (By the end of 1922, three quarters of retail trade was in private hands. Heavy industry, however, remained in the hands of the state.) Taxation in kind replaced forcible exaction of produce from the peasants. The industrial proletariat and the landowning peasant were to work together in harmony (a most un-Marxist innovation).

3) The NEP produced results. By 1923 overall agricultural production had risen to nearly three quarters of that of 1913.

COMMUNIST CONTROL

1) Despite economic concessions there was little freedom in Russia. Mensheviks and Social Revolutionaries were tried and imprisoned; liberals suffered the same fate. Kerensky and David Dallin and many other political leaders fled to the United States. Artists such as Stravinsky and Rachmaninoff were among the great exodus of creative talent. Artists did remain, however, and some fine works were produced during the 1920's, but after 1928 a cultural revolution took place.

2) The Soviet leadership created a monopoly of the interpretation of ideology. A single source of ideology was absolutely necessary to the maintenance of power. This was the heart of the struggle between Trotsky and Stalin, for the man who laid down the party line would be the man who controlled Russia. (This is also the heart of the battle today between Mao, Tito, and Brezhnev.)

International Affairs

THE TREATY OF BREST-LITOVSK   MARCH, 1918

A. Lenin had come to power promising land, bread, and peace. Peace had to be achieved on any terms, and in March, 1918 one of the harshest treaties in history was signed.

B. Russia agreed to the evacuation of the Ukraine, Finland, the Baltic states, Poland, and the Transcaucasus. She lost three quarters of her iron and coal, one quarter of her arable land, one quarter of her population, one third of her manufacturing, and also had to pay a large war indemnity.

C. Since Russia concluded a separate peace, almost all the countries of the world broke diplomatic relations with her, but Lenin succeeded in saving the revolution.

THE QUEST FOR INTERNATIONAL RECOGNITION

A. Russian foreign policy from 1921 to 1924 was aimed at

1) the establishment of relations in order to reduce her economic and political isolation,

2) friendship agreements with neighbors to prevent further Allied intervention,

3) the encouragement of colonial countries to revolt. (The first two were of course a "soft" international policy, but the third contained the ultimate aim of the Communist take-over of the world.)

B. In January, 1921 the Chinese granted *de facto* recognition to the Soviet Government; then Iran and Great Britain followed suit, but it was not until April, 1922 that Russia ended her isolation by signing the Treaty of Rapallo with Germany. By 1924 Britain gave *de jure* recognition to the Soviet Government, and the rest of Western Europe followed her example, but the United States did not recognize her until 1933.

THE COMINTERN

Despite the fact that Lenin's era was a "soft" period in international relations, the Third Communist International (the first was created by Marx 1864–1876; the second was formed 1889–1914), or what was termed the Comintern, was established in 1919, setting up an international espionage system with its main objective the establishment of communism in all countries in the world. Orders were taken directly from Moscow, and the Comintern became a fifth column instrument of Soviet foreign policy. It was agreed that "unreserved support of Soviet Russia is the very first duty of Communists of all countries."

The Battle for Power between Trotsky and Stalin

LENIN'S DEATH

By the end of 1921 Lenin was working only half time; in 1922 he suffered a stroke and was an invalid until his death in 1924, when Stalin and Trotsky began the struggle for leadership of the Soviet Union.

STALIN VERSUS TROTSKY

A. The battle between the two men was personal as well as ideological. Trotsky, the brilliant historian, politician, orator, and military leader, had the army and the youth of Russia on his side. On the other hand, Stalin, the son of a Georgian cobbler, common, calculating, and coarse, had the great advantage of being a consummate manipulator of men. His position as secretary of the Party gave him control over party affairs and access to secret files of information.

B. The Ideological Conflict

The victory was an ideological one. Stalin's theories were appealing to the mass of the people; Trotsky's were not.

1) Trotsky's Theory of Permanent Revolution

A) According to Trotsky, the Communist Revolution had occurred in a country that had a predominant number of peasants, who were petty bourgeois. The proletariat in Russia was a small minority in a hostile sea of peasants. Therefore the Russian revolution was doomed unless there was a Communist revolution in Europe that could support the proletariat in Russia. The U.S.S.R.'s chief aim should be to continue and encourage revolution outside of Russia.

B) Trotsky also believed that the Communist Party should be less tightly knit than Lenin had advocated. Here his philosophy was contradictory, for if a minority were to stay in power it had to be tightly organized and disciplined. This theory was to brand him as the romantic of the revolution and a Menshevik.

C) Trotsky's theory of permanent revolution proved unpopular; for one thing, Russia's energies badly needed to be directed towards improvements at home. For another, revolution was failing in Europe and all over the world. The German Communist revolution in 1923 had failed, and in 1927 the Chinese Communists were slaughtered by Chiang Kai-shek.

2) Stalin's theory of "Socialism in One Country" contradicted Trotsky.

According to Stalin the Russian revolution was not unique; it was the pattern of all Communist revolutions. Russia, in fact, was the vanguard of the revolution; therefore the more rapidly Russia built socialism the better. She could then act as a lever for the disintegration of imperialism. Socialism could exist in Russia without the aid of a world revolution, and revolutions throughout the globe should be supported only if they were in the interests of the U.S.S.R. The Party was the dictator of the Vanguard, and until 1928 Stalin maintained that the peasants and the proletariat were allies.

c. In 1929 Trotsky fled to Mexico, and in 1940 he was assassinated.

The Second Revolution 1928–1938

This period is often referred to as the second Bolshevik Revolution, for it was during this decade that cultural, political, and economic changes took place that transformed Russia and created the state that exists today.

The First Five-year Plan 1928

A. As soon as Stalin was firmly entrenched in power he introduced a program that had two purposes:

1) to force peasants to give up privately held land and to join in collective or state farms,

2) to increase the output of heavy industry.

B. The Collectivization of Agriculture and the Elimination of the Kulaks (Wealthy Peasants) as a Class

1) Stalin's first step in creating Russian socialism was to declare that the peasants were bourgeois and enemies of the proletariat. The peasants were holding back on produce, inflation was resulting, and capital was badly needed to increase industrial production.

2) In 1929 an extensive drive was begun in the country to force the peasants into collective farms. The peasants resisted; they slaughtered cattle, burned their crops, and killed as many officials as they could. The process of collectivization was bloody and violent; armed troops were sent into the countryside; millions of peasants were exiled; war was declared against the Kulak, and most were either slaughtered or sent to prison camps. Figures are doubtful, but probably nearly 3 million peasants died of starvation. By 1939 collectivization was almost universal.

3) The Collective Farm—Kolkhozy

Most land and livestock were owned by the collective, although the peasant was allowed an individual patch of land. Machine Tractor Stations controlled by the Party managed all mechanized farm equipment and thus controlled the collective (the only change in this system has been the abolishment of the MTS by Khrushchev and more direct control of the collectives by the Party). By 1940 there were 250,000 collective farms and 7,000 MTS.

4) The State Farm—Sovkhozy

According to Leninism–Stalinism, the ideal organization of peasants was the state farm. It was owned and operated by the state, and peasants worked for wages and had no freedom to dispose of surplus as they did on the collective. By this means the peasant was to be proletarianized. By 1940 there were 4,000 state farms.

c. Industrialization

1) The First Five-year Plan was to control and direct the entire resources of the nation toward a particular set of goals. Steel was to be increased from 4.2 million to 10 million tons (in 1940 the United States produced 66.9 million tons; by 1960 the U.S.S.R. was producing 65 million and the United States 90 million); coal was to be increased from 35 million to 150 million tons (in comparison, the United States produced 62.4 million tons in 1930); and electric power was to be increased from 5 million to 22 million kilowatt-hours (in 1957 the United States produced 715.7 billion and the U.S.S.R. 210 billion kilowatt-hours). All industry was nationalized and directed by the state.

2) The heart of Marxism is the doctrine *from each according to his abilities, to each according to his needs*. The Russian Communists, however, maintained that equality was alien and detrimental to socialism. Under Stalin wage differentials and rewards such as bonuses and vacations for overfulfilling quotas of production were introduced.

3) The worker's freedom was taken away. The power of trade unions was curbed, and they became tools of the party. The internal passport system was reintroduced, and labor books containing a full record of a worker's employment were neces-

sary to get a job. The worker was pinned to his job, because managers would not relinquish their labor books. By 1940 a state decree bound all workers to their jobs. Thus the worker and the peasant were bound to state service under conditions resembling serfdom in seventeenth-century Russia.

The State

Hand in hand with the First Five-year Plan came a reinterpretation of the role of the state. According to Marxist doctrine the state would wither away, but according to Stalin it would get stronger and stronger because of the danger of foreign capitalistic military attack. Not until socialism was triumphant all over the world would the state disappear.

THE STALIN CONSTITUTION 1936

The Stalin Constitution granted unrestricted universal suffrage (formerly there had been unequal representation of workers over peasants) and secret elections, but this meant nothing, because the system called for a single party. As Stalin said, "in the U.S.S.R. only one party can exist, the Communist." (Khrushchev made a new constitution in 1962, but it is unlikely to alter the dictatorship of the Party.)

The Control of the Arts—Socialist Realism

A. More than force was needed to meet the demands of the Five-year Plan. Propaganda was thrown into the battle for production, and a cultural revolution was forced upon the Russian population. The press, the radio, the arts were now to be dedicated to the purpose of ideologically remaking the people in the spirit of socialism. All art was to depict Soviet reality, optimistic and happy. No experimentation was allowed, jazz was outlawed, artists were arrested and even executed.

B. Men like Boris Pasternak (Nobel award-winner in 1958 for *Doctor Zhivago*) were denounced as unintelligible, introspective, and slanderous. The purges in art reached their peak between 1936 and 1938. In 1937 alone sixty authors were attacked. Many Jewish authors were shot. History was rewritten to inspire nationalism; names of liquidated men were eliminated from all records. Western books were removed from shelves, and history became merely a pawn of politics.

The Great Purge   1934–1938

A. The purpose of the purges was to eliminate those groups of people who might form power factions and oppose the existing regime.

B. The excuse was the murder of Kirov, henchman of Stalin, in 1934. (Khrushchev said Stalin had Kirov assassinated.)

C. The groups eliminated included the Old Bolsheviks, the idealists; the army, the Trotskyites, and the old guard; those who had had contact with the West, particularly prisoners of war in World War I; and the technical intelligentsia. Seventy percent of the Central Committee of the Party was eliminated, and 25 percent of the army.

International Affairs

THE SOFT POLICY AND RUSSIA'S INTERNATIONAL POSITION

From 1928 to 1933, Stalin did not concern himself with the affairs of the world, but when Hitler became chancellor of Germany in 1933 and Japan was threatening Russia's defenseless Pacific flank, he began to look to the West for help. In 1934 the U.S.S.R. even joined that "capitalist club," the League of Nations, and Stalin vigorously made efforts at negotiating security agreements.

THE POPULAR FRONT   1935

The "popular front" tactic was an effort to make it appear that Communist parties were just ordinary political parties and to get all nonfascist parties to work together with one another. The popular front had two purposes:

1) to rally support against Nazism,

2) to create new governments that would lead eventually to Communist triumph.

THE FAILURE OF STALIN'S EFFORTS TO ACHIEVE COLLECTIVE SECURITY IN EUROPE

The West did not trust Stalin. His aid in the Spanish Civil War (1936–1939) and his actions at home did not produce confidence. Stalin's policy of collective security had obviously failed when in 1938 England and France refused his offer of military aid against Germany and gave in to the demands of Hitler for the partition of Czechoslovakia at Munich.

Litvinov, Russia's foreign minister, was replaced by Molotov in 1938, and the change in ministers also signified a change in foreign policy.

World War II 1939–1945

The Nonaggression Pact with Germany 1939
A. The Terms of the Pact

Hitler and Stalin agreed to remain at peace for ten years and to divide Eastern Europe into two spheres of influence. Russia was to have eastern Poland, the Baltic states, and Bessarabia.

B. The Red Army occupied eastern Poland in 1939. Treaties were forced upon Latvia, Lithuania, and Estonia in 1940, and both Poland and the Baltic states were incorporated into the U.S.S.R. The Russo-Finnish War was fought from November, 1939 to March, 1940. The Russian army took a terrible beating but won control of Finland in 1940.

C. On June 22, 1941 the uneasy truce ended and Germany invaded Russia. Stalin had been warned by Churchill and others that Hitler planned to attack, but he refused to believe that his policy would fail, and it was two days after the invasion before he was finally convinced.

The First Phase of the War

In the first year the Germans blockaded Leningrad and came within twenty miles of Moscow; they drove deep into southern Russia in 1942. The Russians played a waiting game until winter, and Stalin appealed to his people to fight for their homes (not for communism); and the Germans created their own destruction by being more cruel and more merciless landlords than the Communists. (They even maintained the collective farm system.)

At Stalingrad in 1943 the Nazi war machine stalled and the Russian counterattack began.

From 1943 to 1945 Stalin drove the Germans from Russian

soil and pressed for political concessions in eastern Europe from the Allies. At the Yalta Conference (1945) the Big Three agreed to settle the problem of eastern Europe by free elections, a coalition government of Communists and non-Communists in Poland, and recognition of the 1941 Soviet–Polish frontier. These agreements were ignored by Stalin.

Internal Policy 1941–1945

During the war all propaganda was directed at increasing nationalism, and there was some diminution of police terror in Russia. Yet there was very little pro-Western propaganda—only two or three times did news of Western feats come to the Soviet population's attention. As far as the Russian people were concerned, the U.S.S.R. was winning the war almost single-handed.

Recovery from the War and the "Cold War" 1946–1953

The Take-over of the Satellites of Eastern Europe 1945–1948

A. Immediately after the war East Germany, Bulgaria, Rumania, Poland, Yugoslavia, Hungary, Albania, and Czechoslovakia fell into Communist hands. (Today Yugoslavia is not considered a satellite and Albania has also deviated from the Russian path.)

B. Eastern Europe was vital to Russia as a buffer zone against the West and as a source of raw materials and manpower. East Germany and Czechoslovakia had enormous industrial capacity; Czechoslovakia had important munition industries as well as rich agricultural and forest lands. Rumania had oil; Hungary had bauxite and fertile plains for agriculture; Poland had raw materials, particularly coal; and Yugoslavia was rich in natural resources. In 1962 the satellites produced 150.9 million metric tons of coal and the U.S.S.R. 517 million. In steel the satellites contributed 24 million metric tons and the U.S.S.R. 76.2; in electricity the satellites' share was 134.4 billion kilowatt hours and the U.S.S.R.'s 369 billion; in cement the satellites produced 25.7 million metric tons and the Soviet Union 57.4 million.

c. Most of the satellites (except Yugoslavia and Albania) were "liberated" by the Russians, and along with Soviet troops came the police and the Party. (Austria was also occupied by the Soviet army, but today she is not Communist and is independent.) Generally there was a pattern of take-over: first, the Communists would gain control of the key posts of foreign minister, minister of the interior (police), and/or minister of defense. Then, with the Red Army to back them, they would push out the moderate socialists from the government and push through nationalization of industry and land reform, gaining the support of labor and peasants. Finally opposition would be outlawed and, if necessary, destroyed by force. Then friendship, military, diplomatic, and economic pacts would be signed with the U.S.S.R., which in effect meant Soviet control.

By 1948 Russia Had Gained as a Result of the War and the Aftermath
A. all of Eastern Europe except Austria,

B. the Kurile Islands, South Sakhalin Island, and Port Arthur.

International Policy
In 1946 Stalin declared that as long as capitalism survived the world was not safe from war. International policy changed abruptly from the "soft" tactics of 1941–1945 to the hardest period in Russian foreign affairs. Aggression was the theme of the cold war.

In 1943 the Comintern had been disbanded, but in 1947 the Cominform (Communist Information Bureau) was established. It was an espionage, foreign policy, and economic coordination center for the satellites and Italy and France. In February of 1948 the Czechoslovakian coup (the take-over of the country by armed force) finally awakened the Western world to the ultimate purpose of the U.S.S.R. Shortly afterwards, Greek and Turkish Communists increased antigovernment agitation, and in China Moscow openly supported Mao Tse-tung and gave her blessing to Communist activities in French Indo-China.

THE BERLIN BLOCKADE

In the spring of 1948 Stalin decided to drive the West out of Berlin, and he closed all surface access routes to the city. A massive airlift was the West's answer to this threat. From June, 1948 to May, 1949 planes flew night and day, saving Berlin by bringing in over 2 million tons of food and coal, and Stalin finally surrendered and lifted the blockade.

THE SINO-SOVIET TREATY AND THE KOREAN WAR

In 1950 Stalin signed the Sino-Soviet Treaty and then encouraged the North Korean army to attack South Korea. His "forward" policy failed, however, thanks to the efforts of the U.N.

TROUBLE IN THE SOVIET BLOC

1) Tito (Josip Broz) of Yugoslavia was one of the few Communist leaders in the satellites who was not under direct control, and in 1948 Stalin tried to get rid of him. Tito was expelled from the Cominform, but Stalin was unable to shake Tito's grip on his party or on Yugoslavia, because Tito turned to the West for aid and received it.

2) Numerous other Eastern European Communists of the same independent leanings as Tito were purged. Executions were brutal. Gomulka of Poland was arrested, and Kostov of Bulgaria, Slamsky of Czechoslovakia, Rajk of Hungary were shot.

Internal Policy Went Hand in Hand with Foreign Policy

The trend toward national patriotism was reversed; Party membership was tightened; and a police crackdown under Beria, the new chief, was instigated (at least 100,000 were deported). Stalin's personal ascendancy became so great that the Politburo rarely met, and the Party was simply an instrument used to carry out orders.

The Death of Stalin   March, 1953

In 1953 a group of Jewish doctors who were accused of trying to poison Stalin were arrested, and it looked as if a new purge was in the making. The wave of terror was just in the planning stage when Stalin conveniently died. It has been argued that his death was not accidental, but so far there is very little proof of this.

Domestic Progress and the "Hot Peace"   1954–1965

The Struggle for Power

The battle for Stalin's power was similar to the 1924 struggle at the death of Lenin and was an ideological, economic, and personal war.

A. The contenders for power were Beria (1899–1953), chief of the secret police and in charge of all atomic installations; Bulganin (1895–   ), leader of the army; Malenkov (1902–   ), leader of the government; Molotov (1890–   ), foreign affairs minister and vice-premier; and Khrushchev (1894–   ), secretary of the Party. (Mikoyan [1895–   ] was first deputy premier but was not really in the competition because he was Armenian.) The key post, as in 1924, was that of secretary of the Party, which was held by the son of Ukrainian serfs, Nikita S. Khrushchev.

B. Beria was arrested and executed a few months after Stalin's death. Georgi Malenkov was the next victim; head of the government from 1953 to 1955, his power was based on the state apparatus. Next to be defeated were Molotov and Kaganovitch (the man responsible for Khrushchev's rise to power during Stalin's rule). Both were old-line Stalinists, and Khrushchev almost lost this battle. He was outvoted by the Presidium on the question of agriculture and foreign policy, but saved himself by bringing the issue to the Central Committee and relying heavily on the support of the army in the form of Marshall George Zhukov, popular hero of World War II. When Zhukov had done his work, he too was removed from office. In 1958 Bulganin "resigned" as head of the government, a post he had held since 1955, and Khrushchev was made both head of the government and general secretary of the Party. He now had the power that Stalin had once held.

C. Like Stalin, Khrushchev had successfully played his rivals against one another and defeated them one by one. Unlike Stalin, he did not find it necessary to kill his opponents (Beria was the only one exterminated). Molotov became ambassador to Mongolia; Malenkov, a manager of a power station in Siberia; Bulganin, the president of the state bank.

Economic and Ideological Warfare and Changes under Khrushchev

One of the main ideological battles on which Khrushchev rose to power was decentralization. Under Stalin the soviet economy had been incapacitated by overcentralization, lack of local initiative, and fear. Khrushchev wanted to decentralize industrial management and thus eliminate the serious waste and confusion and duplicating of functions under the State Planning Commission (Gosplan). He also advocated decentralization of agriculture, and in 1958 the MTS were abolished in order to eliminate inefficiency. His main ambition was to decentralize government control and tighten Party control, and he succeeded. Party authority has grown significantly since Stalin's death.

Khrushchev also promised more food. Forty-five million acres of grassland in North Kazakhstan were opened up to cultivation. This "Virgin Lands Campaign" eventually failed but succeeded long enough for Khrushchev to accomplish his purpose of winning the support of certain elements of the Party. His economic promises could not help but be appealing: soon there would be free rent, free food, and free clothing; socialism was already here.

THE SEVEN-YEAR PLAN (1959)

Khrushchev's Seven-year Plan called for an 80 percent increase in industry and a 70 percent increase in agricultural production. Grain output was to rise from 120 million tons to 175 million; meat from 6 million to 16 million tons; milk from 55 to 110 million tons. Housing space was to be one and a half times what it was in 1958.

ECONOMIC PROGRESS

During the first two five-year plans and postwar reconstruction, the gross national product experienced a 15 percent to 18 percent growth; since 1950 the growth has been somewhere between 10 percent and 12 percent (the United States, by comparison, 4.3 percent). Despite low wage levels and high prices, real wages of workers in the U.S.S.R. have doubled since World War II. Nevertheless, Khrushchev could not achieve the goals desired: In 1961 the U.S.A. had a gross national product of $540 billion, the U.S.S.R. of $264 billion; in 1964 the gap was wider, the U.S.A. $623 billion and the U.S.S.R. $287 billion. Meat production failed to increase by 70 percent, and to make matters worse there were 13 million more mouths to feed. Steel production and housing projects were also too ambitious, and these may in part explain the downfall of Khrushchev in October, 1964.

The Twentieth Party Congress and the "Thaw"

A. The "Thaw," named after a novel by Ilia Ehrenburg, began in 1953 with the death of Stalin and reached its high point in 1956 with the announcements of the Twentieth Party Congress. At the congress Khrushchev announced that Stalin had been a villain, for he had established the cult of personality and allowed no contradiction and no freedom. Khrushchev then declared his opponents to be anti-Party for following Stalin's notions. There was to be a cultural and intellectual as well as an economic change in Russia.

1) Educational reform was passed in which the best students were allowed to go to school full time instead of working part time.

2) Cultural exchange was begun in 1958, and there was a general relaxation of censorship and police control.

3) The Communists were attempting to awaken the intellectual life of the U.S.S.R. without relaxing their ultimate control over creativity. Creative impulses in all fields had been hampered by fear and restriction. In Soviet science, for instance, creativity was minimal. Between 1901 and 1962 only five Russians won Nobel prizes for science. (The University of California alone has won more, and the United States' total during these years was fifty-eight.)

B. With the Thaw, voices of protest against Party dictators got out of hand and even cultural exchange caused problems. The U.S.S.R. wanted to exhibit her cultural advances, but it was very difficult to control the ideas foreigners brought into Russia. In 1958 the leash was pulled tighter, and Khrushchev was forced once again to choke the intellectuals. In 1963 he urged the Party to bar the Soviet writer Victor Nekrasov, who wrote favorably of his visit to the U.S. In his denunciation of Nekrasov, he explained the ultimate philosophy of the Communist state: "The party should get rid of such people, who set their personal delusions above the decision of the party, which represents the entire great army of singleminded people." The loosening of control also caused problems in the satellites.

The Hungarian and Polish Revolutions 1956

A. The revolutions in the satellites of Hungary and Poland were direct results of the de-Stalinization campaign and of tremendous economic discontent.

B. Poland's revolution began with the Posnan Revolts, where workers demanded bread. Ochab became First Secretary of the Party after the Twentieth Party Congress and was wise enough to move with the demands of his people, quickly eliminating the Stalinists and bringing back Gomulka (released from prison in April, 1956) in October as First Secretary. As a result, Poland became the freest satellite in the Soviet bloc.

C. Hungary's revolt began when a group of intellectuals met in June at the Petofi Club and drew up a manifesto demanding the ousting of the First Secretary of the Party, Rakosi, the curbing of the secret police, and the end of radio-jamming. For a while it seemed as if the Hungarians would have their way as the Poles did, but on October 23 students demonstrated in favor of the Polish demands, and the actual revolution began when the new First Secretary of the Party, Gero, called in the Soviet army. Although Nagy was brought in as premier and Gero was forced to resign in favor of Kadar, the regime had not moved in time with the pressures from below. Soviet divisions poured in on November 1, and the revolt ended in bloodshed and terror. (Nagy was eventually shipped to Rumania and killed.)

D. Today the U.S.S.R.'s warmest relations are with Poland, Hungary, and Bulgaria. There is behind-the-scenes friction in East Germany and Czechoslovakia and coolness in Rumania. There is, of course, open enmity in Albania, which has sided with China.

Relations with China

There are many disagreements between the Chinese and the Russians, but few authorities thought that there would be a major break between the two countries. Presumably they have too much in common, both being communistic. Geographically they are back to back. At present China relies heavily on Russian assistance and in the future she may be a market for the U.S.S.R. China needs military aid for penetration into Southeast Asia, and the U.S.S.R. relies on this penetration to spread the Communist doctrine. Yet in July, 1963 there was a decisive clash. Five "undesirable" members of the Chinese embassy in Moscow were sent home, and Khrushchev became more outspoken in his denunciation of China than anyone thought possible. What will occur as a result of this controversy remains to be seen (one possible consequence may be the increasing willingness of Russia to compromise over a workable atomic test ban). The Vietnam situation, however, may again force cooperation between the two countries.

International Affairs

A thaw took place in foreign relations too. Soviet demands against Turkish areas were dropped; a naval base was returned to Finland; in 1955 the Austrian peace treaty was signed, and troops went home; rapprochement with Tito was achieved; and armistices were signed, with Soviet blessings, ending the war in Korea and in Indo-China (1954).

PEACEFUL COEXISTENCE

1) With Khrushchev's rise to power it was announced that antagonism toward the West would be modified. Because of the strength of the Communist bloc the capitalist world would be afraid to start a war; therefore war was not inevitable in all areas. Communism would triumph by socialist competition—cultural, political, and economic.

2) The shattering of Western confidence and alliance systems has been a fundamental aim of this period. In 1955 the Communists tried to combine NATO and the Warsaw Pact of European satellites. This, of course, would have totally undermined NATO. The U.S.S.R. has also attempted to pick away at

African and Asian neutral nations by guerrilla warfare and "aid-plus-trade" tactics, and at the same time to keep the West aware of Russia's military might by rattling nuclear weapons (the atomic bomb "secret" was successfully obtained at the end of World War II) and by assuming control of space (Sputnik I was launched in 1957).

The Fall of Khrushchev

In October, 1964 Khrushchev quietly retired to his country home, and Leonid Ilyich Brezhnev became First Secretary of the Communist Party, while Aleksei Nikolayevich Kosygin assumed the title of premier. The change in leadership has so far meant little change in policy. The cited cause for Khrushchev's downfall was a repetition of the charge against Stalin—"the cult of personality," but more likely he was too old-fashioned (he got his start during the revolution) for the new and younger men rising to power in Russia, the "apparatchiki," or organization man, who is beginning to dominate the Soviet Union.

BREZHNEV

The son of a Ukrainian steelworker, Brezhnev rose to power first as a Red Army political commissar and briefly as a member of the Communist Party Central Committee. Under Khrushchev, Brezhnev was put in charge of the Virgin Lands program; in 1956 he was reinstated in the Central Committee; and in 1957 he was made a full member of the Presidium. In 1960 he was given the honorary title of Soviet President, but he resigned in 1963 to give full attention to the Secretariat. By this time he was slated as Khrushchev's successor.

KOSYGIN

Kosygin was the son of a Leningrad lathe operator and had no formal education except the Leningrad Textile Institution. He received his political training under Stalin, and after many setbacks he became Russia's top industrial expert. In 1957 he returned to the Politburo, and in 1960 he was made deputy premier. Then, when Mr. Mikoyan succeeded Brezhnev as president, Kosygin became sole first deputy premier.

Latin America

ANCIENT, CLASSICAL, AND MEDIEVAL HISTORY
500 B.C.–1500 A.D.

Historical periods in Latin America do not correspond with the arbitrary dates of ancient, classical, and medieval periods. The great Indian civilizations overlap these eras. It makes things much clearer to talk about the entire pre-Hispanic period as a unit. Before the Spanish came to Latin America in 1500, there were three levels of development on the continent. The lowest comprised the food collectors and nomads on the plains of Argentina; the next in development were those who practiced a primitive form of agriculture in the Amazon valley; and the highest level of civilization was attained by the Mayas of the Yucatan peninsula, Guatemala, and Honduras; the Aztecs of Mexico; and the Incas of the Andean highlands (from mid-Ecuador to mid-Chile). Despite the high level of development, all the Indians lacked draft animals, iron tools, and knowledge of the wheel and the keystone arch. All three civilizations were authoritarian with well-organized and controlled economies, pioneering in the field of agriculture. The Aztecs and the Incas were destroyed by Spanish guns and cunning, but the Indian has remained an important part of the Latin American scene.

THE MAYAS OF CENTRAL AMERICA
AND SOUTHERN MEXICO

The first civilization in the Americas that historians have knowledge of is the Mayan. (November 4, 291 B.C., the earliest

267

date in American history, was found on a Mayan altar.) Yet little is known, for only three books escaped the burning of the Mayan library at Yucatan by the Spanish. "Because they contained nothing but superstitions and falsehoods about the Devil, we burned them all."

Copan (Honduras) was the capital of the Old Empire, but in approximately 700 A.D. the Mayans moved northward to the Yucatan peninsula and established the New Empire. No one knows why they abandoned huge cities and made this move.

The Mayans have been called the Greeks of the New World, for they reached a high point of development in the arts and sciences, particularly sculpture, painting, architecture, and astronomy. They were a peaceful farming and trading people. Some say their roads were superior to those of the Romans. They measured time more accurately than the Europeans of their day (note, however, that instead of a decimal system of nine numbers and a zero, they used nineteen numbers and a zero) and developed a calendar with 365 days (also used by the Aztecs). They wrote in hieroglyphics and from about 700 A.D. began to record history. With the use of stone tools they created temples similar to the pyramids.

The Mayan empire fell apart sometime around 1200 A.D. They were probably conquered by the Toltecs.

THE TOLTECS

Almost nothing is known about this tribe, but according to legend they were the traditional founders of civilization in Central Mexico. Their capital was Tula (fifty miles north of Mexico City), and they were skilled in agriculture and weaving, architecture and carpentry. It is supposed that they destroyed the Mayan civilization and were in turn absorbed by the Aztecs.

THE AZTECS OF CENTRAL MEXICO

The Aztecs, unlike the Mayans, were a nation of warriors, merchants, and organizers. They were probably the first Americans to use swords, and their religion was bloody and warlike. (Human sacrifice was the basis of the faith.) Trade was a prestige profession, and the civilization flourished. Tenochtitlan (the Venice of America), their capital, was a remarkable city with a population of around 300,000.

Wandering Aztecs reached Anahuac about 1200 A.D. and learned a great deal from their predecessors, the Toltecs. In 1325 the Aztecs founded Tenochtitlan, and gained a foothold in Central Mexico. In a hundred years they were the strongest tribe in the valley, and by 1440, under Montezuma I, they had moved east and south and controlled most of Central Mexico in a confederation of tribes.

Between 1519 and 1521 Hernándo Cortés and four hundred Spanish troops defeated them.

THE INCAS OF WESTERN SOUTH AMERICA

The children of the sun, the Peruvians of the Andes, were a peace-loving people like the Mayans. A great deal is known about their civilization, since they buried their dead in mummy bundles and interred them in the dry desert.

The Incas were empire-builders, giving a common language and communications system to the territories they controlled. By 1492 their empire extended 2300 miles along the west coast of South America. Their government was a type of benevolent despotism. There was a strict labor code, for example, that forced all to work for the state but exempted Inca nobility, the army on active duty, males under twenty-five or over fifty, women and all who were incapable of hard labor. Land was owned by the state and there seems to have been abundance for all. The Incas were skilled in agriculture, domesticating plants, pottery, inlay, alloying, tapestries, and surgery. They had no system of writing, however.

The faith of the Incas was sun worship with a missionary zeal, but it was because of this faith that the Spanish became interested, for the temple of the sun in Curzo was described by the Spanish explorers as literally a mine of gold. The face of the sun-god looked down from a massive gold disc, encrusted with emeralds. All trees, flowers, vases, and other objects were wrought by hand in pure gold.

By the sixteenth century the Incas had reached their peak of development and controlled the largest area ever united under one government in aboriginal America. But in 1527 civil war broke out at the same time as Pizarro's expedition, and this led to their destruction.

MODERN CIVILIZATION   1500 to the Present

In the 1500's the Spanish arrived, destroyed the Indian civilizations, and created a colonial empire in the New World. The Spaniards, however, were more interested in gold, God, and glory than in colonization, and conquest did not mean effective occupancy everywhere. In some areas of Latin America, Spanish influence was minimal. Even the Catholic Church did not penetrate, although its authority and influence went further than any other European institution brought over by the conqueror. "The church ruled while the state governed." The Indian, when he was allowed to survive, remained an Indian, and even today some of them have not yet become westernized. In the twentieth century there are Indians who continue to fight the white man. These are the Huichol, the Lacandón of Mexico, the Indians on the Upper Magdaléna River in Colombia, and the Aucas in Ecuador.

The Spanish maintained an authoritarian regime in which there was no room for native representation or experience, and in doing this they in no way prepared Latin America for independence or for democratic government. Three centuries of isolation under Spanish rule also left its mark on Latin America by encouraging separatist traditions and eventual political fragmentation. Today much of Latin America is underdeveloped, yet it started out with advantages over North America, for it was rich in gold and silver and had a relatively advanced native pop-

ulation. Here too the Spanish left their mark, for the feudalism they introduced and the systems of land tenure and labor relations they developed in part explain the situation today.

The movements for independence began about 1804 in Haiti, and by 1825 almost all of Latin America had become independent of European rule. Simón Bolívar had dreamed of a Latin America both united and free. The first was certainly not achieved, for the eight Spanish colonies became eighteen separate countries, and the accomplishment of the second is open to doubt. It has been said that independence day was "the last day of despotism and the first day of the same thing."

THE SPANISH ARRIVE

After Columbus' voyage in 1492, the Spanish established an outpost in the Caribbean Islands.

From there, in 1519 Hernándo Cortés led the expedition onto the mainland, and with four hundred men destroyed the Aztec Confederacy and incorporated Mexico into the Spanish empire. (In 1535 Mexico became the Viceroyalty of New Spain.) A united resistance by the Indians would have destroyed Cortés and his small army, but there was strife within the empire and Cortés was clever enough to play upon the jealousy of rival cities, persuading many of the neighbors of the Aztecs to join him. Also, the fear and superstition of the Aztec people played a part in the Spanish victory. European firearms were magic, and horses (never before seen in America) were terrifying.

From Mexico Spanish forces moved south and north. Vasco Nuñez de Balboa discovered the Pacific in 1513 and thus opened the way to the conquest of Peru (coast south of Panama) by Francisco Pizarro.

In 1532 Spanish troops encountered the divided Inca empire. Civil war was raging between the two sons of Huayna Capac. When Pizarro captured the Inca emperor he demanded a ransom of a room twenty-two by seventeen filled as high as a man could reach with silver and gold. He got the ransom but strangled the emperor. The Inca territory became the Viceroyalty of New Castile (later Peru). Although Pizarro captured the Inca empire with only two hundred troops, the feat was not as extraordinary as Cortés', since the Incas were not warriors.

Although the Spanish had conquered, their control remained uncertain until the eighteenth century. British, French, and Dutch pirates raided their ships and their seaports; the war against the Apaches in North Mexico went on until the late nineteenth century, as did the war against the Indians in Argentina and the Arucanians in Chile. It was not until 1717 that the Spanish were able to create the Viceroyalty of New Granada (Colombia, Ecuador, Venezuela, and Panama), and the Argentine was not conquered until late in the colonial period. (The Viceroyalty of the Rio de la Plata, established in 1776, included Argentina, Paraguay, and South Bolivia.)

Territories not Controlled by Spain

Portuguese

By the Treaty of Tordesillas in 1494, Pope Alexander VI had drawn a north-south line running thirteen hundred miles west of the Azores. All lands west of this line were to belong to Spain, and all lands east of it to Portugal. Brazil became Portuguese when Pedro Cabral landed there in 1500.

British, Dutch, and French

Haiti and French Guiana became French; Jamaica and British Guiana (acquired from Holland in 1802) went to Great Britain; and the Dutch kept Dutch Guiana.

By 1575 some 32,000 Spanish families had been established in the New World, but they were more interested in mining than in colonizing. Between 1500 and 1660 Spain acquired 18,600 tons of silver and two hundred tons of gold from the New World. (These were official figures and at least 10 to 50 percent more was smuggled into the realm.)

SPANISH COLONIAL PERIOD

Authoritarianism

Spanish government in the colonies reinforced the authoritarian tradition in Latin America.

A. As the Aztecs and the Incas had been divine-right monarchs, so were the Spanish kings. As life for the Indian had been controlled by indisputable law, so now it was under the Spanish conquistadors.

B. The chief officer in the New World was the Viceroy, who held civil, religious, and military power. The captains-general were of lesser power. Cuba, Santo Domingo (later the Dominican Republic and Haiti), Chile and Guatemala (which included Guatemala, El Salvador, Honduras, Nicaragua, and Costa Rica) were captancies-general. All offices were appointed by the King of Spain.

C. Not only were most officials Spanish, but also most were not permanent residents of the colonies. Of 672 viceroys, captains-general, and governors, only eighteen were permanent residents.

D. The difference between the English colonies in North America and the Spanish colonies in South America in part explains the difference today in their respective political institutions and practices.

The Roman Catholic Church was itself an instrument of authoritarianism. The tradition of militant Catholicism of the Counter-Reformation was carried to the New World. There was no religious freedom allowed, and officers of the Church were Spaniards (of 706 bishops, only 105 were permanent residents). The religion of the Indian was destroyed and with it the very soul of Indian civilization. The Church, however, was wise: it built its cathedrals where the old temples had stood. In some ways the Church was the only force that gave the conquistador and the conquered something in common and gave the Indian a sense of identity with the European (although it required a papal bull to make it clear to the Spanish conqueror that the conquered were human beings).

The Class System Reinforced Authoritarianism in Latin America

THE INDIAN

A. The Indian was in the lowest class. Whenever he managed to retain his land he remained Indian in his ways and attitudes. He was deprived of leadership, religion, and learning, and was forced by the Spanish into service and to pay tribute. The result of this policy created a nation within a nation.

B. Nevertheless, it should be noted that Spanish policy toward the Indian was very different from that of the British in North America. The Latin American Indians were more numerous than their North American brothers and were generally agricultural and urban rather than nomadic. The Spaniards, unlike the English, needed the Indians as a labor force in the mines. The English had to exterminate the North American Indians who, being nomadic and warlike, made an unsatisfactory labor force.

C. Population figures are inaccurate, but Latin America today contains anywhere from 14 million to 30 million Indians (at least 30 percent of the people), who speak over a hundred languages.

THE NEGRO

A. The Negro was brought to the New World as a slave but was treated quite differently from the way the Indian was handled. He became closer to and more dependent upon the white man and eventually became Europeanized. The position of the slave in the Iberian countries gave him a legal personality, rights, and duties. He was allowed to buy his freedom; unusual punishments could be taken to court; and the kiling of a slave was murder. There has never been the problem of segregation in Latin America for the Negro.

B. Today Haiti is 90 percent Negro, the Dominican Republic and Cuba at least 34 percent.

THE MESTIZO

The child of a European father and an Indian mother, the mestizo was one of the most important by-products of the Spanish conquest, for he is the leader in South America today. During the colonial period he was looked upon with hostility and suspicion, and he was a misfit in society. "He had no tradition, no invariable rules, no place in the community comparable with his ambitions" (which were to emulate the role of his Spanish father). The civil wars after the wars of independence gave him his opportunity.

THE WHITES

The whites themselves were divided in colonial Latin America. The peninsulares, those who were born in Europe, had the influence and the power, and the criollos, those who were born in the New World, were resentful. This resentment was one of the factors in the wars of independence, for it was the criollos who led the revolt.

The Spanish Economic Policies

Spanish Feudalism

A feudal landowning aristocracy patterned after Spain's was created in Latin America. With the wars of independence, the serf became a peon and the landlord a patron, but the system did not change, for the peon was tied to the land by debt servitude.

The Urban-Rural Split

The Spanish system of viewing Latin America as a group of cities led to important divisions between urban and rural areas. Laws regulated the cities where the Spanish settled but not the rural areas. The cities, therefore, became linked with the events of Europe—the decline of feudalism, the loss of the economic and political power of the church—but the country did not.

The Class System Effected Economic Growth

The Spanish cultural tradition that the gentleman did not work with his hands meant that the mestizo became the artisan, but educational restrictions limiting education to the upper classes caused a situation in Latin America in which there was little or no skilled labor.

Other Iberian Influences

The fundamental cultural influence in Latin America is Iberian. In Brazil the language is Portuguese, and in almost all the rest of Latin America it is Spanish. The religion of the great majority of the people (over 85 percent) is Roman Catholic. Spanish influence is evident in every aspect of life, from clothing to architecture to the law codes of the countries.

THE INDEPENDENCE MOVEMENTS 1804–1825

Causes

The Napoleonic Wars

In 1807 French troops invaded Spain, and Napoleon placed his brother Joseph Bonaparte on the throne of Spain. Whether the colonies refused to accept this "Intruder King" or whether they grabbed the opportunity to overthrow Spanish rule is a matter of opinion. Revolts, however, broke out in 1809 in Argentina, Ecuador, and Mexico, and when Ferdinand VII was restored in 1814, the revolutionists refused to turn the clock back to the days before 1807.

The Role of the Criollo

Discontent with Spain was developing among the criollos, who resented Spanish commercial restrictions (heavy taxation and extremely restrictive mercantilism) and the fact that the government of the colonies was controlled by peninsulares. For half a century political liberalism had been filtering into Latin America in the form of the writings of John Locke, Voltaire, and Rousseau.

Liberation

Under the leadership of Augustín de Iturbide, Mexico won her freedom in 1821.

Northern South America (Venezuela, Panama, Colombia, Ecuador, and Bolivia) was led into revolution (1810–1825) and freedom by General Simón Bolívar.

General José de San Martín, known as the George Washington of Argentina, won the battle against Spain in Argentina in 1816. Then in 1817 he led five thousand men across the Andes to free Chile and Peru. This campaign is considered to be one of the great feats of military history.

In 1822 Bolívar and San Martín met at Guayaquil (Ecuador), and San Martín withdrew from political and military activity, leaving Bolívar to determine Latin America's future (which he did until his death in 1830).

Brazil declared her independence from Portugal in 1822 and achieved it without bloodshed. The French had occupied Portugal in 1807, and the Emperor João VI established a government in exile at Rio de Janeiro. Returning to Portugal in 1821, he left his son Dom Pedro in charge. Dom Pedro, rather than return to Lisbon, declared Brazil's independence in 1822, and his father could not send troops against his own son.

By 1825 Spain had lost most of her colonies in Latin America. Only a few islands in the Caribbean remained in her hands. The most important, Cuba and Puerto Rico, were lost during the Spanish-American War of 1898.

THE PROBLEMS OF INDEPENDENCE

Due to the limitations of this outline, the reader should keep in mind that simplification is not possible without some distortion. Each one of the countries of Latin America is individual and can be understood only in terms of its own history and present social, economic, and political circumstances.

The Question of Democracy

All the Latin American countries are republics (although Brazil, Mexico, and Haiti have experimented with monarchy); most have constitutions; all have presidents; Argentina, Mexico,

Brazil, and Venezuela have federal forms of government. In theory they are all democracies. But this is only the surface picture.

Very few of the countries are actually democratic. Only Uruguay, Chile, Costa Rica, and possibly Argentina since 1955 and Venezuela since 1958 can be said to be democracies today. Most are military dictatorships, basing their rule on controlled elections. For example, in 1965 Peru's Belaúnde held the first municipal elections in forty-five years.

Most are not totalitarian, although partial totalitarian regimes were established by Juan Manuel de Rosas (1829–1852) and Juan Domingo Perón (1943–1955), dictators of Argentina, and by Castro, dictator of Cuba since 1959.

A. Perón's rule in Argentina was both typical as a military government and atypical because Perón aimed at total control and achieved the nearest thing to fascism on the American continent.

1) The great grandson of an Italian immigrant, Perón's chief pillars of support were the army and labor. Despite army-supervised elections and ecclesiastical influence, Perón seems actually to have been the choice of the people in 1946.

2) Once firmly established in power, Perón aimed at social and economic revolution, attempting to rid Argentina of United States and British investments and to establish state monopolies. Through an Institute for the Promotion of Trade he was given the right to buy practically all the country's wheat and meat and sell it at whatever price he chose. Industrial progress was made during the years 1946–1951, but often at the expense of agriculture. By 1951 the press was brought completely under control, and in 1954 Perón broke with the church and legalized divorce and brothels.

3) In the end Perón was supported by the United States, and he granted the rights to the oil resources of Argentina to the California Oil Company. This aroused nationalistic antagonism toward his regime, which, combined with a drastic economic crisis involving meatless days and the importation of wheat, led to Perón's downfall. Like many Latin American dictators, the army's revolt brought his fall from power. He fled into exile (to Venezuela and then the Dominican Republic), taking with him an immense fortune.

B. Castro's Cuba bears certain similarities to Perón's Argentina.

Militarism is the key to power in almost every Latin American country. (In Peru, for example, 80 percent of the presidents have been military men, although in 1965 Fernando Belaúnde Terry won the election, and one may expect some changes.) The rise of the army was, of course, a result of the independence movement and was also due to the fact that the army was the only secular institution with a national interest and outlook.

Most of the Latin American governments are unstable; coup d'états follow coup d'états. Ecuador is the extreme example. From 1931 to 1940, fourteen presidents were in office; there were twelve foreign ministers in a two-month period in 1933; and September, 1947 saw three successive presidents. Palace revolutions are a common picture in Latin America. Generally they cost few lives and effect only the elite, changing one military dictator for another. In some countries there have been long periods without violence (Guatemala and Mexico for over thirty years).

Almost all the Latin American countries have a republican form of government similar to what Bolívar advocated. "The President of the Republic" should be "the sun, which, firm in the center, gives life to the universe." He should be the "supreme authority," and this authority should be perpetual and he should name his successor.

The whites still dominate in most areas. They own the land, dominate the Church, which in turn dominates the people, and control the army. There is still a caste-like racial and cultural distinction that cuts the urban and rural areas and makes popular sovereignty almost impossible.

Lack of effective leadership is another problem that Latin American democracy faces. By default, since the Spanish and Portuguese aristocracy were so far removed from the masses and generally more concerned with events in Europe than at home, the leadership of the nation fell to the mestizo, who had "neither the tradition, the education, nor the experience for the task." The intellectual is respected, but has not become the leader (except possibly in Brazil and Mexico).

Communism

A. The future of democracy, as in many underdeveloped countries, depends a great deal on the ability to solve economic problems. Nowhere in Latin America is Communism yet a mass party (the one exception may be Cuba today—1965). The United States Senate investigating subcommittee released the following figures on Communist Party membership in Latin America during 1958:

COUNTRY	COMMUNIST PARTY MEMBERSHIP (1958)	TOTAL POPULATION (1957 or 1958)
Argentina	70,000 to 80,000	19,858,000
Bolivia	4,000	3,273,000
Brazil	50,000	63,101,627
Chile	20,000 to 25,000	7,121,000
Colombia	5,000	13,227,000
Costa Rica	300	1,072,000
Cuba	12,000 (today this figure is of little significance)	6,410,000
Dominican Republic	Negligible	2,698,000
Ecuador	1,000	3,890,000
El Salvador	500	2,350,000
Guatemala	1,000	3,430,000
Haiti	Negligible	3,384,000
Honduras	500	1,769,000
Mexico	5,000	31,426,000
Nicaragua	200	1,331,000
Panama	500	960,000

Paraguay	500	1,638,000
Peru	6,000	9,923,000
Uruguay	3,000	2,650,000
Venezuela	30,000 to 35,000	6,134,000

B. The Communist bloc, however, is spending $100,000,000 a year for propaganda in Latin America.

Economic Problems in Latin America

In 1960 it was reported that two thirds of the people (120 million) of Latin America were undernourished; two out of five (70 million) were illiterate; two thirds were working under semi-feudal conditions; millions were landless; many countries depended on a one-crop economy; there was a great surplus of un-used population (about 31 percent) and unskilled labor, and productivity was low.

It is difficult to make generalizations about the economic situation in Latin America, for diversity is the theme, as it is in Africa. Countries range in size from Brazil, with a population of 63,000,000 and a land area greater than continental United States, to Costa Rica, the size of South Carolina, with 1,000,000 people. The rate of population growth varies from 3.5 percent in Venezuela and 3.8 percent in Mexico to 1.2 percent in Guatemala and Bolivia (by comparison, the United States is 1.4 percent, Japan is 1.0 percent, and India is 1.3 percent). Venezuela has a per-capita income of $500 a year, Peru of $250, and Haiti, on the other end of the scale, of $85. (The overall Latin American per-capita income is $225.) Dependence on the foreign market varies from 13 percent in Argentina to 49 percent in Venezuela. Mexico and Venezuela have oil; Venezuela and Brazil have an abundance of iron ore; Bolivia has tin; and Brazil has a tremendous variety of mineral wealth. Chile has nitrate and copper; Mexico and Peru, gold and silver. Argentina, Chile, Uruguay, and Costa Rica have a literacy rate of about 80 percent; Bolivia, El Salvador, and Guatemala about 30 percent; and Haiti and Honduras as low as 10 percent.

Latin America's gross national production rate between the years 1950 and 1957 reveals that in some ways she is as underdeveloped as many Asian countries. Latin America had a gross national product of 4.5 percent, but a population increase of 2.5 percent, which gave her an annual advance per capita of 2 percent. (Without Venezuela it would have been 1.5 percent.) In comparison, the United States' gross national product was 4.2 percent and 2.5 percent per capita. Europe (the Common Market) was 5.2 percent or 4.4 percent per capita. Asia ranged from Japan with 8.5 percent gross national product or 7 percent per capita to Pakistan with 2.5 percent gross national product or 1 percent per capita.

Much of the land in Latin America is still controlled by a very small percentage of the population, and the hacienda system (*latifundios*—great estates) is still in existence. The remainder of the land (about 50 percent) are *minifundios* of less than twenty-five acres—hardly capable of subsistence agriculture.

A. In 1960 big landowners held 40 percent of the land in Venezuela, and in Argentina five hundred owners possessed 18 percent of the land. In Paraguay in 1956 over 5.2 percent of the farms were larger than 125 acres, but these covered 93.8 percent of the area. In Colombia 3 percent of the people still own 55 percent of the land, and the average wage of a worker in the city is only 25 cents per hour.

B. In some countries drastic agrarian reform has begun. Mexico placed 1,922,573 families on 110,000,000 acres, yet 66 percent of the land is still dominated by large estates. In Bolivia in 1959 alone 669,441 acres were distributed at an average of fifty-nine acres per person. In Guatemala between 1955 and 1959 284,696 acres were redistributed, and in Venezuela in 1960 620,000 acres were distributed to five thousand families. In Cuba 13,000,000 of her 28,000,000 acres were taken over by cooperatives. Peru is initiating a vast land reform, but rather than redistribute productive estates the intention is to open up new areas for cultivation, in the interior and in the desert.

The Church

The role of the Church in state affairs is a situation that has not been solved in many countries. Although there is legal separation of Church and state in Brazil, Chile, Cuba, Ecuador, El Salvador, Guatemala, Honduras, Mexico, Nicaragua, Panama, and Uruguay, the Church is so strong in Ecuador and Colombia that it can initiate legislation; and it has the power of veto in El Salvador and Peru.

The Indian

The Indian who has never been assimilated into Spanish culture remains a problem in many Latin American countries. Bolivia, Ecuador, and Peru face the most serious dilemma, with 80 percent of their inhabitants Indian and 10 percent to 15 percent considered white. In Paraguay, on the other hand, the amalgamation of white and Indian has gone the furthest, and the country today is essentially mestizo (mixed marriage) and is the only bilingual country in Latin America, where both white and Indian speak two languages—the Indian language of Guaraní and Spanish. In Peru, on the other hand, in the village of Hualcán, only two hundred miles from Lima, only eight out of nine hundred people can speak Spanish.

The Exceptions to the Rule

Mexico—The Example of Successful Revolutionary Change

The revolution that began in Mexico in 1910 brought fundamental social, economic, and political change.

BACKGROUND TO THE REVOLUTION

General Porfirio Díaz was dictator of Mexico from 1877 to 1911. One percent of the population owned 70 percent of the land; Catholicism was the state religion; and church and state worked hand in hand. The Indian had no rights and had been forced into peonage; foreign companies controlled most of the natural resources of the country.

The revolution began in 1910, led by Francisco Indalecio Madero, whose main complaint was fraudulent elections and who forced the overthrow of Díaz. But the revolution soon got out of hand, for the people wanted more than honest elections. Emiliano Zapata was one of the leaders whose cry was for "Land and Liberty."

CHANGES

1) Land tenure was changed radically. Large estates were divided up, particularly during 1934–1940. Between the years 1915 and 1950, 76,570,000 acres were redistributed. The *ejido* or collective system, where the land was held by the village, was established by 1950 on 27 percent of the land in Mexico.

2) The Church lost most of its power over education and government. Church lands were taken away and the government no longer forced people to tithe (pay one tenth of their income to the Church).

3) The Indian and the mestizo gained the right to vote and to own land.

4) Foreign investors lost, for the government declared that everything that was beneath the surface of the land belonged to the government and the people of Mexico. Oil was nationalized in 1938.

5) Political change eventually meant the fall of military dictatorship. No president could be reelected, and in 1946 President Alemán became the first civilian president of Mexico.

Uruguay—an Example of Stability

Uruguay is unlike any other Latin American country. It has had only one dictator in the twentieth century; its population is predominantly white; it has complete religious tolerance; all education, including college, is free; and it has no mountains, no deserts, and no aboriginal Indians.

Brazil

Brazil's political, economic, and social history differs from the rest of Latin America.

A. One reason for this is that her colonial background was

Portuguese and not Spanish. There were few settlers, and they were mostly confined to the coast; the Church was relatively weaker and poorer and there was no Inquisition in Brazil. The Church today does not interfere in politics, so the country is neither violently clerical nor anticlerical. As one student of art remarked, "In Brazil, even Christ hangs comfortably on the cross."

B. Another reason for the difference between Brazil and the rest of Latin America seems to be attitude toward life and politics. There is optimism and a desire to improve, no matter what the cost and inconvenience. The new capital of Brazilía, built in an underdeveloped area five hundred miles into the interior, is a symbol of this energy. Brazil's diversity perhaps makes her people optimistic. It is the largest country in Latin America, the Amazon is the largest river in the world, the country grows most of the world's coffee and bananas, and one quarter of all known plant species can be found in her interior.

C. Even Brazil's dictators have been unique. Vargas ruled Brazil from 1930 to 1954. Between 1930 and 1937 his rule was not dictatorial, but with the heavy migration between 1890 and 1937 (by 1937 one fifth of the population of Brazil consisted of Italians, Germans, Spaniards, Syrians, and Japanese) he met the crisis by establishing a dictatorship. Yet, as Lewis Hanke says in his work on South America, "it was a most Brazilian kind of dictatorship, with little of the harshness usually found in such regimes." In 1954 Vargas surrendered power peacefully at the army's command. He did not flee with millions of dollars, as Perón and many others had; instead he ran for the Senate and won, and in 1950 he was elected President at the age of sixty-seven. (He committed suicide in 1954.)

D. Brazil has a growing labor class that is now becoming a factor in politics. In August, 1961 President Janio Quadros (elected in 1960) was forced to resign by what he termed reactionary forces because of his prolabor policy. Vice President João Goulart succeeded him but with reduced power. In 1964 President Humberto Castelo Branco toppled the unstable leftist regime.

Cuba

HISTORY

Under Spain Cuba was subject to severe control. From 1868 to 1878 Carlos Manuel de Céspedes led Cubans in an effort toward independence that failed. Then in 1895 José Martí fought the Spanish and was able to gain half of Cuba by the time the war broke out between Spain and the United States. In 1898, as a result of the Spanish-American War, Cuba was placed in the hands of the United States; in 1902 the United States withdrew, and Thomas Estrada Palma was inaugurated as the first president of the Cuban Republic. By the Platt Amendment of 1903 the United States, however, had the right to intervene in Cuba's defense, and she also acquired the naval base of Guantanamo Bay. (This aspect of the treaty was renewed in 1934.) The naval base at Guantanamo was part of the reason for United States concern with Castro's activities, for it is a $70 million installment, with 1550 sailors and marines.

THE CUBAN REVOLUTION

The Republic actually came to an end in 1952 when Major General Fulgencio Batista y Saldívar seized control from Doctor Socarras (elected in 1948) and set up a dictatorship. Under the leadership of Fidel Castro, revolutionary cells opposed to Batista's reign were formed. The revolt staged on July 26, 1953 failed, and Castro was imprisoned (released in 1955). Then, after a fiasco in Mexico, Castro returned to Cuba, and on March 12, 1958 announced total war against Batista. More and more supporters rallied to his cause, Batista resigned, and Castro marched into Havana on January 3, 1959.

CUBA UNDER CASTRO

A. In February of 1959 Castro became premier. Instantly, Batista's supporters and any who opposed the new regime were killed or imprisoned. Then Castro set about badly needed agrarian reform. The size of farms was restricted to one thousand acres (farms of 3,300 acres were allowed for sugar, cattle, and rice). Cooperatives were set up on half the land of Cuba; 2,200 "people's stores," 1,215 new schools, one thousand "alphabetization centers" (for adult illiterates) were established.

In 1960, Fidel Castro confiscated all American property in Cuba. United States sugar mills alone were worth about $275,-000,000. Then Castro turned to Moscow and Peking for economic and technical aid, and was assured that the Communists would give military assistance against any "invasion" from American soil.

B. Cuba's economic situation today is open to doubt. In 1960, the last year of unrestricted trade, the United States imported $375,000,000 from Cuba and exported $223,000,000 to her. Now there is a total embargo. Before confiscation, payments for salaries by United States companies in Cuba were $140 million per year. Seventy thousand were employed with an average wage of $2,000, and of the 70,000 only 320 were from the United States. In October, 1960, in reaction to Castro's flirtation with the Communists, the United States placed a partial embargo on exports to Cuba. Then, in April, 1961, Cuban exiles in the United States, with considerable official support, attempted to invade the island and failed, and in February, 1962 a total embargo was placed on exports to Cuba and the sugar imports were completely cut. Cuba remains today the one Communist outpost in the western hemisphere.

Venezuela

The policy of Romulo Betancourt, President of Venezuela (elected 1959) and his predecessor Raŭl Leoni (1964) is in marked contrast to Castro's. Betancourt was a revolutionary from his university days and he was among the military junta that made possible Venezuela's first free election in 1947. When Jiménez became dictator Betancourt fled. Jiménez was overthrown in 1958, and at the end of that year Betancourt was elected President. He immediately set about to solve the economic situation, balancing the budget by cutting expenditures, adopting a program of public works and diversification of the economy, and introducing a land-reform program by purchasing land holdings from absentee landlords. In 1960 his government defeated the attempt of left-wing students to create disorder and has so far promised and given civil rights and free elections.

Raŭl Leoni has followed in Betancourt's footsteps. As a result, Venezuela has prospered: the gross national product rose 5.8 percent in 1963, 7 percent between 1964 and 1965; oil production was up 5 percent, manufacturing 11 percent, mining 25 percent, agriculture 7 percent, and construction 75 percent.

RELATIONS WITH THE UNITED STATES

The most important country that Latin America deals with is, of course, her neighbor to the north, the United States. A two-way trade exists between them of $8,000,000,000 a year. United States' private investment in Latin America amounts to $9,000,000,000, and Government investment to over $2,000,000,-000.

1810–1930

From 1810 to 1824 the United States supported Latin America's fights for independence but was cautious, for she was purchasing Florida from Spain at the time. In 1811, the No-transfer Resolution was passed, stating that the United States could not "without serious inquietude see any part of the said territory pass into the hands of any foreign power."

The Monroe Doctrine   December 2, 1823

The doctrine presented by President Monroe stated that the United States "should consider any attempt on their [Europe's] part to extend their system to any portion of this hemisphere as dangerous to our peace and safety." This was not interpreted immediately to mean the right of United States intervention in the affairs of Latin America, because the inspiration for the Monroe Doctrine came from Great Britain, and the defense of South America was predicated upon the existence of the British fleet. By 1895, however, the United States position changed.

A. In 1875 Great Britain and Venezuela were having a boundary dispute, and in 1895 the United States wrote a series of strongly worded letters to Great Britain and forced her to settle the controversy by arbitration. This was the first step in intervention, and it also led the United States into a hasty rearmament program.

B. In 1904 the (Teddy) Roosevelt Corollary led to a reinterpretation of the Monroe Doctrine to mean the right of the United States to exercise police power in Latin America.

The History of United States Intervention

A. There were five occasions between 1900 and 1940 when the United States intervened in the Caribbean because the United States felt it was necessary to her security to restore and maintain order.

1) Under Teddy Roosevelt, she gave her blessings to a revolution in Panama, arguing that control of the Isthmus was necessary to her security.

2) She intervened in the Dominican Republic in 1904, in 1912, and from 1916 to 1924. In doing so she ultimately placed political power in the hands of the military and was indirectly responsible for the rise of Trujillo to power.

3) In 1909 the marines landed in Nicaragua and came again in 1912, staying until 1933. Here military dictatorship was also the result (Anastasio Somoza 1933–1956).

4) Haiti found herself under the control of the marines in 1915.

5) Cuba was a slightly different story, for the United States could have annexed her at the end of the Spanish-American War in 1898.

B. Intervention in Mexico

1) The earliest example of American intervention was the war with Mexico (1846–1848).

A) Causes

(1) The United States was annoyed with Mexico's weak governments, which refused commercial treaties and left American nationals and property unprotected during frequent revolutions.

(2) The Mexicans were disturbed when Texas joined the United States, for the United States inherited the Texan claim that the Rio Grande was her rightful boundary. Also,

Mexico was convinced that the United States was instigating a Californian revolt as she had done when Texas won its independence from Mexico.

(3) After negotiation failed, United States troops were sent into the disputed region between the Nueces River and the Rio Grande in January, 1846, in hopes that Mexico would declare war. (She finally did in May of 1846.)

B) The Treaty of Guadalupe Hidalgo   February, 1848

(1) Mexico ceded New Mexico and California and accepted the Rio Grande boundary.

(2) The United States paid $15,000,000 for the territory and $3,250,000 for claims of American citizens against Mexico.

2) The Mexican Revolution

According to Herbert L. Matthews in the *United States and Latin America,* the years between 1913 and 1917 witnessed "the most blatant, inexcusable and futile attempts at interventionism in the history of our [United States] relations with Latin America."

A) The United States had 40,000 nationals in Mexico and investments worth a billion dollars, and with the Mexican Revolution in 1910 there was bound to be trouble.

B) In 1907 Secretary of State Root had referred to the dictator Díaz as "one of the great men to be held up for the hero worship of mankind." When Huerta, a conservative, came to power in 1913, President Wilson refused to recognize him, because his government rested on force. In 1914 American sailors were arrested by Huerta, and the United States occupied Vera Cruz in retaliation. Huerta refused mediation and fled. Carranza then became President of Mexico, and in 1915 Wilson gave him full recognition. Villa, a former bandit who had been attacking the Carranza government, retaliated by raiding New Mexico, killing seventeen Americans. At this point the United States sent a military expedition into Mexico.

c) The United States, however, did pass a resolution in 1927 to settle all disputes in Mexico by arbitration.

Intervention was also practiced by manipulating the diplomatic instrument of recognition. The United States' delay in recognizing a new government in Cuba in 1933 led to the collapse of the government, and her speed in confirming the Mendieta government in 1934 led to the power of Batista.

The Good Neighbor Policy   March 1933

Presidents Coolidge and Hoover, and Secretaries of State Hughes, Kellogg, and Stimson attempted to be good neighbors, but the formulation of the doctrine of nonintervention came in 1933 with President F. D. Roosevelt.

In 1934, the marines were drawn out of Haiti; in 1939 the United States abolished her protectorate over Panama; and in 1941 her treaty rights with the Dominican Republic were abolished.

South Americans were outraged, however, during this period when the United States barred Latin America from the Dunbarton Oaks Conference, where the United Nations was formed.

Dictators in South America created a serious dilemma, for the United States could not decide whether to discourage or embrace them. She probably should have done neither.

The Cold War

Since 1945 the United States has been afraid of Communist penetration into Latin America, but whether she has followed a rational and enlightened policy remains to be seen. Any dictator in Latin America has been able to win her support by saying he is anticommunist. In 1954 the Order of Merit was conferred on the Venezuelan dictator Marcos Pérez Jiménez and he was named "Honorary Submariner" by the United States Navy. In 1955, the United States Secretary of the Navy, Thomas, compared Perón to George Washington.

Since 1960 the United States has tried, not altogether successfully, to disassociate itself from support of military dictatorships and to support moderate, progressive, and constitutional elements and parties in Latin America.

In several cases the United States has tried military intervention (both official and unofficial) as a solution.

A. In Guatemala the United States unofficially engineered the overthrow of the procommunist government of Jacobo Arbenz in 1953.

B. In Cuba the United States officially tried to do the same kind of thing against Castro in April, 1961 and failed.

C. In 1965 the United States once again tried to intervene in the affairs of the Dominican Republic.

United States Aid to Latin America

A. The United States has attempted to help alleviate Latin American problems by increasing her economic and financial aid program. Since the war (June, 1946 to June, 1963) she has given Mexico 0.4 billion dollars, Brazil 1.2 billion, Chile 0.4 billion. (This does not begin to compare, however, with aid to Europe: France, 9.6 billion, the United Kingdom, 7.7 billion, Italy, 5.1 billion and Germany, 4.0 billion.)

B. Under the Alliance for Progress more emphasis has been placed on aid to Latin America.

1) Since 1961 $230 million has gone to Colombia.

2) In 1965 Peru was granted $86.8 million (four times the 1960 figure).

The Organization of American States

From 1889 on, inter-American conferences have taken place in an effort to solve many of the mutual problems facing Latin America and the United States. In 1947 a collective security pact was signed at Rio de Janeiro. Then in April, 1948, at the Ninth International Conference of American States at Bogota (Colombia), the charter of the Organization of American States was signed by twenty-one nations. The charter pledges the American states to a meeting every five years; to a foreign ministers' meeting to settle urgent problems that may occur, and to a permanent council of ambassadors to act as the executives of the Organization. The purpose of the Organization is to settle disputes that may occur between member nations; to achieve economic cooperation and economic and social welfare (includ-

ing the exchange of teachers and students and technical assistance); to fight against colonialism and to maintain human rights;
and to a system of collective security in accordance with the
Rio Pact of 1947. The doctrine of collective security states that
any attack by a non-American country would be considered an
attack upon all, and each state would be obligated to assist. This
agreement has been referred to as the "continentalization" of the
Monroe Doctrine. In 1954 the Organization passed the Caracas
Resolution by a vote of seventeen to one (Gautemala opposed,
Mexico and Argentina abstaining) denouncing communism.

A. In July, 1964 the O.A.S. voted fifteen to four to break
diplomatic relations with Cuba. Only Mexico still retains ties
with Castro's government.

B. In 1965 O.A.S. troops were sent into the Dominican Republic at the request of the United States.

India

ANCIENT CIVILIZATION   3000–1500 B.C.

Little is known of the ancient history of India, and no scientific research was done until the 1920's. Evidence seems to indicate that a civilization called the Harappa, named after the city near which the excavation was conducted, did exist in the Indus Valley. Historians believe that this civilization of dark-skinned Dravidians was thriving by 2500 B.C. and reached a high level of development before it was overwhelmed by Aryan invaders from the north. By 1500 B.C. the Aryans were masters of northern India; the Dravidians had been driven into the south and Hindustan history began. The ancient period of Indian history contributed one fundamental aspect of Indian society: the Dravidian—Aryan schism. This division has caused problems throughout Indian history and continues to do so today. In modern India people speak either a dialect of the Dravidian or of the Aryan tongue and are not able to communicate with one another. (The Aryan tongues are related to Sanskrit and the most important of these are Bengali, Hindi, and Gujarati. The most extensive Dravidian languages are Tamil, spoken in Madras, and Telugu, spoken in Hyderabad). Throughout Indian history the south has been divided from the north not only by the geographical division of the Deccan Plateau but also by this traditional rivalry between Dravidian and Aryan. The caste system of Hinduism may even have originated from the desire of the Aryans to preserve their identity as a ruling class by remaining isolated from their darker subjects.

The Harappa Civilization   2500 b.c.–1500 b.c.

In the 1920's archaeologists excavated a site known as Mohenjo-Daro or Place of the Dead and found evidence of at least seven ancient cities that had been destroyed by floods and then rebuilt on the ruins. Since then they have uncovered two major cities and some seventy towns in the vicinity, but still little is known of this civilization, for as yet the language has not been deciphered.

The Harappa empire was far larger and more tightly ruled than either Sumer or Egypt, encompassing some seventy to one hundred thousand people probably ruled by priest-kings. There appears to have been a uniform system of weights and measures unknown in other ancient civilizations, and the civilization seems to have remained unchallenged and unchanged for a thousand years. It had a bronze age technology with a central government strong enough to keep the peace and organize the economy.

Probably the fact that the civilization had been peaceful and unchallenged by invaders made it unable to cope with the Aryans, who invaded the land around 1500 b.c., for the empire seems to have fallen almost immediately.

CLASSICAL CIVILIZATION   1500 B.C.–500 A.D.

During this period information is also scarce, for the Indians, unlike the Chinese, were not interested in this world or in governmental history and failed to keep full historical records. Yet this is an extremely important era, for it was during these two thousand years that India developed her social system, her philosophy of life, and her religion, all of which were based on Hinduism. It was during this period that another powerful faith evolved, that of Buddhism, which was to be significant in Indian history only briefly but was to have a profound effect on the rest of Asia. From 1500 b.c. to 500 a.d. numerous empires—the Maurya, the Kushan, and the Gupta—rose and fell, but none of

*these were able to establish effective rule over wide areas and
maintain themselves in power for more than a few generations.
India's failure to achieve political stability was perhaps the
major reason for the persistence of regional, linguistic, and
racial differences.*

INDIAN PHILOSOPHY AND RELIGION

Hinduism

Hinduism, the oldest of the major religions of the world,
developed sometime after 1500 B.C. The faith of the Aryan conquerors of India had at first been based on the worship of natural
forces such as rain gods, sun gods, and others, and very early
religious ideas were written down in a series of hymns called
the *Rig-Vedas*. By the tenth book of the *Rig-Vedas* the idea of a
single god had evolved, and with this began the development of
Hinduism.

Hinduism as a Philosophy and as a Religion
BELIEF IN ONE GOD

A. This is perhaps one of the least understood aspects of
Hinduism. A Hindu believes in one god, Brahma, but, in contrast to Western religions, he believes that the creator and what
he creates are one and the same thing and that therefore Brahma
is present in every particle of life.

B. Brahma can be represented by many gods, as many gods
as he has characteristics. The two most popular forms of
Brahma are Vishnu, who is Brahma when he becomes the god of
life, of love, of mercy; and Siva, when he becomes the god of
change, of destruction, and recreation. Siva, in turn, is usually
worshipped not as himself but as one of his characteristics—one
of his wives. Many tribal gods, local deities, nature gods, and
household gods are also worshipped and in theory are part of
Brahma. One might say that there are 330 million such gods worshipped in India, or one for every human.

REINCARNATION, OR REBIRTH

A. Since all things are part of the divine creator, the soul never dies but is reborn into another body. To the Hindu the particular body the soul takes on depends on the past lives the soul has led. (The record of his past deeds is known as Karma.) If his record is good, he may be reborn as a holy man; if it is bad, he may be reborn as a member of a lower caste or an untouchable or an insect or a dog, depending on how evil the record.

B. Since all things have a human soul, an orthodox Hindu regards all life as sacred. He is therefore a vegetarian. Although Hindus have for this reason often been pacifists, they do believe that certain lives are more valuable than others, and in the animal kingdom the cow is the most sacred.

THE CASTE SYSTEM

A. The Hindu word for caste is *varna*, which means *color*, and many historians believe that this must have been the original distinction among the peoples of India.

B. Caste is similar to strict class distinction but is more restricted, for people marry only within their caste, associate only with people of their caste, and live according to the rules, ceremonies, and rituals of their particular caste.

C. There were four major castes in India—the Brahmin or priestly caste, the Kshatriuas or warrior, the Vasiya or merchant, and the Sudra or laboring caste. There were, however, thousands (perhaps seven thousand) of subcastes, and the division was made on professional or occupational lines. The castes were not socially or religiously equal. The Brahmin was the elite. All caste was a matter of birth.

D. The untouchable or outcaste was below caste and no one could associate with him. There were between 45 million and 50 million such people in India. They were barred from temples, schools, village wells, restaurants, and elsewhere. The only jobs they were allowed were those the Hindu would consider unclean, such as tanning, latrine duty, and street cleaning.

E. Today caste and untouchability are officially abolished, but the feeling is still very strong in the countryside of India.

MYSTICISM AND THE RENUNCIATION OF THE WORLD

The desire of the Hindu is to achieve union with God. This can be done only by renouncing the body and the material world and concentrating upon the soul. Denial of the material universe takes many forms:

A. Mortification of the flesh, the attempt to prove, by putting the body through physical tortures such as sleeping on a bed of nails and starvation, that it means nothing.

B. Yoga, which means yoking of the mind to God, is another attempt to have such complete control over the body that it becomes almost superfluous to existence. A yogi has been known to stop his heart beat for a minute and to hold his breath for over an hour.

Hinduism as a Way of Life

THE SACREDNESS OF ANIMALS

This has caused many problems in India: pious men allow poisonous snakes and rodents to live, and the cow, even if diseased and no longer a source of milk, is permitted to live and roam freely. More than half the cows in India are worthless and destructive beasts.

THE HINDU JOINT FAMILY

A. In India, as in China, the individual owed his first loyalty to his family. All needs, such as unemployment and illness, were taken care of by the family. A joint purse was administered by the oldest member of the family.

B. The position of women was inferior to men; they could eat only after their husbands, could not appear in public, and their primary function was to bear sons. If this was not done the husband could take a second wife.

1) Suttee was a Hindu practice whereby a wife of a dead man, in order to show her devotion, would throw herself alive onto her husband's funeral pyre. (Often they had to be tied to the pyre.) This was outlawed by the British.

2) Marriage was arranged by the family, and a woman's worth was based on her dowry. Many families went heavily into debt in order to pay for the dowry, and, as a result, there was a high rate of female infanticide.

3) Child marriage was also customary. Girls of seven, eight, or nine would be married to husbands of twenty or thirty. (Today the law limits marriage age to eighteen for males and fourteen for females.)

MEDICINE

A. There were many taboos against medicine, first because the human body was not regarded as important, and second because Western medicines and treatments often contained animal fats, which were anathemas to good Hindus.

B. Sanitation problems often resulted, since Hindus believed in throwing dead bodies of holy men into the sacred Ganges River and bathing the sick and dying in the river in order to cleanse them of their sins. The Ganges was the source of laundry and drinking water for thousands of Indians.

Buddhism

The Founder, Siddhartha Gautama Buddha

According to legend, Gautama was born in 563 B.C. into the second caste of India, the warrior, and brought up in the luxury of warrior aristocrats. At the age of twenty-nine, while on a journey, Gautama is reported to have seen an old man, a sick man, a dead man, and an ascetic. This worried him, for he could not understand why there should be so much misery in the world. For six years he sought a solution. He tried all the Hindu methods, such as asceticism and mortification of the flesh, in order to understand God. These did not give him an answer to the problem. Finally, again according to legend, he seated himself under a tree—the sacred Bodhi tree—and meditated for forty-nine days. He then achieved enlightenment and became known as Buddha, the enlightened one. For the next forty-five years of his life he traveled, preached, and spread his religion.

Buddhism is similar in many ways to Hinduism, advocating reincarnation, the doctrine of Karma, and renunciation of the world, but Buddha disagreed with the methods of achieving these objectives: he did not believe in mortification of the flesh or in caste distinctions, since all men were to him equal in spiritual potentiality.

The Philosophy of Buddhism

A. The Four Noble Truths: (1) suffering is universal, (2) the cause of all suffering is selfish desire and cravings, (3) the cure to the problem of suffering therefore is to eliminate all selfish desire, and (4) the way to do this is to follow the Noble Eightfold Path.

B. The Noble Eightfold Path for eliminating selfish desire consists of (1) right views or knowledge, (2) right ambition, (3) right speech, (4) right conduct, (5) right means of livelihood, (6) right effort or self-discipline, (7) right thoughts, (8) right meditation or concentration.

C. The achievement of enlightenment is the fundamental aim for the Buddhist, as it is for the Hindu. Once one achieves enlightenment, he is said to have reached Nirvana and is finally released from the wheel of death and rebirth.

The Buddhist Monk

Buddhism became a monastic religion, for the aim of the believer was to detach himself from life. The Buddhist monk's main function is to serve as an example of the Buddhist way of life. Simplicity is his aim. Most are celibate, and their only belongings are a robe, an alms bowl, a needle, a string of 108 beads, a razor, and a filter to strain insects out of water. They can eat only before noon and this food must be begged for. For this reason, they have proved to be an economic drain on countries such as Burma and Thailand. (Except for a period during Japanese feudalism, the Buddhist monk has traditionally been a pacifist.)

Divisions of Buddhism

HINAYANA, THE LESSER VEHICLE

This is the original faith, relying solely on one's own introspection and faith to achieve enlightenment. It is the dominant form of Buddhism today in Ceylon, Burma, and Thailand.

MAHAYANA, THE GREATER VEHICLE

This is the Chinese adaptation of Buddhism, and the primary difference is that it relies on other Buddhas and gods to achieve enlightenment or Nirvana. It incorporates the use of saints called Bodhisattvas, praying to them for aid. It is the dominant form today in Japan and China.

Buddhism in 272 B.C. was the state religion of India; by 65 A.D. it had spread to China; by 600 A.D. it was introduced into Japan and became the state religion during the 700's. By 800 A.D. the faith had spread all over the Far East, but a hundred years before that date it had died out in India. The main reason for its demise in India was its renunciation of the caste system, which challenged the existing social structure.

Islam, the other important faith in India, was not introduced until the medieval era.

INDIAN HISTORY 1500 B.C.–400 B.C.

Unfortunately, the early Aryans left only literary records—the four *Vedas* and two epics, the *Mahabharata* and the *Ramayana* (1000–500 B.C.). Consequently, historical records are minimal up to the fourth century B.C.

By the time of the epics, the Aryans had settled in villages, expanded eastward along the Ganges, and fused their culture with that of the Dravidian. It was during this period that Hinduism was fully developed.

Alexander the Great invaded India in 326 B.C. and occupied the northwestern part of the country. There was little Hellenistic influence, however, since Alexander himself died in 322 B.C., and this part of his empire, left to Seleucus, was soon conquered.

THE MAURYA EMPIRE 321–184 B.C.

This dynasty, founded by Chandragupta Maurya at the death of Alexander the Great, was the first in Indian history to unite all of Hindustan under one effective imperial authority.

The Mauryan empire was a police state with an efficient

revenue system, taxing trade and land and controlling all mines.

The reign of the emperor Asoka (273 B.C.–232 B.C.) was the height of the empire. Although essentially a Hindu, Asoka was devoted to the Buddhist faith and became a missionary of peace, goodwill, and compassion by helping to spread Buddhism into Southeast Asia. His empire at its zenith extended as far south as Mysore.

The dynasty was weak after Asoka's death, and with the assassination of the last Mauryan emperor (184 B.C.), India was once again plunged into a period of anarchy and constant invasion.

THE KUSHAN EMPIRE   50 A.D.–220 A.D.(?)

The Kushans from central Asia were the next group of people who were able to conquer and successfully hold a large area of India for over two centuries, but their rule did not extend as far as Asoka's, nor was it as influential.

Under Kanishka (62 A.D.?–120 A.D.?) the state reached its height, for Kanishka was a patron of arts and learning. The school of art called the Gandharan developed one of the traditional images of Buddha and influenced both China and Japan.

THE GUPTA EMPIRE   320 A.D.–647 A.D.

The Gupta dynasty, founded by Chandragupta II, was much less despotic than the Mauryan and is known as the high point of India's classical period. Medicine, literature, and the arts (particularly Indian sculpture) flourished. Great universities were established, and mathematicians and astronomers were certainly as accurate as their contemporaries in the rest of the world. The decimal, the zero, and Arabic numerals all originated in India. During this dynasty nearly all of north India was united.

In 455 A.D. the white Huns struck a deathblow at the Gupta Empire, and this was probably the most destructive of all barbarian invasions into India. It was a part of the same movement of Mongoloid peoples who set the German barbarians moving into the Roman empire and who themselves looted the city of Rome in 410 A.D.

MEDIEVAL CIVILIZATION   500 A.D.–1500 A.D.

During the medieval period the most important single development was the appearance of the Moslems. India had not developed the concept of a single empire, she had not succeeded in unifying the peninsula or in healing the diverse elements within her people. The coming of the Islamic faith created still another division in Indian society, which in 1947 was to split the peninsula into two sovereign nations. The Hindu-Moslem rivalry was not just a matter of two different religious creeds but also two widely divergent cultures. Islam was a proselytizing faith that demanded doctrinal uniformity with only one God, one book, one duty, while the Hindu allowed latitude, tolerance, and diversity in cult, and was nonmissionary. The Moslem had a sense of community and state and believed that Moslems should be governed only by Moslems, while the Hindu's utopia was "philosophical anarchy." Another, and for many years irreconcilable, division was the Hindu belief in caste and the Moslem belief that all men were equal except heathens.

The Moslem invasions occurred in three stages—first, the invasion of the Sind region by the Arab Moslems, second, the Turkish-Mongol invasions, and finally the conquest by the Moguls.

THE ARAB MOSLEMS INVADE THE SIND IN 712 A.D.

They were not able to push far inland, for they were checked by the desert terrain, but they did retain the area near the mouth of the Indus River as a Moslem foothold in India.

THE TURKISH-MONGOL MOSLEMS

These people from Afghanistan began raiding India across the northwest mountain passes. The terrible and bloody raids were begun in 998 by Amir Mahmud and continued for over four centuries.

One of the most famous invaders was Tamerlane, who massacred thousands of Indians and transported the artisans of the land to his capital, Samarkand (today Russia).

The rite of Janhar, which was practiced by the Indians when they felt there was no hope left, is proof of how devastating the raids were. Men burned their wives and children and then went forth with sword in hand to meet the Moslems and their death.

The result of these invasions was that numerous Moslem kingdoms were established in northern India. The Moslems became the ruling class, the military aristocrats, and the Hindus were used to perform physical and clerical work. The Moslems strongholds were

In the east: central and eastern Bengal, where they had the greatest success at conversion, since the area had been Buddhist and resented its Hindu overlords.

In the west: the Sind, the west Punjab, and Baluchistan.

MODERN CIVILIZATION   1500 to the Present

The beginning of the modern period in Indian history coincides with the establishment of the Mogul Empire, which, according to Gibbon, was "one increasing round of valour, greatness, discord, degeneracy and decay." The Empire contributed very little that was new, and the fact that it ended in 1707 in civil war was nothing unique to India either. But the Mogul's decay also corresponded in time with the arrival by sea of Western Europeans, and this proved extremely significant. From 1857 to 1947 Great Britain ruled India, and during these ninety years India changed fundamentally. She was unified for the first time in her history, with a single law and language for all her subjects as well as a single government for the entire peninsula. The British also gave to India a sense of nationalism, and the Indian struggle for freedom after 1900 proved to be one of the most spectacular mass movements in the history of political nationalism. Under the leadership of Mahatma Gandhi every Indian was united in a common demand for independence, and on August 15, 1947 the imperial flag was hauled down, after ninety years of British rule, and was replaced by the flags of two new nations, India and Pakistan. It was at this point that British rule passed the acid test; both new states remained in the Commonwealth and both adhered to constitutional forms of government; and India maintained another British tradition, democracy. Whether Western ideas of liberty and democracy can endure under conditions of extreme poverty and overpopulation is the major problem faced by both India and Pakistan today.

THE MOGUL EMPIRE 1526–1707

Babur

The founder of the Mogul empire was Babur, a Turk from what is today Russian Turkestan, who claimed descent from both Genghiz Khan and Tamerlane. At the head of 12,000 Moslems he swept down on India, conquered Delhi in 1526 and made it his capital.

The Height of the Empire 1556–1605

The reign of Akbar, the grandson of Babur, is considered the golden age of the Empire. An outstanding administrator, scholar, and artist, Akbar was the equal of contemporary monarchs such as Elizabeth I of England and Suleiman the Magnificent of the Ottoman empire. His administration was well paid and competent, and although he was illiterate he was considered one of the best-read (best-read-to) men of his time. He held a meeting every day for discussions of literature, art, religion, philosophy, and politics.

The central purpose of Akbar's administration was to unite

Hindus and Moslems. Thirty percent of the officials of the Government were Hindu and he even attempted to found a new religion that would combine both faiths.

Despite his tolerance and wisdom, another of Akbar's main objectives was the expansion of the empire, and it was during his era that the Empire reached its greatest size, extending from central Asia to southern India, and from Persia to the Ganges.

Akbar's Successors Failed to Keep Up His High Standards

His son, Jehangir (1605–1627), was indolent, ineffectual, and a drunkard. Jehangir's son, Shan Jehan (1628–1658), was intolerant and came to the throne by bloodshed. He is particularly remembered for his building of the Taj Mahal for his favorite wife, and although a magnificent piece of architecture it also involved an extremely heavy tax on his people.

Aurangzeb (1658–1707) was the last Mogul emperor to control all of India.

A. Aurangzeb was a man of great courage and talent, but he was also a fanatical Moslem, determined to conquer the entire peninsula and to convert all his subjects to Islam. The Hindus naturally objected, and Hindu princes organized the Mahratta Confederacy, with its power centered around the city of Poona. In his attempt to conquer the south of India, Aurangzeb overextended his resources, and ultimately the viceroys of the empire broke away, establishing independent principalities in Hyderabad, Mysore, Bengal, and Oudh.

B. By 1707 India was divided into separate Hindu principalities combined in the loosely organized Mahratta Confederacy, separate Moslem sultanates, and smaller independent warring groups. The Sikhs in the northwest were an independent power, advocating no caste, no idolatry, and forming a strong militant brotherhood. Though the Mogul emperors continued to claim dominion over all of India, their effective rule after 1707 was limited to the Delhi Sultanate, a small area around the capital.

THE COMING OF THE WEST

In 1498 Vasco da Gama reached Calicut and the Portuguese asserted their authority in southern India, controlling trading posts and naval routes. They did not develop a political empire, but they did establish an empire of Indian commerce. It was the sense of security which the mastery of the seas gave them that was their undoing, for soon their power was broken by the Dutch and they retained only Goa, Damao, and Diu. Portuguese influence was considerable, for today India is the most Catholic country in the East outside of the Philippines.

The Dutch encountered interference from the Mogul government during the seventeenth century and therefore concentrated on the East Indies and not on India. This left France and Great Britain to battle for control of India.

THE BRITISH GAIN CONTROL OF INDIA

The British East India Company

In 1600 Elizabeth I of England granted the sole right to trade with the East Indies to a group of businessmen and merchants. This was the organization that was eventually not only to trade with but also to govern India.

The Steps to Complete Control of India

The British East India Company established three major posts for its trade. In 1639 St. George Fort (Madras) was built; in 1660 Bombay was gained when Charles II married a Portuguese princess; and in 1690 Calcutta was founded. This was "the tripod on which England" was to achieve "supremacy in India," for from these points British power fanned out.

Victory over the French

A. The French and the British had become the main competitors for power in India. Before 1754 the French had had the advantage due to the leadership of Dupleix, governor of the French East India Company. The French began to intervene in native politics in order to extend their own commerce and limit that of the British, and they were extremely successful. But they pushed the British too far when control of Madras was threatened, and the British regained the initiative and mastery in 1754 under Clive. Dupleix was called back to France because of his costly policies.

B. The Battle of Plassey   1757

A British force of three thousand men (two thousand were Indians) under the leadership of Robert Clive defeated a large (fifty thousand) native force under the Newab of Bengal (directed and financed by the French) and thus won control of Bengal becoming the kingmaker and acquiring nine hundred square miles of territory.

C. In 1759 the French fleet was driven from Indian waters by the British navy; in 1760 the British defeated them at Wandewash, and in 1761 at Pondicherry. The struggle against France ended in 1763 with the conclusion of the Seven Years' War being waged in Europe, America, Canada, and India. France was pushed out of India politically and militarily and was limited to merely commercial operations.

The Defeat of the Moguls

A. Reasons that a handful of English merchants were able to overthrow the Mogul dynasty:

1) Superior Technology:

As in China during the Opium Wars, British artillery and muskets soon proved too much for the archaic Indian means of warfare. The British also controlled the sea, for the Moguls were landlubbers, and this gave the English the advantage of being able to move troops freely and quickly from one part of India to another.

2) Political Reasons

Indians were divided and had no sense of nationalism, so that many were willing to fight on the side of the British against the hated Moslems. The decline of the Moguls had left India a hodgepodge of small states usually at war with one another. This meant that the East India Company could conquer India piece by piece and principality by principality.

B. The Battle of Buxar   1764

With this victory the rich province of Bengal was brought completely under control of the East India Company, giving them a strong base from which to conquer the rest of India. In 1765 Clive obtained from the Newab of Bengal the right to administer the revenues (known as *dewani*) of Bengal, Bihar, and Orissa, and this meant that the East India Company had in effect become a sovereign power on the mainland of India.

Defeat of the Mahratta Confederacy

In the Battle of Assaye in 1803 the British defeated the main Mahratta forces and thus removed the last serious rival to English control of India. There was, of course, more fighting to be done. For example, the Sikhs of the Punjab offered bitter resistance from 1845 to 1849 before they were finally brought under control. But in the end the East India Company ruled three fifths of India directly and the other two fifths indirectly, through alliances with local princes.

The Exploitation of India

The period from Robert Clive to Warren Hastings has been called the era of the grand conquistadors. The profits were tremendous. Princes were forced to pay heavy tribute, and the Company facilities were often used for private trade. India was ruthlessly exploited, yet what is remarkable is that it caused a reaction in Great Britain. For the first time in history a conquering nation experienced pangs of conscience, and from the start Great Britain maintained the position that her rule was for the benefit of the subject peoples.

Robert Clive, the hero of Plassey and the man who had forecast that "tomorrow the whole Mogul power" will be "in our grasp," was brought before the House of Commons in 1767 for his actions in India and accused of graft and extortion. In 1774 he committed suicide.

Warren Hastings, the first governor-general of Bengal from 1773 to 1785, a remarkable man who learned Urdu, Bengali, and Arabic and who laid the basis for order in India, was also brought before the House of Commons for impeachment but was acquitted and quietly retired.

India Becomes a Crown Colony

By the Regulating Act of 1773 Calcutta was made the seat of government. A governor-general was created and put in charge of three provinces and given much of the East India Company's political power.

By the India Acts of 1784 and 1786, the British Government took over the control of policy-making by establishing a board of control appointed by the crown, and Lord Cornwallis was made governor-general (1786–1793), with orders to reform the administration.

In 1813 the government abolished the East India Company's monopoly of trade and in 1831 took away its authority over all territories.

The final blow to the Company's power came in 1833, when the government of England demanded that all laws made in India be laid before parliament.

In 1858, after the Indian Mutiny, the Company and the Delhi Sultanate were both abolished. From then on India was ruled by two British officials, a Secretary of State for India, who operated from London, and a viceroy (or governor-general), who functioned in Delhi (or Calcutta).

In 1877 Queen Victoria was declared Empress of India.

THE IMPACT OF BRITISH RULE IN INDIA   1857–1947

The Political Unification of India

The British established a government that ruled the entire peninsula. All of India was not ruled directly; some 562 semi-independent princely states were governed indirectly, with the English having control only in matters of defense and foreign policy. (It was up to the Republic of India to abolish these.) The viceroy of India not only governed British India in his capacity as governor-general but also represented the crown in its relations with the princely states.

The restoration of internal order was achieved first by martial law and then by the creation of an efficient police force.

A single law for all was created in 1859. This was truly revolutionary, for now all men and all castes were equal in the eyes of the law. England also passed legislation that prevented brutal punishments and the worst aspects of Hindu family law. As early as Bentinck (government-general 1825–1835), suttee had been abolished (1829), the thugee (ritualistic stranglers) had been suppressed (1830), and infanticide had been counteracted. Murderers could no longer be turned over to the dead man's family for revenge, and child marriage was forbidden, although difficult to enforce.

Reform of the communications system was vital to a unified India and was begun under Dalhousie (governor-general 1848–1856). A network of roads, a canal system, and railroads were built.

The English language was established as the official language of the country in 1835, thus giving Dravidians and Aryans a common tongue.

The Destruction of the Village

The British undermined not only Hindu customs but also the village and the joint family. The government's police force weakened the authority of the elders of the village, and linking India to world markets destroyed the economic independence of the village. The economic self-sufficiency of the village was also upset by the British demand for taxes in cash, not in kind.

Economic Effects of British Rule

The destruction of the ancient landholding system of India and the creation of a class of ruthless and absentee landlords:

A. During the Mogul empire the amount of taxation was elastic, depending on the needs of the Empire and the nature of the harvest. The tax collector or zemindar gathered the taxes and kept one tenth. In 1793 the British converted the zemindar from a tax collector into a landlord. He could then charge the peasant what he wished, thus driving them into bankruptcy. Forty-nine percent of the agricultural land was controlled by the zemindar system.

B. The other 51 percent of the land was somewhat better off, but even here taxes were not adjusted to the harvest, and in bad years the peasant was driven into debt. (In 1911 the agricultural debt amounted to £255,000,000.)

Cheap manufactured cloth from England destroyed the domestic handicrafts, and England tended to keep India an agricultural nation and a closed market for her industrial goods.

Despite the fact that England did not go out of her way to industrialize India, the industrial achievement was certainly not inconsiderable. In 1947 India was the seventh greatest producer of iron in the world, third in the output of cotton yarn and cloth, fourth in extent of railroads, and the most heavily irrigated nation in the world (70 million acres of land under irrigation). Famine had been greatly relieved both by better communications and irrigation and also by a Famine Administration established in 1883. (From 1660 to 1750 there had been fourteen major famines in India and countless minor ones.)

The Philosophy of Nationalism

The British introduced the idea itself, and at the same time they created the conditions of political unity in which the idea of nationalism could develop. They thus helped to create the force that in the end destroyed their power in India.

THE RISE OF NATIONALISM AND THE STRUGGLE FOR INDEPENDENCE

The Indian Mutiny 1857

The Indian Mutiny or the Sepoy Revolt did not begin as a nationalistic uprising. It occurred when a new kind of cartridge was adopted by the British army (the army consisted of British officers and Hindu and Moslem soldiers or sepoys). These cartridges were smeared with grease and had to be bitten before being placed in the rifle. The rumor spread that the grease was a mixture of cow and pig fat, and religiously neither Hindu nor Moslem could touch it. This was the cause of the mutiny among the sepoys. In June of 1857 they revolted, released military prisoners from jail, burned the garrison, and killed any European they could find.

Soon the mutiny spread, and Indian civilians joined because they feared and hated the West and what it was doing in India. (The same superstitions that led the Boxers to war in China also influenced the Indians.) There were over forty thousand mutineers in Delhi alone. The mutiny was finally put down by the British, but not until a great deal of blood had been shed on both sides.

Although the causes of the mutiny had not been nationalistic, the results led to a growth of nationalism in India, for after the mutiny the British developed what was known as a "mutiny complex," becoming less sympathetic to the idea of local self-government, more impersonal, developing a color bar, monopolizing high posts in government, and refusing to share with the Indians in the formulation of public policy. Also, civil service examinations were created, and Indians could not be members of the government unless they passed a test given in England before reaching the age of nineteen. This, of course, eliminated most candidates from the competition. In 1870 there were only seven, and in 1880 only two candidates.

The Indian Nationalist Congress Party

In Bombay in 1885 an Englishman by the name of Hume called a meeting of Indians who were interested in the introduction of democratic and parliamentary government into India. Seventy delegates appeared (only two were Moslem) and the aim of the Congress was stated: "Indirectly this conference will form the germ of a native parliament and . . . will constitute in a few years an unanswerable reply to the assertion that India is still wholly unfit for any form of representative institutions."

After 1907 the Congress split between moderates who wanted to cooperate with British rule and radicals who demanded complete independence. But as the British failed to reform, all groups insisted upon independence and British withdrawal.

The Congress party's membership consisted of the educated classes of India—the lawyers, merchants, students, and journalists. It was not a mass movement until Mohandas Gandhi's return to India in 1919.

Lord Curzon's Reforms and the End of an Epoch

After 1900 nationalism increased in India. Famines, plagues (particularly severe in 1897), and British unconcern made the Indians restless. The humiliating victory of the British in the Boer War (1899–1902) and the defeat of Russia by Asiatic Japan in 1905 tended to make the Indians more vocal and more militant in their demands for independence.

The Curzon Reforms in 1904 and 1905 further inflamed nationalism.

A. Lord Curzon was governor-general of India from 1899 to 1905. He was thoroughly honest and hardworking and he was determined to rule India efficiently, but he had absolutely no understanding of Indian attitudes.

B. Curzon put through many useful reforms. Establishing

rural banks, reorganizing agriculture, strictly enforcing measures against British soldiers who abused Indians, and encouraging the study of Indian history (of which he himself was a student) were all to his credit. Yet there were two reforms that were badly needed but totally misunderstood by the Indians.

1) The University Act of 1904

One was a reform of education. Universities were over-crowded and suffered from poor discipline and poor teachers, and their sole objective seemed to be cramming for exams. So the University Act of 1904 was passed, giving the British government more control of the school system. This "convulsed educated India from one end of the country to another," for the Indians felt that the aim of the British was to control the last semi-independent institution in India.

2) The Partition of Bengal   1905

The second item that was needed was to do something about the administration of Bengal, which was terribly overburdened by 78 million people in the provinces, while the area east of the Ganges was neglected. The partition of Bengal into two administrative units was the final blow to the Indian nationalists, for it divided Bengal into the East, which included 18 million Moslems and 12 million Hindus, and New Bengal, of 42 million Hindus and 12 million Moslems. This not only split an area which had a linguistic patriotism but it also meant that the Moslems now had the majority voice in East Bengal, and this outraged the Hindus. (The Moslem League was formed in part in order to maintain the partition, which was reversed in 1911 and so outraged them in turn.)

The good feeling caused by the reunification of Bengal in 1911 and the Morley-Minto Reforms of 1909 (allowing one Indian to six British on the executive council and twenty-seven Indians to thirty-six British on the legislative council) was completely nullified by the announcement in 1911 that the capital would be moved from Calcutta to New Delhi. This again outraged Bengal nationalists, for they felt it was an insult to their prestige. Also, there was hard feeling, for the Morley-Minto Reforms did not go far enough for most nationalists and the Moslems were given more representatives than they deserved as a result of pressure by the Moslem League.

World War I

During World War I 800,000 Indian volunteers fought with the British against the Germans. India provided foodstuffs, and twenty-seven of the princely states provided troops and money. (The Maharaja of Mysore gave £1,600,000, Nepal gave all its troops, Hyderabad gave £400,000 plus expenses for two regiments overseas.)

At the beginning of the war the moderates were in control of the Congress Party, but even this period was not free of violence.

A. Riots broke out in the Punjab when Sikhs and Moslems were denied admission into Canada under immigration laws of 1914.

B. The Moslem League was quite anti-British, since Turkey was on the side of Germany.

C. By 1918 the moderates had lost control of the Party and a revolutionary situation had developed.

The Amritsar Massacre   April, 1919, and the Increase of Nationalism

The Rowlatt Acts of 1919

In order to curtail lawlessness, particularly in Bengal, these acts permitted the jailing of suspects without trial and took away the right of counsel and the right of appeal. This led to so much agitation that the laws died stillborn, but they had done their harm.

The Massacre

A. The northwest region was aflame with tribal struggles while the Third Afghan War was in process, so military rule was established and a ban on assemblies proclaimed. A crowd of ten thousand Indians nevertheless gathered in a walled courtyard to listen to speeches against the British administration. General Reginald Dyer, who was in charge of the area, ordered the group machine-gunned without word or signal. The walls were too high to scale, the only exit was blocked by British troops, and as Dyer said, "the targets were good"; 379 were killed and 1,200 wounded.

B. Not only did the massacre itself outrage nationalists but its aftereffects did, too. Martial law was strictly enforced, a section where two Englishwomen had been killed in the riots was roped off, and all Indians were forced to crawl by it. General Dyer not only escaped punishment but also became a hero to some Britons in India who presented him with a sword of honor as the "Savior of the Punjab."

Mahatma Gandhi, the Man Who Awakened the Masses and Led India to Independence

Mohandas Karamchand Gandhi (1869–1948)

A. Gandhi was a product of two worlds. He studied law in England, practiced in South Africa, and was a journalist who had been trained in Western party politics and mass propaganda techniques; yet he was also a deeply devout Hindu who believed that industrialization was evil, that violence was wrong, and that an Indian spiritual revival was necessary to save India. The only aspect of Hinduism that Gandhi did not believe in was untouchability.

B. In 1919 Gandhi returned to India from South Africa (where he had been a part of the movement against discrimination) and became the spiritual and political leader of India's fight for independence.

Nonviolet Resistance Was Gandhi's
Major Tactical Weapon

A. Economic strikes and general noncooperation with the British, such as renunciation of titles and honors, the boycotting of law courts, schools, and all British manufactured goods were the means by which Gandhi fought the English. Often, however, nonviolent disobedience led to violence and bloodshed, although Gandhi himself did his best to control his people.

B. The most famous demonstration of civil disobedience came in the Salt March of 1930, when Gandhi demanded the abolition of the state tax on the sale of salt. The salt tax, he felt, was the worst kind of taxation, since it hurt the poorest people in the country. Consequently, Gandhi organized a march to the sea to make his own salt. This 165-mile walk embarrassed the British and brought the plight of India to the attention of the world. During 1930 about fifty thousand political offenders were jailed, including Gandhi and Nehru.

C. To publicize his boycott of English industrial goods and to encourage local village industry, Gandhi began what was to be known as the Homespun Campaign. He dressed himself in a homespun loincloth, took to spinning wherever he went, and lived on goat's milk. The issue of the evils of industrialization was one of the points with which Nehru, his disciple, did not agree.

D. In September, 1932 he went on a "fast unto death" against untouchability. This was another method of getting his way.

The Constitution of 1935

After Gandhi's popularity had gotten out of hand, the Government of India Act was passed giving complete self-government at the provincial level.

World War II

India was declared a belligerent by the British on the day the war broke out, without consultation with the Congress Party and against the wishes of the great majority of Indians. The Congress Party asked England for recognition of Indian independence, in return for which cooperation in the war was to be promised. This was rejected.

As the Japanese made gains in Malaya, Sir Stafford Cripps of the British war cabinet brought proposals to the Congress

Party in March, 1942, giving India more self-government and promising dominion status after the war was over. The Cripps mission failed, and the last and greatest nonviolent resistance campaign began. As a result Congress was outlawed and its leaders jailed. This led to violence; railroads and police stations were destroyed and government officials assassinated. By the end of 1942 order was restored, but as a result sixty thousand Congress members were jailed.

Although the Indian Congress refused to cooperate with the British, the contributions India made to the Allies were considerable. By 1945 India had an army of 2 million volunteers, the largest volunteer army ever assembled. Some of these men played a large part in the winning of Italian East Africa, and 70 percent of the one million troops that defeated the Japanese in Burma were Indian. Besides men, India contributed much to the Allied cause in the way of supplies and became a creditor nation. (At the end of the war she was owed, primarily by Great Britain, £1,250,000,000.)

INDEPENDENCE AND PARTITION AUGUST 15, 1947

Why the British Granted Independence

One of the main reasons was, of course, the growing violence and nationalistic feeling in India. It was quite apparent that Britain could no longer rule India without holding her by military force and producing a great deal of hard feeling internationally. She could ill afford this after a world war of survival, and India was judged not worth the price.

The changing feeling at home was certainly a part of the decision to grant freedom. The most destructive of all wars had been fought to preserve the liberal and democratic world, and it seemed inconsistent for England to champion freedom in Europe and rule India by force of arms. The government of Great Britain changed from the conservative to the labor party at the end of the war, and the new labor government pledged itself to the policy of independence for India.

Partition

Hope that Hindus and Moslems might find a way of living together was doomed as early as 1937, when governments formed by the National Congress shut out Moslems in some of the provinces. At this time Mohammed Ali Jinnah (Moslem League President after 1934) became committed to the concept of a Moslem nation of Pakistan.

In March, 1946 the government of Great Britain dispatched a three-man mission under Sir Stafford Cripps to bring about an immediate transfer of power in India, but the question of partition slowed down the process. That year rioting took place, in which Bengal and Bihar provinces alone suffered nearly ten thousand fatalities in six months. Finally the Congress agreed that no group should be compelled to accept a constitution against its will and, as expected, the Moslem majority areas voted for partition. On August 15, 1947 India was granted her independence and was divided into two separate nations.

INDIA AND PAKISTAN SINCE INDEPENDENCE

The Problems of Partition

Pakistan consisted of two sections a thousand miles apart: West Pakistan (the Sind, the northwest frontier, Baluchistan, and the western part of the Punjab) and East Pakistan (the eastern part of Bengal plus the Sylhet district of Assam). National assets were divided on a ratio of 82.5 to 17.5 in favor of India. Everything (from railroad equipment and the national debt to criminals, lunatics, and office furniture) had to be divided, and Pakistan received her share only after Gandhi insisted.

The transfer of people who were located in split areas caused the most trouble. Rioting and religious wars broke out in the Punjab, which had been divided right down the middle. Approximately 12 million people moved (often fled) from one country to another, and estimates place the number of deaths through violence at 200,000 and others due to dislocation at 300,000.

Economic dislocation was another result of partition. East Pakistan grows 70 percent of the world's jute, but all the mills are in India. Pakistan received the better food- and cotton-growing areas and India the coal, metals, and industrial resources of the peninsula. India received 82 percent of the population but only 69 percent of the irrigated lands.

The status of 562 princely states also caused problems, some of which have not yet been solved. All the princely states joined either India or Pakistan, but trouble arose in Jammu and Kashmir, Hyderabad, Junagadh, and Manavadar.

A. The small states of Junagadh and Manavadar were predominantly Hindu and surrounded by Indian territory. They had, however, Moslem rulers, who joined Pakistan in 1947. The Indian government sent in forces and occupied the countries, granting a plebiscite that resulted in an overwhelming vote to join India.

B. Hyderabad, the largest state in the Deccan and completely surrounded by Indian territory, was also Hindu with a Moslem ruler, and the Nizam felt powerful enough to hold out for independence. Armed Moslem forces terrorized the population, and communists took control of many of the villages. After first trying an economic blockade, the Indian army took over the state in 1948.

c. Jammu and Kashmir

1) The problem of these two princely states has not been totally solved, and the Pakistan government has an excellent precedent in Indian action in Junagadh, Manavadar, and Hyderabad for taking over control of this area, which is predominantly Moslem (three quarters) with a Hindu Maharajah. In 1947 Pakistan invaded the area, and the Maharajah quickly joined India. Indian troops arrived by airlift barely in time to save Srinagar, the capital. Nehru referred the case to the U.N. demanding a plebiscite and the condemnation of Pakistan as an aggressor. The two countries were at war for fourteen months until a cease-fire was arranged by the U.N. in January, 1949.

2) Kashmir is valuable, for it has the rich agricultural vale and a lucrative tourist trade; it controls the headwaters of important rivers; and it is situated in a position strategic to both Pakistan and India.

3) Nothing has been settled, and partition at this point seems the only answer—Jammu to India, the north to Pakistan, and a plebiscite in the vale. Nehru, however, said that partition had to be along the cease-fire line only, which gave India considerably more territory, and in 1957 this area was incorporated into India.

The Death of Gandhi

Another result of the partition was the assassination of Mahatma Gandhi on January 30, 1948. Fortunately for relations between India and Pakistan, he was killed not by a Moslem but by a fanatic Hindu who was confused and frustrated by Gandhi's attempt to stop the violence among Hindus, Moslems, and Sikhs. (In January, 1948 he had begun a fast for the "reunion of hearts.")

The Political Scene in India

The Form of Government

India today is a constitutional federal state. The sixteen states themselves have little power, for, unlike the United States, the residual powers are given specifically to the central government, which has the power to seize and assume the functions of state governments in case of emergency. (This was done in 1959 in the communist-controlled state of Kerala.) The constitution established a bicameral government, with executive power resting in a prime minister who is leader of the majority party in the House of the People, and a Federal Court of Appeals with powers similar to that of the United States Supreme Court.

Political Parties

THE CONGRESS PARTY IS THE ONLY LARGE
AND IMPORTANT PARTY

This party, which led India to independence and of which Jawaharlal Nehru became the head after Gandhi's death, is a litical creed and organization. When Nehru died in 1964 the socialist and secular party favoring government control of basic industry (but not secondary industry) and democracy in its po-leadership of the Congress Party was taken over by Lal Bahadur Shastri, who died in January, 1966 and was succeeded by Nehru's daughter, Mrs. Gandhi (no relative to Mohandas).

THE RIGHTIST HINDUS

Culturally and religiously nationalistic, these parties all favor a revival of Sanskrit culture and a policy of India for the Hindus. The parties are the Jan Sangh (People's party), the Ram Rajya Parishad (God's Rule Party), and the Hindu Mahasabha (Great Society). Another party, which is the most militant of all, is the Rashtrya Smayamsevak Sangh (National Volunteer Association, the R.S.S.).

THE PRAJA-SOCIALIST PARTY (THE PSP)

The socialists, although now united in a common party, are not very strong, because the Congress Party has put through many of the desired reforms advocated by the socialists.

THE INDIAN COMMUNIST PARTY

Although the socialist party carries a larger number of votes than the communist party, in terms of strength the ICP is stronger, for it is a disciplined and devout group. By using China and Russia as examples of what can be done in an under-developed country they have gained support, although their popularity at this point seems restricted to Kerala, Andhra, and the cities of Bombay and Calcutta.

Nehru (1889–1964)

A. Born in Kashmir of the Brahmin caste, Nehru became a westerner when, at the age of fifteen, he was sent to England's Harrow School and then entered Cambridge at the age of seventeen.

B. A democrat and a socialist, prime minister of India, minister of atomic energy, minister of foreign policy and economic policy, he was by far the most powerful person in India. In a very real sense he was the father of modern India.

C. In 1916 Nehru began his political career when he met Gandhi and joined the movement for independence, during which he was imprisoned nine times, the longest from 1942 to 1945.

D. In 1948 he became India's first prime minister and head of the Congress Party.

Lal Bahadur Shastri (1904–1966)
Shastri was also a veteran of jail sentences under British rule, and he was a strong advocate of Nehru's policies, both domestic and international.

The Political Scene in Pakistan

Since independence, Pakistan has not experienced the same stability of leadership as India. In fact, there have been continual changes in government. At first Pakistan was under the rule of a governor-general and a constituent assembly, and a constitution was not accepted until 1956 (and it was very quickly abrogated).

The first governor-general was Mohammed Ali Jinnah (1876–1948), the leader of the Moslem League and the man who was really responsible for the founding of Pakistan. He was not only governor-general but also head of the constituent assembly (formed in 1947). His death in 1948 left the country without a leader who could inspire loyalty and the necessary unity.

Kwaja Nazimudden became governor-general with Liaquat Ali Khan as prime minister (League secretary 1936–1947). A progressive and a moderate in relations with India, Ali Khan was assassinated by a Moslem fanatic in 1951. Nazimudden then became prime minister and nominated Ghulam Mohammed as governor-general.

Because of economic problems and the question of representation in East Pakistan, Governor-General Mohammed dismissed the cabinet in 1953 and appointed Mohammed Ali (ex-ambassador to the United States) as premier. His cabinet lasted only two years (1953–1955). The Governor-General dissolved the legislature and declared a state of emergency in October, 1954.

In 1955 Chandhri Mohammed Ali (finance minister) re-

placed Mohammed Ali as prime minister, and General Mirza
became governor-general when Ghulam Mohammed retired.

The Constitution of 1956

Pakistan was declared to be an Islamic Republic, and General Iskander Mirza was made its first president, with H. S.
Suhrawardy as prime minister. The government was to be
stronger at the provincial than at the central level. The relationship between the president, the cabinet, and the national
assembly was not worked out. In 1958 Mirza took complete control, abrogated the constitution, and dissolved all political parties. He did this with the support of Marshal Mohammed Ayub
Khan, commander of the army. In October, 1958 Ayub withdrew
his support, offered Mirza a trip to England and a pension, and
took over the government himself, ruling by martial law until
the end of 1960. Today (1965) he continues to rule as virtual
dictator of Pakistan, although in 1962 a new constitution was
written and in 1965 elections were held.

The Economic Scene in India and Pakistan

India and Pakistan are both underdeveloped countries.
Yearly incomes in both countries average $66 per person, and
75 percent of the populations are illiterate. Their economies are
still overwhelmingly agricultural (about 70 percent in India),
and 65 percent of their peoples are undernourished, with a life
expectancy of only thirty-two.

The Problem of Overpopulation and Low Productivity

Although India has spent $30 million on birth control clin-
ics, her population today (1965) is approximately 460 million,
and next year it is estimated that she will have 28 million tons
of food too little to keep her people from starving. The average
population density is 356 people per square mile (in the United
States it is fifty), but this is less than many areas (Holland has
948) and would not be a problem if India were not an agricultural nation. Nor would her population growth, which is less

than that of the United States, be a factor if it weren't for the low productivity of her land.

India's Five-year Plans

A. India's first five-year plan was put into operation in 1950. It proposed to do three things:

  1) grow two stalks of wheat where only one had grown before,
  2) have one baby born where two had been born before,
  3) build new industries.

The main emphasis of the first plan was on agriculture.

B. The second plan of 1955–1960 shifted the emphasis to heavy industry, communications, and transportation, with the cost approximately double—11.76 billion dollars as against 5.7 billion.

C. The third plan of 1961 emphasized agriculture once again, but by 1962 many aims had to be abandoned; one of these was to increase the per capita income from $69 to $81.

D. Raising the standard of living progresses slowly. In Calcutta alone, 25,000 people remain homeless.

E. Village Development

Land reform was accomplished by abolishing zemindar landowners in 1953 and setting up a Community Development Program, under which the government gave advice, materials, and initiative. The peasants were free to decide whether they would accept these services. This method of economic improvement is, of course, unlike that in China or Russia and is necessarily slower, for the people must be educated to want reform.

Pakistan's Five-year Plans

A. Pakistan's first five-year plan began in 1956 and placed main emphasis on agricultural improvement and electric power output. Pakistan has food and cloth, but industrial development appears rather hopeless, since practically no industrial base and few power resources exist.

B. Her second plan (1960–1965) emphasizes the same things with an increase in expenditure of over 70 percent. Greater emphasis on education is an essential part of the plan, and the expenditure on health has risen 200 percent. Funds for housing are still very low in spite of pressing needs. Since 1960 Ayub Khan has initiated a land reform. Fifteen hundred acres was made the maximum size for farms and all land over that amount was confiscated. The overall plan calls for a 20 percent rise in the output of the nation.

The International Scene

India has become the leader of the neutral nations, refusing to be committed to either the West or the East. She is an independent nation within the British Commonwealth but other than this has no ties with any country. Despite the fact that it is extremely hard to maintain neutrality, she has so far been quite successful.

A. In 1951 India refused to condemn China as the aggressor in Korea but did provide some aid to the U.N. forces in the form of ambulance units.

B. In 1955 she was present at the Bandung Conference of Asian nations and advocated peaceful coexistence with China, signing the Five Principles of Peaceful Coexistence submitted by Chou En-lai.

C. India advocates the recognition of her neighbor China and maintains an active embassy in Peking, but since 1958 relations have been strained due to serious border clashes along the northeast frontier and the Tibet Revolt, which shocked the neutral world.

D. At the Belgrade Conference of 1962 India was one of the few neutral nations that spoke against the Russian breaking of the atomic test ban.

E. Today, as a consequence of the Chinese invasion of her frontier provinces (1959–1963), India is receiving military aid from the United States and seems to be somewhat more inclined to the Western camp.

Pakistan has not maintained neutrality, although in 1954 she followed India's lead and became a republic within the Commonwealth. She is nevertheless a member of SEATO (Southeast Asian Treaty Organization) and thus allied defensively with the United States, the Philippines, and Thailand. She is also a member of CTO (Central Treaty Organization) and therefore militarily allied with Great Britain, Iran, and Turkey. But since 1960 she has become more and more friendly with China, for she claims that Western military aid to India may be used against Pakistan.

China

ANCIENT CIVILIZATION 2200–1000 B.C.

Information on the first known civilization in China, which developed near the Yellow River, is only about sixty years old, for it was then that certain animal bones were first discovered by peasants. These dragon bones, as they were called, were oracle bones used by the people of the Shang dynasty to ask the gods questions, and it is from them that all that is known of this early civilization has been learned. Possibly there was an earlier civilization, between 2205 B.C. and 1523 B.C., known as the Hsia dynasty, but although there are many Chinese myths about it, historians have little evidence that it actually existed.

THE SHANG DYNASTY AND THE BRONZE AGE
1523 B.C.–1028 B.C.

The Shang dynasty was possibly the first and certainly the most civilized of a number of principalities located in the Huang Ho Valley. (Its capital was near the modern city of Anyang.) It is known to have had a system of writing using a brush on ivory or bronze, domesticated animals, and an organized army of over five thousand men employing the use of the chariot.

The system of writing was perhaps their most important single contribution and was not lost with the end of the dynasty, for historians believe that the Shangs tutored their conquerors, the Chous, in their way of life.

The practice of divination employing the use of the oracle bones to ask the gods questions was combined with the worship of a major deity called Shang Ti. Ancestor worship is believed to have begun during this period.

The downfall of the Shang came when a less civilized principality in the valley of the Wei called the Chou defeated the Shang ruler in battle and took over the principality.

CLASSICAL CIVILIZATION   1000 B.C.–500 A.D.

Most of the chief characteristics of Chinese civilization were developed during the classical era. Chinese political, religious, and social philosophy were established, the highly centralized system of imperial government was formed out of a host of petty principalities, and Chinese imperialistic expansion began.

The Dynasties of the Classical Period

The Chou Dynasty   1124 B.C.–249 B.C.

This period is often referred to as China's feudal period, for it was during the Chou dynasty that China experienced political chaos and decentralization somewhat resembling European feudalism. By 720 B.C. the reign of Chou was weak, and power was distributed among principalities similar to feudal states. But throughout this period there was more uniformity of culture than there was in Europe.

This was also the outstanding creative period of Chinese thought, as it was in many areas of the world; it corresponds in time with the height of Greek culture, the Hebrew prophets, and the flowering of Buddhism in India.

The Chin Dynasty   221 B.C.–206 B.C.

This dynasty is most famous for its contribution to China's political unity.

The ruler of the Chin was Chin Shih (first) Huang (emperor) Ti (deity of the Shang dynasty), and it was he who was solely responsible for the determined effort to unify and establish a central government over all China. It is from the word *Chin* that China is named.

The government allowed no freedom of thought, burning all books in 214 B.C. except those on agriculture, medicine, and divination, killing those who disagreed with the state either by burial alive or by forced labor on the Great Wall (completed in 204 B.C.), which ultimately meant death.

The Han Dynasty 202 B.C.–221 A.D.
(Divided into the Western Han 202 B.C.–9 A.D. and the Eastern Han 25 A.D.–221 A.D.)

This dynasty immediately modified the severe laws of the Chin and eventually adopted Confucianism as the basis of the political structure of China.

The reign of Wu Ti (140–87 B.C.) was the height of the Western Han, witnessing the opening of the great silk route with Rome, the beginning of irrigation projects, the regulation of commerce and coinage, expansion into North Korea, and explorations into Central Asia.

It was during this period that the Chinese invented paper and developed a calendar, and historical records of previous dynasties were begun.

221 A.D.–589 A.D.

During this time there was no unified rule in China, and the territory shrank to the size of China Proper (the eight provinces below the Great Wall).

CHINESE POLITICAL AND RELIGIOUS PHILOSOPHY

Confucianism

Confucius (Kung Fu-tzu 551 B.C.–479 B.C.) lived in the province of Lu and was a minor official of the government, but he quit his job because of the corruption and chaos of the Chou dynasty.

The main purpose of Confucius' philosophy was to bring social order into an era of political chaos and confusion. The code became the most successful of all systems of conservatism, lasting two thousand years as the chief ideology of the world's largest state. Confucius believed that only through harmonious relations among individuals could true harmony between man and nature be reached.

The Five Relationships and the Classes of Society

A. Each person was to assume a specific place in society, with specific duties and modes of conduct known as *li* or propriety. This was accomplished by a system of superiors and inferiors.

B. The Five Relationships of superiors over inferiors were prince over subject; father over son; husband over wife; elder brother over younger brother; and friend over friend.

C. The classes in society were ordered on the Confucian idea of worth: first, scholars; second, farmers; third, artisans; fourth, merchants; fifth, slaves. Soldiers were not even on the social scale, although their position varied throughout Chinese history, on the assumption that "nice boys don't become soldiers." (This attitude is quite different in Japanese history.) Confucianism placed great emphasis on an intellectual and landed elite and depreciated the value of anyone in commerce or manufacturing. Consequently, it succeeded in creating a bifurcated social structure in which 80 percent were illiterate peasants and 20 percent landed upper-class. There was almost no middle class.

The Emperor

A. The emperor received the mandate of heaven, an authorization from the deity to reign, but he ruled by means of his virtue. Thus if he was not virtuous he could lose his mandate.

B. The ruler was considered to be the son of heaven; his only superior was God. He was therefore held responsible for all calamities, and thus revolutions in China often occurred at times of famine or other hardships.

Confucian Emphasis on Paternalism

The emperor of the state was the father of society. The father in each family was the most important person and the family was the most important unit. The family, rather than the individual or the state, was the most significant unit in Chinese society. This was not true in Japan.

MAJOR CHARACTERISTICS OF THE CHINESE FAMILY

1) Group was important, not the individual.

2) Youth was subordinate to age.

3) Ancestor worship was emphasized (subordination of the living to the dead).

4) The wife was subordinate to the husband.

5) The daughter-in-law was subordinate to the mother-in-law.

6) Child-bearing, not love, was the reason for marriage.

The Confucian Classics and the Examination System

No one could become an official of the government without mastering the canonical works of the Chinese classics.

Ceremony Emphasized

Because of the strict relationships among men, Confucianism was based on ceremony and eventually become more form than substance. The Japanese succeeded in borrowing the ceremony and not the philosophy of Confucianism.

Mencius (Meng-tzu 373 B.C.–288 B.C.)

A. Mencius was a Confucian scholar who traveled from state to state preaching good government as Confucius had done, and emphasized the importance of education and self-improvement. He advocated a code of moral righteousness for all, not just for the upper class.

B. Mencius' most important contribution to Confucian theory was the clarification of the Right of Rebellion. He emphasized the importance of the ruler ruling by good conduct; if he did not rule in this way, he could and should be overthrown.

Once he had been overthrown, the mandate of heaven obviously
would go to the conqueror.

Taoism

The founder of Taoism is believed to have been a man by
the name of Lao Tzu (604 B.C.?), but historians are not sure
that he actually existed.

Taoism advocates the subordination of oneself to nature's
ways, for only in this manner can man lead a meaningful life.
The search of the Taoist is to find union with nature, to find
the way, or the tao. This involves something similar to the renunciation of the world.

Taoism was in many ways the opposite of Confucianism,
romantic rather than matter-of-fact, intuitive rather than or-
derly, mystical and vague rather than rational. Yet many Chinese were both Confucianist and Taoist—Confucian during
times of peace and prosperity or while holding government
office, and Taoist during times of trouble and disorder or while
home in the country.

Ancestor Worship

This lasted, despite the introduction of the religious philosophies of Buddhism and Taoism, and Confucius encouraged
it, believing that it would make people more aware of their
responsibility to the family and their duties to their elders.

The Yin and the Yang

A belief in the Yin and the Yang persisted from early
times and was included in the philosophies of Confucianism and
Taoism. The Yang was positive and male, everything that was
warm and active (represented by heaven), while the Yin was
negative and female, everything that was cold or wet or myste-
rious (represented by the earth). These were the two forces in

the universe and were inseparable; therefore man and nature must be harmonious, and heaven and man were in partnership.

Buddhism

The religion from India was not introduced until the end of the classical period and was adapted and changed by the Chinese to include Confucian ethics, Taoist beliefs, ancestor worship, and a multitude of gods.

THE CREATION OF THE CHINESE STATE

The formation of the central government of China and the establishment of the emperor as a hereditary leader was accomplished under the Chin dynasty. The imperial structure, with its all-powerful emperor and its efficient and disciplined bureaucracy, was the Chin's lasting contribution to Chinese history.

Uniformity was achieved by a common tax system, weights and measures, and a uniform written script that gave to China a language by which all could communicate.

China was divided into provinces that could be administered from the central government, and irrigation and canal projects were begun.

This was perhaps the time of the most profound and far-reaching social upheaval in all Chinese history with the exception of the twentieth century.

Confucianism as the philosophy of government was established during the Han dynasty, and the examination system as a means of recruiting government officials was based on the Confucian classics. This persisted until 1900.

The Expansion of the Chinese State

During the Chin dynasty the area of land controlled was extended along the coast and below the Yangtze River and south as far as the Indochina border.

The Han dynasty is particularly famous for its imperialistic expansion in all directions—west into central Asia, north into Manchuria, and south into Indochina. It was equal in size and military might to the Roman Empire.

MEDIEVAL CIVILIZATION 500 A.D.–1500 A.D.

One of the unique characteristics of Chinese history is its continuity. Although dynasties declined, decayed, and were rebelled against from within and invaded from without and finally overthrown, the basic characteristics of the Chinese way of life and the Chinese government did not change. Though anarchy prevailed during the periods between great dynasties, Chinese culture was not destroyed. Though barbarians invaded and conquered the land, they themselves were conquered by Chinese philosophy, and their governments continued to be supported by Confucian doctrine, agricultural revenues, and forced labor. Though there were foreign commerce, migrations, and influence, and though there were material innovations and discoveries, China remained essentially the same. During the medieval period, the greatest influence from the outside world was Buddhism, which the Chinese quickly accepted and adapted to their own use. But even Buddhism could not seriously challenge Confucianism or the structure of Chinese society. So although each dynasty during the medieval period of Chinese history varied in detail, in essence each was the same.

THE DYNASTIES OF MEDIEVAL CHINA

The Sui 589 A.D.–618 A.D.

This dynasty reunified China after over 350 years of civil chaos at the fall of the Han. In this respect it was similar to the Chin dynasty, although certainly not as bloody or as dramatic. It was a military government that served its purpose of reunification and then fell.

The Tang   618 A.D.–907 A.D.

The Tang dynasty resembled the Han in extent of empire and brilliance of civilization. It was a period of foreign expansion into Manchuria, Mongolia, Tibet, and to the Indus. During the reign of Hsuan Tsung (712 A.D.), schools were established all over China, and the world's first newspaper was printed. Japan was so impressed by the dynasty's greatness that she borrowed wholesale from it, imitating everything she saw.

Sung in South China   907 A.D.–1279 A.D.

Political turmoil reigned from 907 to 960, until the Sung dynasty finally was able to reunify and rule part of China proper. The barbarians controlled the north, and in 1123 the Sungs were forced to move even farther south. During this period the south witnessed a flourishing of the arts and some attempts at economic reform; the dynasty is famous for its porcelains and its paintings.

The Yuan   1279 A.D.–1368 A.D.

Kubla Khan led the Mongols against the Sung dynasty in the south of China and successfully established himself as ruler of all China. This was the first time in her long history that China was completely under the control of a foreign dynasty, but the dynasty was short-lived, for the Mongols were few in number and were soon absorbed by the Chinese and their culture.

This was the time of Marco Polo, and it is interesting to note the contrast between Europe and China. In his travels, Polo stated that he had seen in China printed paper money, broad streets, police patrols at night, public carriages, drains under the street, and landscaped roadsides—all of which he had never encountered in Europe.

The Ming 1368 A.D.–1644 A.D.

A revolt in the south of China led by a poor farm laborer established the Ming dynasty in power. The dynasty advocated a return to China for the Chinese and in many ways was reactionary, for it was content simply with reestablishing old ways: civil service exams were stereotyped, there was little philosophic innovation, and creativity was nil. This quality of rigidity and resistance to change became increasingly typical of China and eventually became one of the causes of the downfall of Chinese civilization in the face of the Western impact.

MODERN CIVILIZATION   1500 to the Present

The modern history of China is really the story of the coming of the West in 1514, the dominance of the West by 1900, and the reaction to the West in the form of the Republican Revolution of 1911, the Nationalist Revolution of 1927, and finally the Communist Revolution of 1949; but as Mr. Fairbanks said, "The tragedy of China's revolution is that the modern technology which so obviously makes possible the economic and cultural liberation of the Chinese peasant also makes possible . . . his political enslavement."

In 1500, China still thought of herself as the "Middle Kingdom," the center of the world. She still carried on foreign relations based on the tribute system, a sort of vassal relationship in which China would recognize the legitimacy of a neighboring state in return for tribute from that state. To her, the rest of the world was barbarian and had nothing to offer China. In a letter to George III of England in 1790, Peking announced that there was "nothing we lack, as your principal envoy and others have themselves observed. We have never set much store on strange or ingenious objects, nor do we need any more of your country's manufactures. . . ." This impression was not totally changed until 1900, and it was only then that China became fully aware of how archaic her institutions were in contrast to those of the West (in comparison, see history of Japan). The hope, however, is that Napoleon's forecast of the future was mistaken: "Let China sleep; when she awakens the world will be sorry."

THE CHING DYNASTY   1644–1912

The beginning of the Manchu reign in China is often cited as the commencement of the modern period, but it was not. The Manchus invaded and conquered China, but did not change its ways. China's imperial government remained essentially the same, although the Manchus set up a dyarchy in which there was one Manchu and one Chinese for every post. They attempted to maintain their dynastic identity and not be absorbed as the Mongols had been by Chinese culture. They forbade intermarriage between Manchu and Chinese, retained Manchuria as an exclusive preserve for themselves, and limited the army to Manchurians.

The Chien-lung Period   1736–1795

This was the height of Manchu power. Chien-lung himself is considered the greatest of the Manchus, equal to Catherine the Great of Russia and Frederick the Great of Prussia, his contemporaries. A period of internal peace prevailed, with improvement in the rural situation and religious tolerance. China stood in marked contrast to Europe at the time and she was certainly her equal if not her superior. It was also a period of great physical extension—the Tarim Basin area, Manchuria, Mongolia, Tibet, all were under China's control, and raids even into Nepal were conducted.

The Coming of the West—the Real Beginning of the Modern Era

The Portuguese arrived in China in 1514, followed closely by the Spanish and the Dutch. From 1514 to 1644 there was little direct trade, and when the Manchus came to power in 1644 they prohibited trade by sea for forty years. From 1685 to 1759 there was multiport trade, but by 1670 the Manchu government decided that with the increase of foreigners, particularly British, who were soon to dominate the trade, something had to be done, and the Factory System was introduced.

The Factory System   1760–1842

A. This was a system of trade regulations whereby foreigners, limited to the port of Canton, were not allowed to deal with anyone other than one of the thirteen cohongs who were representatives of the government. The cohong decided not only what China would sell but also what she would buy and for what price.

B. The regulations on foreigners were severe: they could not live in China during the nontrading season, and during the trading season they were forced to live outside of the city in factories or warehouses built for the purpose, and under no circumstances were they allowed to bring women with them. Their goods were taxed at whatever rate the government chose, and they were allowed no freedom of trade.

C. The purpose of the system, as far as the Manchu government was concerned, was to milk the trade and keep the barbarians under control.

D. Despite these restrictions the foreigners, particularly the British East India Company and the Americans, certainly profited.

The Penetration of the West

The First Opium War Between the British and the Manchus   1840–1842

CAUSES

1) The Opium Trade

A) China was not interested in anything the British had to sell, but tea and silk were in great demand in London.

The British were naturally opposed to paying in gold and by the eighteenth century found a commodity that the Chinese were happy to pay for—opium. The opium was grown in east and west India and smuggled into China. In 1729 two hundred chests (one hundred twenty pounds per chest) were sold, and by 1838 the number had risen to forty thousand. The result, of course, was that the Canton cohongs were losing out and the trading balance had shifted—now gold was being drained out of China.

B) The Manchus, since they could not profit from the trade, tried to stop the opium importation. The government succeeded in getting the British to turn over twenty thousand chests to the Manchu officials, but they could not force the British to sign a bond guaranteeing that there would be no more opium sold in China. This precipitated the war.

2) Lack of Diplomatic Equality

The foreigners were definitely considered and treated as inferiors by the Chinese. There was no communication with the dragon throne unless the emperor invited it, and even this invitation involved the humiliating kowtow (prostrating oneself three times and bowing your head nine times to the floor), which most Britishers and Americans refused to perform.

3) Clash Between Legal Systems

The Chinese believed in the doctrine of responsibility: someone had to pay for a crime, whether it was manslaughter or murder. For example, in 1821 a jar fell off a ship and killed a woman in a sampan. All trade was halted until the American ship surrendered a man to be strangled by the Chinese.

THE WAR did not last long, for the British with their gunboats, rifles, and cannons were definitely superior to the Chinese with their spears and junks.

THE TREATY OF NANKING   1842

This treaty ended the Factory System and established what was to be known as the Treaty System. It opened five ports to trade, gave Hong Kong to the British, and promised diplomatic equality along with an indemnity of $21,000,000.

OTHER TREATIES 1843

Immediately, other treaties followed with other countries—the United States, France, Holland, and Germany. Each nation was granted a most-favored-nation clause, which meant that anything one nation received the other nation would also receive.

The Second Opium War or the Arrow War—Britain and France versus the Manchus 1858–1860

CAUSES

1) The primary causes of this war were that the Chinese refused to accept the basic premise of the Treaty of Nanking—diplomatic equality—and that the treaty had never determined the status of opium nor had there been a settlement on whether foreigners were to live in or out of the cities.

2) The Chinese were also annoyed. The coolie trade, or the kidnapping of Chinese by Westerners to be used as cheap labor in South America, Australia, and Malaya (the British and the Americans had banned it), was on the increase. There was piracy along the coast, and the Portuguese had established a protection racket.

THE TREATY OF TIENTSIN 1858

All of the first gains were preserved by this treaty, and in addition eleven new ports were opened, opium was legalized, the tariff was fixed at 5 percent, diplomats were allowed to reside in Peking, and foreigners were permitted to navigate up the Yangtze.

The Treaty did not actually end the war; it took two more years of fighting to have the treaty ratified in Peking, but by 1860 the first chapter of the pressure of the West had ended.

The Second Chapter of Penetration Has Often Been Called the "Scramble for Concessions"

A. From 1898 on China was divided into spheres of influence: Britain—the Yangtze Valley; Russia—Manchuria and Port Arthur; Japan—Korea and the Ryukyu Islands; Germany—Kiaochow Bay; and France—the three southern provinces of Yunnan, Kwangsi, and Kwangtung.

B. 1899 and 1900, the Open Door Notes of the United States Secretary of State Hay called for the treaty powers to refrain from staking out exclusive trading rights and leave the door open for trade. Perhaps United States' action slowed the process of cutting China into many different colonial areas, but probably the major reason for China remaining free was the bitter rivalry among European nations.

Reaction to the West

The Taiping Rebellion 1851–1864

A. This rebellion marks the opening phase in a revolutionary process, and it is in this framework that it is important. It was the beginning of a revolution that would eventually affect all aspects of Chinese society from the economic to the ideological.

B. Led by Hung Hsiu-chuan, a man who considered himself the younger brother of Christ and who aimed at the overthrow of the Manchus and the establishment of the "Heavenly Kingdom of Great Peace" (T'ai-ping tien-kuo), this was the first foreign-influenced ideology to be successful since Buddhism.

C. At first the Taipings were remarkably successful, taking Nanking in 1853, moving thirty miles south of Peking, and consolidating the lower Yangtze valley area.

D. The Taiping rebellion is unique, for it not only professed a pseudo-Christian doctrine but also used military tactics such as guerrilla warfare and fifth columns. It advocated economic reforms, redistribution of land, and a type of socialist state. It also advocated equality of women and language simplification. There are many similarities between the rebellion and the Communist Revolution in 1949.

E. The Reasons for the Failure of the Rebellion

Corruption and dissension among the leadership was part of the reason for failure, but the most important was the fact that the Taipings professed an ideology unsuitable for enlisting the support of the educated gentry, and this was vital. The educated began to mobilize opposition and organize local militias to put the Taipings down, asking for and receiving aid from Europeans.

F. Results of the Taiping Rebellion

1) It further weakened the Manchus, for it led to more foreign intervention and growing decentralization of China, with the development of native Chinese militia from local provinces under the command of the gentry.

2) The Manchus tried to restore Confucianism in the government, to improve the bureaucracy, to reorganize the military by incorporating some Western techniques, and to deal with the West on its own terms by establishing a foreign bureau and an interpreters' college. But the adoption of Western institutions began to undermine the very thing the adoption was supposed to build up.

The Second Major Reaction to the West—the Reform Movement 1895–1900

A. The cause of the desire for reform was not only the further penetration by the West but also the impact of the Japanese victory over the Chinese in 1895. This was the first event that impressed a considerable number of Chinese, for here was an example of the modernization of an Asian country and the final proof of the weakness of China.

B. Hundred Days of Reform   June 14–September 16, 1898

1) Kang Yu-wei, a member of the bureaucracy, was chiefly responsible for influencing the Emperor of China, Prince Kung, to make the reforms. These reforms included a new education system, a Western army, and the cleansing of government by the abolition of some of the more corrupt offices.

2) These reforms, passed from June 14 to September 16, were in direct conflict with the desires of Empress Dowager, Tzu Hsi, who was the real power in China, for the doing away with loyal if corrupt offices as well as the undermining of the Manchu nobility threatened her position. She immediately plotted against the prince and overthrew him, and on September 26 all reforms were abolished, the Emperor was arrested, and she put an end to voluntary reform.

The Third Reaction—the Boxer Rebellion   1900

A. The Boxer Rebellion was another phase in the revolutionary process. It was symptomatic of the growing unrest, the increasing antiforeignism, and it was the last desperate effort to drive out the foreigners.

B. The rebellion was led by a group that called itself the Fists of Righteous Harmony and was supported quietly by the throne. It was directed against all foreigners and any Chinese who had come under the influence of the West (particularly Christians). The foreign legations in Peking were attacked, and 242 Westerners were killed as well as several thousand Chinese converts. The Western governments immediately sent an allied army (the greatest number of men to relieve the legations was sent by Japan—80,000). With this, the movement collapsed.

C. Effects of the Boxer Rebellion

1) The Settlement

An indemnity of $333,000,000 was demanded, forts were dismantled, the foreigners occupied thirteen places around Peking, officials were punished (many were ordered to commit suicide), and a genuine Chinese foreign ministry was demanded.

2) It convinced many of the most conservative bureaucrats that things had to be changed, and it indicated the lack of central authority of the government.

3) The reforms of the Manchus   1901–1910

A) Educational reforms: Schools were established, the examination system was abolished, and students were sent abroad to study.

B) A new army was created, modeled after the German system. Between 1902 and 1907 six modern divisions were created.

C) A constitution was promised, copied from the Japanese, and drafted in 1908, and provincial assemblies were put into operation in 1909 and a national assembly in 1910.

D) Railroads were built, but this led to a contest between central and provincial power.

E) The early reforms had been within the Confucian system. These reforms were not, and the Manchus soon found that drastic change was undermining the very foundations of their government.

THE REVOLUTION OF 1911

Causes of the Revolution

Lack of Leadership

In 1908 the Empress Dowager, Tzu Hsi, died, and her heir was a three-year-old boy who was controlled by the seventy-three-year-old, corrupt, and inefficient Prince Ching. Growing pressure from provincial assemblies and financial problems, along with a lack of central control, further weakened the Manchu government. It was only a matter of time before it would fall.

Revolutionary Developments

A. By the reforms of 1900–1908, new revolutionary groups had been created in China. The students educated abroad returned and demanded radical change, not just reform. The army trained in Japan, the Chinese who lived in treaty ports beyond the reach of Manchu authorities, and the Chinese who lived overseas all demanded violent change.

B. Revolutionary societies developed. The most important was the Teng Meng-Hui (the Together-Sworn Society), formed in 1905 by Sun Yat-sen. This was the party that was later to become known as the Kuomintang or the Nationalist party. By 1912 its membership was approximately 300,000.

Sun Yat-sen and the Three People's Principles

A. Sun was the man who knit these revolutionary groups together. He was definitely a product of Western influence himself. Born in 1866 in south China of upper peasantry, he was sent to school in Honolulu, where he became a Westerner and a Christian, and then attended the Hongkong College of Medicine.

B. In 1905 he organized the Teng Meng-Hui and issued a manifesto that called for the driving out of the Manchus, restoring China to the Chinese, establishing a republic, and equalizing land ownership. His Three Peoples' Principles were formulated at this time and were what he considered the essence of revolution—nationalism, democracy, and people's livelihood. (This is what the Communists advocated in 1949 and the basis on which they claim Sun, as well as Marx and Lenin, as their ideological father.)

c. Sun also mentioned that the revolution would have to pass through several periods:

1) military government,

2) government by provisional constitution, in which the party would lead,

3) the final stage of a democratic republic (the revolution never reached this stage).

The Double Ten and the Revolution Itself

On October 10, 1911 (the double ten—tenth month, tenth day), the Wuchang uprising took place. In May of that year the Manchu government had decided to nationalize all trunk railroads. This led to local opposition in Wuchang, Hanyang, and Hankow. By accident a bomb went off in Hankow, men were arrested by the Manchu authorities, and lists of army officers involved in revolutionary activities were found. This meant that the officers had to mutiny or be caught by the government, and on October 10 the revolution began. The rebels set up a new republic in the south of China with Sun as president, but their forces were unable to take the north.

In the meantime the Manchu government had turned to the leader of the army, Yuan Shih-kai, to save them. They made him premier in November, 1911, but then Sun offered him the presidency of the republic if he would turn against the Manchus. He accepted, and on February 11, 1912 the abdication edict of the Manchus was issued, transferring imperial power to Yuan, while Sun transferred republican power to him.

The Failure of the Revolution

The revolution removed the Manchu dynasty, but did not put in its place a viable political machine. Instead, a phantom republic was created by Yuan Shih-kai, which was in reality a military dictatorship. By 1913 he had ended any pretense of republicanism by dissolving parliament and the KMT (the Nationalist Party).

What unity there was in China quickly disappeared when Yuan's authority was eliminated by his death in 1915. China then broke up into a score of regimes dominated by military men. The period from 1915 to 1927 is known as the era of warlordism, and even Sun became a warlord in Canton.

World War I found China at the mercy of warlords and foreign powers. In 1915 Japan presented her with Twenty-one Demands, to which China was forced to submit.

During this period, however, signs of intellectual change were occurring:

A. The May 4, 1919 Incident was a mass demonstration by students against foreign representatives and a boycott of all Japanese goods, and the results were the refusal by the Chinese to sign the Versailles Treaty and increased anti-Westernism. The other important result was the fact that it made the students more conscious of the situation in China and more determined to do something about it.

B. It was at this time that Marxism-Leninism also appeared in China. The first Marxist study group was formed in 1918, and the Chinese Communist Party (CCP) was organized in 1921.

THE NATIONALIST REVOLUTION

The Triumph of the KMT by Reorganization

Russia had accomplished an impressive revolution with a tightly organized and highly disciplined party. Immediately after this she had renounced her spheres of influence in China. Sun was impressed by both actions, and negotiations were begun with the Soviet government.

The Sun-Joffe Statement   January, 1923

A. An agent of the Soviet Union, Joffe, was sent to Canton, and in return for the U.S.S.R.'s collaboration and aid Sun agreed that Chinese Communists could join the KMT as individual members.

B. A veteran revolutionary agent of the Communist International, Borodin, was then sent to advise Sun in Canton on organization, training, and methods, thus creating a modern totalitarian party that would be capable of taking over all of China. The military was also reorganized; Chiang Kai-shek was sent to Moscow for training and brought back to head the Whampoa Military Academy.

Sun's Death and Disunity

In 1925 Sun Yat-sen died, and an open factional conflict broke out in the KMT between Wang Ching-wei, the new chairman of the government who was a leftist, and Chiang Kai-shek, head of the military forces. In March of 1926 Chiang carried through a coup d'état for leadership of the party when Borodin, the strong man behind Wang, was out of town. Wang fled and Chiang made a temporary compromise with Borodin.

The Northern Expedition

In the summer of 1926 the campaign against the warlords for the reunification of China under Chiang's direction was begun. By March, 1927 Nanking and Shanghai had been taken by Chiang, and Hankow and Wuchang had been seized by the left wing of the KMT, which set up a government independent of Chiang's control in that area. Chiang therefore established his own regime in Nanking. Fortunately for Chiang, the left wing of the KMT split when the Soviet Embassy in Peking was raided and documents were found that showed Soviet Russian control of the Chinese Communists. The Hankow regime then came under Chiang's control, and Borodin and his advisers fled to Moscow (Mme. Sun Yat-sen returned with them). The Northern Expedition had turned out to be a three-way struggle—Chiang versus the Communists and Chiang versus the warlords. By the end of 1928 Chiang was in the saddle, Nanking was declared the new capital of the new China, and most of China had been unified.

The Achievements of the KMT

The Rights Recovery Movement and Foreign Affairs

Not until 1943 did the Chinese succeed in doing away with extraterritoriality, although by 1937 foreign concessions had been reduced from thirty-three to thirteen and by 1933 the government had regained control of the tariff.

Economic reforms were initiated under T. V. Soong (the brother of Mme. Sun Yat-sen and Mme. Chiang Kai-shek).

In 1935 the currency was unified and communications were improved, but nothing was done about either the control of agricultural rents (although the government promised in a land law of 1930 to limit rent to 37½ percent of the crop) or the redistribution of lands. Emphasis was purely on technical improvements, and a high percentage of the annual budget was dedicated to military rather than economic needs. This, in part, reflected the military nature of the origins of the regime as well as the growing threat of war with Japan.

THE GROWTH OF COMMUNISM

The Early Period 1921-1923

In July, 1921 the Chinese Communist Party was founded in Shanghai. Chinese students studying abroad had been exposed to Marxism, but there was very little interest in the ideology before the Russian revolution. Lenin's theory of imperialism was perhaps one of the greatest appeals of communism for the Chinese, for it explained the problem of colonialism and offered the country hope for the end of capitalist exploitation.

CCP—KMT Cooperation 1923-1927

The decision of the Communists to enter the Kuomintang caused considerable debate among the Chinese, but Moscow insisted upon it, for the Chinese Communists were weak and this was believed to be the best way to spread their influence.

By the spring of 1927 both the KMT and the CCP had achieved what they wanted from the union—that is, the KMT possessed a party apparatus and military organization, and the CCP had gained popularity through its work with the peasants and laborers.

Period of Insurrection 1927–1931

This was the era of the Northern expedition, and the Communists were forced underground after the break with the KMT in 1927. Their work was concentrated primarily in the cities and with the labor unions, but in the 1930's the shift toward a peasant base was already becoming obvious.

Period of Kiangsi Soviet 1931–1935

This was the critical transitional period, for the CCP had been forced into the countryside by Chiang Kai-shek's army. A Soviet Republic was organized in Kiangsi in the south of China, with Mao Tse-tung as president.

This was also the time when Japan had taken over Manchuria, and by 1933 she was below the Great Wall. Chiang was willing to trade space for time in order to overcome his internal problems, and he signed the Tangku Truce with the Japanese, demilitarizing the area from Peking to the Great Wall. Then he turned to what he considered to be his greatest problem—the Communists—and in 1933 and 1934 conducted five extermination campaigns (known as bandit suppression campaigns). The Chinese Communists were finally forced to flee from the south of China in 1934 and began the Long March to the north through the foothills of the Himalayas.

The Long March

About 180,000 Communists were in Kiangsi: 100,000 of these defied orders from Moscow and fled the area. Less than 20,000 survived the six-thousand-mile march, and they fought fifteen major engagements against the Nationalists en route.

RESULTS OF THE MARCH

1) During this period Mao became the unquestioned leader of the CCP.

2) The Communists were driven into the northern province of Shensi, where they became completely dependent on agrarian support. This dependency caused them to alter their program and in the end was the very thing that won for them mastery over the country of China.

3) Those who were fit survived. The twenty thousand men who survived the Long March became the hard core of the Chinese Communist leadership, creating a bond that has not yet been broken by factionalism and ambition. Mao Tse-tung, Chou En-lai, Chu Teh, Liu Shao-chi were all to become leaders of Communist China as they had become leaders of the march.

THE TRIUMPH OF COMMUNISM

The Yenan Period   1935–1945 and World War II

The Sian Incident—the Kidnapping of Chiang Kai-shek 1936

Following his kidnapping by a northern warlord, whose troops Chiang had gone to inspect, and the negotiations carried on by the Communist Chou En-lai in order to force him to declare war against the Japanese, Chiang finally realized that he must do something about the Japanese situation, and an agreement was concluded for a united front between the Communists and the Nationalists against the Japanese.

The United Front Against the Japanese

The United Front policy was a Communist offer in February, 1937 to abandon the system of soviets in favor of the Nationalist government, to subordinate the Red Army to the command of the Nationalist Army, and to end their policy of landlord extermination. They did this for several reasons:

A. The U.S.S.R., wanting to keep the Japanese out of Siberia, had ordered the Chinese Communists to cooperate with the Nationalists.

B. Relief from another planned bandit suppression campaign of Chiang's, which might have exterminated them completely.

C. It enabled them to pose as advocates of the interests of the people and to extend their area of control.

The War Against Japan

On July 7, 1937 (the double seven—seventh month, seventh day), the Japanese attacked Marco Polo Bridge. By the end of 1937 they had overrun Nanking, and by 1938 Hankow was taken, a sea coast blockade was established, and all major treaty ports and the main lines of communication were in Japanese hands. China was trisected.

A. The Japanese-controlled areas were all provided with puppet regimes (Wang Ching-wei, the leftist whom Chiang had overthrown, was one of them), but the Japanese were unable to win the population or economically to integrate the south of China with the north.

B. The Nationalist-controlled areas were the largest, containing nearly one half the population of China, but they had been pushed into the country, leaving the areas of their major support and their sources of income from trade. They were without industry or communications and were in the most conservative areas of China. Inflation immediately occurred (in 1945 the Chinese dollar was equal to one one-thousandth of its value in 1936), and this lowered the morale of the intelligentsia (who were dependent upon fixed incomes), and led to defection, which in turn led to more active attempts on the part of the Nationalist Government to control thought, which simply added to the corruption and the disaffection with the regime. The army became corrupt, relying solely on old methods of positional warfare; the peasants were more heavily taxed and the conservative landlords became the pillars of government. The conditions themselves, in contrast to the Communist-controlled areas, were enough to defeat the Nationalists.

The Communist Areas

A. The Communist-controlled areas were rosy compared with the Nationalists'. The Red Army did very little fighting against the Japanese, reserving their greatest strength for the Nationalist war that was to follow. In the areas of Communist control, economic and social reforms were put through under Mao's doctrine of the "New Democracy." The ultimate aims of the Communists were hidden. Moderate economic and political reforms including a ceiling on rent of 33½ percent, a self-sufficient industrial base, a political system whereby no more than one third of the government were known Communists, and a mass cultural movement to educate the people were all established. That this policy was successful is proved by the statistics that in 1937 the Communists controlled 40,000 square miles of territory and one and a half million people, and by 1945 they controlled 225,000 square miles and 85 million people.

B. The five essentials of Maoist strategy that were to win him China were

   1) a fixed territorial base from which to expand;

   2) a highly indoctrinated Red Army using guerrilla tactics;

   3) basing the strength of the Party on the peasants and winning them over by land reform;

   4) making sure that the Party leadership was strong and elite;

   5) ensuring that the Communists were entirely self-sufficient and independent of any outside aid (even from Russia).

The Civil War   1945–1949

During World War II the civil war had already begun. Both the Nationalists and the Communists did everything they could to check the other. The CCP moved into Japanese-controlled areas at the expense of the KMT, and the KMT blockaded Communist areas to prevent trade.

V-J Day led to a scramble for north China. The Nationalists immediately occupied (with United States aid) the major cities of China, but they also wanted to occupy Manchuria. The Communists moved into south Manchuria and the battle began.

The Marshall Mission

In January, 1946 General George Marshall of the United States was sent "to end the civil war and to build a strong, united, democratic China." He was able to establish a cease-fire, but in January, 1947 the mediations collapsed. The possibility of agreement was perhaps out of the question, although the objective had been worthy.

The story of the triumph of the Communists at this point is a military one. In 1948 the Communists took Mukden, and Chiang lost some of his best troops; from then on the Nationalists went downhill. In January, 1949 the Communists crossed the Yangtze, and by April Nanking had fallen (that autumn Chiang had fled to Taiwan). On October 1, 1949 the People's Republic of China was declared, and by the summer of 1949 all China was in Communist hands.

The Failure of the KMT

Domestic shortcomings of the Nationalists were certainly part of the reason for their failure. They had not satisfied the peasants, they had not satisfied those who demanded China for the Chinese and a strong unified country, and they had had to fight Japanese aggression along with inflation and political corruption. They had staved off defeat but had lost the energy required for rejuvenation.

The Communists had the advantages of the support of the rural areas, an armed force based on a guerrilla army, and a unified and dedicated political and military command.

Chiang's mistakes were many. He believed that reforms must wait on unification, and he made no effort to present the people with an attractive postwar program. He was not a great military strategist and refused to give command to those better equipped than he, so although he was superior in both numbers and arms (in 1945 he had three times the number of troops), he over-extended his troops, didn't use his air force, directed battles from miles away, and must be personally blamed for his military failure.

The Communist victory was not a popular revolution. Instead, it was a slow defection because of the lack of another alternative. Once the KMT alienated the intelligentsia of China, the Communists won.

THE SPECTER OF RED CHINA—CHINA SINCE 1949

The Leaders of Red China

Mao Tse-tung: Secretary of the Chinese Communist Party and Chairman of the Politburo—the top man in China.

Born in 1893 in Hunan province, the son of a sadistic and wealthy peasant, educated in a classical tradition and then in technology, Mao became a library assistant in the University of Peking. In 1921 he was present at the formation of the Communist Party, and in 1925 he directed the peasant department of the CCP, where he first became convinced of the necessity of working through the peasant in China. He became leader of the Party on the Long March and was definitely responsible for the New Democracy and the United Front policy. In 1949 he became Chairman of the Central Government of the Chinese People's Republic as well as Secretary of the Party. In 1959 he retired as head of the government, but, as in Russia, real power lies within the Party.

Chou En-lai: Premier of the Government, Minister of Foreign Affairs, and member of the Politburo.

Chou En-lai was raised in a Cantonese family who had been members of the government under the Manchus. He was educated in Japan and then Paris and there became a Communist. In 1919 he was imprisoned during the student riots, in 1921 he was present at the founding of the CCP, in 1923–1927 he was chief of political training under Chiang Kai-shek, and in 1931 he sided with Mao. As foreign minister he negotiated the Sino-

Soviet Treaty, the Geneva Conference, and emerged the hero of the Bandung Conference.

Chu Teh: Former Commander-in-chief of the Red Army, Chairman of the Standing Committee of the Government, and member of the Politburo.

Chu Teh joined the party in 1928 after having been educated in Berlin. He was the man who trained all of China's generals, including Lin Piao, the present Minister of Defense and the man "who never lost a battle." In 1934 Chu Teh led the Long March, in 1947 he fought against the Nationalist forces, and in 1950 he led the Chinese into Korea.

Liu Shao-chi: Chairman of the People's Republic, Commander-in-chief of the armed forces, Chairman of the Council of National Defense, and member of the Politburo.

The son of a well-to-do farmer, Liu began his work for the Party in the Kiangsi coal mines. Today he is the party doctrine and policy specialist and is the possible successor to Mao (although about the same age).

The Transformation of China—"We Must Walk on Two Feet."

Economic Development

All statistics on China's economic growth are open to doubt. Although the Chinese claims are certainly greater than their achievements, some facts are known and others can be safely guessed.

INDUSTRIAL DEVELOPMENT

The development of industry has been the main concern of the Chinese Five Year Plans. Emphasis has been on heavy industry, particularly steel production, coal mining, and electric power output.

1) The First Five-year Plan, begun in 1953, was quite successful. Steel production is the best example of this: in 1952 1.35 million tons of steel were produced, by 1955 2.85 million, and by 1958 over 19 million tons, which exceeded the goal of the Plan to quadruple steel production. By the end of the Third

Five-year Plan in 1967 the Chinese intend to bring steel production to 30 million tons annually (United States production in 1956 was 115 million tons). Between 1952 and 1958 coal production was raised from 63 million tons to 270 million. Between 1951 and 1958 China's gross national product went up 173.2 percent (in contrast to India's 120.3 percent).

2) New railroads and highways are being built in China, but the problem of transportation of goods has by no means been solved—there is not yet one railroad that crosses the country from west to east.

AGRICULTURAL DEVELOPMENT

In 1958 the Chinese Communist Government announced that this was to be the year of the Great Leap Forward, but authorities wonder if the leap has been reduced to a limp in the field of agriculture.

1) Although the Communists in 1949 immediately began an active antilandlord campaign, they at first continued the program of the New Democracy, redividing land and allowing individual ownership. However, as soon as most landlords had been tried and executed and most land redistributed, the government announced that individual ownership was inefficient and bourgeois and began to collectivize, first introducing mutual aid teams and rural producers' cooperatives, and by 1955 full-scale collectivization. Within two years (1957), 92 percent of the land was in collective farms.

2) Between 1952 and 1958 grain production was raised from 163 million tons to 250 million, yet the announced average annual agricultural production growth was only 4 percent, while industrial growth was 17.6 percent.

3) Suddenly, in 1958, it was announced that "true" communism was to be established. The peasant was taken out of the collective and put into a commune. The objectives of this radical step are believed to have been

A) The total mobilization of the 500,000,000 peasants into a massive human work force. The communes were approximately ten times the size of the collectives, and the workers were organized along military lines of companies, battalions, and brigades. Each person's activities were rigidly supervised.

B) An attempt to curtail both rural migration to the cities and rural unemployment, which has been an extremely serious problem in Red China.

c) The destruction of the family as the social unit in China. The communes were completely segregated. Children, wives, and husbands all lived in separate barracks and worked in separate battalions, and old people were assigned to "happiness homes" where they did "light" labor. Communal living was emphasized by eating, sleeping, and working in teams. Husbands and wives were allowed to be alone only at certain times of the month and for only a brief period. Many authorities believe that this was an attempt to curtail the population growth as well as to break down family solidarity.

D) A means of acquiring more capital for industrialization was also an objective. Mess halls facilitated rationing, and the communes were to be self-sufficient units, producing the necessities of life and giving the unskilled worker some training in industry.

E) Another objective was the control of the ideological training of the Chinese masses. The rigid control offered excellent opportunities for indoctrination, and the worker was forced to take part in ideological sessions many evenings a week.

The communes have not proved as successful as the government hoped, but they have not yet been abandoned, although more freedoms have been allowed.

4) Abnormal droughts and terrible famines have been reported and may have seriously slowed up agricultural progress, but the possibility remains that these reports are excuses for the failure of the communes.

POPULATION

Like most Asian countries, China faces a population problem. The 1953 census was 583 million people, with an annual rate of increase of 2 percent or 12 million. With this increase the population would be one billion by 1980 (India would have 520 million, the U.S.S.R. 260 million, the U.S. 228 million). Although some attempts have been made to extend the practice of birth control, it is questionable how successful the government wants them to be, for Mao has said that the greater the population, the stronger the nation. At the moment (1966) the trend seems to be toward greater birth control.

Social Change
A. China, since 1949, has been witnessing a continuing social revolution. Indicative of the fantastic change from old social Confucian concepts is the fact that the daughter of the President of Peking University stood up and attacked her father in public on an ideological question.

B. The Communists in China, as in Russia, have employed "socialist realism" as the basis of all art. In the use of radio, newspaper, and mass organization, the Chinese Revolution has surpassed most others in propaganda techniques.

Communist China's Foreign Relations

General Pattern
A. Few historians or political scientists agree on what China's ultimate goals are, but it is generally assumed that she intends to establish herself and be recognized as a world power with primacy in Asia.

B. The period from 1949–1954 was fundamentally one of aggressive expansion. The major examples of this policy were Tibet, Korea, and Indochina.

1) Korea: By November of 1950 China had sent over a million men to fight in Korea. Her motivations may have involved both fear of United States control of Korea through Japan and the need for a "cause," since she was plagued with enemies from within and without. Undoubtedly, she was closely tied with the Communists in Korea ideologically, but also she considered Korea vital to her security as a necessary buffer area.

2) Tibet: In 1950 the Red Army invaded and took control of Tibet, which had traditionally been a part of the Chinese empire. This was not looked upon as an international affair by China, since she considered it a necessary step in the reunification of her country.

3) Indo-China: China supported the Vietminh rebellion in Indochina, giving sufficient aid to tip the balance against the French. Advisers, equipment, and training facilities were made available to the Vietminh in southwest China, and a strategic railroad to the Indo-China border was quickly completed.

c. The first sign of a shift in tactical policy came with the Korean truce on July 27, 1953 and became quite evident with the Geneva Conference. The period from 1954–1958 was not one of aggressive warfare but instead of "peaceful coexistence."

1) There are several possible explanations for the shift in policy:

A) Aggression in Korea had resulted only in a military stalemate and was costing China important outlays of economic resources: 39 percent of the budget was spent on the military in 1950, and this was hindering internal progress.

B) Stalin's death and the de-Stalinization program may have encouraged Mao to initiate a less aggressive policy.

c) By 1955 at the Bandung Conference, it was quite evident that Asia was not only reacting to Western imperialism but also to Communist imperialism.

2) The Geneva Conference   1954

A) The states represented were Red China, Vietnam, Vietminh, Cambodia, Laos, France, the United Kingdom, the United States, and the Soviet Union.

B) Results: Korea remained divided at the thirty-eighth parallel, and elections for reunification were promised (so far they have not been held). Vietnam was temporarily divided along the seventeenth parallel, with the north going to Ho Chi Minh and the south to Bao Dai. Here again, national elections were to be held (in 1956); again they have not taken place. South Vietnam, Laos, and Cambodia were not to participate in any military alliances and not to allow foreign military bases on their soil.

3) The Bandung Conference   1955

Chou En-lai announced that China would become the defender of peace, the defender of Asia. She would "seek common ground and not create divergence." China would base her new friendship on the Panch Shila or the Five Principles, which included territorial integrity and sovereignty, nonaggression, noninterference, equality and mutual benefit, and peaceful coexistence (signed in 1954 with India and then with Burma).

4) Cultural exchange was encouraged. In 1955 alone China sent groups to twenty-four countries and received groups from thirteen.

D. By 1958 China had reverted to a hard policy and an emphasis on militancy and Stalinism. The explanation for this was probably domestic strain, and a growing sense that she, not Russia, was the leader of militant communism throughout the world. The offshore islands, controlled by Chiang Kai-shek, were shelled, and the Tibet revolt of 1959 was put down without mercy. China attempted to arrest the Dalai Lama (religious and political leader of Tibet), but he fled to India. The same year, she demanded areas in Nepal and Ladakh (on the Tibet border) and sent troops into mountain areas claimed by India; her relations have been strained with India ever since. In 1964 China became even more aggressive, placing further pressure on India, fanning the Indian-Pakistan controversy over Kashmir, and using North Vietnam and the Viet Cong as her instruments of war against the U.S.A.

The Dragon and the Bear—Sino-Soviet Relations

The relations between Moscow and Peking were crucial to China's foreign policy. Together the two countries formed an ideological, military, and economic union of 850 million people.

A. In 1950 the Sino-Soviet Treaty was negotiated. Directed against the Japanese and their allies (the United States), it gave military and economic aid to China. In return, joint-stock companies and joint Chinese-Russian railroads in Manchuria were to be maintained (these terminated at the death of Stalin).

B. China has never been a satellite of the U.S.S.R. Ever since 1934, the Chinese Communists have kept Moscow-trainees out of the government. In 1954 the joint-stock companies and close technical supervision were ended, and control of Port Arthur was returned to China. In 1955 the Chinese received experimental atomic piles from the U.S.S.R., and in 1958 there was an obvious ideological split between the two countries over the issue of the communes. In 1960 another ideological dispute occurred over the question of peaceful coexistence and revolutionary change. Although China agreed to an official statement of compromise, evidence of a breach and a challenge to the leadership of the Soviet Union was clear, and in 1963 a definite break occurred. The Vietnam situation has not helped Sino-Soviet relations and has put Moscow in a very difficult position. The issue of Russian assistance to North Vietnam in its conflict with the U.S.A. is causing tension since China claims Southeast Asia as her historic sphere of influence and resents any foreign interference.

c. Soviet aid to China has been rather niggardly. In technical assistance only about 80,000 advisers have seen sent, military assistance in weapons and planes has come slowly, and the U.S.S.R. has been quite reluctant on the question of atomic weapons. In 1959 financial aid amounting to one and one quarter billion dollars was promised over a period of nine years, and approximately 250 industrial projects have been aided by Russian finances, but there is evidence that China is using her trade surplus with Russia to pay for Soviet assistance (in 1958 China exported $900,000,000 worth of merchandise to Russia and imported $600,000,000). Despite the suspension of Soviet aid, China has been able to raise its overall national income about 9 percent each year, has succeeded in exploding an atomic device, and has become a world power, a leader in the Afro-Asian world.

The United States and Red China
A. The United States does not recognize China, she carries on no diplomatic or trade relations with her, and she is bound by treaty to support the Republic of China on Taiwan (Formosa).

B. To the Chinese Communists America is the leader of the imperialist world, and if she is defeated all other imperialists will fall. She is the target of Chinese anti-Western propaganda, and her position in both Japan and Taiwan is useful for stirring up mass support for the regime.

c. Southeast Asia is the critical area in the economic, ideological and military conflict between Red China and the U.S.A., and in 1964 South Vietnam became the major battleground in this struggle. In a world deeply disturbed by the possible consequences of a rapidly escalating war, it appears as if both countries have determined on a policy of calculated risk: the U.S.A. that Chinese pressure on Southeast Asia can be checked by an overwhelming show of force; and China that the Western giant can be made ridiculous by prolonged and unvictorious guerrilla warfare in South Vietnam.

Japan

ANCIENT AND CLASSICAL CIVILIZATIONS
660 B.C.–500 A.D.

Japan has no ancient and little classical history. By 500 A.D. she had not yet developed a mature civilization, but certain characteristics had evolved that were to influence later Japanese history. The first Japanese, probably from Korea, drove the Ainu, the aboriginal inhabitants of the islands, into the north of Japan. Although there was a certain amount of influence from Korea, Japan was geographically and culturally isolated at a time when other peoples were migrating, transmitting cultures, and intermarrying. For this reason Japan developed a uniformity not found in many countries. Her people became homogeneous—a mongoloid type with no significant additions to the blood for over a thousand years. She eventually developed a homogeneous culture as well, which remained intact until the Western occupation of Japan in 1945. Japan's isolation from the outside world made these periods of foreign contact generations of frantic borrowing, but at the same time reaction to outside influences made her even more determined to preserve the native elements of her culture—her emperor and her religion, Shintoism.

Shintoism—the Religion of Japan

Little is known about the origins of the native religion of Japan. Shinto itself means *way of the spirit,* and it was originally and still is a form of pantheism, a simple faith concerned with the powers of nature. Anything that is a part of nature is awe-inspiring or *kami*; a tree, or a rock—each has a spirit. It does not involve great reaches of the mind, a definite idea of the soul, or a speculative philosophy; only a strong sense of the beauty and richness of the environment.

The concept of the emperor sprang from Shintoism. The ancestor of the imperial line was believed to be the Sun Goddess. The emperor, therefore, was considered divine or semidivine. This theory was pursued to its fullest by the militarists of Japan in the 1930's and 1940's in order to arouse devotion and a sense of obedience in the people.

The chief sin of Shintoism is uncleanliness. Death, wounds, diseases, and lack of personal hygiene were considered not only unclean but also ungodly and could be cured only by ritualistic ceremonies. Therefore the Japanese were very clean people, but they never developed a scientific attitude toward sanitation or medical care for their sick and wounded.

Early Shintoism did not involve ancestor worship. This was imported from China. There was no organized church as such, although there were Shinto priests. There was no concept of sin in the ethical sense, only in the ceremonial, and prayer was made outside a shrine after offerings and personal purification had taken place.

THE YAMATO CLAN AND THE CREATION OF THE EMPEROR

During the precivilized period of Japanese history, the people who had settled on the islands lived in clans and fought among themselves. Gradually, certain clans in Kyushu began to extend their power, reached the province of Yamato, and established a central state there. According to legend, the emperor Jimmu celebrated his conquest on February 11, 660 B.C. (the official date of the foundation of the Japanese empire—it was actually about the time of Christ). In order to maintain the supremacy of the Yamato sovereigns the two histories, the *Kojiki* (712 A.D.) and the *Nihon-shoki* (720 A.D.), were compiled, recording the history of the imperial line from its mythical origins.

Under the rule of Empress Jingo (360 A.D.) the Japanese

were united and brought into contact with the Asiatic mainland. An envoy from Korea was sent in 405 A.D. to educate the heir-apparent in the Chinese language and script. This prepared the way for the rapid absorption of Chinese culture more than a century later.

MEDIEVAL CIVILIZATION   500 A.D.–1500 A.D.

It was not until 550 A.D. that Japan, through the influence of Chinese-Buddhist missionaries, became fully aware of the existence of the outside world. It was then that she began to borrow extensively from Tang China in hopes of creating a comparable civilization. Although the history of the medieval era from 618 A.D. to 906 A.D. is a record of this borrowing, Japan was not simply an imitator, for the remaining six hundred years were spent in developing a culture that was truly Japanese. The medieval history of Japan is therefore most significant, for it was during this period that she developed her art, her language, and her social and political structure. National characteristics that were to make Japan unlike any other Eastern nation were also developed—her sense of conformity, her acceptance of hereditary authority, her devotion to the soldier, her Spartan ideal of self-discipline, and perhaps most important, her sense of nationalism and the superiority of the political unit over the family.

THE IMPACT OF BORROWING FROM THE TANG DYNASTY
618 A.D.–906 A.D.

When Japan became aware of the brilliance of the Tang dynasty, she immediately began to send missions of specialists to investigate and bring back the glories of China. Obviously what she gained was not a real picture of China, for both distance and language changed the image. The final result was the borrowing of the forms of Chinese culture rather than the essence. This slavish imitation often led to the borrowing of things that were not suitable to Japanese society and had to be modified. This process was to be repeated in 1868 with Western culture.

The First But Not the Most Permanent Result of "Cultural Piracy" Was a New Concept of the Position of the Ruler

Japan borrowed the imperial concept from China but retained the notion of the ruler as a high priest. Eventually this imperial ideal began to disappear, and though the emperor retained his title, he lost his imperial powers and became ruler in name only.

Another Result Was the Change in the Position of Women

This was one of the consequences of contact with China that most people in the modern era would consider undesirable. Before 600 A.D. Japanese women often held important positions in society (it is even believed by some historians that many of the clans were matriarchal), but with the introduction of Confucian philosophy the position of Japanese women sank to an even lower scale than in China.

The Third Result Was the Development of Central Government

The Japanese modeled their entire central governmental organization on that of China, including all the bureaucratic red tape and the hierarchy based on rank and scholarship. The central government was too big and too complicated for the needs of Japan, and a good example of borrowing form without essence is the fact that she retained bureaucratic rank without the Chinese emphasis on scholarship. In the building of Nara in 710 and then Kyoto in 794, Japan imitated down to the last detail the capital city of the Tang, Ch'ang-an.

The Japanese System of Writing Developed

Another disastrous innovation was the Chinese system of writing. Japanese could have easily been written phonetically, and a system of phonetics might have developed had not Japan adopted the Chinese characters, which were entirely unsuited, since Chinese was a monosyllabic language with no written inflections. Eventually Japan developed a system of writing that included both Chinese characters and phonetics.

The Confucian System

Japan also borrowed the Confucian class system but made it more inflexible and more unsuitable, for the scholar never became first in importance. The traditions of clan loyalty and hereditary rights were too strong, and in most cases scholars were given the humble clerical jobs. During the feudal era the military assumed the primary social position and retained it until after World War II.

The Arts

The one area Japan seemed capable of understanding and really profiting from was the arts. Here Japan borrowed wholesale for a while and then perfected and developed her own style. The long horizontal scrolls of narrative are unlike any others in the world. In sculpture, she used a new technique in wood, and in painting developed an interest in humanity.

Buddhism

Buddhism, although Indian in origin, came to Japan from China. Japan later made her own modifications and innovations such as Zen, which stressed the virtues of mental concentration and physical self-discipline.

THE LOSS OF POWER BY THE COURT AND THE DUAL
SYSTEM OF GOVERNMENT—THE SECOND MAJOR
DEVELOPMENT OF MEDIEVAL CIVILIZATION

The Fujiwara Clan

A dual system of government in which the emperor held
the power in name but someone else held it in fact developed
when the Fujiwara family won complete mastery over the imperial family through intermarriage. A daughter of the Fujiwara
clan would marry the emperor and then as soon as a son was
born persuade her husband to abdicate. Naturally, the head of
the Fujiwara family would then act as regent for the small boy.

The Fujiwaras retained a monopoly of all high court posts
from the seventh century to the early nineteenth century. But the
court did not always retain the power in Japan.

The Military Aristocracy Develops

In the countryside noble families and Buddhist monasteries
became autonomous centers of authority. By the eleventh century real power passed to a rising military aristocracy. Tax-free
estates grew up as the emperor had to give away more and more
land in hopes of gaining loyal support against disruptive clans.
When knights had to be called in to settle disputes between two
court factions in the capital, the beginning of military rule in
Japan was not far away.

The Shogunate Established and the End
of the Court's Power

Two military clans, the Taira and the Minamoto, began
to compete for power in Japan around 1150. At first the Taira
defeated the Minamoto in 1160 and settled in the capital, taking
over the position of prime minister and controlling the govern-

ment until 1185. The Minamoto retaliated by crushing the Taira in a war that lasted from 1180 to 1185. Minamoto Yoritomo, leader of the clan, did not attempt to control Kyoto, the capital; instead he built his capital in Kamakura and, assuming the title of Shogun (generalissimo), created the first military dictatorship of Japan. This was the beginning of seven hundred years of rule by warrior aristocrats.

But even the Shogun was unable to create an effective central government for long, for in 1219 the Minamoto line ended and his wife's relatives, the Hojo, became regents of Japan, ruling through a puppet shogun. In other words, the emperor was controlled by the Fujiwara, the government was controlled by the Shogun, and the Shogun was controlled by the Hojo regents. This was more than dual control, it was a tripartite government.

FEUDALISM AND JAPAN'S MILITARY TRADITION

The Minamoto Period

The ethical code or chivalric code was first established. The concept of a warrior's duty to his master was introduced. This is significant, for it also implied that there was a loyalty greater than that owed to one's family.

Zen Buddhism was created and became practically an official religion under the Ashikaga.

During this period the custom of suicide, of self-inflicted death preferable to capture, of death better than disgrace, was developed.

The Mongol Invasions

The failure of the Mongol invasions in 1281 further increased the prestige of the warrior class but revealed the growing dependence of the Shogunate upon this military element in society.

The Ashikaga Shogunate   1338–1615

This was really feudalism, for after defeating the Minamoto the Ashikaga clan was never able to achieve central control of Japan. From 1467 on there were constant civil wars and shifting feudal allegiances. Feudal lords known as daimyo rose to power, and eventually this led to the financial ruin of the court aristocracy. (One emperor was reduced to selling calligraphy in order to keep himself alive.)

Although this was a period of political chaos, it was also an era of great art in the form of architecture, painting, and the native Japanese theater. Trade and manufacturing flourished, and it was a time of migration to the Philippines and Southeast Asia and contact with Europeans through Christian missionaries. (By 1580 there were approximately 150,000 Japanese Christians and in the early 1600's twice that number.)

MODERN CIVILIZATION   1500 to the Present

The modern history of Japan should be divided into three major periods: the first from 1615 to 1668, the Tokugawa regime; the second from the Meiji Restoration in 1868 through World War II; and the third from 1945 to the present. During each of these periods change in Japan was overwhelming.

THE TOKUGAWA REGIME   1615–1868

Japan ended the medieval age in some ways more modern than she was to be for the next 250 years. She did not have political unity, but she had witnessed a lively cultural development, an expanding economy, and a growing sense of her own importance in relations with the outside world. In 1615, however, the Tokugawa Shogunate claimed control of Japan and attempted, until its downfall in 1868, to halt the expansion of Japan, to close the door to foreign influence, and to maintain the domestic status quo.

The Rise to Power of the Tokugawa Shogunate

The story of the success of the Tokugawa was, of course, a military one. A daimyo by the name of Oda Nobunaga seized the capital and most of central Japan. After his death, his general Hideyoshi defeated the Satsuma clan in 1587 and by 1590 controlled most of eastern and northern Japan. In 1597 Hideyoshi died, and Tokugawa Ieyasu, one of his vassals, destroyed his family and took over control of the rest of Japan.

Tokugawa's main purpose was to keep his own family in power and to maintain political stability. He thus created a system that remained almost unchanged for two and a half centuries.

The Tokugawa System of Control

A system of checks on and controls over the population was established. An extensive and efficient secret police patrolled Japan, and members of important, if unreliable, families were held as hostages in Edo (Tokyo), the capital. The inner circle of people around Edo were those whose loyalty could be depended upon, and the outer circle, or Outer Daimyo, were kept under constant surveillance and strict control.

The Confucian class system was rearranged and strictly maintained: first was the warrior or the samurai; second, the peasant; third, the artisan; and fourth, the merchant. No one could leave his employment and no one could change his class by law. The peasant was forced to hand in his arms, and the sword could only be worn by the samurai. The system was entirely artificial and real wealth was still in the merchant class, but it was an effective means of maintaining the status quo.

The warrior code of Bushido, the unwritten ethical code of the samurai, was reestablished to control the warless warriors.

Japan was closed to the rest of the world. Foreign trade was eliminated, except for a restricted Dutch port; Japanese were not allowed to travel abroad, and those who lived overseas were not allowed to return. Christianity was outlawed, and many Japanese Christians were martyred. Punishments for Christians who would not renounce their faith were severe, including crucifixion with the head downwards, sawing off limbs with bamboo saws, roasting, boiling, and slicing. (It should be remembered that these punishments were no more terrible than those found in Europe during the same period.) Priests, however, were only exposed or banished. The dramatic end to Christianity in Japan came in 1637, when an economic revolt led by Christians near Nagasaki took place and 37,000 were slaughtered.

The Downfall of the Tokugawa

The new economic system was probably one of the most important causes for the downfall of the Tokugawa, for as the nation began to build a more complex economic system with exchange based on money instead of rice, the daimyo (feudal landowners) and the samurai classes went further and further into debt to their social inferiors, the merchants. Many of the poorer samurai were among those who led the opposition to the Tokugawa.

The opening of Japan by Commodore Matthew C. Perry of the United States in 1854 proved the Tokugawa regime militarily impotent. By 1858 treaties were concluded that allowed foreigners permanent residence at five ports and at Osaka and Edo, and unrestricted trade relations were sanctioned.

The samurai of the Outer Daimyo were the most important cause of the Tokugawa fall from power. For two and a half centuries they had been forced to recognize the regime, but now there was hope, for the coming of the West had proved that the Tokugawas were vulnerable to attack.

In 1867 a bloodless revolution took place when the new Shogun voluntarily surrendered the rule of the country to the Emperor. Until 1868 there was some fighting between Tokugawa and imperial forces, but seven hundred years of military rule had ended.

JAPAN BECOMES A MODERN NATION   1868–1945

The imperial revival or the Meiji Restoration of 1868 ushered Japan into the modern world. The contrast between Japan's reaction to the threat of Western control and China's reaction was staggering. The explanation for Japan's more rapid progress in modernizing her country and driving out foreign control is found in a combination of two factors. One, the Meiji government was politically unified and efficiently administered by young and talented leaders, while the Manchu dynasty, after two hundred years of strong rule was decaying; and two, Japan had had a tradition of borrowing in the past, recognizing the superiority of other nations and quickly imitating them, while China had for centuries thought of herself as the Middle Kingdom, or the center of the world, and had had no equal.

The Meiji Restoration   1868

The imperial restoration, named after the young Emperor Meiji, did not really restore authority to the throne. The system of dual control continued, and the leadership of the new regime was actually taken over by a group of young samurai from the Outer Daimyos of Satsuma and Choshu.

The altering of the political and social structure of Japan was the first thing the Meiji Restoration accomplished.

A. The feudal system was eliminated by decree in 1871, when an imperial edict abolishing all fiefs and transferring all taxes to the national government was proclaimed.

B. The samurai were deprived of their economic and military privileges.

1) In 1873 they were forced to commute their pensions to money bonds, and in the same year universal military conscription was passed by the government. In 1876 the samurai could no longer wear their swords, the final act that was to make them ordinary citizens.

2) Obviously, the samurai fought this change. The Satsuma Rebellion of 1877 was the last attempt by the warriors to reassert their historic position. They were defeated by the government's peasant conscript army.

c. Political parties were formed by the discontented samurai who were not in power. The Liberal Party, formed by Itagaki, and the Progressive Party, formed by Okuma, were nevertheless soon destroyed by the government either by political suppression or by splitting the party leadership or the party itself. The result was that from the very beginning no strong political parties existed to oppose the government in Japan.

d. The Meiji Constitution   1889

A man by the name of Ito, who was made prime minister of Japan in 1885, was primarily responsible for the writing of the constitution, and in February, 1889 it was given as a gift to the people from the Emperor. It in no way altered the structure of power, for the Diet, consisting of a House of Peers (appointed by the emperor and elected by the nobility) and a House of Representatives (elected by the political parties), had very little actual power. Real authority remained in the hands of the cabinet or the oligarchy.

The early Meiji period was an age of reform. Many significant changes and additions were made to Japanese society.

A. Military Reform

The Japanese army was patterned after the German system and the navy after the British. The army and the navy were in theory to remain independent of politics.

B. Educational.Reform

One of the most important and influential reforms was put through in 1871, when the Ministry of Education was created and education was made compulsory for nine years. Because of this reform Japan became one of the first nations to have a literate population. By borrowing from the French and thus establishing a highly centralized and controlled system that was geared to the needs of the nation, the government had at its disposal a powerful means of molding public opinion and persuading the populace to accept whatever policies it decreed and whatever image of the outside world was deemed politically advisable. It was for this reason that Japan went into World War II with little notion of the real strength of the United States.

c. Every Western nation contributed its share to the reforms passed by the Meiji:

The United States, her postal service and her notion of public education;

Great Britain, her cotton mills and mint, her railroad system and her navy;

France, her administrative and educational systems and her criminal code;

Germany, her pattern for local government and constitution and cabinet system as well as her army;

Italy, her sculpture and painting were imitated.

D. Industrialization

1) Unlike China, Japan began a rapid program of industrialization, with the expressed objective of building a modern nation. The government immediately began forced industrialization and was very fortunate, for the necessary capital was found not only by taxing the peasant but also through a sudden demand on the world market for silk because the mulberry blight all over Europe created a scarcity of domestic silk.

2) When the government decided to sell its industry to individual citizens, manufacturing soon fell into the hands of a few wealthy families who formed monopolies known as zaibatsu. (The Mitsui family, for example, became so wealthy and so powerful that it employed 1,800,000 people in Japan and another 1,000,000 overseas.)

Japan's Foreign Relations 1894–1918

The Sino-Japanese War 1894–1895

The cause of this war is open to debate. Some historians believe that political leaders precipitated the war in an effort to stop political opposition at home; others believe that it was entirely the rivalry between China and Japan over Korea; and still others say that Japan was attempting to show her strength to the outside world.

THE RESULTS OF THE WAR

1) A resounding Japanese victory.

2) The Treaty of Shimonasiki, 1895: Korea was declared to be independent, and Japan was given Formosa, the Pescadores, and a huge indemnity. The Liotung peninsula was given back to China as a result of Western pressure, and this inflamed Japanese nationalism.

3) Japan was recognized as an important, and possibly Western, nation. By 1899 all occidentals were once again subject to Japanese law, and in 1900 Japan fought with the West against the Boxers in China. Perhaps the most significant proof of Japan's importance was the Anglo-Japanese Treaty signed in 1902. Not only did this break Britain's splendid isolation, but it also signified to the world that Japan had become a Westernized nation. By 1911 Japan had also succeeded in terminating all tariffs imposed by treaties with the Western world. China did not eliminate her fixed tariffs until 1933 and did not eliminate extraterritoriality until 1943.

The Russo-Japanese War   1904–1905

A. This was definitely a conflict waged for imperialistic motives. Japan wanted to prevent Russian control of Korea, and most nations supported her (the United States and Great Britain provided money).

B. In 1904 Japan attacked Port Arthur, and in the Battle of Mukden in 1905 she won a glorious and overwhelming victory and initiated negotiations for the end of hostilities.

C. The Results of the War

1) The Portsmouth Treaty, 1905: Japan gained rights in southern Manchuria and the southern half of Sakhalin Island, as well as recognition of her position in Korea, which she annexed in 1910.

2) The war amazed the world, for here was an Eastern nation, a small island, that had defeated the largest Western na-

tion. To much of the world this was proof of what industrialization could do, and it was proof to non-Westerners that the white man was not as superior as he tended to assume.

World War I

A. Japan was on the side of the Allies, doing no fighting but profiting by taking over property, mining, and land controlled by the Germans in China. In 1915 Japan presented the weak Chinese government with Twenty-one Demands, which included a ninety-nine-year lease on Port Arthur instead of a twenty-five-year one; control of industry and mines in Manchuria; and Japanese military advisers in China.

B. By the Treaty of Versailles Japan gained the German Pacific islands as mandates and a seat on the League of Nations council.

The Road to Totalitarianism

The Liberal Era of the 1920's

A. From 1890 to 1918 the clans of Choshu, Satsuma, and Hizen had dominated the government, but during the 1920's political parties had a chance to share in the government of Japan, for the old oligarchs had died out and the army had lost some ground for the first time because of a costly failure in Siberia during the Russian Revolution and also because of the general world attitude toward disarmament. Hara Kei (1918–1921) was the first party premier.

B. In 1925 a Universal Manhood Suffrage Act was put into effect, and in 1924 the army and the navy were reduced in size; earlier in 1922, at the Washington Naval Conference, Japan had agreed to limit her growing navy on a 5–5–3 ratio with the United States and Great Britain.

Signs of Change

A. The liberalism of the 1920's was for the most part limited to the cities. Although the army was reduced, ROTC programs were increased, a strict Peace Preservation Law designed to control thought by complete censorship of the press was passed, and prime ministers were regularly assassinated.

B. The military was still immune from civilian and political control and in actual fact held a veto power over the cabinet.

C. The transition to militarism was not unexpected, for Japan had had seven centuries of rule by the sword, her oligarchs were all ex-samurai, and there was a history of devotion to the military and the emperor.

D. The army became more and more extremist and broke into two factions:

1) The Control Faction made up of high-ranking officers, advocated a reconstruction of society along totalitarian lines and expansion into China and Southeast Asia. This was the group that eventually won control of Japan.

2) The Imperial Way Faction consisted of younger, lower-ranking officers who were against capitalism, against parliament and political parties, and for direct and immediate action and expansion into Russia.

Outside Influences Leading toward Totalitarianism

DISILLUSIONMENT WITH DEMOCRACY

There was no disarmament, and democratic governments seemed to be failing all over the world. The greatest democracy of them all, the United States, had deeply insulted the Japanese when in 1924 she negotiated the "Gentlemen's Agreement" barring Asiatic migration into the country. Fascist totalitarian regimes, on the other hand, were proving quite successful, and also friendly toward the island nation.

THE DEPRESSION OF 1929

The collapse of international trade started Japan on her own depression. A small country like Japan, which was completely dependent on the outside world for many of her raw materials as well as for a market for her goods, was entirely at the mercy of the tariff policies of other nations. Japan's price level fell 35 percent as compared with 27 percent in the United States, her export trade decreased 27½ percent, and the export of raw silk fell by 50 percent in 1930. Rice fell from twenty-nine yen per koku to seventeen, and this ruined both peasant and landlord.

THE CHANGES TAKING PLACE IN CHINA

The rise of the KMT (Nationalists) posed a serious threat to Japan's control and interests in Manchuria.

The Turning Point—the Manchurian Incident of 1931

A. The military of Japan decided to take matters into their own hands and start their own imperialistic war. They did not have the backing of the civilian government, and the fact that they were able to get away with it proved the weakness of the party government of Japan and led the country into a war that was to last fourteen years.

B. In September, 1931 Japanese army units, stationed in Manchuria to protect Japanese interests there, started out on their own conquest of all of Manchuria. The pretext for the Manchurian Incident was a trumped-up charge that Chinese agents had attempted to blow up a railway line.

C. Early in 1932 the Lytton Commission was sent by the League of Nations to investigate the incident and sharply criticized Japan's actions, but it had no power to do anything; and Japan's answer was simply to withdraw from the League (establishing a precedent that Italy, Russia, and Germany soon followed).

The End of Civilian Government

A. After the Prime Minister and various members of the cabinet had been assassinated in May, 1932 by radical members of the army, party government collapsed. A compromise national government was established in which the military element increased and the party element slowly dwindled in number throughout the 1930's.

B. The showdown between military and civilian elements in the cabinet came on February 26, 1936, when young officers of the Imperial Way Faction mutinied and martial law was declared in Tokyo by the Control Faction. This was followed by a series of trials in which thirteen of the officers and four civilians were executed. The significance of the event was the final intimidation of the population and their realization that only the military could control the military.

c. In 1940 all parties were disbanded and the Imperial Rule Assisting Association, which was a military dictatorship, emerged. In 1941 General Tojo Hideki became prime minister, ending any pretense that the government was not a military dictatorship.

Japan's Wars: Undeclared and Declared

The China Incident   1937

THE FIRST PHASE: THE MARCO POLO BRIDGE INCIDENT

This was war, although undeclared, against China. In July, 1937 Japanese troops overran the northern cities of China and established their control.

THE SECOND PHASE: DECEMBER, 1937—OCTOBER, 1938

A long and drawn-out battle was waged at Hankow, and finally in October the Japanese succeeded in capturing the city.

THE THIRD PHASE: OCTOBER, 1938—DECEMBER, 1941

The Japanese began their move towards Chungking.

The Pacific War   1941–1945: Japan Enters World War II

At first Japan did not intend to go to war against the West. The outbreak of war in Europe seemed a welcome event to her, for she had joined Germany in the Anti-Comintern Pact in 1936, and Germany was certainly keeping the rest of Europe's minds off Japanese affairs. The surrender of France in 1940 gave Japan the opportunity to gobble up French Indochina; she had signed a neutrality pact with the U.S.S.R., which meant that she did not have to worry about her Siberian flank.

WHY JAPAN WENT TO WAR

1) There are many possible explanations for the decision to enter the war. For one thing, the United States refused to condone Japanese aggression into Indochina; she froze all Japanese assets in the United States in July, 1941 and put a partial economic embargo on Japan as well. For another, the Tripartite Pact of October, 1940, in which Germany, Japan, and Italy agreed to aid one another if attacked by a power not involved in the European or Chinese conflicts, appeared to protect Japan against United States technological superiority. The military was faced with a costly stalemate in the China War and needed further victories to sustain their political position at home and their aggressive policy abroad. The Japanese were also victims of their own propaganda, which was aimed at convincing them that they were superior to the Western world.

2) In October, 1941 General Tojo replaced Premier Konoye, who had hoped to avoid war, and on September 6, 1941 the Japanese government became committed to a policy of military action against the United States if diplomacy should fail. War at this point was almost inevitable, for neither the Americans nor the Japanese would yield over the issue of Japan's withdrawal from China, which the United States insisted upon before she would unfreeze Japanese assets or lift the embargo.

THE WAR ITSELF

Pearl Harbor, December 7, 1941, was followed by amazing Japanese successes against the British in Singapore and the Malay peninsula. In 1942 the Philippines fell, followed closely by the Dutch East Indies and most of Burma. The main Japanese objective was to secure control of a wide perimeter around the home islands and to carve out an empire in Southeast Asia. The plan failed, because the Japanese were too successful in their first steps and attempted to expand the perimeter. They struck at the Coral Sea in the spring of 1942 and were defeated, and then at Midway in mid-1942 they lost their crucial aircraft carrier force. After this battle they never again regained the initiative and were on the defensive. They also failed in their efforts to establish an economic empire in Southeast Asia. The very forces of nationalism, which they had deliberately set astir, turned against them.

DEFEAT AND SURRENDER

1) In July, 1944 Koiso replaced Tojo and constructed the Supreme War Council in an attempt to harmonize political, economic, and military elements. The Council consisted of the foreign minister, the prime minister, the ministers of the army and navy, and the chiefs of staff of the army and navy. The de-

feats of 1945 brought the eighty-year-old Admiral Suzuki to power, and he became a wavering advocate of peace.

2) On August 6 the first atomic bomb fell on Hiroshima; on August 8 Russia declared war on Japan; and on August 9 Nagasaki was hit with the second A-bomb. On August 9 the Supreme War Council was deadlocked three to three on whether to accept the Allied terms of surrender. The army minister and the two chiefs of staff voted against it. That night Premier Suzuki called another meeting of the War Council and dramatically called upon Emperor Hirohito to vote. The Emperor voted for acceptance of the Allied terms of unconditional surrender. The United States tacitly agreed to allow the Emperor to remain on the throne.

3) Although the military extremists still did their best to change the decision, they were unable to do so, since most of the cabinet was behind it and all of the princes of the blood were for the Emperor's decision. Consequently, if the militarists had attempted a coup there would have been no one they could have put in Hirohito's place.

4) On August 15 the surrender proclamation was issued, and on September 2, on board the U.S.S. Missouri in Tokyo Bay, Japan formally surrendered.

1945 TO THE PRESENT

From September, 1945 to April, 1952 Japan was occupied by a foreign power—the United States of America—and as Edwin Reischauer said, "Never before in so short a space of years has so much that was old and accepted been burned out and so much that was new and unfamiliar poured in." The aims of the occupation were both negative and positive: to demilitarize by disarming and punishing, to decentralize and to democratize. What the military occupation accomplished was one of the most profound revolutions in the history of the twentieth century. Nor could this have been done without the cooperation of the Japanese people. When, in August, 1945, the Emperor Hirohito announced that the Japanese should unite their "total strength to be devoted to the construction for the future, cultivate the ways of rectitude; foster nobility of spirit, and work with resolution" in order to "enhance the innate glory of the Imperial state and keep pace with the progress of the world," the Japanese obeyed the imperial mandate and cooperated with their conquerors in a fashion unique in history.

Punishment and reform were accomplished between 1945 and 1948; reconstruction was begun between 1948 and 1950; and revision as well as reversal took place after 1950, when Japan suddenly became the friend and ally of the West and not the enemy.

THE UNITED STATES OCCUPATION OF JAPAN

The Means of Accomplishing the Objectives

Thirty thousand men occupied Japan, and the man who headed the job was General MacArthur. The group of men who had fought under MacArthur at Bataan and the General himself were really responsible for the ruthless reform.

Punishment and Disarmament

This was one of the failures, for the repatriation of Japanese troops and civilians from overseas, the destruction of major industries with war potential, and the dismemberment of the empire led to serious economic problems in Japan. Those who had led Japan to war were tried for war crimes by an international tribunal (1946–1948). This did not accomplish its purpose, for Japan had no fascist party nor definite organization that had led her into war, and given the dual nature of the Japanese government, it was difficult to pinpoint responsibility.

Key Reforms

The Constitution

A. The constitution was written by MacArthur's staff with the help of Japanese advisers and was constructed and presented to the Japanese people in much the same manner as the Meiji constitution.

B. There are five major differences between the Meiji constitution and the MacArthur constitution:

1) Redefinition of the emperor's position—he was no longer divine and this was publicly announced by Hirohito himself.

2) Transfer of basic political powers out of the hands of the oligarchy into the hands of the Diet; under the new constitution, both houses are elected, with the prime minister selected from the Diet. A party government based upon parliamentary majority was created.

3) For the first time citizens were protected by a bill of rights, which included academic freedom, equal education for all, rights of labor, and women's rights, as well as freedom of speech, religion, and so on.

4) The judicial system was altered and made independent of the executive. A supreme court was modeled after that of the United States.

5) Article 9 of the constitution called for the renunciation of war forever and made illegal a standing army. (This has been reinterpreted so that a police force is now considered constitutional.)

Economic Reforms

A. Land reform was one of the most drastic, revolutionary and successful of all the reforms put through by the occupation. All nonresident farmers had to sell their land, except for 2.45 acres, to elected local land commissions, who then sold the land to tenant farmers at fixed prices. The purchaser had thirty years in which to pay. Rent was fixed at 25 percent of the rice crop. The result of this reform was that 5 million acres changed hands, and that today only 10 percent of the farmers of Japan are tenants, while approximately 80 percent had been before.

B. In 1946 a trade union law was passed that gave people the right to join unions, bargain collectively, and strike.

c. An attempt was made to dissolve the large family economic combines of Japan. Their assets were frozen and a liquidation commission was established. This was one of the reforms that did not succeed; today the zaibatsu (family monopolies) have reconsolidated themselves, and their financial power is greater than ever before.

Educational Reform

An effort was made to decentralize control of education, to purge teachers and textbooks and revise the curriculum, and to organize education on the American plan. The educational reform did not really succeed in decentralization of the school system; the local boards are now appointed by the mayors of Japan. But education is no longer a tool of the state.

JAPAN SINCE 1950

Peace with Japan

In 1949 the United States decided to sign a separate peace with Japan. The Japanese were hesitant to accept this, for it meant taking sides in the cold war. They feared the Russians, because in February, 1950 the U.S.S.R. had signed the Sino-Soviet Treaty, which was directed against Japan. In June, 1950 the Korean incident began, and Japan's fears of invasion from the mainland increased. In August the government announced that it would choose the West rather than remain neutral in the cold war.

In 1951 at San Francisco, a meeting of all nations involved in the war against Japan was called to sign a treaty of peace. On September 8, 1951 forty-nine nations signed the treaty, and on the same day the United States concluded a security pact with Japan. Japanese independence and full sovereignty were granted April 28, 1952.

A. Neither Nationalist nor Communist China was invited to the meeting.

B. India and Burma did not attend.

C. The Philippines were induced to come only after the United States had signed a security pact protecting them against any invasion.

D. Australia was also induced to come as a result of a similar United States pact (the Anzus Pact), signed September 1.

E. The U.S.S.R. came, but did not sign the treaty.

On April 29, 1952 Japan signed a separate peace with the Republic of China (Formosa).

In December, 1954 a settlement with Burma was reached, after the promise of $250,000,000 in reparations in ten years.

A reparations settlement with the Philippines was not reached until 1956, when Japan agreed to provide the Philippines with $550,000,000 in goods and services over a period of twenty years and to loan her $25,000,000.

In April, 1955 $41,666,000 was promised to Thailand.

The U.S.S.R. peace declaration was not agreed upon until 1956, after a bitter struggle between 1951 and 1955, during which time Russia vetoed Japan's entrance into the U.N.

Social and Intellectual Changes in Japan

One of the greatest changes between prewar and postwar Japan is social mobility. Equal education, destruction of wealth during the war, the changed attitude toward superiority, and the weakening of family control have all contributed to this.

Intellectually Japan has changed. Widespread devotion to pacifism and internationalism is found among the intellectuals. Radicalism is also prevalent. Although there is historic fear and dislike of Russia, there is still a great deal of admiration for the Chinese, and although less than one third of the people vote socialist or communist, support for the left may be as high as 90 percent among the intellectuals. The fact that there is an abundance of scholars with no jobs and that there is a sense of guilt among intellectuals for having failed to speak out against the war has led to discontent with existing institutions.

Economic Changes in Japan

Japan has made an amazing economic recovery since the end of the war.

Her population problem was more acute at the end of the war, with the addition of 6,000,000 Japanese from abroad and a birthrate of more than a million a year. The Japanese government has made an active attempt to control the problem by legalizing abortion and maintaining offices of information on birth control all over the country.

By the end of the occupation, production in industry was above the prewar peak of 1934–1936 and has continued to rise. The Korean War caused a boom that made it possible for Japan to accumulate capital, buy new machinery, and raise her standard of living. Her unfavorable balance of trade fell from $1.1 billion in 1953 to $770 million in 1954, and in 1955 ideal weather conditions resulted in the largest rice crop in her history. In 1955 she also began to reestablish trade relations with Southeast Asia.

There are, of course, many problems still facing the Japanese economy. She is dependent on the United States for trade, she still must import much of her food and materials, she must be able to compete with China for the Asian market, and she is totally dependent on the fluctuations of the world market. She is also receiving a good deal of aid from the United States. Between June, 1946 and 1963 this amounted to 4.8 billion dollars.

The Political Scene in Japan

Major Political Parties

CONSERVATIVE

The two major parties of the right in Japan were the Progressives (sometimes called the Democrats) and the Liberals. They joined in 1955 as the Liberal-Democratic Party. Leaders such as Yoshida, Ashida, and Shidehara were "liberals" of the

1920's, advocating parliaments and civilian rule, and they have
all been trained as foreign diplomats.

SOCIALIST

The Socialist party is the second major party in Japan. Today it is a unified party, although it was split during much of
its postwar history. Katayama, the leader, Mrs. Koto (founder of
the birth control movement in Japan), and Kagawa were important in the party and were acclaimed in the United States.

COMMUNIST

The only organized group immediately after surrender was
the Communist, but they have failed to gain much popular
support. In 1949, at the height of their power, they won only
9.6 percent of the electorate. Yet they are financially well off and
certainly a party to keep an eye on.

Major Political Trends

A. The first trend in Japanese politics was toward the extreme left, but in the first general election in 1946 the Communists won only 3.8 percent of the vote, whereas the Socialists
won 17.8 percent, tying for second place as the largest party in
the Diet.

B. In 1947 the Socialists won 25.8 percent of the vote, and
this made them the largest party in the Diet, but because of
difficulties under the occupation, Katayama was forced to resign in
1948 and Ashida became premier in a coalition Democratic-
Socialist government. Finally, under an attack of corruption, he
resigned, and Yoshida, head of the conservative Liberal Party,
took over.

C. The Liberal Party, which had ruled from 1946–1947, took
over once again in 1949. The trend during this election was
away from the middle parties; the Communists won 9.6 percent
of the electorate, and the Democrats and Liberals gained a
majority of seats at the expense of the moderates.

D. The shift back toward the center in the 1952 elections
caused Yoshida to resign in 1954 and Hatoyama (Democrat) to
take his place. The shift toward center led to a coalition of
Liberals and Democrats and the reunification of the Socialists.

E. Since 1956 the conservatives have remained in power. Hatoyama was replaced by Ishibashi and then Kishi in 1957, followed by Ikeda until his retirement in 1964. Eisaku Sato (younger brother of Kishi) was next in line.

The International Scene

Relations with the United States

Japan imports more from the United States than any other country. The problem is that the United States buys relatively little in return. Tariffs and quotas on items such as Japanese textiles not only strain Japanese-American relations but also seriously hurt them. American bases, although vital to Japanese security and economy (as a source of dollars with which to buy American goods), also strain relations, and the question of the return of Okinawa is perhaps the sorest point.

Relations with Southeast Asia

Japan is slowly reestablishing relations with the countries of Southeast Asia and trade is beginning to be resumed, but it is still a long uphill battle against resentment and fear. In 1965 she finally resumed trade relations with South Korea.

Relations with Red China

In Japan there is continuing pressure for normal trade relations with Red China, and restrictions on trade with Communist China are slowly being relaxed. So far, Japan has continued to follow the United States lead and does not recognize mainland China.

Southeast Asia

ANCIENT, CLASSICAL, AND MEDIEVAL CIVILIZATION

There is little recorded history in the Southeast Asian areas before the coming of the West in 1500 A.D. Until well into the medieval period, the Southeast Asian areas remained in small tribal groups, and some of them were under the political domination of the mightier empires to the north—China and India. Migrations, religious missionaries, and traders played an important role before 1500, bringing to Southeast Asia her people, her faith, and her social structure. To Vietnam came Confucianism and Buddhism from China, and to Cambodia, Laos, Malaya, Indonesia, Burma, Thailand, and even the Philippines came the Indians with their religions (first Buddhism and then Islam) and their way of life.

THE PHILIPPINES

Before the coming of the Spanish and Portuguese, the Philippine Islands (a group of seven thousand islands, its two largest being Luzon and Mindanao) had been controlled by a number of Malay principalities, absolute monarchies whose subjects ranged from free peoples to slaves acquired in wars with neighboring principalities. Islam reached only the southern island of Mindanao (where there are today about one million Moslems).

Indonesia

The group of islands (the Larger Sunda Islands of Borneo, Sumatra, Java, Madina, and the Celebes; the Lesser Sunda Islands; the Moluccas; and the island of New Guinea) known as Indonesia or the Spice Islands had witnessed two waves of Malay immigration that destroyed the tribal Negrito types on the islands.

In the eighth century A.D. the Indians came to the archipelago, first to Java, setting up their princely states, then to Sumatra. Two migrations of Indians seem to have come, one establishing Hinduism in the interior of Java and the other, Buddhism on the coastal areas.

In the twelfth century A.D. merchants from Persia, Arabia, and India arrived for the purpose of acquiring pepper from Sumatra and spices from the Moluccas. With the traders came Islam, and this became the dominant religion of the area.

In the fourteenth century Java, an agricultural state, gained control of the coastal trading states and established the empire of Majapahit. This was the first time that the islands were under one government. But the empire lost control over its vassal states, and the division between the agricultural inland areas and the trading coast made it easier for the Dutch to gain control in the 1600's.

Indochina

Annam (Vietnam)

Annam was not only subject to Chinese influence, but from 181 B.C. to 939 A.D. she was a part of the Chinese state.

Annam always suffered from division between north and south, and in 1673 she split into three parts, with three rival dynasties struggling for power until the eighteenth century. This struggle led to an excuse for French intervention.

Cambodia and Laos Were Influenced by India

The descendants of the Cambodians were the Khmers who ruled south Annam at one time but were forced back by the Annamese in the sixteenth century.

BURMA

Burma, like other areas, was a conglomeration of tribes and ethnic groups—the Karen tribes in lower Burma, the Shan tribes in the mountain plateaus, the Chin and Kachin tribes on the Indian-Tibetan borders. A Sino-Tibetan tribe, the Mons, ruled the greatest section of Burma before the eleventh century A.D.

At the beginning of the Christian era the Indian merchant arrived in Burma. His faith, Hinayana Buddhism, the Pali script (derived from Sanskrit), as well as his customs, his art, and architecture were borrowed by the Burmese.

In the eleventh century A.D. the first Kingdom of Burma was established. The many ethnic groups were unified under a Sino-Tibetan dynasty, the Pagan. The Pagan dynasty was destroyed by Mongol invasions from China in 1287, and the Mons were left in control of the south and the Shans in the upper Irrawaddy area.

In the middle of the sixteenth century Burma was once again united under the Toungoo dynasty, but it suffered from constant invasions from China and Siam and soon fell. In the middle of the eighteenth century reunification was accomplished under Alaungpaya, and Burma became strong enough to challenge her Indian borders.

SIAM (THAILAND)

Thailand's people, the Thais, originally from Laos, intermixed with Khmers and by the eleventh century A.D. had established a state.

In the fourteenth century the Mongol conquests in China led to heavy Chinese immigration into Siam and the establishment of a Chinese-dominated government in 1351. This government was an absolute monarchy; as in China the land was divided into provinces and six ministries; there was no nobility, and the monarch appointed all offices of state and disposed of officials who did not suit him. Labor, taxes, and conscription were required of all subjects, but the Thailand government was subject to attacks from all sides, and in 1767 the capital was destroyed by Burmese invaders. Reunification followed, then dethronement of the monarch, and in 1782 the present house of Chakkri was established with its capital at Bangkok.

MALAYA

The Malayan peninsula was settled by peoples of Malay stock, but two groups of people were believed to have been there first—the Negritos and the Sakai.

Like most of the rest of Southeast Asia, Malaya was subject to Indian influence at the beginning of the Christian era. These Indians were primarily traders, priests, and scholars—not conquerors, and a Malay-Hindu upper group was established and a state formed.

In the eleventh century Islam arrived, and the Malayan states became sultanates. Some sultans were vassals of other sultans, and all paid tribute to China or were controlled by Indonesian principalities (primarily in the fourteenth century). Malacca, founded in 1403 by a refugee from Malaya, became the center of Moslem influence.

MODERN CIVILIZATION 1500 to the Present

At the beginning of the modern era Southeast Asia was brought under Western control; with the exception of Thailand, the countries became colonies of the European powers. By the time rule was established and effective economic exploitation begun, World War I had arrived and with it demands by Asians for independence. The idea of nationalism was a Western gift to Southeast Asia and was further intensified by the ideals of the war itself. The prestige of Europe also dropped considerably because of the war. Economic expansion, caused by the war, strained the Southeast Asian economy and led to further resentment on the part of the native-born against foreign control and the Chinese or Indian middle man. Throughout the period from World War I to World War II Europe spent its energies in maintaining control of its colonies, but World War II brought drastic change in Southeast Asia. The Japanese occupied the areas under the slogan "Asia for the Asiatics." The Vichy French cooperated with the Japanese and further lowered European prestige, and an Asiatic power, Japan, succeeded in driving the Westerners out, thus convincing Southeast Asia that it could be done. At the end of the war the withdrawal of the Japanese forces created a temporary power vacuum into which nationalist leaders stepped. By the time the Europeans returned they had to face organized national resistance. By 1955 almost all Southeast Asia was free.

SOUTHEAST ASIA COMES UNDER WESTERN DOMINATION

Indonesia Becomes a Dutch Colony

Division in Indonesia facilitated foreign control. In 1596 the Dutch arrived; in 1602 the Dutch East India Company was formed, and the Portuguese were driven out of southern Moluccas; Spanish garrisons were wiped out; and inter-Javanese rivalries were played upon. By 1618 the fortress at Jakarta (Batavia) was built, and during the 1650's the Dutch subjugated the island's sultanates. By 1705 the Dutch East India Company had total control of Java.

The Dutch East India Company Rules the Spice Islands

A. In the eighteenth century the Dutch introduced agricultural exploitation, demanding forced deliveries from the local sultanates, whom they allowed to rule in name only. The Chinese were brought in as a favored economic group and became the intermediaries between the Dutch and the Indonesians.

B. Unlike the Spanish, the Dutch retained Malay law for the Indonesians, Chinese law for the Chinese, and, of course, Dutch law for the Hollanders. This did not encourage a Western cultural tradition.

The Netherlands Government Rules Indonesia

A. In 1796 the Netherlands government took control from the Dutch East India Company and established more direct rule of the area. Eventually it turned over the Company's commercial monopolies to private individuals. Villages became responsible for taxes in kind and labor services.

B. Between 1811 and 1818, as a consequence of the Napoleonic Wars, the Dutch lost control to Great Britain. When European peace was established and the colonies returned, the Dutch met resistance from Javanese princes, which was not suppressed until the 1830's.

C. In 1830 the "culture system" was introduced. Peasants were forced to plant crops for export and sale in Europe. The Dutch did bring new lands under cultivation and introduce new agricultural plants such as tea, tobacco, and the cinchona tree (quinine), but the profits flowed into Dutch pockets, and by the 1850's liberals in Holland began to attack the system.

D. In 1860 the first steps were taken to abolish forced labor, and the agrarian law of 1870 forbade the sale of land to non-Indonesians. (It had to be leased instead.) Land was in the hands of the village, not the private farmer, and thus no tradition of independent farming was developed. A new system of private plantations under European control brought no benefit to the Indonesian, and the European continued to gain sole profit from tin and oil.

E. By 1914 the economic situation in Indonesia was such that the Europeans controlled the capital; the Chinese were the middle men; and the Indonesians, with the exception of a small group of aristocracy, were the workers.

The Philippines Under Spain

In 1521 Magellan arrived in the Philippines, and between 1556 and 1571 the Spanish established their rule of the islands.

The Spanish, unlike the Dutch, created not only a new ruling class but also brought the Philippines into the Western cultural tradition, establishing Western law and the Christian faith. (Today the Philippines are 90 percent Christian and 80 percent Catholic). The area was ruled, however, as an appendage to the Spanish colonies in Central America, and it was not until 1862 that six ports were opened up to free trade. The opening of the ports led to prosperity for the Filipinos but increased dissatisfaction with Spanish rule, for they were still under strict political and cultural control.

Movements for Independence Began Very Early in Philippine History

A. Jose Rizal y Mercado (1869–1896), who had studied abroad, created the Liga Filipina in 1892. The organization demanded liberal political institutions and more educational facilities. Mercado was arrested and deported and finally executed after his involvement in the Cuban Revolution of 1896.

B. With Mercado's arrest the Philippine nationalist movement became more radical. The Katipunan party was established, demanding the redistribution of land as well as complete independence. It is believed to have had fifty thousand members in 1896. Under the leadership of Emilio Aguinaldo, fighting broke out against the Spanish, and in 1897 a truce was negotiated but no reforms followed.

C. In 1898, during the Spanish-American War, Aguinaldo helped American troops drive the Spanish out of Luzon and then immediately declared the Philippines to be a republic. When the United States would not grant independence, Aguinaldo led military action against American troops from February to November, 1899. In 1900 the United States declared local self-government for the Philippines, and the last of Aguinaldo's followers surrendered in 1902.

Indochina Under France

In 1789 the deposed king of Annam was reinstated with the help of the French, and in return France was allowed to maintain bases in the area. In 1801 she helped the king extend his control northward, but in 1858 attacks upon French and Spanish missionaries led to military action. French troops captured Saigon in 1859 and Cochin China in 1860. In 1867 Cambodia was made a French protectorate; in 1874 extraterritoriality was acquired in North Annam; in 1882 the French took Hanoi; in 1893 they acquired Laos, and by 1907 conquest of Indochina was complete.

The colony of Cochin China and the four protectorates of Annam, Cambodia, Tongking, and Laos became the colony of French Indochina, with a governor-general over the entire area. The French followed the same policy as in Africa and the Middle East—a strong centralized rule, European ownership of production, and the creation of a small number of French citizens.

Burma Becomes British

Britain Conquered Burma in Three Stages

A. Border troubles with the British East India Company in India led to war in 1824. In 1826, as a result, Burma lost Tenasserim, the coast of Arakan and the Assam border area and was forced to allow a British resident in the capital city of Ava.

B. War was again waged in 1852, after the Burmese refused to allow British economic penetration.

C. A third war broke out in 1885 and resulted in the destruction of the Kingdom of Burma. However, the Burmese resisted with guerrilla warfare until 1895. In 1897 Burma was included in the administration of India.

The economic situation led to further antagonism on the part of the Burmese, for the Indian merchant was favored and soon became the moneylender, and in time controlled the land, while the British owned the oil and teakwood. Buddhist monastaries also objected to British rule, for although Buddhism was not suppressed, it was no longer the state religion.

Malaya and the British

The creation of British Malaya was fundamentally the work of Sir Thomas Stamford Raffles. After failing to persuade the British government to maintain control of the Dutch East Indies, Raffles turned his interest to the Malayan peninsula.

A. In 1786 the British had acquired Penang.

B. In 1819 Raffles gained the uninhabited island of Singapore by negotiation with the Sultan of Johore and created a free port, which not only prospered but was strategically located, for it controlled the Malacca Strait and the eastern approach to the Indian Ocean.

C. In 1824 Britain exchanged Benkoelen on Sumatra for Malacca. (In 1511 the Portuguese had conquered Malacca and in 1641, the Dutch.)

D. Then began the penetration of the Malay peninsula itself. First came economic penetration, then treaties (1874), and finally, total control.

By the beginning of the twentieth century there were three patterns of British rule in Malaya:

A. The Straits Settlement—a crown colony under a governor-general (who was also the most important power in all the areas)—which included Singapore, Malacca, Penang, the province of Wellesley, and the area south of Penang.

B. The Federated Malay States—under a British resident-general—which included the states of Negri, Sembilian, Selangor, Perak, and Pahang.

C. The Unfederated Malay States, which were protectorates.

The British introduced a plantation economy to Malaya, and, as in their other colonies, used the Chinese and the Indian as the moneylender, the merchant, and the middleman. Eventually the Straits Settlement area became 80 percent Chinese, and this caused problems with the modern independence movement. To compensate, the British tended to favor the Malays culturally and politically.

Thailand Remains Independent

The only country in Southeast Asia able to maintain at least partial independence was Siam. Her independence was due to a number of factors:

A. She had shrewd diplomats who successfully played England off against France and persuaded the two nations that Thailand was best left as a buffer zone.

B. She rapidly put through some timely domestic reforms and allowed liberal trading concessions to the British (in 1826) and the Americans (in 1833). She also opened up the country to foreign missionaries.

In 1851 a rapid program of westernization was begun under King Mongkut. The army and navy were modernized, currency reform was introduced, a foreign language school was built, communications were improved, hospitals were established, and extensive irrigation projects were begun. From 1868 to 1910 Mongkut's son, Chulalongkorn, created a ministry, an efficient tax system, and, most important, codified law, and sent students abroad to study. Extraterritoriality had been granted, however, in 1835, but under Vajiravudh (1910–1925) Thailand regained full sovereignty.

THE BATTLES FOR INDEPENDENCE
AND INDEPENDENT SOUTHEAST ASIA

Thailand

Political History

A. In 1932 King Prajadhipok had been deprived of any real power by a coup d'état of Western-trained intellectuals and military men—the People's Party. By 1940 political parties were allowed and reform was initiated. Education was to be in Thai; foreign control of industry (the British and American oil, the British and Chinese rubber, and the Chinese teak) was to be eliminated; and Buddhism was to be stressed.

B. In 1941 an area with about a million and a half population in Cambodia and Laos was ceded to Thailand by the Japanese. Then came a Japanese ultimatum demanding that Thailand allow her to move troops through the country to Malaya. Pridi, the prime minister, refused to declare war against the United States and was forced to resign. He and his men, representing the king, went underground, and Pibul became prime minister. The new government sided with Japan and thus suffered less of the ravages of war. In 1944 Pibul was ousted in turn by Pridi, but in 1947 he staged a military coup that ended Pridi's rule. (Pridi fled to China.) In 1952 Thailand rounded up all Communists, but in 1957 they were released, and in reaction the military staged a coup d'état. Since 1958 the government of Thailand has been in the hands of the army.

Economy

Thailand's economic resources are plentiful, and she does not suffer from overpopulation. She is more pro-Western than other Southeast Asian countries; she supported U.N. action in Korea and in 1954 joined SEATO. However, she has been worried by her neighbors, her weak border defenses, the United States' equivocal position in Vietnam, the forty thousand Vietnamese refugees living on the Thai side of the Mekong River, and the general pattern of communist infiltration in Southeast Asia.

The Philippines

Under United States Control

A. Under William Taft, the civil governor, the Philippines had been granted local autonomy. Public health had been improved; education had been made free and universal (one third of the children were enrolled); and agrarian reform had made some headway, if only against church held (friar-held) land. In 1907 the first representative Philippine assembly was granted.

B. Immediately after World War I Governor-General Francis Burton Harrison further increased Philippine representation by opening up most of the offices of the government to Filipinoes. They now became the majority in the upper house as well as the lower house.

c. In 1934 an independence act was passed, promising independence in ten years after preparation. From 1934 on the Philippines were to have commonwealth status; the United States was to control foreign affairs and defense only.

During World War II

When the Philippines were attacked by Japan, defense was an American responsibility. Bataan surrendered in April, 1942; Corregidor, in May of 1942. The Philippine government went into exile, but many of the government employees collaborated with the Japanese. Guerrilla resistance was led by tenant farmers organized into the Hukbalahap, controlled by the Moscow-trained Communist, Luis Taruc.

Independence

In 1946 the Philippines were declared independent under the following conditions: American bases were to be allowed; the United States agreed to pay $400,000,000 in war damages; and United States tariff on Philippine goods was free until 1954, to be increased gradually until a full tariff would be assumed by 1874. Nevertheless, the Philippines are not totally independent, for they are dependent on United States markets, and one third of their economic interests are still in American hands and one third in Chinese.

The Philippines Since Independence

THE PHILIPPINES HAD TROUBLES IMMEDIATELY FOLLOWING THE WAR.

1) The two-party system of liberals and nationalists was plagued by factionalism and corruption. Manuel Quezon died; and President Osmena could not keep his party united and was defeated in 1946 by the Liberal Manuel Roxas. The new government was also unable to maintain law and order.

2) The most serious disorder in the country was the activities of the pseudo-communist Hukbalahap party. During the war its energies had been directed as much towards killing its political rivals as killing Japanese (out of twenty-five thousand killed only five thousand were Japanese). The Huks came into conflict with United States guerrilla forces. After the war they continued their program of slaughter and destruction, and the Communist leanings of the organization were more pronounced. By 1950 the situation had reached a crisis (the Huks at this time numbered forty thousand fully armed members, with about 2,500,000 reserves). Ramon Magsaysay, minister of defense, offered the Huks a chance to surrender, and when they refused he sent in the regular army against them. Magsaysay soon ran into trouble with the party machine that controlled the Philippines.

MAGSAYSAY BECOMES PRESIDENT

In 1952 Magsaysay used the army to guarantee free elections, and he himself shifted to the Nationalist Party and in 1953 became president of the country. He then began an active campaign against the Huks. He finally destroyed them and attempted, by land reform, to satisfy agricultural discontent, which had gained the Huks the support of the tenant farms. In foreign policy he abandoned the neutralist policy of his predecessors and favored closer relations with the United States. Magsaysay died in 1957 and was replaced by his vice-president Carlos Garcia, who followed Magsaysay's policies. In 1962 the Liberal Party defeated the Nacionalista and placed Diosdad Macapagal in power.

Burma

Independence Movements

A. The British made concessions where the French had not, but the tension between Burmese tenant farmers and agricultural workers and their Indian landlords and moneylenders increased during the 1930's. Serious uprisings led to the Burma Act of 1935, in which Burma was separated from India.

B. In the 1930's nationalist parties were formed.

1) The Poor Man's Party (later the Freedom Block) was founded by Ba Maw, who became prime minister of the country in 1937, advocating rebellion against the British. When the

Japanese occupied Burma in 1942 they declared Burma independent under Ba Maw.

2) The Patriotic Party was founded by U Saw, who became prime minister in 1939.

3) The Thakin Party was a group of students who were primarily critical of British education. Some of them became Marxists; others went to Formosa in 1941, where they were trained and organized by the Japanese for the conquest of Burma.

World War II

The Japanese occupation of Burma was not what the Burmese expected; all the major cities and much of the industry were destroyed by bombing, riceland was overgrown by jungles, and many water buffaloes were slaughtered. In 1943 the Anti-Fascist League was organized, as was also the Communist Party of Burma.

Independence

At the end of the war (1946) negotiations were carried out between the British and General Aung San, head of the Anti-Fascist League (AFPFL). Aung San agreed to a peaceful settlement and called off the threatened general strike designed to force the British out of Burma. In 1947 a meeting set up self-government for the Burmese. Independence was delayed, however, for U Saw, head of the Patriotic Party, endeavoured to assassinate every member of the proposed government, and he succeeded, with the exception of the Vice-President of the AFPFL, U Nu, who was not at the meeting. U Nu became the successor of Aung San, and in 1948 Burma was declared independent.

Independent Burma

A. Factionalism continued to be a major problem in Burma. By the summer of 1949 there were at least five insurrections in progress: the Orthodox Communist Party, the dissentient Communist Party, the mutinous army, the Karen minority, and the rightists. The government held only Rangoon and its surrounding area.

B. Since 1949 the government has gained power and is still

controlled by the AFPFL, with U Nu, a Socialist, as the most popular figure. But the regime has continued to be plagued by instability, and in 1958 and again in 1962 General Ne Win (rightist, head of the army) replaced U Nu as leader of the government, not only because of internal problems but also because of Red Chinese occupation of areas of Burma's borders. Since 1963, however, Burma and Ne Win have become more and more anti-Western.

Indochina

Under the French
A. French policy was to exploit the economy of Indochina. In thirty years of rule the rice export had tripled, but it was a Chinese monopoly; by 1939 the rubber industry exports equaled 78,000 tons and coal two and a half million tons, but these were totally under French control. Indochinese goods were restricted by French tariff but the reverse was not true. The French not only dominated the economic scene but also the political scene, and thus alienated the intelligentsia of Indochina.

B. The fundamental influence toward nationalism came from China. In 1912 the Nationalist Party of Indochina held its first meeting in Canton. In 1920 Ho Chi Minh, who had been trained in both France and China, organized the first Communist Party. By the beginning of World War II, however, the French administration had curbed the Communist Party and destroyed the Nationalist Party.

During World War II
The Vichy French capitulated to Japanese demands that the defense of Indochina be left to Japan. In July, 1941 the Japanese took all of Indochina. Resistance movements sprang up, the Communist Party declared a united front, and in 1944, under the command of Vo Guyen Giap (trained at Yenan), engaged in active battle. In 1945 the Japanese set up puppet governments under Bao Dai and the kings of Cambodia and Laos, but the nationalists refused them support.

Independence and Division in Vietnam

A. In September, 1945 the Nationalists established a government. After the Japanese surrender the south was occupied by British troops and the north by Chinese troops. The Chinese immediately recognized Ho Chi Minh's government, but in the south the British sided with the French. War between the north and south broke out in 1946. In 1949 the French granted semi-independence within the French Union to Cambodia and Laos, and set up Bao Dai as chief of state of Vietnam (both North and South). But despite his imperial descent he was obviously the wrong choice. Bitter fighting continued until the truce of 1954, when the French pulled out completely; Laos and Cambodia were given total independence; Vietnam was divided at the seventeenth parallel; the Communists agreed to give up their projected invasion of Cambodia and Laos; and North and South Vietnam promised to allow civilians to move from one side to the other and to hold elections in 1956 to reunite the area (they never did).

B. The uneasy partition between North and South Vietnam continued. In the north, Ho Chi Minh led the Communist government which was closely allied with Red China and continued to penetrate into the south and Laos. In the south Bao Dai was replaced in 1955 by Premier Ngo Dinh Diem, and a constitution was approved in 1956. Among other political disadvantages, Diem was a Roman Catholic and antagonized sections of the Buddhist faith. He was supported by almost no one except the Americans. The United States continued to support the regime financially (in 1954–1955 she sent $320,000,000 worth of aid, and between 1955 and 1956 another $196,500,000).

C. In 1960, however, the Communists in North Vietnam decided on more aggressive action. In 1961 the United States increased her military advisers from 685 to 2,000, and the first combat support units were sent in. The Communists in turn decided on full-scale guerrilla warfare. In 1962 the United States increased the strength of the army to 11,000 and aid to $500 million a year. The Chinese and North Vietnamese sent arms to the Vietcong (South Vietnam guerrilla rebels). In 1963 the United

States had 15,500 men, and the Communists built up their forces. By 1965 the Communist guerrillas gained control of most of central South Vietnam and the United States commenced the bombing of North Vietnam military bases, and a heavy military buildup.

Laos

Laos was supposed to be evacuated by the Communists under the terms of the Geneva Conference in 1954; this has not been done. The Vietminh (Communist Party of Vietnam) supports Pathet Lao (Communist Party of Laos) which continues to wage war against the kingdom and controls two provinces. Laos has received 56 million dollars in economic and military aid from the United States, and its armed forces are entirely paid for and equipped by the United States. Laos receives more aid per capita than any other nation. It now has a coalition government between the Communists and Prince Souvanna Phouma. Out of twelve ministers and four vice-ministers, eight are nationalists, three are "independent" (fellow travelers), and five are members of the Pathet Lao, but since 1962 the strength of the Communists has diminished.

Cambodia

Temporarily, Cambodia fared better, and its king Sihanouk was able to maintain both an anti-communist and anti-American policy. Since the Vietnam crisis, however, Sihanouk has refused United States aid and become cozy with the Chinese.

Indonesia

The Dutch East Indies and Independence Movements

A. Agitation for educational and commercial improvements and greater autonomy began in 1908 in Indonesia.

B. In 1916 the Dutch created the Volksraad, a council for the expression of public opinion. But even by 1928 the council was not representative of majority opinion for there were fifteen Dutch, four Chinese, one Arab, and thirty Indonesians (and of this thirty, ten were appointed by the Dutch government).

c. In the 1920's political "study clubs" led to the organization of the National Indonesian Party (the PNI), with Sukarno, an engineer, as head. The party was dissolved by the government in 1929, and the Dutch created a prison camp in New Guinea for certain revolutionary leaders, while others were banished from Java (Sukarno was banished to Flores and then to Sumatra). It was these revolutionaries whom the Japanese freed.

World War II

Japan attacked in March, 1942, and the Indonesians did not defend their country, welcoming the invaders as liberators. It soon proved, however, that Japan was not going to permit as much local participation as was originally hoped or promised, and some nationalists did not cooperate with the invaders. (Sukarno, however, did.)

The Wars of Independence

A. At the end of the war in August, 1945, the Indonesian Republic was proclaimed by Sukarno, and after six weeks he gained control. The British then arrived to evacuate the Japanese forces and recognized de facto the Sukarno government. This forced the British into the position of mediator with the Dutch.

B. In 1947 the Linggadjati Agreement was signed, giving Sukarno's government de facto authority on Java, Madura, and Sumatra, but retaining Borneo and the Great East State for the Dutch. Sukarno's three islands were declared the United States of Indonesia; Dutch prisoners, who had been held as hostages by the nationalists, were freed; and Holland immediately established an economic blockade of the three islands and puppet governments. In July, 1947 war broke out; the Hollanders won, and the United States took up the job of mediator. War continued, and in December, 1948 the situation was brought before the United Nations.

C. By the Hague Agreement of 1949 Indonesia was declared free.

Independent Indonesia

The independent state of Indonesia is racked with problems.
A. The outer islands problem is perhaps one of the most

serious and has even led to rebellion and war. The outer islands, particularly Sumatra, resent Javanese control, both political and economic.

B. Diversity and factionalism within the government, ranging from orthodox Moslems to Chinese Communists, have caused Sukarno to become more and more dependent upon dictatorial methods.

C. Poverty is still prevalent, both in industry and agriculture.

D. In foreign policy, Sukarno for a while maintained a neutral position, but his relations with Red China were complicated by a 1,500,000 Chinese minority in the country, and since 1964 he has become more and more anti-Western. He objected violently to the incorporation of North Borneo into the Malaysian federation and has been sending bands of guerrillas against the British troops defending Borneo. The culmination of his attacks against Western influence came in January, 1965, when he announced the withdrawal of Indonesia from the U.N. In March of 1966 he was forced to step down when the military took control as a reaction to Communist influence.

Malaya

The first modern political activities occurred among the Chinese, who outnumbered the Malays in the cities and constituted about 44 percent of the population. The KMT (Chinese Nationalist Party) founded branches in Malaya, and the Chinese Communists followed suit in 1921.

During World War II
In February, 1942 Singapore surrendered, and the Japanese occupied Malaya. The Japanese favored the Malays and heightened Malay distrust of the Chinese. The Chinese Communists were the ones who organized the anti-Japanese underground movement.

Independence
A. After the war a proposed Malay union in which everyone

would be a citizen (immigrants as well as native-born) was objected to by the United Malay National Organization. In 1947 a new plan was introduced. Citizenship would be given to all who had been born in Malay or who had lived in the area for fifteen years. The Malay Federation also excluded Singapore, which was heavily Chinese.

B. Before the Federation could be put into operation, the Chinese Communists led a planned military attack of murder, ambush, and guerrilla warfare against plantations, mines, officials of the government, and the Chinese KMT members. They used 300,000 Chinese squatters who had been driven inland during the war as the center of their power. In 1950 the British sent in 18,000 troops; in 1952 they resettled 100,000 of the Chinese squatters. Finally, after a major military effort (35,000 British soldiers, an extra police force, the air force, and the expense of £100,000,000 a year) the military threat of the Communists was destroyed by 1954. In 1955 plans for the Federated Malay States could be continued and elections held.

c. The Problem of Singapore

1) The merger of Singapore with Malaya would have meant the extinction of the majority position of the Malays in the Federation and the extension of Chinese influence into southeast Asia. In 1955 there were serious riots in Singapore, and in 1957, under the leadership of Lim Yew-Hock, an independent state of Singapore was formed with internal freedom but with British control of foreign policy.

2) In September, 1963 a proposed federation, known as Malaysia, was approved by the British. The federation, within the Commonwealth of Nations, included North Borneo (Sabah) and Sarawak, Singapore, and the Federated Malay States.

A) North Borneo and Sarawak were included in order to counterbalance the heavy Chinese majority in Singapore.

B) Although both Indonesia and the Philippines objected to the inclusion of Borneo, the U.N. investigated and found that the majority preferred to belong to Malaysia.

c) In 1965, Singapore pulled out of the Federation.

GENERAL PROBLEMS OF INDEPENDENT SOUTHEAST ASIA

Poverty is the common denominator of all Asia, and along with a need for improved methods of agricultural production and industry goes an extremely rapid population growth (in Malaya, for example, it is 3 percent a year, and in Singapore it is 4 percent). The per capita income ranges from $50 per year in Burma and Laos to $400 in Singapore.

Another special problem in Southeast Asia is the large number of minority groups and the Chinese problem. The Chinese generally maintain allegiance to either Chiang Kai-shek or Mao Tse-tung, and they attempt to remain culturally distinct from the rest of the population by using the Chinese language and establishing their own schools.

Democracy is rare in Southeast Asia. Only Malaya and the Philippines can be said to be democratic. In Malaya the framework that makes democratic politics possible is provided by emergency regulations adopted in response to the Communist insurrection that started in 1948. In the Philippines it was the army that broke the back of the Communists. Most Southeast Asian governments would today agree with Sukarno who said in 1957: "The experiences of these eleven years have convinced me that the democracy we have adopted . . . is not in harmony with the soul of the Indonesian nation. This is what I call Western democracy—for that matter you may call it parliamentary democracy . . . an import democracy, not an Indonesian one." Sukarno's government ruled by decree and relied totally on the support of the army, which took over in March of 1966.

Sub-Sahara Africa

ANCIENT AND CLASSICAL CIVILIZATION
1000 B.C.–500 A.D.

This chapter is limited to sub-Saharan Africa because the area has developed separately from the northern and Mediterranean parts of the continent. The people of the north were influenced by the Greeks, the Phoenicians, the Romans, and the Moslems, and belong to the Mediterranean world. On the other hand, Africa south of the Sahara was relatively isolated by its vast expanse of desert. Almost nothing is known about tropical Africa before the Arab chronicles of the ninth century A.D., and very little is known until the coming of the Europeans in the sixteenth century. Most of what historians know about pre-European Africa is based on archeological discoveries, since few African tribes or civilizations developed a system of writing and still fewer a calendar. Consequently, all that remains is oral history (legends) and artifacts (weapons, cooking implements, and so on).

About ten thousand years ago, four racial types had appeared in Africa, and the migration and intermingling of these groups are the story of Africa's early history: (1) the ancestors of the modern Bushmen probably occupied most of the drier areas of the east and south; (2) the Negroid type emerged in the west central forested regions; (3) the Pygmies' ancestry is open to doubt, but probably developed in the forests of the Congo and Guinea; and (4) a race akin to the Caucasian (called proto-Hamite) appeared in the north and east. The areas of densest population seem to have been the savanna regions and the Nile river valley.

413

*There was little or no population on the southern tip of Africa
until the Negroes moved down some time before the coming of
the Portuguese in the fifteenth century* A.D.

*African development was by no means uniform over the
entire continent. The people of Khartoum on the Nile reached
the neolithic stage by the second half of the fourth millennium,
whereas the Pygmies in the Congo are today still in the Stone
Age, since they are hunters and food gatherers. From the time that
the peoples of the savanna areas first experienced the food-produc-
ing revolution (farming) to the moment when such knowledge
came to the forest regions of Africa, three thousand years elapsed.
Between 3000* B.C. *and 100* B.C. *the art of cultivation came to the
Bantu-speaking Negro of the savanna in a series of slow and
easy stages. The advent of even primitive "civilization" produced
a population explosion, and by the beginning of the Christian
era the Bantu had begun to move south. The migration into the
warmer and more moist southern regions of Africa was made
easier by the introduction of two important Southeast Asian food
plants—the banana and the yam. In the course of the Bantu dispersal other racial stocks were absorbed, except in inhospitable
areas.*

*During the ancient and classical period, Africa was never
entirely isolated. Greeks traveled across the desert, and people
from Indonesia, Malaya, and Polynesia reached Madagascar and
penetrated the east coast of Africa. There are even indications of
trade between east Africa and China, but the first civilization to
influence African development fundamentally was the Egyptian.
The Meroe civilization on the upper Nile and the Sudanic civilizations of West Africa were directly influenced by Egyptian political theories.*

THE RACIAL TYPES OF AFRICA

The Pygmy

The typical Pygmy now numbers only about thirty-five thousand to forty thousand. His average height is four feet, six inches

and his average weight is eighty-eight pounds. He has a yellow-ish-brown skin and is still a food-gatherer in the forest.

The Bushman

The Bushman is somewhat taller than the Pygmy and is noted for his wrinkled skin. There are probably no more than ten thousand to fifty thousand Bushmen living in the south of Africa (particularly the Kalahara desert).

The Negro

The Negro is today the major physical type in sub-Sahara Africa. There are three main groups:

The West African Negro, called the true Negro.

The Bantu, who are a linguistic, not a racial grouping, but who do seem to be somewhat lighter-skinned than the true Negro.

The Nilotes of east Africa, who are tall, slender, and long-headed.

THE MEROE OR KUSH CIVILIZATION   800 B.C.–300 A.D.

In 666 B.C., in the face of an Assyrian invasion, the pharaoh of Egypt retreated southward up the Nile to Kush, establishing Egyptian influence in the Kush area or what is today the Sudan.

Around the sixth century B.C. Kush began to push its frontiers southward into the wooded areas of Africa and founded the new capital of Meroe, henceforth ruling over a mixed population of Caucasoids and Negroes. The Meroe had an Iron Age civilization and were able to defend themselves from Egyptian pressure in the north and to expand into the south.

We know very little about the Meroe, but they seem to have been a trading civilization, directly influenced by Egyptian ideas, and their kings were considered to be divine.

Axum

By the middle of the first century A.D. Meroe society was in decline, probably because of the rise of a rival trading empire, Axum.

Axum, located in the north corner of the Ethiopian highlands, was the great ivory market of northeast Africa. During the second and third centuries A.D. its power rose, and by the fourth century it had conquered Meroe and burned the city to the ground. During the fourth century Axum became Christian (the Coptic church) with strong political and religious links with Byzantine Egypt.

Sudanic Civilizations

From the Red Sea to the mouth of the Senegal River, African peoples formed states "so similar that they must have been derived from a common source." There is little doubt that the ideas of ancient Egypt, transmitted through Meroe, formed the basis of these Sudanic civilizations, but there was also a southwest Asian influence that must have come from Axum.

The greatest of early Sudanic civilizations was Ghana, founded in the fourth century A.D. on the main caravan route to north Africa. At its height in the tenth century Ghana's capital city had a population of close to thirty thousand people and controlled an area extending from the Atlantic Ocean almost to Timbuktu.

Ruled by divine kings, concerned with the fertility of the land, the Sudanic state was not feudal, for power was not hereditary but wielded by officials who held office at the king's pleasure and were transferred, promoted, and demoted at his bidding.

The Sudanic states are believed to have been parasitic growths fastening themselves upon existing agricultural societies, probably with the aid of cavalry warfare.

MEDIEVAL CIVILIZATION   500 A.D.–1500 A.D.

There is evidence of regular contact between Mediterranean and Negro Africa from at least the fifth century B.C. The agents of this contact were the Berbers of the desert. The social and political organization of the sedentary Mediterranean Berber was fundamentally democratic, but that of the desert Berber, the Tuareg, was hierarchical and authoritarian. The western Sudan exported gold, ivory, and slaves to the north, in return for luxuries and salt. With the beginning of the medieval era the Arabs invaded north Africa. By the ninth century the Moslems had made contact with both Ghana and Kanem (two centuries later Kanem was converted to Islam). By the eleventh century Islam had made progress among members of the Tuareg (who became known as the Almoravids).

MOSLEM INFLUENCE IN WEST AFRICA

Ghana

The Almoravids moved against Ghana in 1062, but not until 1076 were they able to capture the capital. Yet the nomads were unable to benefit from their conquest, for they soon ended up fighting among themselves, and Ghana became independent once again. However, the kingdom was never able to recover its trade or repair the damage done to its agriculture, and the empire began to break up into tribal units.

Mali

The Mali empire was established on the upper Niger valley (1230–1255) by members of one of the Mande clans that had ruled Ghana. Sundiata, their leader, adopted Islam. By the fourteenth century Mali controlled the upper Niger west to the Atlantic and all the land north of the forest and east along the Niger valley to Hausaland.

Songhai

Mali collapsed when one of its vassals, the king of Songhai, broke away in the fifteenth century and eventually captured Mali territory, ending up with an empire even greater than Mali. The capital of Songhai was Goa, and its wealth was based on control of the salt mines. King Mohammed Askia's reign (1493–1528) was exceptional. The city of Timbuktu became his center of learning, a university was built, and clerics, judges, and scholars flourished under his patronage. Songhai fell to the Moroccans in 1591.

Without losing their Sudanic characteristics, the states of the western Sudan became part of the Islamic world.

EAST AFRICA AND THE MOSLEMS

Moslems had little influence in east Africa until the thirteenth century. Although they occupied the coastline and most of the land along the eastern frontier of Abyssinia (Ethiopia), and although by the tenth century a series of Moslem trading states had been built, Christian Abyssinia was able to dominate them and force them to pay tribute. (Ethiopia became Christian during the fourth century A.D.)

This domination eventually led, in the fifteenth century, to religious wars between Abyssinia and the Moslems. Ifat, the largest Moslem community, was destroyed in 1415 and the Moslems retreated temporarily to Yemen, but returned and founded Adel.

From the fourth to the tenth century, Bantu Negroes were spreading into Tanganyika and Kenya, and the number of Arab colonists was extremely small. From the middle of the thirteenth century, however, to the coming of the Portuguese, wealthy Moslem states grew up all the way down the coastline and experienced a period of prosperity, trading in slaves and ivory. The

Portuguese left no deep mark on east Africa. The essential cultural and commercial contact was Islam.

GUINEA AND THE EXPANSION OF THE NEGRO

By the thirteenth century a growth of population in the Sudan led gradually to the infiltration of the forest lands; the governments of the forest regions were modeled on the older Sudanic states. North of the Gold Coast forest the Akan state of Bonot Banda was founded, but it was not until the fifteenth century that the forest was penetrated. The city of Ife, close to the edge of the forest, was the dispersal point for the Benin dynasty, which controlled the Nigerian forest lands. The Oyo, who held supremacy in the area in the seventeenth century, also had their center to the north of the forest.

These Guinea states were patterned after the Sudanic civilizations. They were urban in character, for the nucleus of each was a town surrounded by a wall. They established an extensive network of trade routes and exported gold dust, kola nuts (one of the few stimulants tolerated by Islam), and ivory. They imported salt, which came from the sea and the Sahara via the Sudan, and horses and cattle.

MODERN CIVILIZATION 1500 to the Present

At the beginning of the modern period in African history Africa was not the most backward of the continents. Most Africans were using iron while the American Indians and the Australian aboriginals were not, and most were organized into states powerful enough to deter invaders until the late nineteenth century. Yet Africa was the last of the continents to experience the impact of European peoples and ideas. For one thing, Africa had less to offer Europe than the East (only ivory and gold), and because of climate, disease, and lack of communications, Europeans were prevented from entering Africa and producing what they wanted. It was not until the seventeenth century, with the in-

creased demand for labor on plantations in the New World, that Europe's interest in Africa began to grow. Yet three centuries of European trade in slaves on the coasts of Africa resulted in little penetration of Western influence. Ironically, it was not until the antislave movement in Europe (in 1807 the slave trade was outlawed in Great Britain) had won great victories that European culture began to affect the indigenous civilizations of Africa. The exploration of inner Africa at the beginning of the nineteenth century was a manifestation of new European humanitarianism, of missionary zeal to convert the dark continent to Christianity, and of the effort to establish legitimate trade in place of the slave trade. But even as late as 1874 the Ashanti was the only Negro kingdom to have fought a European army, and little had been done to bring Africa into European hands; only a very small portion of the continent was actually under Western rule. It was not until Belgium and Germany became interested in Africa in the 1880's that the scramble for colonies began, and by 1914 almost all Africa was under European political domination.

During the years between the two world wars Europeans controlled everything, no African was in a position of responsibility, and there was little financial assistance to stimulate economic development. With the Second World War and its need for strategic raw materials and foodstuffs Africa suddenly became important, and Africa and her people began to change. With Westernization came inevitable reaction and challenge to Europe's political domination of Africa. The disintegration of the colonial system began in 1957, when the British colony of the Gold Coast became the independent state of Ghana. By 1961 almost all Africa was independent.

THE COMING OF THE PORTUGUESE

Henry the Navigator (1394–1460) of Portugal had a scheme to circumvent the Islamic middleman by traveling around Africa to the Far East. In 1444 the Portuguese reached Cape Verde; by 1471 they were at the Gold Coast and building forts to protect their rights to the gold they found there. In 1488 Diaz rounded the Cape of Good Hope, and in 1497 Vasco da Gama made his famous trip to India.

Angola

The Portuguese discovered the kingdom of the Bakongo, one of the largest states in Africa (it was bounded by the Atlantic Ocean, the Congo, the Kwango and the Dande rivers, and had a population of close to two and a half million). The Bakongo kingdom was a typical Sudanic state. Its capital was the modern Sao Salvador. Around the state were clusters of small states owing nominal allegiance to the Bakongo (one of these was Ngola, the origin of the present day word Angola).

Missionaries were sent in 1490, and the king of Bakongo was converted to Christianity. From 1491 to 1543 an "ardent and enlightened" Christian sat on the throne, but the Portuguese were more interested in the slave trade than in the establishment of a Christian state, and by 1660 they were at war with the Bakongo.

By the eighteenth century there was no Christianity and no state, and the Portuguese retained Angola merely as the supply base for the Brazil slave trade.

Mozambique

The Portuguese took control of Sofala at the beginning of the sixteenth century and soon came into conflict with the Vakaranga people (whose ruler was known as Monomatapa), who controlled the Zambezi valley, the north and east parts of the southern Rhodesian plateau, and the lowlands of southern Mozambique.

In 1560 the Portuguese occupied territory ruled by the Monomatapas. The military strength of the Portuguese and their assistance against the rising power of the Changamires made the Monomatapas dependent upon them, and by 1629 the Monomatapas had become Portuguese vassals. This, of course, meant the end of the kingdom and Portuguese supremacy in the area.

The Portuguese Achievement in Africa

Though the Portuguese were the first West Europeans to arrive in Africa, they made no significant contributions to African history from the fifteenth century to the end of the eighteenth century. In Angola they exported their own Portuguese criminal classes and then used them to incite natives to fight among themselves so as to make it easier to carry on the slave trade. In Mozambique the situation was less bloody, for it was gold rather than slaves that the Portuguese were interested in, but again exploitation was the theme of Portuguese control.

The opening up of trade and slave routes by the Portuguese did, however, bring Africa into contact with the outside world and with its own peoples. Moreover, the Portuguese did introduce new plant foods (coffee, tobacco, and others) from South America.

THE SLAVE TRADE

The need for labor on the sugar plantations in the New World led to the growth of European interest in Africa. The Europeans sailed to the Gold Coast and bought their slaves from African kings or merchants. The slave trade was pioneered by the Dutch, who had ousted the Portuguese from the Gold Coast by 1642. Soon, however, the British and French became interested, and by the eighteenth century they controlled the major portion of the trade. (England controlled more than 50 percent).

Effects of the Slave Trade by the Eighteenth Century

A. Depopulation

This was not as great in West Africa as in Angola and East Africa, but by 1600, 900,000 slaves had been taken to America; during the 1600's, another 2,750,000; during the 1700's, 7,000,000 more; and by 1900, another 4,000,000. For every West African on a plantation in the New World, it is estimated that one died in the slave wars or en route; for every East African taken by the Arabs, five to twelve died.

B. The Slave trade moved the centers of African wealth and trade from the Sudan to the coast.

C. Tribal war and conflict in the interior were also results of the slave trade. At first the slaves who were sold to Europeans were probably slaves in the African communities, but with the increased demand chiefs resorted to the use of their newly purchased firearms to raid one another's tribes for slaves.

THE ANTISLAVE MOVEMENT

In 1807 the British parliament passed a bill outlawing the slave trade, but England felt the need for suppressing the trade not only among her own people but also, for commercial reasons, among the other European nations. Legitimate trade could only be developed after the more profitable and much easier slave trade had been eliminated.

In 1808 the United States followed suit; in 1814 so did the Dutch; and after the Napoleonic wars most other European nations, except Spain and Portugal, outlawed the slave trade. Great Britain set up naval patrols and persuaded or forced African rulers to outlaw the export of slaves, but it was not until the United States Civil War in 1865 and the final abolition of slavery in Cuba and Brazil in the 1880's that the picture really changed.

The antislave movement was part of a larger humanitarian movement in which the revival of Christianity played a major role. Missionary activity in Africa began to gather momentum in the 1850's and had spread rapidly by the 1870's.

EXPLORATION

Commercial and missionary interests led to the opening up of Africa. The geographical exploration of the interior started in the 1790's, but it took seventy-five to eighty years to learn the main facts about the continent.

The British led the way in the exploration of Africa, for it was in the pay of the British government that:

Mungo Park sailed most of the course of the Niger in 1805;

Denham and Clapperton explored Bornu and Hausaland in 1823–1825;

The Lander brothers followed the lower Niger to the sea in 1830;

And the German Heinrich Barth explored central and west Sudan in the 1850's.

The French contributed little despite their interest in Senegal. René Caillié's journey in 1827 was the only one that compared with the British feats, and it was a private venture.

Some of the earliest pioneers in east Africa were German (Knapf and Rebmann found Kilimanjaro), but again exploration of the south and east was done primarily by the British. The Royal Geographical Society financed David Livingstone's trip to Victoria Falls in 1853, Burton and Speke's trip to Lake Tanganyika in 1858, and Livingstone's expedition of 1859–1864.

David Livingstone was probably the symbol of his age, for he was both a medical missionary and an explorer, and it was his task to look for trade routes that would permit English manufactured goods to supplant the slave trade.

POLITICAL ANNEXATION AND THE SCRAMBLE FOR COLONIES

Not until the 1870's did the European nations become involved in schemes for political annexation in Africa. Two countries, which had heretofore not been interested in Africa, suddenly entered the picture.

King Leopold of Belgium decided to develop the Congo as his commercial monopoly, and as Roland Oliver and J. D. Farge said in *A Short History of Africa,* "Probably it was Leopold, more than any other statesman, who created the 'atmosphere' of scramble."

Between 1883 and 1885 Germany annexed southwest Africa, Togoland, the Cameroons, and East Africa.

At the Berlin Conference of 1884–1885 the actions of Germany and Belgium were legalized and an international code for the partition of Africa was established. This attempt at internationalism failed because there was no machinery to enforce international law, and in the fifteen years following the conference, the entire continent with the exception of Ethiopia was divided among the great powers.

The Process of Acquisition

A. Treaties granting rights to European powers were signed by the tribal chiefs of the interior, whom the white man insisted had the authority to convey land, grant mining concessions, and so forth (by tribal law they had in fact no such power).

B. The system of indirect rule was established in most territories, whereby the Europeans built up the power of the chief and ruled through him. By this means a labor force was acquired to work the mines and the plantations.

French Interests

France had turned to West Africa in order to compensate for the loss of her empire during the Napoleonic wars. In 1854 Senegal was developed as a French colony and as a base for the French conquest of the western Sudan. Logically, France should have expanded quickly into West Africa. By 1883 she had fought her way (against the Ahmadu) to the upper Niger, but she did not succeed in reaching Timbuktu until 1893, for the western Sudan had witnessed a new advance of Islam and the Mande tribes were too strong.

British Interests

British initial interests had been on the western coast of Africa. Sierra Leone was colonized by the British at the end of the eighteenth century and Freetown was established. It was a private venture of antislavery humanitarians. (Liberia was the American equivalent in 1821 and Libreville the French copy of Freetown in 1849.) By 1860 seventy thousand Negroes freed from slave ships had settled in Sierra Leone, and the British became convinced that the most effective way of stopping the slave export was to establish rule over the coast. But it was not until 1874, after the Danes and the Dutch had handed over their forts and the British had defeated the Ashanti, that the Gold Coast was declared a British colony. In 1851 Legos was captured, and in 1861 it became a colony.

From 1886 to 1892 British African policy was based on the retention of Egypt at all costs. This meant that she was willing to allow French expansion in the west, despite the fact that it involved the encirclement of four British spheres on the coast. Great Britain herself turned to the east coast of Africa, although it was commercially almost valueless.

South Africa

South Africa was the one exception in the period prior to the scramble for concessions.

A small Dutch colony had been planted at the Cape in 1652 in order to supply food for passing ships. The Dutch East India Company found it necessary to attract colonists to the Cape in order to create a labor force and to defend the settlement against the Bantu, who had moved into the south. However, the settlement soon became too large, and opposition grew to the Company's rule. Some of the colonists decided to seek liberty and a new life in the interior. These colonists, known as the Trek-Boers (migrant farmers), moved east to Natal and established the Boer Republics of Fraaff Reinet and Swellendam. In 1779 they first came in conflict with the Bantu tribes (the infidel wars).

THE ZULUS

The advance of the Boers cut off new lands available for the Bantu tribes, forcing the various tribes to fight among themselves for the remaining land. The victor of these wars was the Zulu clan in northern Natal, led by Shaka, who created a Zulu empire. Two areas that withstood Zulu pressure were Swaziland and Basuto. It was not until 1838 that the Zulus were challenged by the Boers.

During the Anglo-French wars of 1793–1815, the Cape came

under British control, and so did the independent Boer republics of Swellendam and Fraaff Reinet in 1795.

THE GREAT TREK

A. The Boer farmers were as unhappy under British rule as they had been under the Dutch East India Company. When British humanitarian colonial policy favored returning disputed frontier land to the Bantus in 1836, the Boer farmers decided on a second trek.

B. The Great Trek (1835–1837) was the exodus of the Boers living along the frontier to the lands across the Orange River, where they established the virtually independent Republics of Natal, Transvaal, and the Orange Free State. In December, 1838, the successor of Shaka, King Dingaan of the Zulus was defeated by the Boers, led by Andries Pretorius, and the Africanders were able to settle in Natal. (In 1879 another war was fought against the Zulus, but this time by the British.)

BOER VERSUS BRITISH

A. The Boer republic of Natal was established in 1839 but was annexed by the British in 1845. The Transvaal and the Orange Free State became independent republics in 1852 and 1854, but they were so poor that they were incapable of coping with the wars of the Bantus. Despite Boer opposition the ideal solution, according to the British, was a federation of the British colonies and the Boer republics.

B. In 1877 the Transvaal was annexed, and the British found themselves at war with both the Zulus and the Boers. In 1881 the British decided that the Transvaal was not worth the military effort and recognized its independence once again.

C. Hostility between Boer and British was further increased by British (Anglican) missionary work, for the Boers were strict Calvinists, believing in racial segregation.

D. The Boer War

1) The discovery of gold of the Witwatersrand in the Transvaal in 1886 again caused trouble. Kruger (president of the Transvaal from 1883 to 1902) and Rhodes (a British settler in South Africa, who had acquired mining rights in the Kimberley diamond mines and was prime minister of the Cape 1890–1896)

soon clashed. Rhodes succeeded in encircling the Transvaal and persuading Great Britain to annex Bechuanaland in 1885, to declare a sphere of interest extending from Bechuanaland to the Zambezi River in 1888, and to acquire northern Rhodesia and Nyasaland in 1889–1890. But Rhodes had to fight the Portuguese in Mozambique and to overcome an uprising of the Matabele and Mashone tribes (1897) in order to achieve his policy of encircling the Transvaal.

2) Kruger retaliated by building a railroad to the Portuguese port at Delagoa Bay, and Rhodes answered by attempting to instigate a revolution in the Transvaal, supported by hired mercenaries under Dr. Jameson. The Jameson Raid of 1896 failed, and this ruined Rhodes' political reputation and career.

3) Gold, however, continued to attract English settlers into the Transvaal, where the Boers treated them as second-class citizens. War between Boer and British came in 1899. In 1902, after three years of inglorious war in which the Boers were regarded as the heroes by the rest of the world, the Boers sought peace, and the independent republics and the British colonies became a federation.

By 1902 the scramble was over, and the only sub-Saharan countries that remained independent were Ethiopia (which had defeated the Italians and limited their expansion to the coastlines of Eritrea and Somalia) and the republic of Liberia.

THE COLONIAL PERIOD

The First Years of Colonial Rule

Once the colonial powers had taken their share of Africa, they lost interest in their acquisitions. In nearly every territory only a serious military crisis brought reinforcement or economic grants-in-aid. With the establishment of civil administration over a colony the grants-in-aid ended, and the colonial administration was generally expected to pay for itself out of custom duties and taxes.

During the first years of the colonial period the great powers had no positive policy and were concerned only with maintaining peace and security and making their territories economically self-supporting. Since taxation was to be the basis of self-sufficiency, some European nations encouraged African production and others encouraged white immigration. Which policy they followed generally depended on the governor of the territory. (For example, the British government encouraged European plantations in Kenya and Nyasaland but not in Uganda, and it disallowed them in West Africa.)

1918–1940

With World War I Came a Change in Attitude

The great colonial powers suddenly were no longer so self-confident as in the past, and they began to feel that colonialism required a goal and a justifying moral and political philosophy. After the war the decision to break up the German empire also had to be rationalized. Togoland and the Cameroons were divided between France and Great Britain; Southwest Africa went to the Union of South Africa; German East Africa was divided between Britain and Belgium. These territories became mandates under the League of Nations, and the trustee nation had the obligation to govern justly and to carry them forward economically and politically. They were viewed as "a sacred trust of civilization."

This view implied an extension and change of the functions of the colonial governments. Education is perhaps the best example. In all of the colonies there was some attempt to educate the native.

A. Britain used the already established missionary schools, insuring that about one quarter of her Africans received from two to four years of education—some received from eight to twelve.

B. Belgian policy was similar, although the emphasis was on primary education.

C. France made no use of the missions, but established state schools for the select minority.

D. Throughout Africa most of the European powers followed the doctrine of assimilation, the philosophy which assumed that the African would grow into citizens of the mother country. Britain was an exception, for she never assumed that the African would become a Britisher. This is perhaps one of the reasons why Britain accepted independence as an ultimate goal much more readily than did Portugal, France, or Belgium.

Economic aid, however, did not come, although railroads were built by most colonial powers. Nor did European private investment flourish. With the exception of South Africa, Europeans did not migrate to Africa readily (by the 1930's there were only 60,000) and the few who did had neither skills nor capital. The only exception to this was in the mining industry (which consumed two thirds of European investment), but this, of course, was limited to South Africa, the Rhodesias, and the Katanga province of the Congo. Only in these territories did secondary industry develop (by the mid 1930's South Africa accounted for more than half of Africa's international trade).

World War II

The Great Depression of 1930–1936 led to the realization on the part of the European governments that they could not depend on private investment in Africa to develop their colonies, and then World War II followed and changed both Europe's and Africa's attitude toward the nature of colonial responsibility and the right of Europeans to be there at all. During the war Africa became important as a future supplier of industrial raw materials and unprocessed foodstuffs. She suddenly became known as "the continent God kept in reserve." The need for raw materials (the value of the Congo's exports increased fourteenfold) and greater private investments led to rapid economic change in Africa. Europe also felt a strong moral obligation to the colonies, and this ultimately led to political and social change in the form of the founding of universities, the training of doctors, and the liberalizing of political control. Results of the change varied from colony to colony according to the mother country's colonial aims and the number and influence of European settlers in each colony.

Here again education is a good example of varied colonial achievement.

From 1946 to 1954 in British Ghana the number of children in school increased from 147,447 to 521,989; in the Belgian Congo, from 885,038 to 1,138,700; in French West Africa, from 107,470 to 284,441; and in British Nigeria, from 614,173 to 1,114,985. By 1954 twenty-five universities and technical schools had been established, but this figure is misleading, for ten were in British territories, ten in the Union of South Africa (only three of which were for Negroes), three in Liberia, and only one in Belgium and French territories.

Europe's exhaustion following World War II, Asian independence, which was granted at the end of the war, the increasing number of Africans who left their villages for the cities, the mounting discontent caused by postwar inflation and demobilization, and the growing number of young Africans who had been educated in the Western liberal tradition—all these factors led to the rise of political agitation among Africans and the demand for independence throughout Africa.

INDEPENDENCE

South Africa

South Africa had become a self-governing union in 1909 within the British Commonwealth of Nations, and in 1923 South Rhodesia had gained virtual self-government, but in both cases self-government was for whites only.

The three Bantu territories—Basutoland, Bechuanaland, and Swaziland—remained under British protection because of South Africa's attitude toward nonwhites (that is, treating Negroes as inferior human beings). Since 1948 the majority of the electorate in the Union has voted for apartheid, the principle of total separation between white and black.

In May, 1961 the South African Republic broke with the

British Commonwealth on the issue of apartheid, and its Nationalist government has stated that no nonwhite shall have a share in politics and that the Bantus shall be confined to separate areas. How long this can go on is a question that remains to be answered.

South Rhodesia

Since 1923 Southern Rhodesia Has Had Two Main Aims
A. To stay out of the Union of South Africa;
B. At the same time to maintain power in the hands of the white minority.

With this purpose in mind a federation of the two Rhodesias and Nyasaland was proposed, with hopes of getting rid of British surveillance and of creating a bloc strong enough to stand against the Union of South Africa.

After World War II Southern (white) Rhodesians renewed their campaign, stressing the economic advantages of the union, and in 1953 the British government finally agreed to this policy, which most Africans in the three territories were opposed to. The situation could not long remain static, with 300,000 Europeans and 7,000,000 Africans. The Federation called itself a partnership of black and white in government; this was definitely a misnomer. Only fifteen out of fifty-nine seats in the Federal Assembly were reserved for African interests, and only twelve of these were actually held by Africans.

On December 31, 1963 the union broke up. Nyasaland became the independent state of Malawi and North Rhodesia became the independent state of Zambia. South Rhodesia remained a white self-governing colony. In 1965, in defiance of both the British government and world opinion, Rhodesia declared its independence.

The Sudan

In 1953 the Sudan received from Great Britain and Egypt the agreement that she could decide her future after a three-year transitional period. In 1956 she voted to become an independent republic.

West and East Africa

There had been reactions in West and East Africa to colonial control and alien pressures before World War II. In 1915 a rebellion led by John Chilembwe in Nyasaland had a political-religious orientation (the Mau Mau uprising of 1952–1956 in Kenya was also a pseudo-religious and political movement), and in British West Africa the newly educated Africans formed political associations and hoped to convert the legislative councils into African parliaments. In the French colonies, authority had always been centered in France, and therefore African intellectuals sought to secure greater influence in Paris. During the 1930's they had little support and no means of influence.

With World War II, however, the French Africans' attitude changed. During the war French territories had been controlled by the Vichy government, and this produced a severe shock among the Africans. In French Equatorial Africa, Africans led by Felix Éboné joined the Free French movement, and in Brazzaville in 1944 declared that Africa's future would be decided by Africans. This led to the establishment of the French Union after the war, in which Africans were to be partners in government, and more important, it led to decentralization within the French colonial empire. An interterritorial party was founded (the Rassemblement Démocratique Africain), which continued agitation in France (between 1948 and 1950 it was suppressed because of its militant association with communism), but what happened in the British colonies changed the French Africans' outlook.

British West Africa

A. In the British colonies on the coast, World War II had led to an increase in income, more contact with the outside world (particularly among Africans fighting in the Burma campaign), and a desire for independence. When the war ended

there was growing agitation for independence; there was economic discontent (new wealth but nothing to buy); and there
was a growing demand that Britain fulfill the ideals laid down
in the charter of the United Nations. Great Britain, however,
continued to move slowly, and Africans became increasingly
frustrated.

B. On the Gold Coast in 1948 in response to this frustration, there was boycotting and rioting. Kwame Nkrumah returned from England to organize political opposition, and in
1949 the British agreed to an all-African committee to devise a
new constitution for Ghana. Nkrumah, however, was not satisfied and demanded self-government. In 1957 it was granted, and
this was the beginning of the end of colonialism in Africa.

C. Independence followed in most of the British colonies
but at a slower pace than in Ghana since many of Britain's
African colonies faced special problems. Nigeria was separated
into three districts, and therefore time was needed to form some
kind of a federation. Sierra Leone and Gambia were poor and
small. Uganda had four kings (the kingdoms of Toro, Bun-
yoro, Ankole, and Buganda) who all claimed power. Kenya had
a white settler problem, and in 1953 the Kikuyus (about 1,200,000
natives) had formed a terrorist organization called the Mau
Mau and revolted against white supremacy in the highlands;
Tanganyika was a huge trust territory with a small population
and at least 120 different tribes.

French Africa

In 1956 the French granted more local autonomy, but this
did not satisfy the new nationalists inspired by Nkrumah and
the independence of Ghana. In 1958 French colonies were given
a choice of independence or remaining within the French
Community (a position similar to being in the British Commonwealth). All except Guinea voted to stay in the Community. But
the example of Guinea and the influence of her president, Sékou
Touré, led to the withdrawal of nine of the fifteen nations forming the French Community. In 1959 Senegal and the French

Sudan formed the Federation of Mali, independent within the French Community. By 1960 all the former French colonies were independent, some within and some outside of the Community.

The Accra Conference 1958

Ghana decided to direct all her resources against colonialism, and in 1958 the first African conference (representing twenty-eight territories) met; and Nkrumah announced that "Our task is not done and our own safety not assured until the last vestiges of colonialism have been swept from Africa."

The Belgian Congo

A. Independence in the Belgian Congo was the pan-African movement's "greatest triumph and its most serious test." The Belgian Congo had been under strict paternalistic control since 1885, but in 1955 the Belgian government finally bowed to nationalistic pressure and allowed a few political groups to exist. In 1958 Patrice Lumumba began to agitate for independence, and in 1960 the Belgian government granted free elections and independence.

B. Lumumba became the first premier, with Kasavubu as president. Conflict between the two men developed, since Lumumba tended to be pro-Russian and pseudo-Marxist, and Kasavubu was more favorably inclined toward the West. In a heavily tribal country the government was totally dependent on the army, which was still led by Belgian officers. When the army mutinied against their officers the regime collapsed, and the Congo broke into warring tribes. The province of Katanga, led by the pro-Belgian Tshombe and supported by Belgian mining interests, declared its independence, and the Africans turned to the U.N. for support in bringing their country back together.

C. The years 1960–1961 witnessed chaos, murder, and war in the Congo, in which Lumumba was killed (February, 1961) and U.N. troops endeavoured to maintain the peace and crush the independence of Katanga by force of arms. Gizenga, a pro-

Lumumba man, tried to succeed him but was ousted in January, 1962. The situation was temporarily solved and the country united under Prime Minister Cyrille Adoula, but U.N. troops remained for two more years.

    D. Ironically, Tshombe, the separatist leader of Katanga, was made premier of the Congo in 1964. That same year U.N. troops withdrew, but the Congo's troubles were far from over. Tshombe was not trusted by many African leaders: he had been on good terms with some of the most hated white men (Welensky of the Federation and Verwoerd of South Africa), and the rebels who were pro-Lumumba held him responsible for their hero's death.

    E. The rebellion in the Congo continues. Rebels hold the area around Stanleyville in the north, Albertville in the east and Kwilu province in the west. When the rebels took Stanleyville at least fifty-eight whites were massacred, but the entry of the United States and Belgian paratroopers saved the lives of thousands. The treatment of those who died at the hands of the rebels was as gruesome and terrible as anything in history.

The Nations of Africa and Their Leaders at the Dates of Independence

(Nations are starred if they are members of either the French Community of Nations or the British Commonwealth)

NATION	DATES OF INDEPENDENCE	LEADERS
Ex-French Nations		
Guinea	1958	Sékou Touré
Mali (Sudan)	1959	Modibo Keita
*Senegal	1959	Sedar Senghor
Cameroon	1960	Ahmadou Ahidjo
*Central African Republic	1960	David Dacko
*Chad	1960	Francois Tombalbaye

NATION	DATES OF INDEPENDENCE	LEADERS
*Congo (Republic of)	1960	Fulbert Youlou, president until August, 1963 replaced by Premier Alphonse Massamba-Debat
Dahomey	1960	Hubert Maga
*Gabon	1960	Leon M'Ba
Ivory Coast	1960	Felix Houphouet-Boigny
*Malagasy Republic	1960	Philibert Tsiranana
Mauritania	1960	Mokhtar Ould Daddah
Niger	1960	Hamani Diori
Togo	1960	Sylvanus Olympio, assassinated
Upper Volta	1960	Maurice Yameogo

Ex-British

NATION	DATES OF INDEPENDENCE	LEADERS
South Africa (Union of)	1909	Hendrik F. Verwoerd, prime minister, 1963
Sudan	1956	General Abboud (1963)
*Ghana	1957	Kwame Nkrumah
*Nigeria	1960	Abubakar Tafawa Balewa
Togoland (joined Ghana)	1960	
*Sierra Leone	1961	Milton Marqai
*Uganda	1962	Milton Obote
*Malawi (Nyasaland)	1964	Dr. Hastings K. Banda
*Zambia (N. Rhodesia)	1964	Kenneth D. Kaunda
*Tanganyika } became Tanzania 1964	1961	Julius K. Nyerere
*Zanzibar	1963	
*Kenya	1963	Jomo Kenyatta
*Gambia	1965	David K. Jawara

Ex-Belgium

NATION	DATES OF INDEPENDENCE	LEADERS
Congo Republic	1960	Kasavubu, president; Cyrille Adoula, prime minister, 1962
Rwanda (Ruandi)	1962	Gregoire Kayibanda, 1963
Burundi (Urundi)	1962	Chief Bagaya

NATION	DATES OF INDEPENDENCE	LEADERS
Ex-Italian		
Eritrea (part of Ethiopia)	1952	
Somali	1960	Aden Adbullah Osman
Ethiopia		Emperor Haile Selassie
Liberia		William Tubman
Remaining Colonies		
Bechuanaland		British protectorates
Basutoland		British protectorates
Swaziland		British protectorates
Rhodesia		Self-governing colony (status uncertain)
Rio de Oro (Sahara)		Spanish
Rio Muni (Guinea)		Spanish
Mozambique		Portuguese
Angola		Portuguese
Guinea		Portuguese
Cabinda		Portuguese
Somaliland		French
Southwest Africa		Union of South Africa (mandate)

The Leaders

The leaders of the countries of Africa reveal the diversity and the depth of nationalistic feeling characteristic of the continent.

Felix Houphouet-Boigny of the Ivory Coast was not from a poor and illiterate family as were Nkrumah and Nyerere; he was the son of a wealthy chief. He was one of the few leaders in ex-French territories who was dedicated to the French Community, yet he could not keep his own country in it.

Kwame Nkrumah, president and prime minister of Ghana, holds both a M.A. and a M.Sc. degree. In 1960, at the U.N. General Assembly, he tried to lead the African bloc to win their support for Patrice Lumumba of the Congo and to create and control a neutral bloc of African nations. In this he failed. While on a trip to China in February of 1966 he was ousted by a military coup in Ghana.

Kenneth Kaunda of Zambia is the son of a preacher and a strong advocate of Gandhian nonviolence. He is a dedicated Pan-Africanist, and believes in protecting the rights of white settlers. (In fact, only three thousand of seventy-seven thousand Europeans in Zambia have emigrated). Recently his tolerant policies have been strained by the extreme actions of the whites in the neighboring state of Rhodesia.

Julius K. Nyerere of Tanganyika holds a M.A. in history and economics from the University of Edinburgh. He has been a teacher and has successfully maintained peace between white and black in Tanganyika.

PROBLEMS OF INDEPENDENT AFRICA

Pan-Africanism

The desire to form large political units in Africa and eventually create a United States of Africa is a problem and has caused difficulties. The argument for a united Africa is that small countries cannot afford large-scale development programs and Africa will never be totally independent until a confederation has been achieved.

A. At the Casablanca Conference in 1961, the group of states who favored pan-Africanism and an extreme anti-Western policy met. They included Guinea, Ghana, Mali (which had broken with Senegal), Morocco, and Egypt.

B. That same year another group met at the Monrovia Conference. These states felt that internal problems should be tackled first; that there should be cooperation with Europe; and that regional, tribal, ethnic, or language interests should be recognized.

C. In May, 1963 the Organization of African Unity was formed. The explosive emotional forces that hold it together are hatred of remaining colonialism and racism in South Africa and Rhodesia.

Tribalism
A force equal to that of pan-Africanism is tribalism. Africa is composed of hundreds of different tribes with diverse cultures

and languages. There is a desire to unify these tribes (irredentism) which often cut across existing state boundaries. For example, the Bakonga live in three areas, North Angola and the ex-Belgium and ex-French Congo. The Ewe spread across the boundaries of Ghana and Togoland, and the Masai of Kenya also live in Tanganyika. There are many Africans who have little loyalty to their nation and still think of themselves first of all as part of the tribal people to which they belong.

Religious rivalries also split Africa, and political divisions within Africa contribute to diversity. Mali, Guinea, and Ghana generally adhere to an anti-Western policy, while Mauritania, Senegal, Gambia, the Ivory Coast, Upper Volta, Niger, Chad, Cameroon, Dahomey, the Central African Republic, and Gabon appear pro-West; and the other independent nations follow a middle-of-the-road policy.

The Future of Democracy

Many African states are adopting democratic political institutions patterned after Western models. National legislatures are based on adult suffrage and free elections. Civil and social rights are protected through courts. Nevertheless, African leaders argue that internal stability must be achieved at all costs. In many states there are no opposition parties allowed and freedoms are curtailed. Many Africans agreed and still agree with Nkrumah when he said (in 1956) that "Even a system based on . . . a democratic constitution may need backing up . . . by emergency measures of a totalitarian kind."

There is the threat that if African leaders fail to make headway in achieving effective economic and social programs, the path may be wide open for extremists or demagogues who want to seize power. So far communism has not made serious gains in Africa, but during the past few years Soviet activities have been considerably stepped up. When Guinea became independent in 1958 and the French withdrew all assistance, the Sino-Soviet bloc gained its first major foothold in sub-Saharan Africa. In Burundi, however, which had become the biggest base for Red

Chinese subversion, the government succeeded in booting the Chinese officials out of the country. One hundred million dollars in Soviet aid has gone to Ethiopia, radio broadcasts are beamed to Africa, there are numerous scholarships for Africans to study in Moscow, and money to support the pan-African movement.

There is an insufficient number of educated leaders throughout Africa. When the Belgian Congo became independent, for example, there were only sixteen Congolese college graduates. Africa also lacks an effective locally recruited civil service. Many African states have had to retain or hire European administrators.

Economic Problems

The future of African democracy may rest on the solution of pressing economic problems.

There is lack of technical training and there are inadequacies in education, sanitation, power, transportation, and investment capital.

There is an uneven distribution of wealth among African countries. South Africa, the Rhodesias, and the Katanga province of the Congo have the lion's share of gold, industrial diamonds, cobalt, copper, platinum, and uranium.

The other countries have their wealth and economic future tied up in a one-crop economy and are consequently totally dependent upon the price of that crop on the world market. For example, Liberia depends on the rubber market, Ghana on cocoa, Uganda on cotton, Tanganyika on coffee and mica, Sudan on coffee, the Cameroons on cocoa and coffee; and Somalia on fresh fruits and nuts. Even the Rhodesias are almost completely dependent on the copper market. Ghana, with one of the most prosperous economies, has a per capita income of only $150 a year.

Large portions of the population are still engaged in subsistence agriculture, and the forces of nature are unfavorable in many parts of Africa. Yellow fever, malaria, and sleeping sickness still plague large sections.

The Whites and Multiracial Territories and Unsolved Problems of Colonialism

The whites still control South Africa, South Rhodesia, Angola, and Mozambique. Each country has evolved policies that provide for the subordination of the African majority.

A. Assimilation is the method used in Portuguese territories. One percent of the Africans are *assimilados,* who speak Portuguese, have been educated in Portugal, and who have full citizenship and equality with the Portuguese; the rest are *indigenatos,* subject to severe control and obligatory labor requirements.

B. Apartheid in South Africa involves total segregation, political and geographical and social. All nonwhites are disenfranchised, trade unions are forbidden, and Africans are tied to their jobs.

c. The government of Rhodesia has white supremacy policies and has been the subject of attack by Commonwealth members. It threatened to declare its independence without British consent rather than give voting rights to the Africans, and in 1965 Ian Smith broke with England.

As long as these conditions exist there will certainly be no peace in Africa. South Africa has approximately 9,000,000 Africans, 1,500,000 colored (mixed), 400,000 Asians, and 3,000,000 Europeans. Rhodesia has 250,000 Europeans and 3,800,000 Africans; Angola has 80,000 Europeans to 4,500,000 Africans; and Mozambique, 49,000 Europeans to 5,500,000 Africans. Some day the tables will turn. This is one of the avowed aims of the pan-African movement.

Kenya, a multiracial nation with 6,000,000 Africans, 62,000 Europeans, 150,000 Asians and 30,000 Arabs has perhaps solved the problem by granting representative government. But here the Europeans had never been able to acquire exclusive rights, and they were never a large majority. How long whites will be protected remains to be seen, for in November, 1964 Kenya became a one-party state.

The Cultural Impact of the West

Economic and political change has brought with it cultural change. The destruction of the old way of life has been more rapid than in most civilizations, and the reaction has been varied. Some tribes have lost their traditional rules of conduct without working out new ones. (In 1948–1949 in Elizabethville, 88 percent of the cases before the police courts were instances in which Africans had not done things in the "western way," for example, cases of polygamy, breaking of labor laws).

Traditional African Culture—Tribalism

A. The African tribe was organized and highly developed in politics, human relations, and culture. The chief's power varied from tribe to tribe, but in almost every case it was not absolute, for religious men (witch doctors) and tradition influenced his decisions.

B. In African culture there was no written law, and power rested primarily on the control over people rather than ownership of things. Chiefs, for example, usually lived in the same type of dwelling and wore the same clothes as their subjects, but they invariably had more wives, more children, and more people who owed them special duties. Land was not a saleable product, and there was relatively little difference in wealth among Africans in a particular village. Group responsibility was more important than individualism, and usually the tribe was a kin group who lived together in a village.

C. Polygamy was a common practice, and bridewealth (cattle or produce paid by the groom's family to the bride's family) ensured that the bride had a certain amount of protection and independence. (If she was mistreated by her husband she could return to her own family, and her family was not obligated to return the dowry.) Even today Tom Mboya of Kenya paid a "brideprice" of sixteen cows for his wife, Pamela Odede (an American college graduate).

D. Religion was often a highly developed ritualistic system, involving ancestor worship and spirit worship, in which the duty of the witch doctor was to manage the spirits. Religion was one of the elements that bound clans together.

The Impact of the West

The cultural and economic impact of the West upon Africa is best epitomized in the words of Henry Morton Stanley: "There are 40 millions of people beyond the gateway of the Congo, and the cotton spinners of Manchester are waiting to clothe them. Birmingham foundries are glowing with the red metal that will presently be made into . . . trinkets that shall adorn those dusky bosoms, and the ministers of Christ are zealous to bring them, the poor benighted heathen, into the Christian fold."

THE INFLUENCE OF THE EUROPEAN TRADER

The slave trade had little cultural influence, except perhaps to give Africans a preconceived notion of Western materialism. In some cases Africans, in order to regain freedom from Western domination, tried to adopt Western ways, but this was not usually the case.

THE INFLUENCE OF THE MISSIONARIES

The missionary deliberately set about to change the African way of life by education, medicine, and religion. Educated Africans moved away from their traditional culture; medicine changed the Africans' attitude toward illness, family, and agriculture. Christian converts became isolated from their kin group because they could no longer participate in religious ritual.

THE INFLUENCE OF THE EUROPEAN COLONIES

A. Western education has probably been one of the most significant forces in challenging the traditional African way of life. The idea of democratic government, of progress through science, of the importance of the individual, and of industrialization have all had their effect on Africa, as on the rest of the non-Western world.

B. Working for the white settler on a plantation or in a mine has undermined the African way of life. The introduction of wages and a money economy has weakened the influence of the father, since sons who earn their own money can challenge his authority, and has decreased the size of families and the number of wives a man can afford, since today bridewealth is often paid in cash, not kind.

c. The Europeans deprived chiefs of their traditional authority and established Western notions of law and order that outlawed many of the traditional ways.

d. Urbanization has led to the greatest change in Africa.

1) The African has been separated from the traditional kin group and he has been exposed to Western ways as well as to the ways of other tribes. With the rapid growth of cities has come the most rapid change. (Dakar and Elizabethville doubled their population between 1945–1955; from 1947 to 1950 Northern Rhodesian towns doubled in size. In 1935 Leopoldville had only 26,600 people, but by 1955 it was thirteen times that size.)

2) As in the West urbanization and industrialization have been the instruments of vast social change and the seedbed of most problems, so in Africa the full impact of these forces for both good and evil are only just beginning to be experienced. For less than 10 percent of Africa's 175 million people live in communities of five thousand, or more, and with the exception of Johannesburg (which has a population of 2,100,000 including suburbs), Ibadan, Nigeria, is the largest city in sub-Sahara Africa, with a population of only 533,000.

African Nationhood

Most of the boundaries of the states of Africa are the result of the accident of Western colonialism. They do not necessarily represent ethnic, linguistic, or economic divisions. As a consequence, a number of African countries are not viable political, economic, or cultural units, and the boundaries of most African countries may well be changed in the course of time.

African Politics Since Independence

African politics since independence have been so unstable that it is impossible to keep abreast of current leaders and governments. Between November 25, 1965 and February 24, 1966 there were six revolutions in Africa: in the Congo Republic,

Kasavubu was replaced by military rule; in Dahomey, the same kind of military takeover occurred; in the Central African Republic, President Dacko was also replaced by a military figure; in the Upper Volta, Yameogo was ousted by Lt. Col. Lamizana; in Nigeria, Prime Minister Abubakar Tafawa Balewa was assassinated as a consequence of a military coup; and in Ghana, Nkrumah's government was taken over by army leaders. Given the events of 1965–66 it is questionable how long the civilian governments of Africa can survive.

CONCLUSION

World history is still in its infancy. Measured by the scant three hundred years of global unity, or by the forty-five centuries of recorded civilization, or even by the fifty millenniums of human existence, the history of man's world is young. Brief as are the annals of the human race, it is clear that those of us living in the twentieth century stand upon the threshold of a future so filled with change that the horrors and wonders of the past seem petty in comparison. From time out of mind, our battered earth has lived with the perpetual fear of hunger, pain, repression and indignity, evils which were accepted as being as much a part of life as birth and death. Today fear remains, but it has received a new urgency and a new dimension. For the first time in history, man must fear for the survival of his species, but at the same time he has been offered the knowledge that suffering, starvation and slavery need not be his fate if he moves with sufficient speed and confidence. The marvels of medicine, the engineering ingenuity of man, the scientific wonders of an age which has extended man's horizons deep into the limitless unknown of the universe—all these have made it possible to re-create the globe in a new image—the republic of plenty, well being and dignity for all.

Today it lies within the power of scientists and statesmen to transform such a vision into reality; but the dream can equally well become a nightmare. The wellspring of science, which has done so much to save life and relieve suffering, has also produced the uncontrolled explosion of a world population which doubles itself every thirty-five years, the dread of nuclear holocaust, and the bloody spectre of racial and national strife. As the world becomes more unified and territorial history gives way to terrestrial, and as the technological instruments of human progress are thrust into man's hands, the possibility remains that this globe will grow even more politically fragmented, even more at odds with itself.

The statistics of potential world starvation, as birth rates and life expectancies out-distance food production, are stark reminders that the utopias of the future may well be populated by hordes of impoverished, bitter and envious peoples who will use any means to save themselves. Once the starving waited patiently to die; once the chasm between squallor and riches was accepted as part of God's design; but today the submerged masses of Africa, Asia and South America demand heaven here on earth. Economic and material wellbeing are the minimal prerequisites to a society fit for the dignity of man, but full bellies and fat babies can be hollow achievements if economic security is purchased at the price of liberty—liberty to think, to speak, to criticize, to worship, to elect one's own way of life, and to choose between right and wrong.

Yet hope remains. Dreary as the annals of man have been, the pattern and the theme have been constant—as men have learned more, they have drawn closer and closer together, moving steadily from tribal to civic to national and finally to global associations and history. This was the faith expressed by Adlai Stevenson in one of his last speeches (June 17, 1965). "The art of government has grown from its seeds in the tiny city-states of Greece to become the political mode of half the world. So let us dream of a world in which all states, great and small, work together for the peaceful flowering of the republic of man." Attain that vision, and world history will no longer be the figment of the historian's organizational mind but an historic reality.

SELECTED BIBLIOGRAPHY

Useful reference works for world history are W. Langer, *Encyclopedia of World History* (Houghton Mifflin, 1940, 1st ed.), and John Bowle, *Concise Encyclopedia of World History* (Hawthorn Books, 1958). Atlases are R. R. Palmer, ed., *Atlas of World History* (Rand McNally, 1962), W. H. McNeill, M. R. Buske and A. W. Roehm, *The World: Its History in Maps* (Denoyer Geppert, 1963), and J. P. Cole, *Geography of World Affairs* (Penguin Books, 1959) for the contemporary period.

The best general survey of world history are W. H. McNeill, *The Rise of the West: A History of the Human Community* (University of Chicago Press, 1963) and Leften S. Stavrianos, *The World Since 1500* (Prentice-Hall, 1966). H. G. Wells, *The Outline of History* (Garden City Publishing Co., 1920, 1st ed.) is a classic. Other analyses are J. Bowle, *Man Through the Ages* (Little, Brown, 1962); A. J. Toynbee, *A Study of History* (Oxford University Press, 1934, ff. 1st ed.); Will Durant, *The Story of Civilization* (Simon and Schuster, ff. 1935, 1st ed.). Interpretations of the contemporary world from a global viewpoint are V. M. Dean, *The Nature of the Non-Western World* (Mentor Book, 1957); K. Jaspers, *The Future of Mankind* (University of Chicago Press, 1961); R. L. Heilbroner, *The Future as History* (Harper, 1959); H. Stuart Hughes, *An Essay for our Times* (Knopf, 1951); E. H. Carr, *The New Society* (Beacon Press Paperback, 1957); Raymond Aron, *The Dawn of Universal History* (Praeger, 1961); and D. Thomson, *World History 1914–1950* (New York, Oxford University Press, 1954).

Selected Bibliography for the Middle East

PREHISTORIC PERIOD
V. Gordon Childe, *Man Makes Himself* (Mentor, 1951)

ANCIENT AND CLASSICAL PERIODS

H. Frankfort, *The Birth of Civilization in the Near East* (Doubleday Anchor Books, 1950)

H. Frankfort, et al., *Before Philosophy* (Pelican, 1963)

P. K. Hitti, *The Near East in History* (Van Nostrand, 1961) [the best general survey]

R. Turner, *The Great Cultural Traditions* (McGraw-Hill, 1941, 2 vols.) [includes more than the Middle East]

MEDIEVAL PERIOD

P. K. Hitti, *The Arabs: A Short History* (Gateway Editions, 1956)

MODERN PERIOD

E. Atiyah, *The Arabs* (Pelican Books, 1955)

S. N. Fisher, *The Middle East* (Knopf, 1959)

H. A. R. Gibb and H. Bowen, *Islamic Society and the West* (Oxford University Press, 1950)

D. Lerner, *The Passing of Traditional Society: Modernizing the Middle East* (Free Press, 1958)

O. I. Janowsky, *Foundations of Israel: Emergence of a Welfare State* (Anvil No. 41, 1959)

L. V. Thomas and R. N. Frye, *The United States and Turkey and Iran* (Harvard University Press, 1952)

Selected Bibliography for Western Europe

ANCIENT AND CLASSICAL PERIODS

W. R. Agard, *The Greek Mind* (Anvil No. 17, 1957)

V. Gordon Childe, *What Happened in History* (Pelican Books, 1942)

R. M. Geer, *Rome* (Prentice-Hall, 1950)

Michael Grant, *The World of Rome* (Weidenfeld and Nicholson, London, 1963)

H. D. F. Kitto, *The Greeks* (Penguin Books, 1951)

W. Miller, *Greece and the Greeks: A Survey of Greek Civilization* (Macmillan, 1941)

MEDIEVAL PERIOD

Ferdinand Lot, *The End of the Ancient and the Beginnings of the Middle Ages* (Harper, 1961)

J. R. Strayer and D. C. Monro, *The Middle Ages: 395–1500* (Appleton, 1959, 4th ed.)

MODERN PERIOD

Raymond Aron, *The Century of Total War* (Doubleday, 1954)

T. S. Ashton, *The Industrial Revolution 1760–1830* (London, Home University Library, 1948)

Crane Brinton, *The Anatomy of Revolution* (Vintage, 1957)

Herbert Butterfield, *The Origins of Modern Science* (Macmillan, 1952)

Winston Churchill, *The Second World War* (Bantam, 1962, 6 vols. 1948–53)

Cyril Falls, *The Great War 1914–1918* (Putnam, 1961)

Cyril Falls, *The Second World War: A Short History* (London, Methuen, 1948)

E. Fischer, *The Passing of the European Age* (Harvard University Press, 1948, rev. ed.)

Ortega y Gasset, *The Revolt of the Masses* (London, Allen and Unwin, 1961)

M. Gilmore, *The World of Humanism 1453–1517* (Harper, 1962)

J. H. Hayes, *The Generation of Materialism: 1871–1900* (Harper, 1941) [a provocative account]

Hajo Holborn, *The Political Collapse of Europe* (Knopf, 1951)

W. L. Langer, *European Alliances and Alignments* (Knopf, 1931)

P. T. Moon, *Imperialism and World Politics* (Macmillan, 1939)

Samuel E. Morison, *Admiral of the Ocean Seas* (Little, 1942, 2 vols)

R. R. Palmer, *The Age of the Democratic Revolution* (Princeton University Press, 1959)

R. R. Palmer and J. Colton, *A History of the Modern World* (Knopf, 1956) [the best general survey]

K. M. Panikkar, *Asia and Western Dominance* (London, Allen and Unwin, 1959, rev. ed.) [the best work on Europe in Asia]

J. H. Parry, *The Age of Reconnaissance: Exploration, Discovery and Settlement 1450–1650* (London, Weidenfeld and Nicholson, 1963)

M. E. Townsend and C. H. Peake, *European Colonial Expansion Since 1871* (Lippincott, 1941)

André Siegfried, *Europe's Crisis* (Eng. trans. London, 1935) [economic study]

John Strachey, *The End of Empire* (Random, 1960)

Alexis de Tocqueville, *The Old Regime and the French Revolution* (Doubleday Anchor Book, 1960)

Barbara Ward, *The Interplay of East and West* (W. W. Norton, 1957)

Selected Bibliography for Russia

ANCIENT, CLASSICAL, MEDIEVAL, AND MODERN UP TO 1914

Michael T. Florinsky, *Russia: A History and an Interpretation* (Macmillan, 1947, 2 vols.) [the best study]

A. G. Mazour, *Russia Past and Present* (Van Nostrand, 1951)

George Vernadsky, *Ancient Russia* (Yale University Press, 1943)

W. B. Walsh, *Reading in Russian History* (Syracuse University Press, 1950)

SOVIET RUSSIA

E. H. Carr, *The Bolshevik Revolution, 1917–1923* (Macmillan, 1951–1953, 3 vols.)

Edward Crankshaw, *Khrushchev's Russia* (Penguin Books, 1960)

Merle Fainsod, *How Russia is Ruled* (Harvard University Press, 1963, rev. ed.)

R. N. C. Hunt, *Marxism: Past and Present* (Macmillan, 1954)

A. Inkeles and K. Geiger, *Soviet Society: A Book of Readings* (Houghton Mifflin, 1961)

G. F. Kennan, *Russia and the West Under Lenin and Stalin* (Little, 1961)

P. E. Mosely, *The Kremlin and World Politics* (Vintage Russian Library, 1960)

W. W. Rostow, *The Dynamics of Soviet Society* (Mentor Books, 1954)

Georg von Rauch, *History of Soviet Russia* (Praeger, 1954) [brief]

Bertram Wolfe, *Three Who Made a Revolution* (Beacon, 1956)

Selected Bibliography for the United States and Anglo-Saxon Migrations

F. L. Allen, *Only Yesterday* (Harper, 1931)

F. L. Allen, *The Big Change* (Bantam, 1961)

S. F. Bemis, *A Diplomatic History of the United States* (Holt, 1955)

Cambridge History of the British Empire, Vol. II, *Australia and New Zealand* (Cambridge, 1929); Vol. VI *Canada and Newfoundland* (Cambridge, 1930)

D. G. Creighton, *Dominion of the North: A History of Canada* (Macmillan, 1958)

George Dangerfield, *The Era of Good Feelings* (Harcourt Brace, 1952)

J. K. Gilbraith, *The Great Crash, 1929* (Houghton, 1961)

Arthur Link, *American Epoch: A History of the United States Since the 1890's* (Knopf, 1950)

William Miller, *A History of the United States* (Dell Publishing Company, 1958) [A good brief account]

E. S. Morgan, *The Birth of the Republic 1763–89* (University of Chicago Press, 1956)

C. P. Nettels, *The Roots of American Civilization* (Appleton, 1938)

Allan Nevins, *Ordeal of Union* (Scribner, 1947, 2 vols.)

Clinton Rossiter, *Seedtime of the Republic* (Harcourt, 1953)

Selected Bibliography for Latin America

S. F. Bemis, *Latin American Policy of the United States: An Historical Interpretation* (Harcourt, 1943).

Joâo P. Calogeras, *A History of Brazil* (University of North Carolina Press, 1937)

R. T. Davies, *The Golden Century of Spain* 1501–1621 (St. Martin's, 1954, new ed.)

Luis Galdames, *A History of Chile* (University of North Carolina Press, 1939)

C. H. Haring, *The Spanish Empire in America* (New York, Oxford University Press, 1947)

Ricardo J. Levene, *A History of Argentina* (University of North Carolina Press, 1937)

F. Macdonald, *Latin-American Politics and Government* (Crowell, 1954)

Henry B. Parkes, *A History of Mexico* (Houghton Mifflin, 1950)

W. L. Schurz, *This New World: The Civilization of Latin America* (Dutton, 1954)

Arthur Whitaker, *The United States and South America: The Northern Republics* (Harvard University Press, 1948)

Selected Bibliography for India

ANCIENT, CLASSICAL, AND MEDIEVAL PERIODS

W. T. de Bary, ed., *Sources of the Indian Tradition* (Columbia University Press, 1958)

S. Piggott, *Prehistoric India to 1000 B.C.* (Pelican Books, 1952).

T. Walter Wallbank, *A Short History of India from Ancient Times to the Present* (Mentor, 1958) [the most available]

MODERN PERIOD

W. Norman Brown, *The United States and India and Pakistan* (Harvard University Press, 1955)

V. M. Dean, *New Patterns of Democracy in India* (Harvard University Press, 1960)

Jawaharlal, Nehru, *The Discovery of India* (John Day, 1946)

L. S. S. O'Malley, *Modern India and the West* (London, Oxford University Press, 1941)

K. M. Pannikar, *A Survey of Indian History* (Asia Publishing House, 1956)

Percival Spear, *India, Pakistan and the West* (Oxford University Press, 1952) [the best general survey]

Percival Spear, *India: A Modern History* (Univ. of Michigan, 1961)

Selected Bibliography for China

ANCIENT, CLASSICAL, AND MEDIEVAL PERIODS

W. T. De Bary, ed., *Sources of the Chinese Tradition* (Columbia University Press, 1960)

L. Carrington Goodrich, *A Short History of the Chinese People* (Harper, 1959, 3rd ed. rev.)

H. G. Creel, *The Birth of China* (F. Ungar, 1954)

K. S. Latourette, *The Chinese: Their History and Culture* (Macmillan, 1946, 3rd ed. rev.)

MODERN PERIOD

A. Doak Barnett, *Communist China and Asia: Challenge to American Policy* (Harper, 1960)

H. L. Boorman, A. Eckstein, P. E. Mosely and B. Schwartz, *Moscow-Peking Axis: Strengths and Strains* (Harper, 1957)

Conrad Brandt, Benjamin Schwartz and John K. Fairbank, *A Documentary History of Chinese Communism* (Harvard University Press, 1952)

J. K. Fairbank and Ssu-yü Teng, *China's Response to the West* (Harvard University Press, 1954)

J. K. Fairbank, *The United States and China* (Harvard University Press, 1958) [the best introduction to modern China]

H. B. Morse and H. F. MacNair, *Far Eastern International Relations* (Houghton Mifflin, 1931)

Robert C. North, *Moscow and Chinese Communists* (Stanford University Press, 1953)

W. W. Rostow, R. W. Hatch, F. A. Kierman, Jr., and A. Eckstein, *The Prospects of Communist China* (J. Wiley, 1954)

Selected Bibliography for Japan

ANCIENT, CLASSICAL, AND MEDIEVAL PERIODS

W. T. de Bary, ed., *Sources of Japanese Tradition* (Columbia University Press, 1958)

K. S. Latourette, *The History of Japan* (Macmillan, 1957, rev. ed.)

E. O. Reischauer, *Japan Past and Present* (Knopf, 1953, rev. ed.)

G. B. Sansom, *Japan: A Short Cultural History* (Appleton, 1962, rev. ed.) [the best study]

MODERN

Edwin O. Reischauer, *The United States and Japan* (Harvard University Press, 1957, rev. ed.) [the best survey]

Robert K. Reischauer, *Japan, Government–Politics* (Nelson, 1939)

G. B. Sansom, *The Western World and Japan* (Knopf, 1950)

R. Scalapino, *Democracy and the Party Movement in Prewar Japan* (University of California Press, 1953)

R. Scalapino and Junnosuke Masumi, *Parties and Politics in Contemporary Japan* (University of California Press, 1962)

Selected Bibliography for Southeast Asia

There are no good general surveys of Southeast Asia. For the subject see the following:

CLASSICAL, MEDIEVAL, AND MODERN PERIODS

John K. Fairbank and Edwin O. Reischauer, *A History of East Asian Civilization* (Houghton, 1960, 2 vols.)

Fred Greene, *The Far East* (Holt, Rinehart and Winston, 1957)

Sir John T. Pratt, *The Expansion of Europe in the Far East* (London, Sylvan Press, 1947)

George E. Taylor and Frank H. Michael, *The Far East in the Modern World* (Holt, 1956)

G. Wint, *The British in Asia* (Faber, 1954, rev. ed.)

Selected Bibliography for Africa

The American Assembly, *The United States and Africa* (Columbia University Press, 1958)

P. Bohannan, *Africa and Africans* (Am. Mus. Sci. Books, 1964)

R. Emerson, *From Empire to Nation: The Rise to Self-Assertions of Asian and African Peoples* (Harvard Univ., 1960)

J. D. Fage, *An Introduction to the History of West Africa* (Cambridge University Press, 1959)

Lord Hailey, *An African Survey* (London, Oxford University Press, 1957)

G. Grove Haines, ed., *Africa Today* (John Hopkins, 1955)

T. Hodgkin, *Nationalism in Colonial Africa* (New York Univ., 1957)

Roland Oliver and J. D. Fage, *A Short History of Africa* (Penguin, 1962)

Roland Oliver, *The Dawn of African History* (London, Oxford University Press, 1961)

C. W. Stillman, ed., *Africa in the Modern World* (University of Chicago Press, 1955)

I. Wallerstein, *Africa: The Politics of Independence* (Random, 1963)

INDEX

NOTES

NOTES

NOTES

NOTES

NOTES

NOTES